Gordon Noble is Professor of Archaeology at the University of Aberdeen and has undertaken award-winning landscape research and field projects, working on projects from the Mesolithic to Medieval periods. He is author of *Neolithic Scotland: Timber, Stone, Earth and Fire* (Edinburgh University Press 2006), *Woodland in the Neolithic of Northern Europe: The Forest As Ancestor* (Cambridge University Press, 2017) and co-author of *King in the North: The Pictish Realms of Fortriu and Ce* (Birlinn, 2019). He works on two current major projects: Northern Picts and Comparative Kingship, the research for which won the *Current Archaeology* Research Project of the Year 2021, a highly prestigious accolade. His research has featured on BBC 2 *Digging for Britain*, BBC Radio 4 *In Our Time* and many other media outlets.

Nicholas Evans is a Research Fellow on the Leverhulme Trust funded Comparative Kingship: the Early Medieval Kingdoms of Northern Britain and Ireland project at the University of Aberdeen. A historian whose research and teaching have focussed on the medieval Celtic-speaking societies of Britain and Ireland, he is the author of *The Present and the Past in Medieval Irish Chronicles* (Boydell Press, 2010), *A Historical Introduction to the Northern Picts* (Aberdeen University/ Tarbat Discovery Centre, 2014) and co-author of *King in the North: The Pictish Realms of Fortriu and Ce* (Birlinn 2019).

PICTS

SCOURGE OF ROME
RULERS OF THE NORTH

GORDON NOBLE
AND
NICHOLAS EVANS

BIRLINN

First published in
Great Britain in 2022 by
Birlinn Ltd
West Newington House
10 Newington Road
Edinburgh
EH9 1QS

www.birlinn.co.uk

ISBN: 978 1 78027 778 3

British Library Cataloguing-in-Publication Data
A catalogue record for this book is available on request from the British Library

Typeset by Mark Blackadder

Printed and bound in Britain by Bell and Bain Ltd, Glasgow

This book is dedicated to Anna Ritchie, an inspiration to any archaeologist studying Pictland. Her work has enriched Pictish studies for many decades and will do so for many more to come.

This book is also in memory of Caroline Wickham-Jones, another equally inspiring archaeologist, a great friend and sorely missed colleague.

Contents

List of Illustrations

In-text illustrations

Colour plates

Acknowledgements

This book contains a study of multiple facets of Pictish society from archaeological, historical and other perspectives, seeking to present a rounded analysis from the emergence of the Picts *c.*AD 300 to their disappearance in the 10th century. It is based on years of research and work by the authors and many individuals, both scholars and other members of the public, who have contributed in various ways.

Sincere gratitude to Anna Ritchie for reading through the entire book, providing timely comments and help. Isabel and George Henderson and Adrian Maldonado also read through chapters and provided very helpful comments. Obviously all errors and opinions remain our own.

This book would not have been possible without generous funding and support through the University of Aberdeen Development Trust from Don and Elizabeth Cruickshank, both born and educated in the north-east of Scotland and graduates of the University of Aberdeen, who helped establish the Northern Picts project. The generous funding of Iain and Nancy McEwan also through the University of Aberdeen Development Trust, along with funding from the McKay–Ardmay Fund, will open a new chapter in Pictish studies in the coming years.

The new discoveries outlined in this volume have also been generously funded by the Historic Environment Scotland Archaeology Programme, the Leverhulme funded Comparative Kingship project, the Strathmartine Trust, the British Academy, the Society of Antiquaries of Scotland and Aberdeenshire Council Archaeology Service. In particular, the writing of this book was supported by a Leverhulme Trust Research Leadership Award (RL-2016–069).

Many thanks to all those who provided images or facilitated access: Andy Hickie, Matt Ritchie, Kelly Kilpatrick, Hugh Levey, Holger Becker, Margaret Wilson, James O'Driscoll, Davy Strachan, Martin Cook, AOC Archaeology, Steve Birch, Eric Grant, Jane Geddes, Cecily Spall, Ian Tait, Mark Hall and Gail Drinkall. Sesilia Niehaus helped with some of the image production. Alastair Reid also provided a very fine gift that helped with the research for the book.

GN: To all at the University of Aberdeen who make our research possible – our wonderful students and volunteers who work on our projects, to my colleagues who provide inspiration, knowledge and fun! Thanks to all at Birlinn, especially Hugh and Andrew, and Patricia Marshall, who produce these wonderful books at affordable prices. To Jane Geddes who started this journey in Pictish studies. Thanks to colleagues who have either worked on the projects highlighted here or for amazing Pictish chats or both: Meggen Gondek, Ewan Campbell, Gemma Cruickshanks, Martin Goldberg, Daniel Maclean, Cathy MacIver, James O'Driscoll, Edouard Masson-MacLean, Samantha Jones, Kate Britton, Andy Seaman, Paddy Gleeson, John Borland, David McGovern, Zack Hinckley, Derek Hamilton, Simon Taylor and many others. No thanks whatsoever to anxiety which has attacked body and soul throughout this Pictish journey. Finally and most of all, love and gratitude to Marianne, Elliot, Magnus and Stella. I couldn't do this without you.

NE: Thank you to everyone in Archaeology at the University of Aberdeen and those involved in the Comparative Kingship project – especially Gordon, Samantha Jones, James O'Driscoll, Edouard Masson-MacLean and Patrick Gleeson – for providing a very welcoming and stimulating environment for a textual historian, albeit at a distance in the last few years! I am also very grateful to everyone at Birlinn for their enthusiasm and industry. I really appreciate more than ever the chances I have had to discuss the subject with so many over the years, most notably Dauvit Broun, Thomas Clancy and Simon Taylor among many others. I am also grateful for the kindness and help of our local community in Stirling but, above all, for the support of my family, especially Sarah, Lachlan and my parents, and the contribution of Pangur, whose paws have made their mark all over this work.

CHAPTER ONE

'From Every Cranny of the North'

The Picts

> Originally those islands were inhabited by Peti and Pape. One of these races, the Peti, only a little taller than pygmies, accomplished miraculous achievements by building towns, morning and evening, but at midday every ounce of strength deserted them and they hid in fear in underground chambers.

This is how the writer of the late 12th-century *Historia Norwegie* described the *Peti*, the Picts, who, along with the *Pape*, presumably clerics, had inhabited the Orkney, Shetland and the Western Isles of Scotland before supposedly being wiped out by the Scandinavians in the reign of the semi-legendary Norwegian king, Harald Fairhair (*c.*870–932) (Ekrem and Mortensen 2003, 64–67). By the 12th century, the Picts were, at best, a very dim memory so Orcadians assumed that they had inhabited the prehistoric monuments, like Maes Howe, on their islands, while perhaps building the pre-Viking settlements whose foundations still survive in the landscape today. Combined with ideas about strange peoples and monsters on the edge of the world, the Picts became the 'wee dark folk' of folklore, a creative, enigmatic, strange, lost people, located out of time, but still present through their creations.

We can chuckle at this Norwegian depiction, but the Picts have long been a puzzle, the creators of a fascinating society that have both intrigued and confounded. Even now, while scholars explode myths built over centuries with evidence-based analysis, the attraction of the Picts is not just academic. When people encounter Pictish sculpture (Figure 1.1), with the patterns, symbols, monsters and people inscribed in stone, it often sparks once again a need to understand this ancient society and to connect with those who created these wonderful carved stones over a thousand years earlier. And it is easy to comprehend why people desire to find out more about the creators of such monuments, for one fundamental issue is why the Picts, the last major ethnic group to disappear from Britain and Ireland, are no longer with us.

This book sets out some of the major advances that have been made

1.1 A Pictish symbol stone from Broomend of Crichie, Aberdeenshire.

which enable us to say much more than was possible even ten years ago on many aspects of Pictish life, but first, in this chapter, we set the scene, introducing the evidence for the Picts, both textual and archaeological, and providing a historical framework up to the Viking Age, since we discuss the end of the Picts in Chapter 7.

The nature of the written evidence

The literacy of the Picts has been questioned in the past, with little surviving in the way of a written legacy apart from a small collection of difficult to interpret inscriptions alongside the enigmatic symbol tradition. There is, however, one surviving group of texts, the Pictish king-lists, which originated in Pictland, and there is good evidence that the Picts wrote in Latin and perhaps Gaelic too (Forsyth 1998; Evans 2011). It is true that most of our documentary evidence for the Picts was produced by writers based elsewhere, but sometimes we can assume that, like the Iona chroniclers recording Pictish events, information from Pictland was utilised for contemporary records (Evans 2017; Evans 2018), or that an actual Pictish source was adapted, as was the case with Bede's account of Pictish origins (Fraser 2011). We are lucky to have such evidence, since it means that we can build up a partial picture about the Picts, to an extent not possible for all parts of Britain in this era.

However, there are still large gaps for some geographical areas – for example, there are virtually no records for the Western Isles or mainland Scotland north of Ross – and for certain periods, especially *c.*AD400–550. The texts often mainly just enable us to reconstruct a sequence of kings. There were many barriers to the survival of Pictish sources, including the disappearance of the Pictish language, culture and the political ideology related to it, political upheavals, such as the rise of new dynasties like the descendants of Alpin *c.*842/3, and Scandinavian attacks and settlement, while later substantial transformations of the 12th and 13th centuries meant that Gaelic culture in turn was less prestigious, and there were substantial changes in the state. Where there are such discontinuities, it is not surprising that few Pictish documents survive, the exceptions being texts or fragments linked to the royal dynasty and Church institutions, as well as historical texts of interest outwith Scotland.

The texts we have were often written considerably after the events they described, for various purposes, and the past was often re-imagined to explain later situations. An exception might be the Irish chronicles, containing brief descriptions of secular and ecclesiastical events from a source written at the monastery of Iona from the late 6th century to about AD 740 (Evans 2018). This source includes a string of often quite tantalising references to Pictish events such as the following:

> *Annals of Ulster* (hereafter *AU*) in the year 558
> (repeated in 560): 'and the flight before the son of Maelchon'
> *AU* 580: 'Cennalath, king of the Picts, dies.'
> *AU* 664: 'The battle of Luith Feirnn, that is, in Fortriu.'
> *AU* 681: 'The siege of Dunnottar.'
> *AU* 682: 'The Orkneys were destroyed by Bruide.'

While the lack of detail in these accounts is frustrating, sources such as these are extremely important in providing us with a chronological framework for understanding Pictland. The Pictish king-lists, including kings with reign lengths, offer us an alternative viewpoint, mixing a royal ideology with the perspective of the monastery of Abernethy by the Tay, where it was kept in the 9th century and later. It survives in later medieval and early modern manuscripts from Scotland, Ireland and England, being altered over time for various purposes, but comparison of the surviving copies enables us to often reconstruct the form of the text before AD 900, when it was a Pictish document. Its evidence, therefore, can be combined with the Irish chronicles to enrich our understanding of Pictish politics, while also giving us useful insights into how the Pictish past was perceived. In addition to these, other sources then occasionally supplement these partial records, allowing us to understand some broader developments, the richest of which is Adomnán's *Life of Columba*, written *c.*700.

Some potentially valuable evidence for the Picts can also be derived from sources for later Scotland, usually created in the period after 1100, when the number of surviving documents increases exponentially. This includes charters which describe transactions in many areas of Scotland, providing invaluable local detail. We can often use such texts to reconstruct the society of the 12th and 13th centuries and place-names can be helpful in indicating not only the earlier linguistic situation, but also in providing us with useful evidence for settlement, uses and perceptions of the landscape. Such documents can be difficult to interpret and date, as several centuries separate them from the time of the Picts, so considerable caution is needed, but they offer important alternative methods of shining light on the earlier period. Saints' dedications can also be helpful (Clancy *et al.* 2022), though scholars are now more likely to regard them as evidence for the veneration of particular saints over many centuries, than for the contemporary world of the actual holy people. This means that, in practice, extreme caution is needed when suggesting that such dedications, nearly always first attested in the later medieval or modern eras, can be dated to the Pictish period. However, in a few cases, especially if combined with other evidence such as place-names, it is possible to produce a plausible explanation of dedications as early and Pictish (see Chapter 4).

When investigating our surviving sources, scholars are now much more sceptical about accepting texts at face value. Texts were written, copied and adapted for various reasons, reflecting different interests, mindsets and genre expectations, as well as the available sources. Therefore, we should regard our texts as primarily evidence for the time of composition and for later societies as they were subsequently maintained and altered. Nevertheless, through considering different fragments of evidence, we can sometimes build up a picture that is likely to be closer to the reality behind their subject matter. Thus, while our surviving textual sources are often difficult to interpret and are very limited, considerable advances are still possible, especially when they are studied in combination with archaeological and other evidence.

The painted people

> But at that time Britain was not prepared with ships for any kind of naval contest . . . In addition to this, the nation of the Britons was still at that time uncivilised and used to fighting only with the Picts and the Hibernians, both still half-naked enemies; and so they submitted to Roman arms so easily that the only thing that Caesar ought to have boasted of was that he had navigated the Ocean.

In this anonymous panegyric for Constantius Caesar, written in AD 297 or 298, possibly at Trier, the Picts, *Picti* in Latin, first enter the historic record (VIII (V), 11, 4: Mann and Penman 1996, 46). The author, in their praise prose, back projected the Picts to the time of Julius Caesar's invasions of Britain in the 1st century BC. However, prior to the late 3rd century AD, the people of northern Britain had been known as Britons and Caledonians and in Ptolemy's *Geography*, of mid 2nd century AD date, the area of Scotland that became the mainland territory of the Picts was listed as being inhabited by various groups – the Creones, Carnonacae, Caereni, Cornavii, Caledonii, Decantae, Lugi, Smertae, Vacomagi, Venicones, Taexali and the Damnonii (Rivet and Smith 1979, 140–41) (Figure 1.2). The Romans, during the invasion of Scotland in the late 70s to about AD 86 or 87, would have encountered some of these peoples. However, shortly after they made gains in north-east Scotland, the Romans withdrew south of the Firth of Forth. Later, the empire expanded north again, most notably with the creation of the Antonine Wall after a new advance in 138 and the destructive campaigns led by the Emperor Septimius Severus and his son Caracalla in AD 208–211, but Roman gains were often followed by tactical retreats, usually back to Hadrian's Wall (Maxwell 1989). Despite this, Roman influence on the areas north of the frontier was ever present. Military campaigns, outpost forts and imperial agents provided direct contact, bribes and gifts to favoured or troublesome local groups, having both a stabilising and destabilising effect on the composition of local society (Hunter 2007a).

As elsewhere on Roman frontiers (Heather 2009, 36–93), one result of the Roman presence may have been the amalgamation of polities bordering Roman Britain, into fewer but larger units. While describing the major Roman campaigns under Septimius Severus and Caracalla north of Hadrian's Wall from AD 208–211, against the Maiatai and beyond them the *Calidones*, that is the Caledonii, Cassius Dio, in the mid 3rd century, noted that 'the names of other British groups had been merged' into these two main polities (Cary 1927, 262; Fraser 2009a, 15–17, 23–29). As a

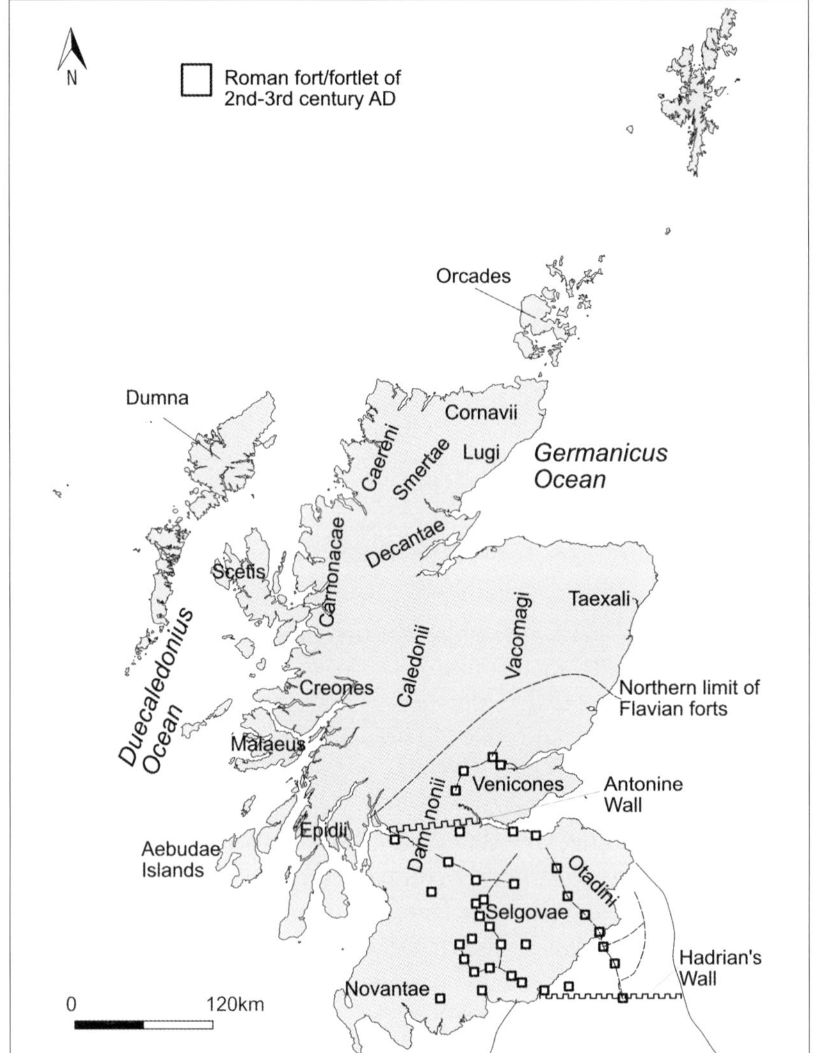

1.2 Population groups, oceans and selected islands in Ptolemy's *Geography* (AD 140×150) and Roman fortifications of the 2nd and 3rd centuries AD.

result of the Roman intervention, the Maiatai seem to have lost land, perhaps territory south of the Forth given to other, more compliant groups, resulting in them being focussed more around the Forth in what became Manaw. Here, their name was remembered, surviving in the place-names Dumyat, on the south side of the Ochils, and Myot Hill, west of Denny (Taylor *et al.* 2020, 52), both prominent hilltop sites. They continued to exist until at least around AD 600 when Adomnán states that they lost a bloody battle against the Gaelic Argyll dynast Áedán mac Gabráin (Taylor *et al.* 2020, 52–54). Ultimately, into the medieval period, the inhabitants of the Maiatai territory predominantly continued to speak British – also known as Brittonic – a P-Celtic language from which modern Welsh,

Cornish and Breton are descended. In this book, adhering to medieval practice, the terms 'Britons' and 'British' will be used specifically to relate to these Celtic-language speakers rather than to the general inhabitants of Britain. The use of British as far north of the Ochils was perhaps due to cultural connections with southern neighbours, until most of the former Maiatai territory was conquered by the Pictish kingdom of Fortriu after 685.

By the end of the 3rd century, the name *Picti* had come into use, representing a still more encompassing term for people in northern Britain, but other groups remained. Ammianus Marcellinus, writing *c.*AD 392 about the Picts involved in what he described as the 'Barbarian Conspiracy' of 367–368, stated that they were divided into two *gentes*, 'peoples' – the Verturiones and Dicalydones. The Verturiones were probably based around the Moray Firth, where their successors, the early medieval kings of Fortriu, were based. Ptolemy called the sea to the west or north of Scotland *Duecaledonius*, a name related to the later Dicalydones, which in turn seems to have meant something like 'twin' or 'double' *Calidones* (Rivet and Smith 1979, 132, 338). The term *Calidones* – or the earlier *Calidonii* – does not occur frequently in the ancient era but the related adjective *Caledonia*, 'Caledonian', is common in classical sources for the 'Caledonian forest' and, in Tacitus's *Agricola*, written in the 90s AD, in relation to the inhabitants living north of the Firth of Forth.

It has been argued (Hind 1983; Fraser 2005a, 33–35, 48) that the Calidones lived in the eastern Lowlands north of the Forth, partly on the basis that not enough people inhabited the Highlands to make that a viable powerbase. However, that downplays the population and potential of the Highlands (Southern 1996, 384), which contains a number of straths with potential for both arable and pastoral farming, and the extent to which these interconnect with their Lowland hinterlands. The textual evidence also places the Calidones firmly in the Highlands, since Ptolemy stated that they occupied the land from the *Varar* estuary (Beauly Firth, near Inverness) to Loch Long off the Clyde estuary. References to the Calidones survive inland in place-names in Perthshire, at the edge of the Highlands at Dunkeld and Rohallion, and at its heart, at the mountain of Schiehallion (Watson 1926, 21–22). The most natural explanation of all the evidence is that the Calidones were located primarily in the Highlands and neighbouring Lowland areas, such as around the Tay, but that the term could also be used for wider confederations north of the Forth, including some of the other Lowland polities mentioned by Ptolemy. At the time of the 'Barbarian Conspiracy' of 367–368, it may have been the Dicalydones who were able to impose their leadership over many of the others in this Caledonian zone, though perhaps the Verturiones also included lands and peoples which had previously contributed to earlier confederations.

Unlike the Maiatai and the Verturiones, the Calidones and related terminology do not appear in medieval sources, apart from one 9th-century reference in the Welsh *Historia Brittonum* to a battle by King Arthur in the Caledonian Wood, *Coit Celidon* (Morris 1980, 35, 76). Why the Calidones disappeared is uncertain; perhaps the term lost its appeal, as different confederations, like the Verturiones and Dicalydones, emerged and, as its former territory north of the Forth was divided among the Gaels, Britons and Picts. Both would explain why it was a new term, *Picti*, not *Calidones*, that emerged as the name for the main enemies of the Romans.

From the late 3rd century to the 6th century, *Picti* was an ethnic term in wide circulation in the Late Antique world (Evans 2022). Fifteen texts by eleven different authors refer to the Picts in this period, from poems produced for elite audiences, such as the florid and bombastic poems of Claudian composed around AD 400, to cataloguing works, like a version of *Nomina Provinciarum Omnium*, 'The Names of All the Provinces', (written AD 312–314), which lists the *Picti* among the barbarian *gentes* which had emerged under the emperors. In these sources *Picti* is found either on its own or in combination with other large ethnic groups, like the *Hiberni* (Irish) or *Scotti* (Gaelic-speakers, perhaps particularly raiders) primarily in negative contexts, fighting the Roman Empire or slave trading for example. The term *Picti* was used as an ethnic term, the Picts being described as a *gens* by Ammianus, albeit one that was divided into two groups, the *Verturiones* and *Dicalydones*.

One notable event in the 4th century suggests the Picts were powerful enemies of the military and cultural might of the Romans in Britain. Ammianus Marcellinus records the Picts taking part in the 'Barbarian Conspiracy' of AD 367–368 when the Picts colluded with the *Scotti*, the *Attacotti*, Saxons and Franks, as well as Roman scouts beyond Hadrian's Wall, to attack Roman Britain and neighbouring territories (*Res Gestae* xxvii.8.1–10; Seyfarth *et al.* 1979, II. 46–48). During this episode, Hadrian's Wall was overrun, a Roman general was killed and many of the Roman outposts and settlements of Britannia were overwhelmed. The strife lasted for around a year before order was restored. Ammianus is likely to be a relatively reliable source as he was a high-ranking soldier in the Roman military and member of the ruling curial class in Rome who wrote his *Res Gestae* after his retirement from the army. He wrote the work using military sources, including his own contemporary notes, dating back to at least the mid 4th century AD (Evans 2022). Ammianus's text suggests the Picts were a highly effective foil to the Roman Empire – a significant group capable of participating in coordinated attacks on provincial areas, causing extensive disruption to the Roman province.

Material culture of the 4th century also points to the wide currency of the term *Picti* and their infamy in Roman circles. A dice tower from a

Roman rural settlement at Vettweiß-Froitzheim, near Cologne, of 4th century date, has the inscription 'PICTOS VICTOS HOSTIS DELETA LVDITE SECVRI' inscribed on it – 'The Picts are beaten, the enemy annihilated, let us play without a care' (Hunter 2007a, 4–6) (Colour Plate 1). The Vettweiß-Froitzheim dice tower indicates that the Picts were not just a literary phenomenon but an identity that had made an impact on popular culture and the empire's mindset near the Roman frontiers (Hunter 2007a, 4–5).

Indeed, the term *Picti* itself was probably Roman, meaning 'painted people' in Latin and perhaps referring to the practice of tattooing or body painting. It has been suggested that the Romans encountered a Pictish word which was similar sounding and reinterpreted it as *Picti* (Watson 1926, 67–68; Evans 2022), but it was more likely a Roman pejorative name in origin, coined for the more 'barbaric' people outside of the Roman cultural zone (Fraser 2009a, 44–54; Fraser 2011). In the period before the late 3rd century, the Romans had used the general ethnic name *Britanni*, later *Brittones*, for all the inhabitants of the island they called *Britannia*, including those, like the Calidones, living in the northern part of the island (Rivet and Smith 1979, 39–40, 280–82). However, a new term was needed once the Britons inside the Roman province (and in the area south of the Forth which had a substantial Roman presence) ceased to seem as 'barbaric' or were identified as less of a threat to Rome; the inhabitants of the island were now divided into those inside the Roman cultural sphere and those still regarded as living outside the empire to the north. Though the earlier, broader use of 'Britons' (*Britanni* or *Brittones*) did persist in some texts, often the name no longer seemed adequate for all inhabitants of the island, so a new word was needed for those beyond the Britons who were still 'barbaric' and more hostile in the eyes of Rome; *Picti* filled that gap.

It has been argued that that there is no evidence that people in northern Britain called themselves *Picti* until the late 7th century (Fraser 2009a, 44–54; Fraser 2011; Woolf 2017b). However, the Roman origin of the word *Picti* does not mean that it was unknown amongst those beyond Hadrian's Wall. In other regions beyond the frontier, for instance in Germany, Ireland, and even further away in Scandinavia, the Romans had a substantial political, economic and cultural impact, including the spread and use of Latin. Scotland north of the Forth has been considered to have been less connected to the Roman Empire but there is increasing archaeological evidence for contacts (see Chapter 3). We can, therefore, suggest it is plausible, if not provable, that *Picti* came to be adopted as an 'endonym', a name applied by people in northern Britain to themselves, in the 4th century by those most in contact with the Romans, and that its use, alongside vernacular ethnic names, survived due to the adoption of Christianity, which more firmly established Latinity in the region (Evans 2022).

After the end of Roman rule in Britain in the early 5th century, there is a dearth of reliable sources for over 150 years, until we start to get a substantial corpus of medieval texts written in Britain and Ireland. This lack, combined with narratives of the fall of the Roman Empire which stressed its cataclysmic nature, has led to the assumption that the immediate post-Roman period saw a similar decline among the Picts. However, recent archaeological discoveries indicate that such a perception needs to be at least qualified, if not rejected (for example, Noble *et al.* 2019b; Hall *et al.* 2020; see also Chapter 3). Indeed, in spite of the paucity of the surviving textual evidence, the Picts continue to appear in Late Antique sources such as the *Gallic Chronicle* of 452 (Burgess 2001, 67) and Constantius's *Life of Germanus*, a hagiographical biography of Bishop Germanus of Auxerre (Levison 1920). What both these texts demonstrate is that the Picts were still clearly part of the Roman view of Britain in Christian elite circles at the time when the Church was attempting to incorporate Britain and Ireland into orthodox Christendom.

Moreover, there are contemporary references to the Picts from Britain. St Patrick, in his *Letter to the Soldiers of Coroticus*, railed against those who had seized his followers in Ireland and were about to sell them to *apostatae* identified as *Picti* (Hood 1978, 35–40, 55–59). This text implies that some Picts at least had knowledge of Christianity at this stage (see Chapter 4; Fraser 2009a, 112). In Gildas's *De Excidio Britanniae – On the Ruin of Britain* written in the mid 6th century – the Picts make several appearances (Winterbottom 1978). Gildas was a monk from western Britain and his book was a lengthy sermon that included a history of Roman Britain and the century following Roman withdrawal, as part of an extended diatribe against five western British kings and members of the clergy for poor conduct. In the *De Excidio*, the Picts are described as a 'savage nation' living in the northern part of the island of Britain who, along with the *Scotti* and Saxons, are depicted as barbarians taking advantage of the Britons' weaknesses, both during the Roman occupation of southern Britain and afterwards. In contrast to Roman sources that refer to the Picts in the late 3rd century, Gildas claimed that the Picts had settled in the north of mainland Britain at the end of the Roman period. His account thus reflects knowledge of the contemporary people called *Picti* alongside ignorance of their origins: clearly by the 6th century the term had a role in contemporary society that had a life of its own beyond Roman era literate sources.

Language

What language or languages the Picts spoke has long been a matter of great debate, and importance, since it has been regarded as a significant aspect of Pictish identity, distinguishing them from their British, Gaelic, English and later Scandinavian neighbours. Partly this derives from Bede's famous statement (*HE* I.1, Colgrave and Mynors 1969, 16–17) that there were five languages in Britain, which were English, British, Gaelic and Pictish, alongside the universal language, Latin. The view articulated by the great linguist, Kenneth Jackson, that the Picts spoke a non-Indo-European language alongside a P-Celtic tongue closest to ancient Gaulish (Jackson 1955) also indicated that the Picts were very different from their neighbours, including the Britons (who spoke British, the ancestor of Welsh, Cornish and Breton). However, this interpretation is deeply problematic for various reasons (Rhys 2015).

Jackson's analysis of the Pictish language was partly a reaction against a wild variety of opinions expressed previously but it was not a complete study of the evidence. In particular, his argument for a language unrelated to any previously known had a wholly negative basis, used to explain words and texts that he could not identify as Celtic or from the broader Indo-European language family. For example, Jackson made much of the fact that ogham inscriptions from Scotland were very difficult to interpret but it may be that we simply have not found the correct key to unlocking the evidence of undeciphered parts of Pictish ogham inscriptions, where there may have been unusual spelling and abbreviation systems in use (Forsyth 1997a, 32–36). On occasion, Jackson also sometimes stated that a word used in sources was unintelligible when it was probably Celtic (Forsyth 1997a, 20–26, 29), and he did not really consider sufficiently the place-name evidence, which makes it clear that a P-Celtic language was in use from the Forth to at least Sutherland (Taylor 2011). The non-Indo-European hypothesis still has its adherents and it cannot be completely dismissed since such languages, for instance Basque, did survive into the medieval period, and some of the earliest names of peoples, islands, rivers and coastal features in northern Britain in Ptolemy's *Geography* (AD 140×150) do not seem to be Celtic in origin (Isaac 2005). However, it is possible that such pieces of evidence are relics of earlier linguistic strata, which is likely to be especially the case for names of rivers and islands which can be very conservative throughout Europe. In the absence of positive evidence for another, otherwise unknown language being spoken in Pictland, it is best to focus on what we do know.

The most recent studies have shown that there was, indeed, a Celtic language spoken in ancient Pictish territory and that, in the medieval period, this was clearly closest to British rather than Gaulish (Rhys 2015). The similarities with British render it possible that it was simply the most northern form of British (James 2013; Rhys 2015). In terms of place-names, there are many features which are found on both sides of the Forth – for instance, *aber*, 'river- or burn-mouth', *ecles*, 'church', and *pen*, 'head, end, promontory' (Taylor 2011; Taylor with Márkus 2012, see Elements Glossary). The only element not found outside Pictland is **cuper*, 'confluence', which appears in Cupar in Fife and Coupar Angus, Perthshire (Taylor with Márkus 2012, 347). Therefore, place-names indicate that Pictland formed part of a linguistic continuum with British lands to the south. However, when British changed in the period from the 4th century AD to *c.*600 AD, partly under the influence of Latin, medieval Pictish speech did not always follow that of the Picts' southern neighbours, instead becoming more divergent (Rhys 2020a; Rhys 2020b). It is likely, therefore, that Pictish was in essence a dialect of British that was less Romanised than its southern neighbour, perhaps on the route to becoming a separate language.

Understanding that the Picts predominately spoke a Celtic language enables us to gain further insights into how they perceived themselves and their relationships with their neighbours. We can presume that Latin *Picti* had a vernacular equivalent. A Pictish version of the Celtic word for Britons, originally **Priteni*, is the most likely candidate, since the Britons (*Pryden* meant 'Pictland' and 'Britain') and Gaels (*Cruithni* meant 'Picts') both used such words for them while the Romans adapted the same name, creating *Britannia* for the island, *Britanni* for the inhabitants (Jackson 1954; Broun 2007, 81–84). *Cruithne* also appears as the name of the first Pictish king in the Pictish king-lists (Anderson 2011, 79–84), placed deep in the ancient past, so it may be that, in being **Priteni*, the Picts could stress their own antiquity. They were the 'real' Britons who remained unconquered by the Romans, both giving their kings a right to rule and a prior claim on the land of northern Britain, using a word known to their neighbours.

The Late- and immediate post-Roman period, whether regarded as a period of dramatic social, cultural and economic decline or not (Esmonde Cleary 1989; Dark 1994; Fleming 2010, 22–29; Halsall 2013, 87–101, 174–81), involved a number of crucial transformations in Britain and Ireland, with which northern Britain was intrinsically engaged (Charles-Edwards 2003). Roman culture survived in many respects but was modified. Many Britons who had inhabited the Roman province continued to speak Latin until the 7th century but increasingly the British (Celtic) language became dominant again (Charles-Edwards 2013). Anglo-Saxons also settled in the south and east of former Roman Britain and, by AD 700, their kingdoms came to dominate nearly all of what became England – apart from Cornwall and some land by the Welsh border – as well as most of Scotland south of the Forth, except for the lands of the remaining kingdom of the Britons centred on the fort of Dumbarton Rock by the River Clyde. This supremacy resulted in the spread of the English language over the bulk of the island's territory formerly in the Roman Empire.

In the west, there was also settlement in Cornwall, Wales and the Isle of Man, this time by Gaelic speakers (Charles-Edwards 2013, 174–81) who spoke a Celtic language which, by around AD 600 and probably centuries earlier, was very different from British. In Scotland, by this time,

Gaelic speakers inhabited Argyll and the southern Hebridean islands but there has been considerable debate regarding when and how this took place (Campbell 2001; Woolf 2007a, 332–40). By the end of the 6th century, the dynasty of Dál Riata was clearly also established in western Scotland as well as in County Antrim in Ulster. By 700, it was claimed that this Gaelic royal dynasty had seized land in Britain from the Picts around AD 500, but we should be very sceptical – migration and conquest were frequent, often erroneous, explanations for ethnic change in early sources. Ptolemy described the population group in Argyll as the *Epidii*, using a P-Celtic form closer to Pictish and British than Gaelic, but that is slender evidence for their language in the 2nd century AD. The classical sources suggest that some *Scotti*, the Latin term used for Gaelic-speaking raiders in the 4th and 5th centuries, are likely to have been settled in northern Britain by the end of Roman Britain, as they also were on the Isle of Man. If, as seems most likely, the Gaelic language did expand in Scotland in the Late Antique period, it was probably the result of close cultural contacts with Ireland and the Irish Sea area, as much, or more so, than political conquest and settlement.

The existence of these neighbours of the Picts in the Late-Roman and post-Roman periods in turn casts important light on the Picts. In the classical and later sources, the description of *Picti* as a *gens* and the term's use alongside other identities such as the Saxons, *Scotti* and the obscure *Attacotti* imply that the Picts were a recognised ethnic group. This is not to say Pictish identity was unchanging, nor that the Pictish identity fully supplanted a range of regional and local identities, or that the Picts always lived within the same geographic boundaries. Classical writers could often generalise when writing about their neighbours, but the Picts were not simply a catch-all term for 'barbarians' of northern Britain, as the texts distinguish them from the Britons and *Scotti* also living north of Hadrian's Wall. The Picts were clearly an identifiable group throughout the period, although, as with modern identities, we are unlikely ever to be able to fully categorise or single this group out using a rigid set of criteria.

Picts and Christianity

In addition to ethnic change, the early medieval period in which the Picts lived was also marked by the spread of Christianity, a far-reaching process of change that affected world-view, culture and the economy. It has been argued (for example, Grigg 2015) that the Church also supported royal power, partly by claiming that kings acting in their favour were divinely blessed. However, conversely the Church could become a drain on royal resources and a potential rival power source, and was sometimes antipathetic to the violence that was a key feature of the political sphere and the success of powerful kings. As will be discussed more fully in Chapter 4, the process of Christianisation in Pictland was probably lengthy and its impact is uncertain, though we are gradually gaining a greater understanding of the belief systems that were replaced, altered or continued, and we have fragments of evidence for the uptake of the new religion. Our perceptions are clouded by later accounts which attributed the conversion to a few key saints, particularly Columba and Ninian, but it is likely that many early Christians were involved and that the origins of the missionary activity lay in the twilight of the Roman Empire, especially the 5th century, when there was a strong evangelisation campaign in Britain and Ireland coming from the papacy, Gaul and Britain itself (Evans 2022). The success of the missionary activity is difficult to trace, partly because the early Church did not create many distinctive building, burial and sculptural practices, until the growth of Insular monasticism in the mid 6th century. However, it is clear that, by the later 7th century at the latest, Pictland had been converted and was characterised by substantial ecclesiastical institutions and settlements, like Abernethy by the Tay, Ner near Fetternear in Aberdeenshire, Kinneddar in Moray, Rosemarkie on the Black Isle, Portmahomack in Easter Ross and Applecross in Wester Ross.

The magnificent sculptures at such locations and at Meigle, St Vigeans and St Andrews, along with single finds at other sites, stand as testimony to the resources, artistry, ideology and contacts of Christian Pictland (Henderson and Henderson 2004). These connections were multiple, even though it is clear from the names of local saints' cults that Pictish holy figures were themselves significant. The Gaelic world was probably especially important in the conversion process and early Church life. By 700, Iona had a significant role in the Pictish Church with a network of subordinate institutions among the Picts and a series of dedications of places to Ionian clerics in the later 7th and early 8th centuries indicates a continued Gaelic influence in local Pictish communities (Taylor 1997; Taylor 2000a). However, by the late 9th century, Pictland also had other connections – to Bangor in Ireland (County Down) at Applecross and to Kildare through the cult of St Brigit at Abernethy. The cults of Palladius at Fordoun and Laurence at Laurencekirk in the Mearns reflect connections with Irish establishments dedicated to St Patrick, whose cult was dominated by Armagh (Clancy 2009). Moreover, Iona's power was also limited in the early 8th century by King Nechtan when he changed monastic tonsure and the method for calculating Easter away from Iona's practice to that maintained in Rome and most of the western Church, expelling the Columban community in the process. While the expulsion was probably temporary, this enhanced royal control, weakened Iona's influence and also involved Northumbrian English clergy. In the 8th and 9th centuries, the Pictish Church had its own practices, such as the distinct form and iconography of its sculpture, which utilised panels beside crosses not only for interlace but also figures and fantastic beasts, as well as, at least initially, Pictish symbols. However, it also had strong links with the wider Church, as shown by the St Andrew's shrine, being part of wider European developments, even if the Gaelic dimension increasingly came to the fore, part of the broader process by which Pictland became Alba (see Chapter 7).

Pictish kingship and the rise of an over-kingship

It is in the 6th century that clear evidence for Pictish kingship commences – the item in *c.*580 for Cennalath in the Irish chronicles being the first of many – with some given the title *rex Pictorum*, 'king of the Picts'. The Pictish king-lists, an early version of which was in existence by the reign of King Gartnait son of Donuel (*c.*656–663), included many kings before this, some with plausible names and reign lengths, stretching back into the ancient past for many centuries. However, some of the early kings – occasionally with reigns of fifty or a hundred years! – were clearly later additions, possibly included from other regnal lists, so we cannot rely on that as evidence for such a continuous, ancient line of kings.

The first contemporary item involving a Pict in the Irish chronicles, 'the flight before the son of Maelchon' recorded in *AU* 558 and *AU* 560 seems to refer to an obscure event involving Bridei son of Maelchon, a king based in northern Pictland, whose death is recorded in *AU* 583. He was a key figure in later sources, including Adomnán of Iona's *Life of Columba*, written *c.*700, and the Northumbrian Bede's *Ecclesiastical History of the English People*, finished in 731, but for slightly different reasons.

In Adomnán's *Life of Columba*, Bridei was a powerful king residing in a fort by the River Ness in the Great Glen, in *prouincia Pictorum*, 'the territory of the Picts', whose *magi*, 'wizards', sought to defeat the saint (I.37, II.32–34; Anderson and Anderson 1991, 70–71, 138–47). Columba prevailed, winning the assistance and respect of the king, as well as some converts, but the conversion of Bridei himself is not mentioned. Bede also described Bridei as a very powerful king but stated that Bridei was converted by Columba, along with the broader northern Pictish territories (*HE* III.4, Colgrave and Mynors 1969, 220–23). In return, Columba is said to have been given the island of Iona, which was to become the most important early-Christian centre in northern Britain. The contradictions in these two texts may not just be due to the saint's *Life* having a different emphasis from a text that sought briefly to explain Christianity in northern Britain as part of a wider scheme of salvation history, but may also result from Adomnán being conscious of the (probably correct) view that Iona was a Gaelic donation, whereas Bede repeated a Pictish claim to overlordship of northern Britain.

Such views of supremacy, perhaps resting on the idea that the Picts preceded the Gaels in the west, in the area that was, by 700, called Dál Riata, were a product of the power of the Pictish realm in Bede's time. Before the late 7th century, it is difficult to define the status of kings in Pictland, since the Irish chronicles either did not give titles to Pictish rulers or simply called them *rex Pictorum*. The Latin is inherently ambiguous – *rex Pictorum* could mean 'the king of the Picts', representing a Pictish overkingship, but, alternatively, it may have simply denoted 'a king of the Picts', that is, one of many. The latter meaning is more likely since, elsewhere in our early sources, we have the titles *rex Britonum*, 'king of the Britons', and *rex Saxonum*, 'king of the English', when we know that there were multiple kings of these ethnic groups. However, there remains the question of why these particular kings were recorded, so it is plausible that they were particularly powerful rulers in Pictland, who had gained the notice of Iona's chroniclers.

In the mid 7th century, the expansionist Anglo-Saxon kingdom of the Northumbrians achieved a dominance over much of northern Britain, including at least parts of Pictland, though it is uncertain how this hegemony operated in practice. In the later 7th century, that overlordship was shattered by Bridei son of Beli, a ruler of Fortriu, a territory now recognised as located around the Moray Firth, perhaps extending from Ross to Moray (Woolf 2006). The rise of Fortriu, which became the pre-eminent Pictish province, was one of the most notable developments of early medieval Scotland (Figures 1.3 and 1.4).

The formation of the entity known as Fortriu can be traced back to the Roman Iron Age. Our first reference to this region is when Ammianus Marcellinus named the Verturiones (hence the adjective 'Verturian' used in some recent scholarship) as one of the two Pictish peoples, along with the Dicalydones, involved in the 'Barbarian Conspiracy' of 367–368. After this, our next reference is in 664 in the Irish chronicles, which gives the related territorial name, Fortriu in a Gaelicised form. Bridei's stronghold was located, according to Adomnán, by the River Ness, perhaps at Craig Phadrig, Torvean or nearby Inverness, in or close to the power base of Fortriu. If Bede and Adomnán were not simply projecting back Fortriu's later power here, then Bede's description of Bridei as '*rex potentissimus*', a 'very powerful king' (*HE* III.4, Colgrave and Mynors 1969, 222), and Adomnán's portrayal of Bridei as the overlord of a *regulus* or 'underking' of Orkney (*VSC* II.42, Anderson and Anderson 1991, 166–67) indicate that Fortriu's wider power had a precursor in the late 6th century (Figure 1.3).

While their earlier history may be somewhat obscure, it is clear that the power of the kings of Fortriu in northern Britain was secured in the late 7th century with the famous victory at the Battle of Nechtanesmere. Early in his reign, Ecgfrith, king of the Northumbrians (671–685), crushed what

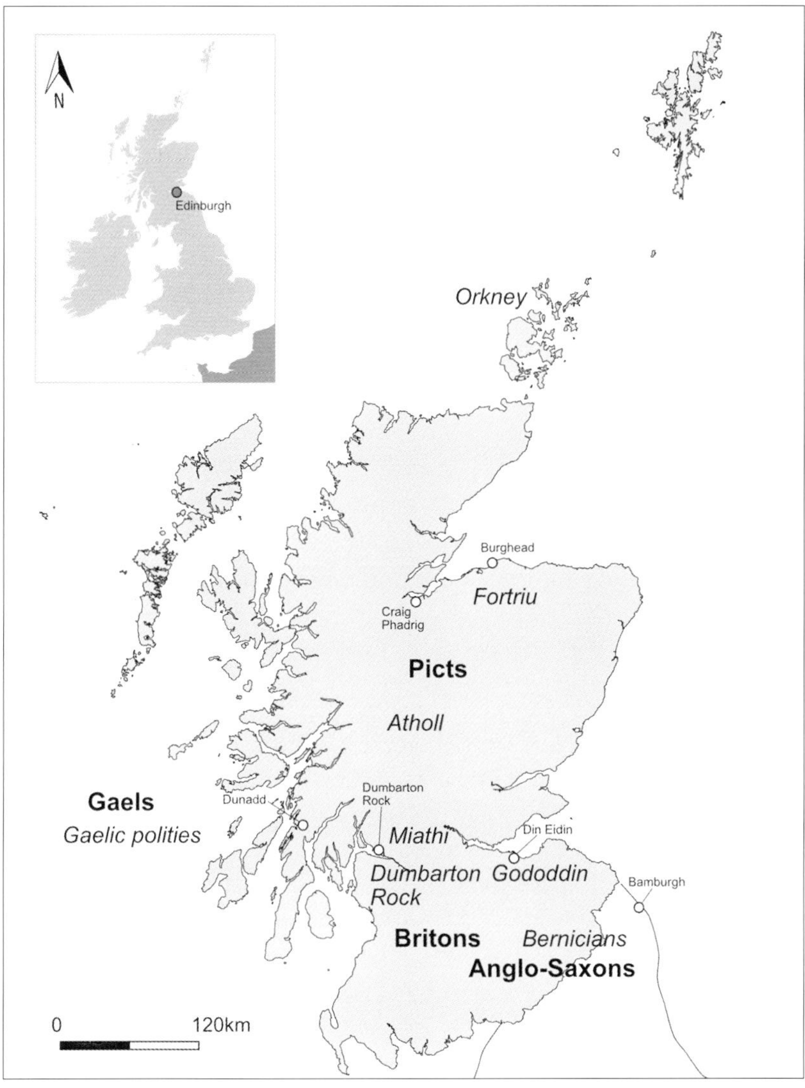

1.3 Map showing Picts and their neighbours in the early 7th century.

Stephen of Ripon regarded as a Pictish rebellion, after 'swarms of them gathered from every cranny of the north' (Stephen, *Life of Wilfrid*, ch. 19, Webb 2004, 128). However, from 679 onwards, the Irish chronicles start to record conflicts in northern Britain that appear to have been preludes to the Pictish victory at Nechtanesmere. Sieges are noted in 679 at Dún Baitte (*AU* 680.5, see Chapter 3) and, in 680, there was a siege of Dunnottar near Stonehaven (*AU* 681.5). Then, in 681 (*AU* 682.4), Orkney was 'destroyed' by Bridei (presumably the son of Beli). In the following year, in 682, there were sieges of Dunadd in Mid Argyll and Dundurn in Strathearn (*AU* 683.3). While these campaigns cannot with certainty be associated directly with Bridei, they can plausibly be linked with Bridei growing his power base and taking the fight to the Northumbrians.

Bridei's activities in Pictland certainly caught the attention of the Northumbrian ruler Ecgfrith who launched his own campaign in Pictland. This resulted in the Battle of Nechtanesmere (Dún Nechtain in the Irish chronicles), in which Ecgfrith was killed and his army defeated (see also Chapter 3). After his victory, Bridei ended Northumbrian rule north of the Forth, extending Fortriu's control southwards. On his death in 692 (*AU* 693.1), the Iona chronicler called Bridei 'king of Fortriu' and it is from his reign that we can see clearly that there was a powerful over-kingdom of the Picts.

The extent and power of the expanded (or partially restored to its former extent) 7th-century kingdom of the Picts is indicated in a number of written sources (Figure 1.4). One of Bridei's immediate successors, Bridei son of Derilei (696–707), was a signatory to Adomnán's 'Law of the Innocents', also ratified *c.*697 by kings in Ireland and Dál Riata. King Bridei was the only Pictish participant, apart from Curetán, a cleric of Rosemarkie on the Black Isle (Márkus 2008, 17–18; see also Chapter 4). This law prevented minors, women and clerics from participating in warfare while also protecting them during conflict. The clerics of the Columban community were to collect the fines designated for infringements, but ultimately rulers were expected to ensure adherence, indicating that kings such as Bridei son of Derilei felt able to assert their rule throughout their realm, in aspiration at least. Similarly, in the 710s, King Nechtan son of Derilei (707–724, 729–732) decided not only the Church practice in his realm, relating to the tonsure and the date of Easter, but Bede states that he then ordered copies of the new Easter tables to be distributed 'throughout all the provinces of the Picts' (*HE* V 21, Colgrave and Mynors 1969, 532–53). Clearly the over-kings of Pictland, in the later 7th and 8th centuries AD, were able to decide law and policy throughout their hegemony.

In the 730s, the Pictish kingdom expanded further, to include Gaelic Dál Riata in the west. King Onuist son of Uurguist (732–761) invaded and conquered the Gaels of Dál Riata in Argyll after a number of campaigns from 731–741. This conquest was not permanent – kings of Dál Riata appear again in the 770s until 792, in a period when Pictland was itself divided, but, by the 9th century, Dál Riata again seems to have come under Pictish rule (Broun 1998; Clancy 2004). This period, therefore, can be regarded as the height of Pictish royal power, but Pictish control might not have been very stable, perhaps being maintained largely through local leaders, even before the Scandinavians presented an existential threat to the kingdom from the mid 9th century onwards (see Chapter 7).

Indeed, throughout the 8th century, there were periods of conflict, such as a major civil war with a three-way leadership battle from 728 to 729. Later, in the 770s and 780s, Pictland seems to have been divided, as indi-

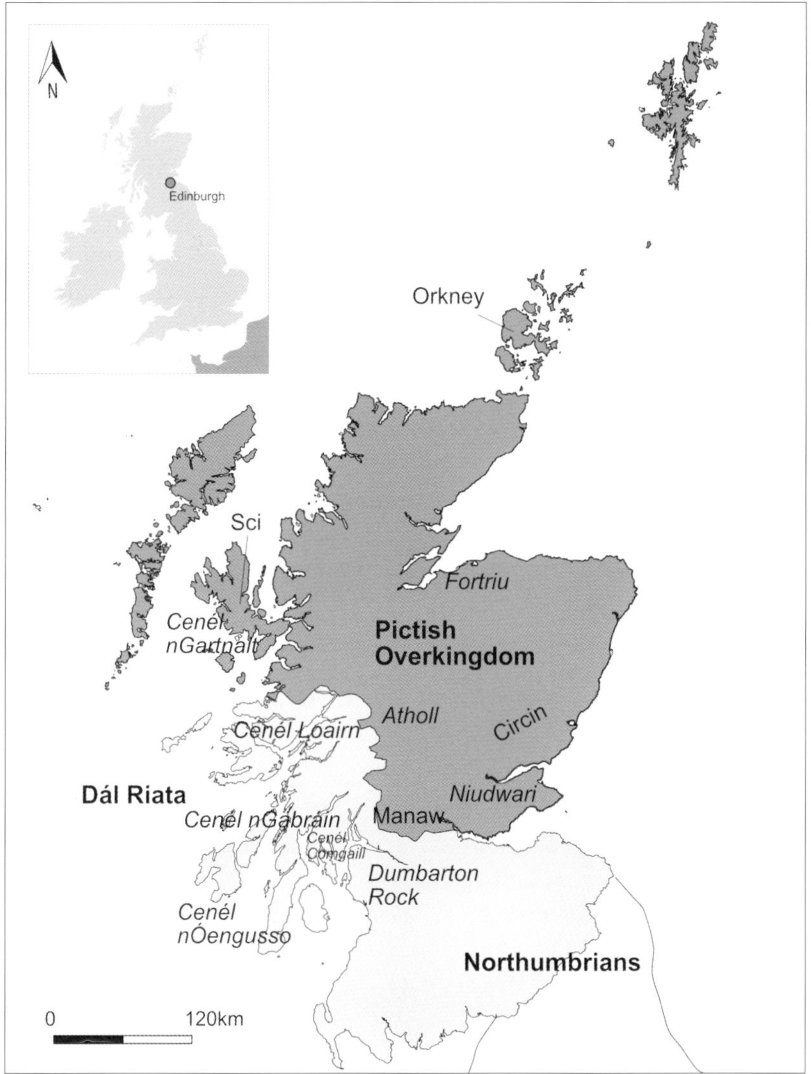

1.4 Map showing Picts and their neighbours *c*.AD 700, when Pictish over-kingship was consolidated.

cated by a reference in the *Annals of Ulster*, *AU* 782.1, to 'Dubthalorc, king of the Picts this side of the Mounth', demonstrating that the Highlands could be a political dividing line. That potential division may also be reflected in Bede's *Ecclesiastical History*, in which he stated that the northern Picts had been evangelised by St Columba, whereas the southern Picts were converted by St Ninian (*HE* III.4, Colgrave and Mynors 1969, 220–23; see also Chapter 4). Similarly, a Gaelic text, *Senchas Síl hÍr*, which might have elements from before the mid 10th century, stated that the *Cruithni* (the Picts) in the ancient period settled in *Mag Fortrenn* and *Mag Circin* (Dobbs 1923, 64–66), the plain of Fortriu in the north, and of Circin, including the Mearns, Strathmore, Gowrie and perhaps Strathearn south of the Mounth. This reflected a similar division to Bede's, with the Highlands again being the dividing line (Evans 2013).

Moreover, even when undivided, Pictish kings faced internal threats, since our sources indicate that a number of kings were expelled from the kingship. In the period before 730, it is likely that father-to-son succession to the kingship of Fortriu was prevented by a wider dynasty or the nobility in order to stop a single narrow lineage dominating at their expense (Evans 2008). How exactly the next king emerged from the royal dynasty is not clear, though recent scholars have argued that the suggested evidence for the Picts practising matriliny, where the succession went through the female line, is weak, to be explained by the brothers Bridei (696–707) and Nechtan (707–724, 729–732) having their claims to the throne through their Pictish mother Der-Ilei (Ross 1999; Woolf 1998). However kings came to power, the pattern of succession changed after the mid 8th century, probably caused by an outsider, King Onuist son of Uurguist (732–761), attempting to position his children on the throne (Evans 2008). After his reign, it seems that his family (with a few exceptions) came to dominate the succession, with sons of previous kings succeeding, albeit with an intervening ruler. Thus was begun the system of alternation between two branches of the royal dynasty, which became standard practice among the dynasty established by Cináed mac Alpín until the 11th century (Woolf 2007a, 220–71), deep into the period of the Gaelic kingship of Alba.

We have a limited understanding of the regional political organisation of Pictland and the political structure of Pictish rulership and kingship. The appearance of a *regulus* of Orkney in Adomnán's *Life of Columba* indicates that some regions could retain local royal dynasties. This is supported by the existence of a king of Atholl, a title given in *AU* 739.7 when recording the drowning of Talorgan son of Drostan, king of Atholl, by Onuist son of Uurguist, king of the Picts. However, this is the last surviving reference to a Pictish king of a specific region. There may have been other forms of local and regional governance, though. From 918 onwards, just after the end of Pictish identity, people with the Gaelic title *mormáer* (meaning 'great steward' or 'sea steward') begin to appear in our sources, associated with regions like Angus, Gowrie and also Atholl, showing that, by this period at least, local kings had been replaced by non-royal officials. Probably these were originally royal officials but, by the 12th century, they had become hereditary positions, controlled by local elites (Broun 2015). In the 12th century, a *mormáer* would lead his province in war, as well as having a judicial role (Taylor with Márkus 2009, 234–36, 274, 285; Taylor 2016, 25–53, 91–113). It is likely that the *mormáer* had Pictish origins and, in one region where there was later a *mormáer* – the Mearns – the name itself means 'the stewartry', indicating an earlier phase in this region when there was a *máer*, 'steward', responsible for smaller areas, perhaps appointed in the era of Northumbrian domination or as Fortriu expanded in the 7th century (Broun forthcoming a).

By the 12th century, there was quite a varied patchwork of relationships and obligations connecting local communities, lords, churches and the king in Alba, which may give clues as to how society may have been organised in the Pictish period. Kindreds – wide familial relationship groups – were central to society, though individuals and settlements usually, but not always, had a lord of some kind (Broun 2015; A. Taylor 2016, 59–60, 146–48). Apart from ecclesiastical institutions, the king and the *mormáer* were also important local leaders, owning lands not only through their positions but also as heads of kin. The lesser lord – the *toísech* (plural *toísig*), also called a thane – was often also head of a kindred, though could manage lands for a king or *mormáer* (Broun 2015). The *toísech*, *mormáer* and king directly controlled some estate centres (*maneria*) but there were other lands (appendages) whose inhabitants brought renders to the *manerium*, such as the annual *cáin* render to the lord. This whole complex of *manerium* and appendages, which could change as relationships altered, was called a 'shire' (Broun 2015). This system's origins certainly lie before 1100, but whether a similar system operated in the Pictish era is not known, and the earliest associated terms were in Gaelic and English.

A more promising Pictish survival is the davoch (from Gaelic *dabach*, 'vat'), a small local unit which is probably earlier than the parish, which itself was firmly established in the 12th and early 13th centuries for organising Christian pastoral care (Ross 2015). The davoch was important as it was the basis for the 'common burdens' of the realm: military service, labour works (such as castle and bridge building) and 'aids' – renders to supply the army (Taylor 2016, 91–111). The first clear references to this relate to the late 11th century, though it was a term which spread to other areas, such as south-east Scotland (Broun forthcoming b). It has been argued to be Pictish, since it appears in a place-name, *Doldauha* in the St Andrews Foundation Legend B, which states that the text was written by a Cano son of Dubabrach for King Uurad son of Bargoit (839–842) in Meigle (Ross 2015, 178–98; Broun forthcoming b) but, unfortunately, this source is an amalgam of multiple available texts, including a later Pictish king-list, so it is unclear what exactly was written by Cano. Nevertheless, the units called davochs vary in their nature, indicating that they existed before the name *dabach* was connected to them (Woolf 2017a). In the Irish legal tract *Críth Gablach* (written *c.*700), it was expected that a *mruigfher* (a wealthy farmer) and an *aire* (a noble) would own a *dabach*, which was the largest type of vat (Binchy 1979, 7, 14; *eDIL* s.v. *dabach*) so, in addition to being a suitable size for quantifying and transporting various food renders, one such vat could have been available among a group of settlements. The word *dabach* is Gaelic but the St Andrews Foundation Legend B states that *Doldauha* ('water-meadow/haugh of the davoch') is now called *Chendrohedalian*, a Gaelic name (now Kindrochit, Braemar), perhaps reflecting an early phase when the davoch was less universal (Broun forthcoming b). This increases the possibility that the davoch had a Pictish precursor. It can be expected that, with interdisciplinary research, it will be increasingly possible to produce a more precise picture of whether units like the davochs and the shires and officials such as the thane and *toísech* represent survivals in some form from the Pictish era or were solely later innovations.

The geography of Pictland

As we have seen, the geographical extent of the Pictish realm changed over time. Not everyone inside the kingdom's boundaries would have regarded themselves as Pictish, although our evidence for self-identity throughout northern Britain is too limited to judge this except in a few cases. One exception is the prehistoric section of the longer (*Series longior*) Pictish king-list, added in the reign of Constantín mac Cináeda (862–876) (Broun 2007, 78). This insertion begins with Cruithne (the Gaelic word for 'Pict') son of Cinge but then lists his seven sons, who each reigned in succession after him. The names of the seven sons are actually not real personal names but Gaelicised forms of Pictish provinces. The provinces are: *Fib*, Fife; *Fidach* which may survive in the place-name Glen Fiddich in Banffshire or may simply mean 'woody'; *Floclaid* or *Foltlaid* is Gaelic *Fotla*, another name for Ireland but perhaps denoting Atholl (*Athfhotla*, 'Second Ireland') or simply a Gaelic-speaking territory; *Fortrenn* refers to Fortriu around the Moray Firth; *Got* or *Cat* equates to Caithness and Sutherland (which are called *i Cataibh* in Scottish Gaelic); *Ce* seems to have been a region which may survive in the Aberdeenshire hill name Mither Tap o' Bennachie; and *Circin* was a region in southern Pictland, a term used for the large Lowland area from the Mearns, Angus, Stormont, Gowrie and perhaps Strathearn (Broun 2000a; Evans 2013). This list was essentially a geographical statement referring to at least some of the core territories of the Pictish kingdom during Constantín's reign, ranging from Caithness to Fife (Figure 1.5). It gave each mentioned region a potential share in the kingship. Fortriu had the longest reign and Circin the second longest, indicating that these were considered to be the most important. Circin was also listed as reigning directly after Cruithne, reflecting the fact that this text was written in Abernethy, in that territory (Evans 2013, 7–10). However, the list of Pictish territories was not comprehensive, since only territories that began with *F* or *C* were recorded, suggesting that literary alliteration decided which names were selected. Other probable Pictish territories such as Orkney were not mentioned. Indeed, our early sources are almost silent on areas outside of central and southern Scotland.

1.5 The geography of Pictland and the probable location of Pictish regions including the over-kingship of Fortriu. (© University of Aberdeen)

Apart from the longer Pictish king-list, when defining Pictland we rely on statements by outside authors about the location of Picts and Pictland. Adomnán of Iona, in his *Life of Columba*, stated that the Gaels and Picts were divided by *Dorsum Britanniae*, 'the ridge of Britain' (later found in Gaelic as *Druim Alban*), which was the watershed line between rivers flowing west and east, north of Loch Lomond (Dunshea 2013). This watershed forms the boundary between Argyll and Perthshire, before it crosses the Great Glen (between Loch Lochy and Loch Oich) and continues northwards (Dunshea 2013, 288). Bede had a similar conception of the extent of Pictland, specifying that the Picts lived north of the Forth estuary (*HE* I.12, Colgrave and Mynors 1969, 40–41). However, Bede also seemed to place Iona in Pictland (*HE* III.4, Colgrave and Mynors 1969, 220–23) but, as already stated, his view on Iona may have been a result of reproducing a Pictish viewpoint, since it is clear from other evidence that Iona was strongly Gaelic in culture. There is also strong evidence for the mainland around Iona being the home of Gaels. Gaels are cited as inhabiting Ardnamurchan in Adomnán's *Life of Columba* (II.10, II.22; Sharpe 1995, 161–62, 171–72); and the existence of later names including Báetán, the ancestor of a Cenél Loairn kindred, indicates that Morvern and Ardgour parish on the mainland west of Loch Linnhe were part of Dál Riata (Watson 1926, 122–23; Fraser 2009a, 245–46). Notwithstanding the possibility that Gaelic-speaking people could regard themselves as Picts or be part of the Pictish kingdom, it is most likely that these areas were outside of Pictland.

Nevertheless, there is some evidence that to the north of Ardnamurchan cultural features common east of the watershed were also found on the north-western seaboard and in the northern Hebridean islands. The place-names Applecross (*Apurcrosan*) and the name Lochaber contain *aber*, 'mouth' or 'confluence', found in eastern Scotland and British areas but not in Ireland or Argyll. Similarly there are Pictish symbols found in the Hebrides, which indicates that the artistic practice, and probably ideology, underlying them spread to Skye and the Western Isles. For Skye, we have references in Irish chronicles to a kindred, Cenél nGartnait, which was regarded by the early 8th century as a branch of the powerful Gaelic Cenél nGabráin kindred (Fraser 2004, 84–86; Fraser 2005b). However, it is striking that many of the names of Cenél nGartnait figures, for instance Cano, Gartnait and Tuathalán, are found in this period among the Picts, but not in Ireland, indicating cultural connections with the east, though we do not know whether they were recent or longstanding (Evans 2019a, 31–32). It is therefore justifiable to include the north-western seaboard and northern Hebridean region as part of Pictland in the analysis of this book, while recognising that we do not know for sure whether or when the inhabitants regarded themselves as Pictish.

In the Northern Isles, the evidence varies according to the archipelago. The name Orkney itself partly derives from a Celtic word found already in ancient sources as *Orcades* from **orcos* (Rivet and Smith 1979, 40, 433–34). Orkney was connected repeatedly in contemporary texts to Pictish kingdoms, not only in Adomnán's *Life of Columba*, where its ruler was present near the River Ness as a subordinate to King Bridei son of Maelchon (*VSC* II.42; Sharpe 1995, 196), but also in the annalistic record that Bridei son of Bile 'destroyed' Orkney in 681. A late 8th- or early 9th-century Anglo-Saxon source also stated that Orkney was in the land of the Picts (Dumville 1976). We do have evidence for Gaelic involvement too (Plumb 2020, 146–50), including clerics being active there before the Viking Age (*VSC* II.42; Sharpe 1995, 196–98; see also Chapter 4). As with Orkney, Scandinavians replaced or transformed pre-existing place-names in Shetland so it is difficult to identify the languages of their predecessors, though, like Orkney, *petta* and *papar* names indicate that there was a later perception that Picts and clerics had once been inhabitants (Wainwright 1962, 100; MacDonald 2002). Gaelic clerics may also have been present in Shetland, since the Gaelic writer Dicuil stated in 825 that hermits had, for nearly a hundred years, sailed from *Scottia*, 'Gaeldom', to live on a previously uninhabited archipelago in the north, probably the Faroes (Tierney and Bieler 1967, 74–77), so clearly Shetland would be another viable destination. Interestingly, Dicuil did not comment on the origins of other clerics who had written to or told him about travels to 'Thule' – here referring to Iceland – and other islands, probably the Faroes again (Lamb 1995, 13), perhaps because these informants were Pictish. This could be evidence for an otherwise overlooked ascetic *peregrinatio* dimension to the Pictish Church. Moreover, as will be seen, archaeological evidence indicates that there were strong connections with mainland Pictland, so it is relatively safe to regard both Shetland and Orkney as Pictish territories, prior to Scandinavian settlement.

After the victory of Dún Nechtain in 685, territories around the Forth estuary and river and its tributaries, such as the Teith, came to be at the southern edge of the Pictish kingdom. Flanders Moss to the west of Stirling presented much more of a barrier to north–south travel than it does today. This frontier area had been predominantly British but, in the late 6th and 7th centuries, we have evidence for Anglo-Saxon conquests from the southeast, as well as Gaelic and Pictish activity. Until the British kingdom of Strathclyde ceased to exist in the 11th century, it was a borderland, a melting pot of different cultures, languages and polities. By about AD 700, Fife seems to have been regarded as part of Pictland (Duncan 1975, 78) but to the west was the area called Manaw straddling the Forth from Clackmannanshire (Clackmannan means 'Stone of Manaw') to Slamannan in Stirlingshire. Manaw was regarded as the northernmost British outpost in Welsh literature as late as the 10th-century poem *Armes Prydein* ('The Prophecy of Britain') (Williams and Bromwich 1982, 12–13, 66). Moreover, the place-names of Clackmannanshire contain a British stratum and Gaelic coinings from the 8th century onwards, but no distinctive Pictish names (Taylor 2020, 70–77).

Much of the area between Loch Lomond and the Forth estuary still requires a full survey to see whether distinctively Pictish place-names were created there, but in Menteith (to the west of Stirling, including Callander, Aberfoyle and Doune) at least such an analysis has been undertaken (McNiven 2011, 45–55, Map 5 at 547). In Menteith, as well as a large corpus of Gaelic names, there were P-Celtic (British or Pictish) names, some with predominantly British elements, like **lanerc*, but many others (such as *aber*, *eccles*, **carden* and *monadh*) found mainly among both the Picts and the northern Britons. The evidence sometimes points southwards to the Britons, sometimes northwards to the Picts, so we cannot impose a hard linguistic boundary in this area between Pictish and British, or indeed with Gaelic (McNiven 2011, 52). Nevertheless, this region was divided into Pictish and Northumbrian zones of control by 700. Bede stated that, after Nechtanesmere, Northumbrian clerics were forced to evacuate Abercorn, the centre of the Northumbrian bishopric of the Picts on the south side of the Forth, now in West Lothian (*HE* IV.26, Colgrave and Mynors 1969, 426–29). This was followed by another Pictish victory in 698 (*AU* 698.2) but, in 711, there was 'a slaughter of the Picts in the plain of Manaw by the Saxons' (*AU* 711.3), which English sources stated took place between the Carron and Avon rivers (Fraser 2009a, 272). The implications of this for political boundaries are uncertain but Bede, in his *Ecclesiastical History*, finished in 731, seems to have placed the boundary between the Picts and their southern neighbours at or close to the Antonine Wall (*HE* I.12, Colgrave and Mynors 1969, 40–43). Bede may have been simplifying but there is no reason to dismiss the possibility that this was a real medieval reuse of this Roman frontier as a political boundary.

The western end of the Antonine Wall, which terminated at Old Kilpatrick on the Clyde, bisected British territory controlled by Dumbarton Rock. On the north and west sides of Loch Lomond are *Clach nam Breatann* and *Clach nam Breatunnaich* (or *Clach a' Bhreatunnaich*), both massive natural features with names meaning 'Rock of the Britons', indicating that these were places Gaelic speakers associated with that ethnic group (McNiven 2011, 46). Moreover, in Welsh literature, *Mynydd Bannog*, probably the high ground from the Campsies to the Gargunnock and Touch hills whose name survives in Bannockburn, was a significant boundary (Charles-Edwards 2013, 6–7). In the Forth valley area, Cenél nGabráin kings won a victory against the Miathi (the earlier Maiatai) in the late 6th century but suffered a major defeat against the Dumbarton Britons *c.*640 in the Battle of Strathcarron when their king Domnall Brecc was killed. Taken together, this activity probably reflects some Cenél nGabráin control east of Loch Lomond in this period. However, both Cenél nGabráin and especially the Dumbarton Britons soon had to contend with the Northumbrians, advancing from the south-east, who, by the 650s, were using the unlocated *Urbs Iudeu* by the Forth estuary as a centre and controlling at least part of Manaw (Taylor 2020, 52–57).

In the same period, Pictish rulers appear in the region fighting against Gaels and Britons. In 654, the Irish chronicles refer to the killing of a certain Dúncath son of Conaing, most likely another Cenél nGabráin dynast (Fraser 2004, 82–84), by the Pictish king Talorgen son of Enfret, at *Srath Ethairt* (*srath*, 'broad valley') or *Rath Ethairt* (*raith*, 'earthen rampart') (Taylor 2011, 477, 504), probably referring to Strathyre (Fraser 2009a,

183), one of the main routes down to the Forth valley from the Highlands. Later, after the rulers of Fortriu defeated the Northumbrians in 685, the Picts fought against the Dumbarton Britons at Mugdock north of Glasgow in 750, and in 756 attacked Dumbarton Rock in alliance with their former enemies, the Northumbrians (Fraser 2009a, 312–18).

To summarise, we have evidence for conflict between Britons, Gaels, Northumbrians and Picts in the zone north of the Clyde and around the Firth of Forth. These episodes of warfare and conflict suggest that there were rough and perhaps ever-changing boundaries, not necessarily reflecting the ethnic or linguistic situation on the ground. In the 650–730 period, Pictish territory was extended south to the Campsie Fells to Forth valley area, with probably Loch Lomond, and, as argued earlier, the Highland watershed forming the boundary to the west. Pictish expansion from the 730s into Argyll resulted in the northern Britons being increasingly surrounded by the Picts to the north and the Northumbrians to the south.

Overall, it is clear that the geographical spread of Picts and the boundaries of their kingdoms changed over time. The extent of Pictland used in this book broadly reflects the situation when Bede wrote in 731, on the eve of the dramatic expansion of the Pictish over-kingdom through the conquest of Dál Riata. It is largely for practical purposes, since the degree to which the people of Argyll and the southern Hebrides came to regard themselves as Pictish after the 730s is an open question, not to be dismissed too readily. It should be stressed that the reconstruction of Pictland is not a precise process, since the evidence is often scanty and inconclusive.

Elsewhere in Britain and Ireland, there was a flourishing vernacular written culture among the early medieval English, Gaels and, to a lesser extent, among the British (where Latin retained a prestige position as a spoken as well as written language) (Charles-Edwards 2013, 75–115). By the late 7th century, a close correlation existed among groups speaking a particular language and their ethnic identity, indicating that language was an important identity marker (Evans 2019b, 154–56). However, we should be wary of assuming that this correlation was present within Pictish territory, for only inscriptions survive as examples of their vernacular texts and there were large areas of the Pictish kingdom with British and Gaelic speakers. In addition, ogham inscriptions, Gaelic place-names present in Pictish areas by the 8th century (Taylor 1996), and the Pictish origin legend's account of a sojourn in Ireland before the Picts took northern Britain, all indicate that Pictland was strongly influenced by Gaelic culture by at least AD 800 and probably much earlier (see Chapter 7). There is no evidence that these cultural influences and strata were in any way regarded as 'non-Pictish' (Charles-Edwards 2008, 185–88).

The complicated relationship between language and kingdom and the Pictish reality is highlighted in relation to a place-name Bede actually described as Pictish. In naming the place at the eastern end of the Antonine Wall, modern Kinneil, which he regarded as dividing the Picts and Northumbrians, Bede gave its Pictish name as *Peanfahel* and its English form *Penneltun* (I.12; Colgrave and Mynors 1969, 42–43). *Pean-* could represent a Pictish form of British *penn*, 'end, head', but *–fahel* is a Gaelic version of British *guual*, rather than the correct Pictish form (Watson 1926, 346–48). It seems that Bede assumed that a name on the border of the Pictish kingdom would have had a Pictish language form, at least in part, in the same way as the English element *–tun* had been added to Celtic *Pennel-*. *Peanfahel* was located in a British area with Gaelic-speaking incomers, so none of the name was in the Pictish language. However, in one sense Bede was not mistaken – if the inhabitants who used *Peanfahel* thought of themselves as Picts (or its vernacular equivalent) because they supported the Pictish kings, then their speech could be regarded, as a result, as 'Pictish'. Clearly, there were Gaelic-speaking Picts and British-speaking Picts, as well as Picts speaking what we assume was 'Pictish'. For this reason, it may be that there was a far less strong connection between language and identity among the Picts than elsewhere in Britain and Ireland – and the increasing need to account for this diversity may have had important implications in the late first millennium AD (see Chapter 7). That greater ability to include new members into the 'imagined community' (Anderson 1991) that this flexibility provided would have been an asset when the Pictish kingdom was expanding and potentially when trying to build coalitions against common enemies, like the Northumbrians and later the Dublin Vikings. However, as will be seen in Chapter 7, it also made it more possible for Pictish identity to shift away from elements like the Pictish language, if it ceased to be the main tongue spoken in the kingdom.

Discovering the Picts through the archaeological record

As well as a relatively limited historical context for the Picts, the other major limiting factor in our understanding of the Picts has been a very meagre archaeological record. In the oft-referred-to volume *The Problem of the Picts* edited by Wainwright, the paucity of the archaeological record was laid bare (Wainwright 1955a; 1955b, 87; see also Chapter 3). In 1955, not a single dwelling could be confidently associated with the Picts and, in the subsequent years, the situation only improved a little and the settlement record has lain markedly behind that of early medieval England, for example, where hundreds of Anglo-Saxon buildings are known, or Ireland, where tens of thousands of early medieval ringforts, settlement cemeteries and other dwellings have been identified (Hamerow 1993, 2012; O'Sullivan 2008; O'Sullivan *et al.* 2014, 49). In contrast, in Pictland, the number of Pictish-era dwellings in Lowland eastern Scotland can be counted on a few

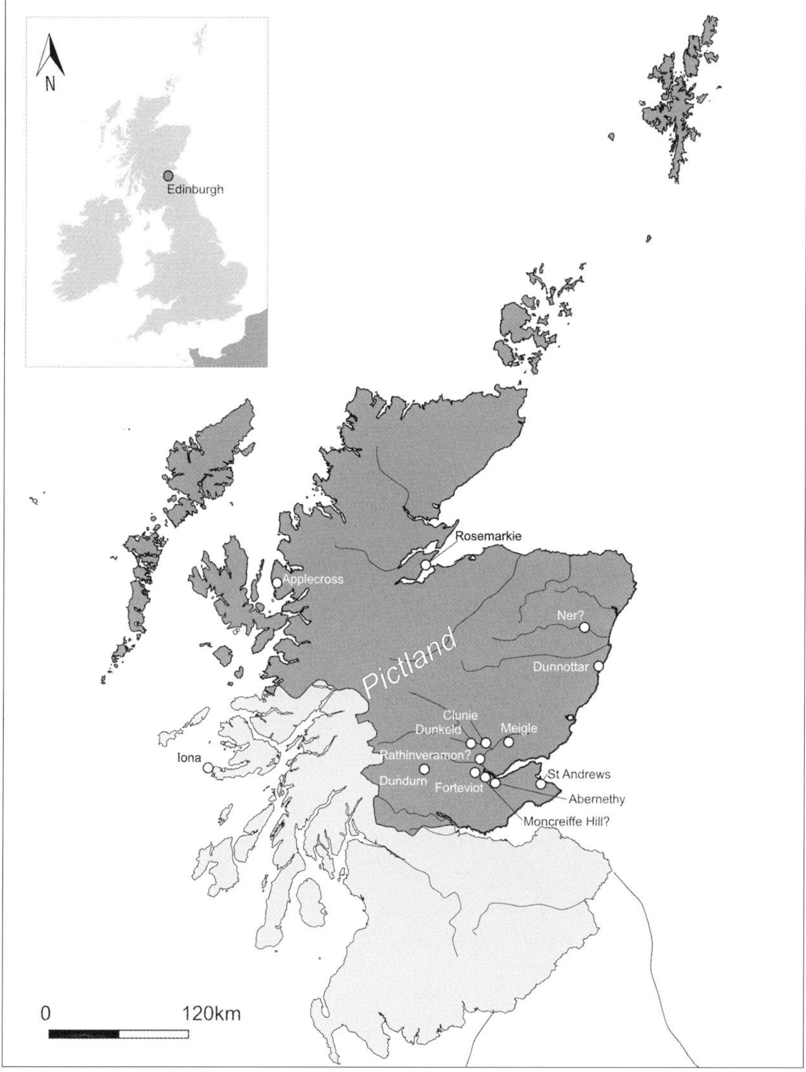

1.6 Sites in Pictland referenced in early sources: Dunnottar (referenced 7th and 9th centuries AD); Dundurn (7th and 9th centuries AD); *Rathinveramon*/*Cinnbelathoir* (9th century AD) – exact site disputed; Forteviot (9th century AD); Moncreiffe Hill (8th century AD); Meigle (9th century AD); Clunie (9th century AD); Ner (Fetternear) (7th century AD); St Andrews (8th century AD); Dunkeld (9th century AD); Applecross (7th–9th centuries AD); Abernethy (Gowrie) (9th century AD); Rosemarkie (8th century AD); Iona (referenced 6th entury AD onwards).

hands (Chapter 2). Progress has been better in the Northern Isles of Orkney and Shetland in particular with a tradition of cellular, figure-of-eight and rectilinear settlement types known. In eastern Scotland, the structural evidence has generally been limited to buildings found within hillforts but, in recent years, a tradition of longhouses in the uplands of Perthshire and Angus has helped to flesh out the settlement record. Although our knowledge of Pictish-era settlement is still relatively scanty, major leaps forward are within our grasp (see Chapter 2).

In the absence of a wider settlement record in Pictland, attention has focussed on Pictish sites mentioned in historical sources, though these are also few and far between (Figure 1.6). The hillfort of Dundurn (Figure 1.7)

1.7 Aerial image of Dundurn hillfort looking down the Strathearn river valley.

is mentioned as being under siege in AD 682 in the *Annals of Ulster* and Dunnottar, a promontory fort, has records in the same source for sieges in AD 680 and 693 (see Chapter 3). In the *Life of Columba*, King Bridei's fort is said to have been located beside the River Ness in the Great Glen – a prime candidate for this fort is Craig Phadrig (Figure 1.8), overlooking modern-day Inverness, and this, along with Urquhart Castle on Loch Ness, has confirmed early medieval activity in the form of objects and dated deposits (Small and Cottam 1972; Alcock and Alcock 1992; Peteranna and Birch 2018).

The lack of identifiable unenclosed settlement has meant that enclosed and fortified sites have occupied a central role in the study of Pictland and the same goes for Scotland more generally with settlement remains difficult to identify in most regions. However, early medieval fortified sites are not numerous – dozens of sites have been identified at best, compared to the many hundreds of hillforts that are likely to date to the Iron Age (Ralston 2004, 2015). Nonetheless, forts are key sites for the early medieval period, for they appear to be deeply implicated in the emergence of early medieval power structures where warfare, the conquest of land and growing hierarchies allowed the growth of royal power (see Chapter 3).

The evaluation through excavation of the defended settlements that had

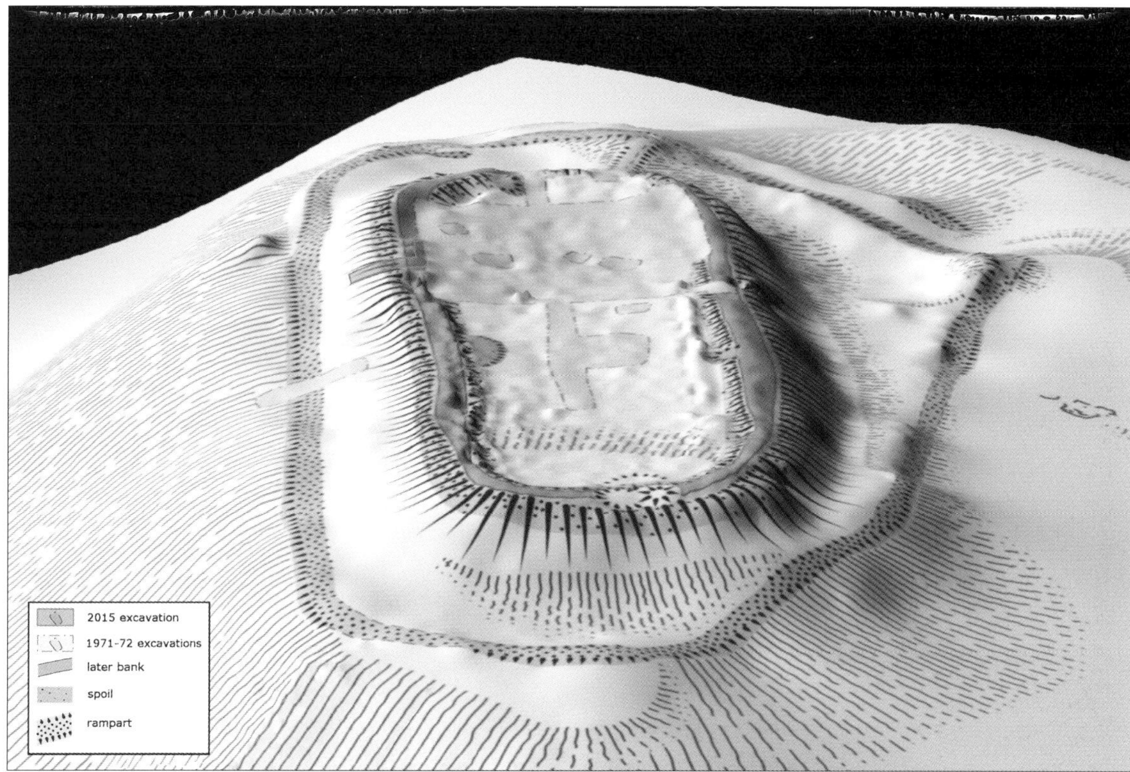

1.8 Craig Phadrig – survey data showing the outlines of Craig Phadrig hillfort – an Iron Age oblong fort re-used in the Pictish period. (© Forestry and Land Scotland by Rubicon Heritage using Historic Environment Scotland plan)

contemporary historical or literary references formed the pioneering work of Leslie Alcock on the early medieval period in northern Britain. In the 1970s and 1980s, Alcock undertook a series of keyhole excavations, some of these at historically documented hillforts. His work involved a programme of investigation explicitly aimed at identifying early medieval phases of occupation at these forts (Alcock 1988a, 2003; Alcock and Alcock 1990, 216; Alcock *et al.* 1989). Alcock's campaign of excavations included a number of sites in Pictland – Dundurn (1976–1977), Forteviot (1981), Urquhart (1983) and Dunnottar (1984). Alcock's work at Forteviot and Dunnottar largely drew a blank but both Dundurn and Urquhart Castle proved to have surviving early medieval deposits. The investigation of potential fortified sites using textual references was successful in providing evidence for the early medieval period in a context of little prior excavation but, in the long-term, it has become obvious that it was essential to broaden the search to include comparatively neglected regions and site types, particularly when it became clear that the historical sources ignored large areas of Scotland (see Chapter 3).

One of the main reasons for the dearth of Pictish-period settlements is archaeological survival. The majority of the Picts would have lived in lowland settlements near rivers and water sources rather than in hillforts

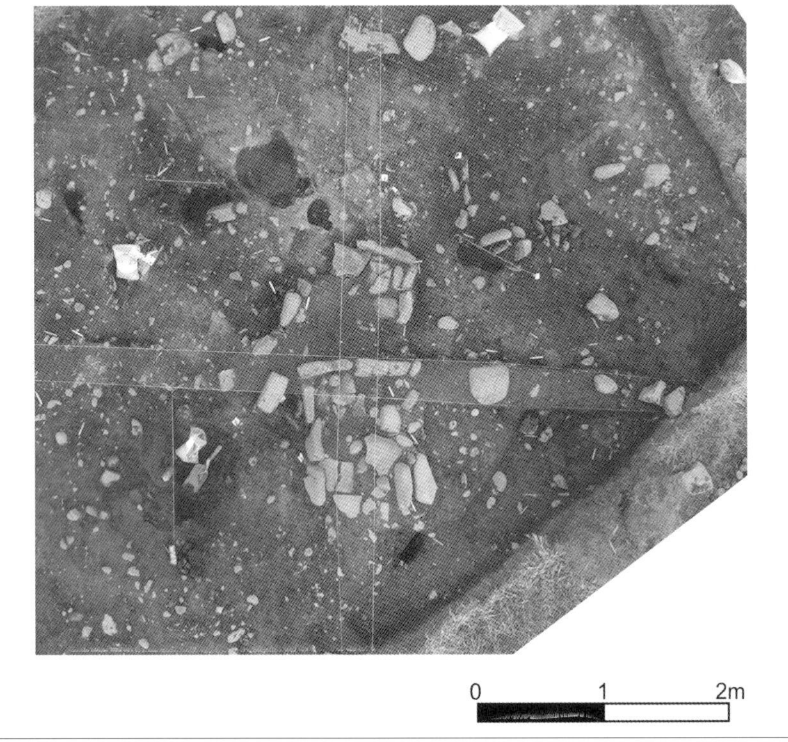

1.9 Dwelling within Dunnicaer promontory fort under excavation in 2017. The central hearths are surrounded by darker floor layers that have been largely removed by this stage of the excavation. Only shallow postholes defined the structural elements of the dwelling.

but these same areas are also the most intensively farmed areas of recent centuries. Hundreds of pre-Pictish timber roundhouses of the Bronze and Iron Ages are known but, after the 3rd century AD, the settlement record becomes very sparse indeed (Hunter 2007a, 48–50). This is probably due to a change in methods of house construction with non-earthfast construction methods such as turf walls and postpads becoming more common (see Chapter 2). With construction methods like this, where the foundation elements do not generally go beyond the contemporary groundsurface, modern agricultural practices such as ploughing can make short work of ancient dwellings and it is likely that most of the Pictish settlement record has been removed in a lowland context (Figure 1.9). It is only in unploughed areas that buildings from the Pictish era tend to survive – in the interiors of relatively inaccessible hillforts or promontory forts or in upland locations only lightly used today. One other factor may be at play – settlement conglomeration. The recent discoveries of potentially hundreds of first millennium AD dwellings at Tap o' Noth, Rhynie (see Chapter 2) suggest that centralisation of settlement in the first millennium AD may be another factor in the relative paucity of Pictish structures in the Lowlands.

Knowing which sites to target is also one of the major challenges of an archaeologist interested in the Pictish period. Morphologically undated

1.10 Craw Stane complex aerial photo – the circular enclosures of the Pictish high-status complex are evident mid centre, located to the east of the modern road, looking west. (© Aberdeenshire Council Archaeology Service)

hillforts can look very similar to documented early medieval sites but the testament of the spade and trowel can prove that forts that superficially look similar can date from very different periods. In the Lowlands, thousands of sites are known as cropmarks and are listed in the National Record of the Historic Environment (NRHE) (accessed through the canmore.org.uk website). Cropmarks represent sites that have been partly removed by the plough and lie buried under the topsoil. These sites become visible in certain conditions, primarily in hot weather when differentials in growth of a crop or grass can reveal the outlines of structures, monuments, enclosures and a whole host of different kinds of site. The Rhynie Craw Stane enclosures, for example, were first identified as cropmarks (see Chapter 3) (Figures 1.10 and 1.11). Cropmark sites are invariably damaged sites – the plough having removed the upper surfaces and deposits. Nonetheless, the well-drained lowland soils of Scotland can help to reveal some of these, with aerial reconnaissance one highly effective methodology for recording plough-truncated sites (Cowley 2011, 45).

Pioneering aerial reconnaissance in Scotland was undertaken by Crawford and Insall in the 1930s and by J. K. S. St Joseph in the 1940s, but it was the Royal Commission for Ancient and Historical Monuments of Scotland (RCAHMS) programme established in 1976 by Gordon Maxwell,

1.11 The Craw Stane complex under excavation in 2016 with Tap o' Noth hillfort in the background.

along with regional programmes of flying, that led to a huge increase in numbers of cropmark sites identified in Scotland (Maxwell 1978). Through the 1970s and 1980s, the spread of identified cropmark sites expanded rapidly, creating distributions that still broadly hold today (Cowley 2016, 62). The success has been such that, to date, over 9,000 cropmark sites have been recorded, the majority of which remain in cultivated fields. Over 1,000 of these are Scheduled Ancient Monuments (Dunwell and Ralston 2008, 69). Undoubtedly, these thousands of cropmarks include Pictish-period sites but again there are few sites you can point to from cropmark remains alone and confidently identify as Pictish. Some cropmark enclosures and sunken floor structures may be of this date (Chapters 2 and 3) but investigation is likely to be hit and miss, and all excavations require considerable resources to fund them. Some cropmark sites are tackled through developer-funded archaeology in advance of construction. These processes of mitigation have revealed some early medieval sites in eastern Scotland but generally only very small numbers and these have tended to be highly truncated and difficult to interpret.

Once a Pictish site has been identified, excavation is a powerful tool for its understanding (Figure 1.11) but that process can be lengthy and expensive and the evidence gained might only be partial. The University of Aberdeen excavations at the Craw Stane enclosures at Rhynie, for example, took five seasons with large field teams and a budget that amounted to tens of thousands of pounds. Excavation at the Craw Stane enclosures from 2011 to 2017 followed a strip-and-map methodology with large trenches opened, cleaned and mapped and select features excavated (see Carver 2009, 101). This approach characterised a large proportion of the complex but left more than 80% of the archaeology in situ – in the future, techniques will undoubtedly advance and it is important to leave deposits for future generations to investigate. The evidence from the Craw Stane enclosures is very rich but it is only a partial record of what was there. No contemporary landsurfaces survived within the enclosure due to modern ploughing, and the process of ploughing clearly had a very detrimental effect on the survival of artefacts that made their way into the ploughzone, destroyed by further ploughing and by the acidic soils that tend to characterise Lowland Scotland (Noble *et al.* 2019a). The lack of contemporary groundsurfaces at sites such as the Craw Stane enclosures means that it is difficult to directly compare the evidence from a site such as this to a hillfort, for example, where occupation deposits may have escaped modern impacts.

Once a Pictish site has been identified, excavation can reveal the groundplans of structures, allowing the architecture of the period to be assessed. This has its challenges too – for example, the buildings at the Craw Stane complex survived only as heavily truncated postholes, which could have been roof supports, the outer walls of buildings, or structural elements of a particular room within a much larger building that has left little trace. Charcoal from domestic fires or the destruction of buildings can be used to date the settlement remains, as can animal bones from middens (rubbish heaps). Radiocarbon dating has been around since the 1940s but really only began to have an impact on early medieval archaeology in the 1970s with Leslie Alcock and others' work on fortified settlements (for example, Small 1969; Small and Cottam 1972; Alcock 1976, 104; Ralston 1980, 1987). Unfortunately, a lot of the early radiocarbon dates have very wide margins of accuracy meaning that a site could only be pinpointed to a three- to four-century bracket in some cases. Nowadays, single radiocarbon dates can have much better accuracy through Accelerator Mass Spectrometry (AMS) methods that can have probability ranges that fall within a century or less. Combining AMS dated samples into a Bayesian model provides new chronology-building tools that enable estimated dates for specific events, often with sub-century precision and even to the generational level (for example, Hamilton *et al.* 2015), meaning that absolute dating from archaeological contexts is getting closer to the generational and annual events recorded in historical sources such as the Pictish king-lists and the Irish annals. Thus, for well-dated sites such as the Craw Stane complex at Rhynie, the start and end dates for the construction and abandonment of the enclosures can be estimated at the decadal level. Likewise very accurate dates have been obtained for the Pictish fort of Clatchard Craig where good animal bone samples allow the less accurate dates from older samples from wood charcoal to be modelled and constrained (Noble *et al.* forthcoming). Alternative absolute dating techniques have also been used on Pictish sites, with techniques such as archaeomagnetic (dating the last firing of a kiln or hearth for example) and optically stimulated luminescence (OSL) techniques (dating the last time that materials such as quartz and feldspar were exposed to light) having been used effectively in Pictish-era sites in Orkney and Shetland (for example, Outram and Batt 2010).

Dealing with death

As well as settlements of the living, the way the Picts dealt with their dead can tell us a great deal about Pictish ways of life, revealing Pictish conceptions of the afterlife, the care for loved ones lost, social stratification and status in Pictish society. In Pictland, only a small number of cemeteries have been excavated to date but there is a growing corpus of cemeteries identified from both upstanding remains and through the cropmark record. The study of the latter has been particularly important for expanding the number and diversity of Pictish cemeteries known (for example, Winlow 2011; Mitchell and Noble 2017). The Picts buried their dead within barrows and cairns, at field cemeteries consisting of multiple long cists and at churches (Maldonado 2013; see also Chapter 5) (Figure 1.12; Colour Plate 2). Unfortunately for archaeologists, the Picts did not tend to bury their dead with objects as was the case in contemporary cemeteries in Anglo-Saxon England. This has been one factor in the difficulty in dating Pictish material culture to particular chronological horizons (see below) and it has also limited the opportunities to read the motivations, ideologies and status signalling that may have been at the root of particular burial traditions. However, the architecture of the graves gives a potential routeway into examining some of these social and cultural trends (Winlow 2011; Maldonado 2013; Mitchell and Noble 2017). Certain individuals were buried in barrows or cairns that were much more monumental than others while some were buried as part of group burials under distinctive monuments – these choices give us clues as to how the individuals and mourners saw themselves and their community both in life and in death.

The survival of skeletal material provides excellent opportunities for a greater understanding of the lifeways of the Picts through direct analysis of the remains of Picts themselves (Figure 1.13). Radiocarbon dating of the interred can provide important dating information on the creation of

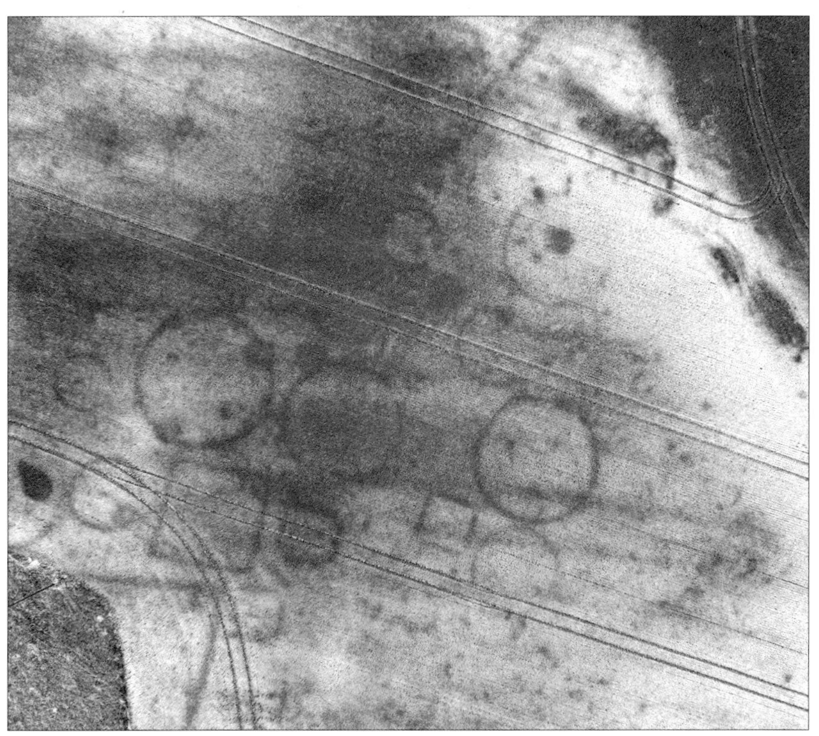

1.12 Aerial photograph showing the traces of the Pictish barrow cemetery at Tarradale, Beauly, as evident in the differential growth of crops in the field. (© Andy Hickie / Tarradale Through Time project)

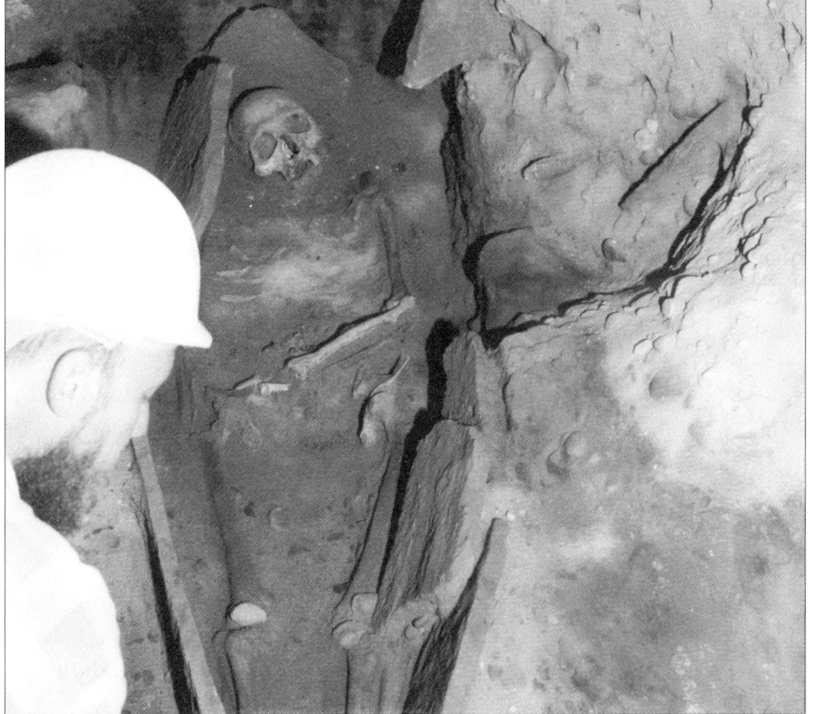

1.13 A long cist under excavation at Portmahomack, Tarbat. (© University of York / FAS Heritage)

1.14 A reflectance transformation image (RTI) of a Pictish symbol stone from Dandalieth, Moray. (© Michael Sharpe)

new styles and traditions of burial (for example, Maldonado 2013; Mitchell and Noble 2017). We can also tell more about the individuals themselves through techniques such as isotopic study and ancient DNA extraction. Isotopic research has had an impact on Pictish research, with a recent study of individuals from Portmahomack showing that individuals in the Pictish phases of the settlement and monastery ate a terrestrial-based diet with very little marine consumption evident. The diet is likely to have comprised cultivated crops such as barley, along with animal protein from cattle, pigs and lamb (Curtis-Summers *et al.* 2020). Mobility evidence has also been procured for Portmahomack showing that a number of individuals at the monastery were incomers (see Chapter 4). In the future, ancient DNA (aDNA) research may also tell us more about Pictish lifeways and genetics. Ancient DNA can be used to trace familial relationships, ascertain the sex of an individual and their relationship to others in cemeteries, assess the long-term genetic inheritance of the Picts and identify the presence or absence of pathogens or genetic disorders. Nonetheless, we have to be wary of how genetic evidence is used and presented. Social and cultural identity is different to genetic inheritance – how people were brought up, the language they spoke, their cultural traditions and their relative levels of freedom and standing within society are amongst the factors that would have defined identity (Crellin and Harris 2020). Many genetic studies also rely on modern DNA evidence and can tell us very little about the early medieval period, despite what is read in the headlines of newspapers and on the internet (Kennet *et al.* 2018).

The Picts and their symbols

In terms of archaeological traces, there is one body of evidence that has dominated Pictish scholarship for more than 150 years – the iconic body of carved stone monuments found across the former area of Pictland. The most distinctive carvings are those with a range of symbols carved on the stone – from abstract motifs (Figure 1.14) to stunning animal depictions (Henderson and Henderson 2004; RCAHMS 2008). The enigma of the Pictish symbol stones has attracted scholars attempting to understand the meaning of the symbols system since the mid 19th century (Noble *et al.* 2018; see also Chapter 6). The stones are beautifully carved, capturing the interest of most who view them, with many Pictish symbol stones carved with a stunning economy of line and an elegance that has made Pictish art loved across the world.

A number of differing monument types were carved in Pictland comprising Pictish symbol stones, carved with a range of abstract and other symbols; symbol-bearing cross-slabs that displayed the symbols along with a Christian cross carved in relief (Figures 1.15 and 1.16); cross-slabs without

1.15 (*Left*) The Maiden Stone, Aberdeenshire. Pictish cross-slab with symbols.

1.16 (*Above*) (a) Pictish symbol stone, Aberlemno, Angus. (b) Pictish symbol-bearing cross-slab, Dyce, Aberdeenshire. Image (a) based on photo. (© Hugh Levey)

symbols; and finally cross-marked boulders or slabs with small crosses marked by incision or relief and no other decoration. Other monuments are also known – recumbent grave-markers and corner-post shrine monuments, for example (see Chapter 4). Traditionally, these monument types were classified as part of a typological scheme first introduced in 1903 by Allen and Anderson that comprised:

> Class I – monuments with incised symbols only
> Class II – monuments with symbols and 'Celtic' ornament carved in relief
> Class III – cross-slabs without the symbols of the other two classes
>
> Allen and Anderson 1903, xi

Allen and Anderson introduced the scheme to describe the types of early medieval sculpture that are unique to Scotland. In 1987, Isabel Henderson

1.17 (*Above and opposite*) Examples of Pictish symbols.

introduced Class IV to describe cross-marked boulders or slabs with small crosses marked by incision or relief and no other decoration – a category of evidence that Allen and Anderson had simply termed 'stone with crosses but no ornament' (Henderson 1987, 46). While the classificatory scheme is still used today, it has its limitations (Henderson and Henderson 2004, 10–11). In this book, the terms Pictish symbol stones (equivalent to Class I), symbol-bearing cross-slabs (Allen and Anderson's Class II), cross-slabs (Allen and Anderson's Class III) and cross-marked stones (Henderson's Class IV) are used instead.

The Pictish symbol stones are thought to be the earliest form of the carving tradition and may date back to at least the 3rd to 4th century AD, and were certainly in wide use by the 5th to 6th centuries AD (see Chapter 6). The symbol-bearing cross-slabs, cross-slabs and cross-marked stones are obviously Christian monuments and are unlikely to date any earlier than the 6th century AD, with most likely to be 7th century AD in date or later (see Chapter 4). The symbol-bearing cross-slabs are generally thought to be earlier than cross-slabs without symbols, with the lack of symbols often thought to be a late phenomenon associated with the demise of Pictish as the dominant language in eastern Scotland – though it may not be as straightforward as this (see Chapter 7). Simple cross-marked stones are unlikely to be chronologically sensitive and were perhaps erected from the earliest stages of Christianity in Pictland through to the end of the first millennium AD. The generally modest size of these latter stones suggests they were predominately grave-markers.

The monuments bearing symbols, Pictish symbol stones and symbol-bearing cross-slabs are the most iconic and distinctive monuments associated with the Picts. Around 30 symbols appear regularly on the stones (Samson 1992, 37; Forsyth 1997b, 93) (Figure 1.17). These include abstract designs such as the so-called 'double disc and Z-rod' and the 'crescent and V-rod', names coined by archaeologists and antiquarians to label these enigmatic symbols. Animals are also carved on the stones and include naturalistic depictions of boars, wolves or dogs, eagles, snakes and bears. What may be mythical animals also appear such as a Pictish beast that may be a representation of a water horse, or kelpie, as they were known in later Scottish folklore. Some objects from the everyday world also appear – mirrors and combs, hammers, tongs and anvils, for example.

The symbols are all incised on the Pictish symbol stones but begin to appear in relief on the symbol-bearing Christian cross-slabs. The latter monuments show the influences of the wider networks that the Christian faith allowed the Picts to engage with. Sculptors adopted more complex styles of carving using low- and full-relief carving methods to bring a new vibrancy to Pictish stonecraft. The motifs and decorative traditions found on cross-slabs became more international too, representing the circulation of Continental books, reliquaries and other forms of Christian art within native Pictish tradition which constituted at times direct inspirations for Pictish designs (Henderson and Henderson 2004, 31–58, 83–85). Hippocamps, griffins and centaurs make appearances, marking this internationalising wave in Insular art. Another important trend was a stronger commitment to depicting the human figure, with clerics, apostles, biblical figures, secular elites and a range of other figures carved on stone.

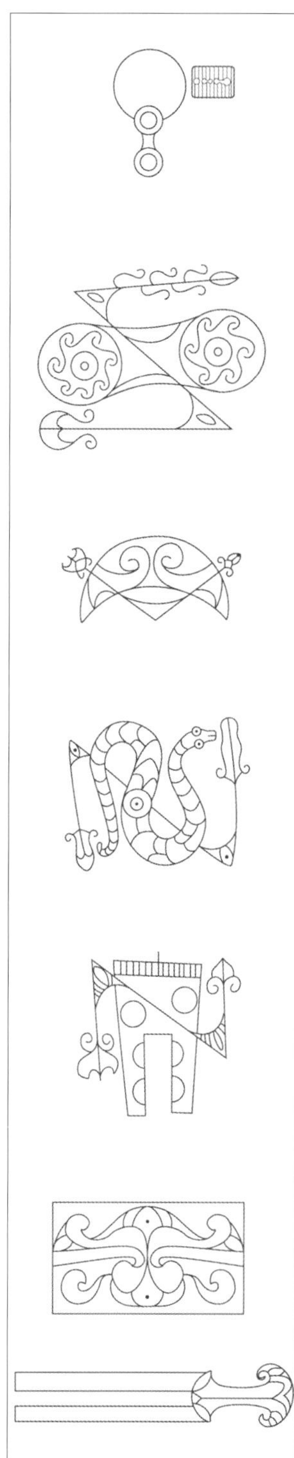

Carved stones are highly likely to have been coloured, traces of pigment having been found on a small number of examples (for example, Carver *et al.* 2016, 164, 174), and other stones carved so shallowly that it seems likely that pigment was used to highlight the lines traced by the hammer and chisel. The symbols found on metalwork are also picked out with colour – as occurs at Norrie's Law where red enamel was used (Colour Plate 3). Painted examples of carved stone monuments are unlikely to have retained their pigments after long periods of standing in the harsh Scottish climate – the more elaborate cross-slabs may well have stood inside Pictish church buildings. With both interior and exterior examples, it is possible that the stones' paint schemes were regularly refreshed, perhaps on major feast days or in the run-up to other major events and celebrations at churches and within the grounds of secular estates.

The distribution of Pictish symbol stones and symbol-bearing cross-slabs is heavily concentrated in eastern Scotland, including in the fertile river valleys of the Tay, the Don, the Spey, and the firths of the north (Figure 6.1). The distribution extends to the Northern Isles, with a few examples also found on islands of the Inner and Outer Hebrides, around Skye and on the Western Isles. Pictish symbol stones tend to dominate in the more northerly areas of Pictland, while more examples of cross-slabs are known in Angus and Fife in southern Pictland. As well as occurring on stones, the symbols are also found on the walls of caves and, as noted above, on objects too. New stones are found fairly regularly and form important additions to the corpus (Figure 1.18).

The symbols may also have appeared in other media – on wood, leather and clothing – and were perhaps even tattooed on the bodies of Picts. We can probably dismiss Isidore of Seville's statement in his *Etymologies* (written in the early 7th century) that the Picts had tattooed (*pictus*) bodies (Barney *et al.* 2006, 386) because of his love of verbal similarities. For instance, 'wine (*vinum*) is so called because it replenishes the veins (*vena*) with blood' (Barney *et al.* 2006, 3). Nevertheless, Herodian's statement in his history (written in the mid 3rd century) that the Britons of the early 3rd century AD (before the first surviving reference to the Picts) 'also tattoo their bodies with various patterns and pictures of all sorts of animals' (III.14.7; Whittaker 1969, vol. 1, 359) seems to correspond strikingly with the imagery of the Pictish symbols. However, tattooing is just one of the stereotypical features

1.18 The discovery of a new Pictish symbol stone at Aberlemno during University of Aberdeen excavations in 2022. The stone was built into the paving of an 11th–12th-century building, with Pictish settlement layers below.

in the description of Britain that classical writers associated with 'barbarians' (Whittaker 1969, vol. 1, 360, n. 1), and Herodian uses the tattoos to explain why the Britons supposedly lived naked, which is perhaps less than ideal in Scotland's climate, though naked warriors do appear in Pictish art (see Chapter 3). Pictish tattooing, with symbols, seems plausible, especially if the people in northern Britain internalised classical stereotypes (Fraser 2009a, 335–36, 376–79), but the evidence is, sadly, inconclusive.

The symbols were in use for many centuries – perhaps five centuries or more – and retained a remarkable degree of regularity in form throughout this time (see Chapter 6). The stones have been found through a variety of means – still standing in the landscape today, through agricultural processes such as ploughing, as chance finds in field walls and clearance heaps and built into the walls of medieval and modern structures. More rarely, carved stones are also found during archaeological excavation. Dating for Pictish sculpture has traditionally relied on art historical methods. For example, Pictish animal art has been compared to the probable 7th-century manuscript the Book of Durrow, with Stevenson arguing that Pictish sculpture was derivative of Northumbrian–Irish illuminated manuscript art (Stevenson 1995, 1971, 1993; see also Chapter 6). Comparison relied on examining conventions such as the use of scrolls to indicate the muscles and joints of animals in manuscript art and similar styles in Pictish stonecraft. However, there has not always been consensus on the dating of manuscript sources or, indeed, the date of particular types of decorative metalwork that Pictish sculptural motifs are also compared with. Motifs and artistic conventions could also endure for centuries making it difficult to assess date from visual analysis alone. Who influenced who can also be uncertain. Isabel and George Henderson (2004, 33–35), for example, in contrast to Stevenson, have identified the vibrant animal depictions of the Picts as a long-lived tradition that influenced manuscript art rather than vice versa. Thankfully, archaeology is increasingly able to contribute to the debate. While dating of the stones themselves or the carving of the motifs upon them is currently beyond accurate archaeological dating techniques, dating the context in which symbols were deployed is possible and this approach has begun to shed new light on the origins and development of the symbol tradition (see Chapter 6).

The rich sculptural traditions of the Picts can provide hints and clues to many facets of Pictish life – from pre-Christian belief to the adoption of Christianity to everyday dress and appearance. Picts themselves are depicted in a range of guises from weapon bearers on standing stones next to cemeteries, to elites and clergy shown on cross-slabs. Hunt scenes tell us about the life of the elite or at least how they liked to be portrayed, while battle scenes and weaponry tell us about warriorhood and warfare. The animals depicted tell us a little about Pictish fauna and the domesticated and wild animals that would have inhabited the woodlands, fields, sky and coastlines of Pictland. The use of classically inspired motifs on cross-slabs are important reminders that some of the motifs found on Pictish monuments may have been exotic but there is plenty of detail, such as the use of local weaponry and dress styles, to suggest that the everyday objects, surroundings and life of the Picts were a main driving inspiration for Pictish art styles and motifs. This is important as sculpture brings the world of the Picts to life.

On stone, we also have inscriptions – many of which are likely to have been recording the name of a person who lived in Pictland, perhaps as a form of memorial or a mark of ownership or status – this goes for the Pictish symbols where a naming tradition is the most likely interpretation of the symbol system (see Chapter 6) (Figures 1.19 and 1.20). There are also a smaller number of ogham inscriptions in Pictland – just under 40 in total (Forsyth 1996, 1997a, 33). Ogham was an epigraphic tradition developed to write the Old Gaelic (Old Irish) language. Some of the inscriptions in Pictland appear to be in Old Irish but others may be in Pictish, after the system was adapted by Pictish speakers for the Pictish language (Forsyth 1997a, 33). Around half a dozen inscriptions in Latin are also known from Pictland (Allen and Anderson 1903, xxv; Higgitt 1982; Henderson 1994; Forsyth 1995a; Carver *et al.* 2016, 124; Clancy 2017). These are located on cross-slabs or free-standing crosses and, where identifiable, contain

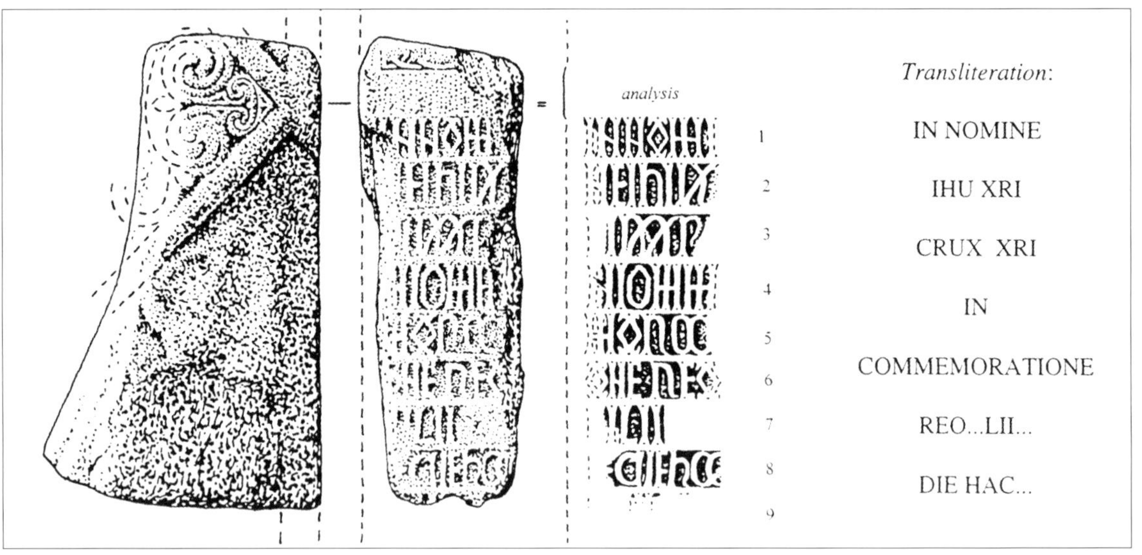

1.19 Fragment of decorated cross-slab from Portmahomack with inscription. (© University of York / FAS Heritage based on an Ian Scott drawing)

personal names, some of which are likely to be of contemporary kings or clerics.

A very unusual script is found on the Newton Stone, Aberdeenshire, which, as well as an ogham inscription and a carving of a mirror, has an alphabetic inscription that has long defied interpretation (Figure 1.20). However, Kelly Kilpatrick (2021) has successfully demonstrated that the alphabetic inscription and the ogham are in the Pictish language and that the alphabetic letters appear to represent an otherwise unattested Pictish monumental alphabetic script derived from the Late Roman cursive. The adoption and adaption of Late Roman traditions appear to reflect a similar development of a local variant comparable to the creation of Insular, Visigothic and Frankish scripts across Western Europe. The Newton Stone provides important evidence that the early Picts not only had access to texts but also gained enough familiarity with the script they encountered to transform it into their own medium, utilising it for messages in the vernacular. Overall, the variety of scripts used in Pictland is another potential indicator of a multilingual Pictland – a particularly important observation with regard to the demise of the use of the terms Picts and the Pictish language (see Chapter 7) but also for the potential diversity of language use and cultural identity within Pictland during the development and height of the Pictish kingdoms.

Crafting kingdoms

As well as being master crafters in stone, the Picts were also accomplished metalworkers. Brooches, pins and a range of other objects were crafted in silver and bronze for personal adornment, and tools and decorative items were also forged through the art of the smith (Youngs 1989a, 1989b, 2013). Metalworking in Scotland goes back to the Chalcolithic around 4,500 years ago but the arrival of the Roman army in Scotland in the 1st century AD brought new metals, new sources of inspiration and greater access to raw materials. Silver first arrived in Scotland with the invading Roman armies and became the dominant metal in the first millennium AD for elite expressions of power and status through the craft of the metalworker (Blackwell *et al.* 2017, xiii). Roman frontier policy sent bribes of silver coinage and hacksilver – hacked up pieces of silver Roman vessels – to local elites in the north throughout the Roman Iron Age (Hunter 2007a, b; Hunter and Painter 2013). Generations of recycling subsequently occurred, transforming Roman raw materials into new, local types of objects in Pictland and elsewhere in early medieval Scotland. Bronze, utilised for thousands of years previously, also continued to be an important metal alloy in crafting and, with this metal more accessible than silver, raw materials were more readily obtainable.

1.20 Newton Stone, Aberdeenshire, with ogham inscription on the left and on the right a Late Antique style Latin alphabet inscription. The ogham contains at least two personal names while the discernible words in the alphabetic inscription are Pictish. (© Kelly Kilpatrick)

From the 3rd to 4th centuries AD, the elite metalworking traditions of Pictland took shape – pins, brooches, chains and bracelets were made of Roman silver and bronze. In the post-Roman period, certain artefact types dominate the archaeological record – penannular brooches, hand-pins and other types of dress accessory foremost (Youngs 2013). Designs for brooches and other objects were developed and practised on bone or slate trial pieces using compasses and fine carving tools. Two-piece clay moulds were used for casting objects. Balls of clay were pressed flat, then a template of wax or lead was pressed into the soft clay and the clay allowed to dry. Pouring channels were added to the mould and keying enabled the moulds to fit together and align (Craddock 1989) (Colour Plate 4). The metals were turned to liquid in crucibles made of fired clay that were set into the smith's fire to heat (Figures 1.21 and 1.22). Cylindrical and triangular shaped crucibles, some with lids, were used and constitute important finds on archaeological sites. The crucibles were lifted by tongs – a set of which has been found in a 6th-century context at the Craw Stane complex at Rhynie (see Chapter 3) (Figure 1.23). In early Pictish styles of metalwork red enamel, a glass paste was used to infill panels on brooches and chip carving was also used to create curvilinear and geometric designs on metal jewellery. In later Pictish brooches, new skills were adopted – the application of gilding and gold filigree added new dimensions to the metalwork of elites (Ó Floinn 1989, 108–16). Highly skilled blacksmiths also created fine objects as well

1.21 (*Above left*) Metal-working crucible sherds recovered from the ditch fill of one of the enclosures at the Craw Stane complex, Rhynie.

1.22 (*Above right*) Ingot mould – a mould for casting the solid bars of bronze or silver used in trading – from the Craw Stane complex, Rhynie, Aberdeenshire.

as everyday tools – a remarkable axe-shaped pin has been recovered from Rhynie, for example (Figure 1.24). The axe pin from Rhynie was not cast – instead, the iron for the pin was carefully and skilfully hammered out and shaped from an iron rod. Silver and bronze bowls, church reliquaries and other objects were also created by hammering metal sheets to shape.

One of the most popular dress accessories in early medieval Scotland was the penannular brooch – an innovation of the Roman Iron Age (Colour Plate 5). These were used to fasten cloaks and other clothing. One of the early forms of penannular brooch in Pictland consisted of thin hoops of bronze or silver with abstract animal-like designs at the terminals. Through time, the hoops, terminals and pins of brooches became larger and more elaborate with large beast or bird heads characterising some of the later Pictish brooch types (Youngs 1989a, 21–22). Another popular object type was the hand-pin – so called because of its resemblance to a clenched fist (Youngs 1989a, 23–27). These developed from projecting ring-headed pins of the early centuries AD. Other forms of personal adornment were also clearly popular but few complete examples have survived. Silver bracelets, for example, are known from both the Gaulcross and Norrie's Law hoard, but are very rare finds elsewhere (Noble *et al.* 2016, 732).

Objects for the house or hall were also created. The front half of a bivalve mould for a hanging bowl escutcheon has been found at Craig Phadrig, for example (Small and Cottam 1972, 43). Hanging bowls were thin copper-alloy vessels with decorative mounts used for suspending the

1.23 Conserved iron tongs from Rhynie for gripping the crucibles used in precious metalworking.

1.24 An iron axe pin from Rhynie – iron could not be cast in this period so this fine object would have been hammered out by a skilled blacksmith. (© University of Aberdeen)

vessel from a tripod (Youngs 1989a, 47–53). No complete vessel has been found in Pictland but hanging bowls appear complete in Anglo-Saxon graves of the 6th and 7th centuries AD, allowing archaeologists to recognise fragments of such vessels and the moulds for making them in Pictish and other contexts and to date them through typological dating. The purpose of hanging bowls is uncertain – they may have been for hand washing during feasts but other purposes are possible (Youngs 1989a, 22).

One category of object in circulation in Pictish society outshines all the others known – the massive silver chains. The majority of these objects have been found outwith Pictland but the findspots of a small number and the presence of Pictish symbols on two chains implies that they were an item of silverware that had important roles in Pictish society. They consist of massive double-lined silver chains with penannular terminal rings and represent the very conspicuous consumption of a precious resource (Youngs 1989, 26; Blackwell *et al.* 2017, 95) (Colour Plates 16 and 24). The weight and form of these suggest they may have had very important roles in elite culture in Pictland (see Chapter 3).

Overall, the study of the material culture of the Picts is important for it reveals much about everyday lives and social status. Metalwork in the form of material possessions, for example, whether in a secular or church context, would have been an important indicator of status and wealth in a coinless economy (Ó Floinn 1989, 72). In addition, the production and circulation of metalwork between a leader and his followers appear to have been an important means of cementing the relationships of hierarchy and subservience in the early medieval period (Nieke 1993, 128–29).

Excavating early medieval settlements rarely turns up complete silver objects like the chains or the elaborate penannular brooches highlighted above. This is for obvious reasons – these were precious and valuable objects and were handed down from generation to generation or recycled into new objects. Occasionally, however, single or hoards of objects were hidden away for safekeeping or were deliberately deposited as gifts to god(s) (for example, Noble *et al.* 2016, 738). A small number of Pictish-era hoards are known – the Norrie's Law hoard from Fife and the Gaulcross hoard from Aberdeenshire are two prominent examples (see Chapter 3). Later hoards from Pictland include examples from St Ninian's Isle, Shetland, Broch of Burgar, Orkney, and Croy, Inverness-shire (Wilson 1973; Graham-Campbell 1985; Blackwell *et al.* 2017, 122) (Colour Plate 6). The Broch of Burgar hoard was clearly a spectacular find, consisting of multiple vessels, combs, pins and brooches of silver and a large number of amber beads (Graham-Campbell 1985, 250), but no trace of the original discovery survives today. Hoards give us a snapshot of what was in circulation in early medieval society – the sort of detail usually lost to the smith's crucible when objects were recycled and the raw materials recast. Thus our archaeological record is a very partial picture of what was once in circulation and is subject to biases of survival – most of our surviving metalwork in Pictland, for example, is secular, with very few finds to reveal the fittings of churches or the reliquaries and other portable objects that would have been used in the Christian Mass and other ceremonies (see Chapter 4).

The power of the exotic

As well as metalwork, other categories of finds are present on Pictish sites

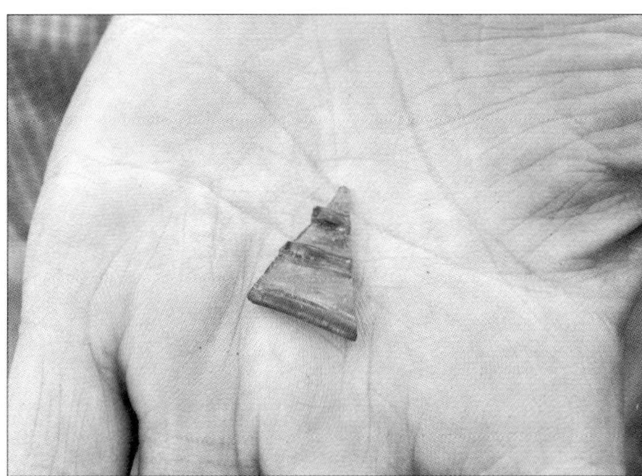

1.25 (*Left*) A sherd of Roman Samian Ware – a type of fine tableware mainly made in Gaul – from Dunnicaer. The Roman imports to the far north largely consisted of objects for feasting and dining.

1.26 (*Right*) A small sherd of a fine Anglo-Saxon glass claw beaker from Rhynie.

and can reveal important detail regarding Pictish lifeways. These finds include pottery, spindle whorls, bone and antler objects, gaming pieces and quernstones (Chapters 2 and 3). Many of these were locally made but imported material culture provides important evidence for long-distance connections. In the early Pictish period, Roman glass and pottery sherds occur on sites such as Dunnicaer (Figures 1.25 and 1.26; Colour Plate 7) and Tap o' Noth, and the nature of the imported material can tell us about some aspects of the site and its occupants. For example, there appears to be a preponderance of Roman objects associated with feasting and fine dining on native sites (Hunter 2007a). Roman finds also provide an important additional strand of dating evidence in addition to radiocarbon dating. In the post-Roman period, finds of Mediterranean and Continental pottery and glass can likewise provide important markers of status and again an important dating measure for imported pottery tends to come from coin-using cultures and more accurately dated cultural sequences (Campbell 2007). At Pictish sites, finds of imported pottery and glass from sites dating from the 5th to 7th centuries AD have been found. Imports tend to be restricted to elite centres of power, residence and enclosure in Britain and Ireland (Campbell 2007, Tables 16–19). The processes of trade and exchange that these objects represent are important, for Campbell's studies have placed imports and their circulation in a central position in understanding the early medieval period, suggesting these were important dimensions of the means by which post-Roman successor kingdoms began to use surplus wealth to develop more hierarchical power networks (Campbell 2007, 140).

The path ahead

The Picts inhabited a substantial part of modern Scotland. As discussed above, there is no perfect way of defining this area precisely, but it is impor-

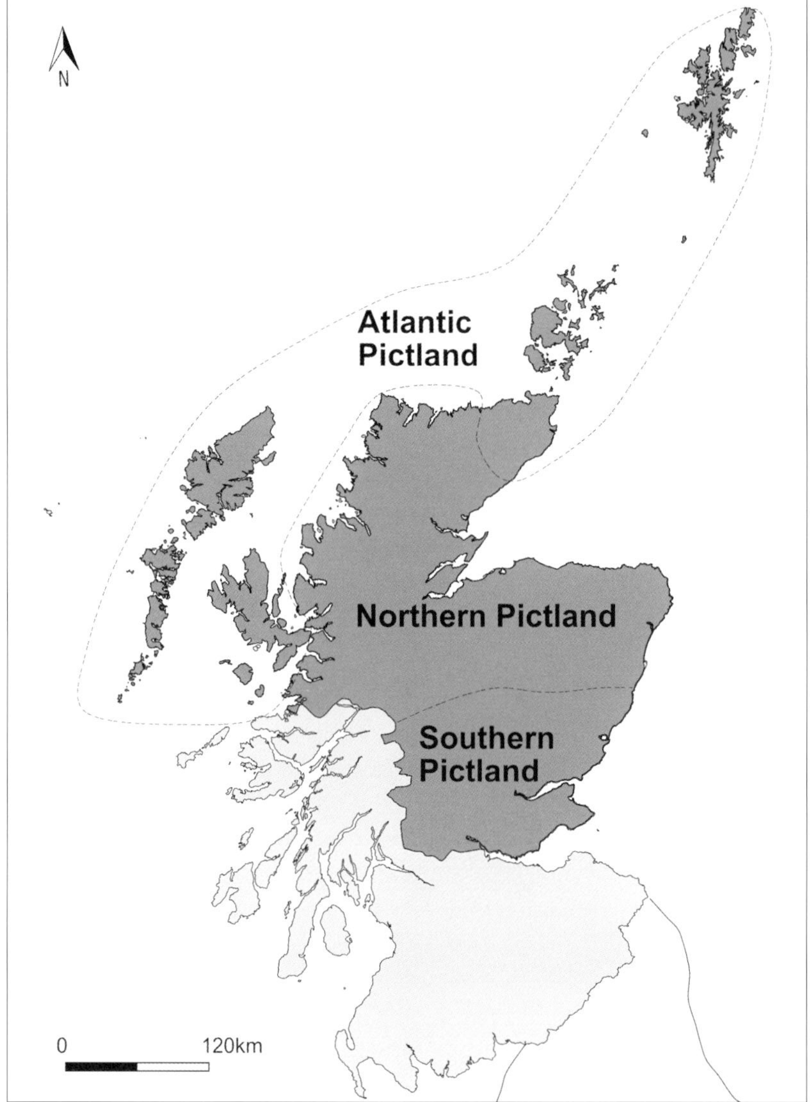

1.27 The zones of Pictland used in the book. (© University of Aberdeen)

tant for the purposes of this book that limits are placed on the analysis – for instance, by excluding Dál Riata since it was only incorporated into the Pictish realm from the 730s onwards. For practical reasons, it is sometimes necessary to subdivide Pictland into zones – southern Pictland, northern Pictland and Atlantic Pictland – and then further more locally (Figure 1.27). In certain chapters, where a regional character to the evidence is particular marked, these divisions are utilised.

Southern Pictland is defined to the north by the Mounth, the range of hills and mountains which starts just west of the North Sea town of Stonehaven, and heads due west from there, forming the watershed boundary of Angus and Perthshire. Then, crossing the Drumochter Pass, the Perth and Kinross Council boundary is followed to Loch Ericht, before heading south along the east–west watershed, known in medieval times as *Druim Alban* (Dunshea 2013), between the councils of Perth and Kinross and Stirling, to the east, and Argyll and Bute and Highland Councils, to the west. Finally, Stirling Council's boundary is used running down through Loch Lomond before heading to Strathblane and east along the Campsie Fells before ending at the River Forth opposite Alloa. Northern Pictland is north of this zone but with its boundary heading west from Loch Ericht so that it includes the Spey basin, and Lochaber at the southern end in the Great Glen, heading west north of Loch Shiel, but including Moidart, finally reaching the west coast at Loch Moidart. Northern Pictland includes all of mainland Scotland to the north of this line, excluding Caithness. Atlantic Pictland consists of Caithness, the Northern Isles (Orkney, Shetland), the Western Isles and the northern Inner Hebrides as far south as Rum, Eigg, Muck and Canna. It is important to stress that these boundaries relate only very approximately to where the Picts lived and that the divisions should primarily be regarded as aids for analysis, rather than necessarily reflecting important medieval divides.

Overall, this book is designed to provide a broad but detailed introduction to the Picts and their ways of life, emphasising the archaeological evidence. The lack of archaeological evidence has repeatedly been highlighted in reviews of Pictish archaeology, from Wainwright to more recent periods – Wainwright (1955a), Crawford (2011, 7) and Carver (2011) – but, in the last decade, the archaeology of the Picts has been reinvigorated and this volume is designed to showcase some of the advances in knowledge which that work has provided, though grounded in the historical context where possible. While a historical overview of the Picts has been provided in this chapter, and their demise will be a focus of Chapter 7, those who seek more detailed considerations of the historical evidence are directed to Woolf (2007a) and Fraser (2009), while Márkus (2017) provides a useful focus on belief and society. Art history is touched upon in the volume but again the reader is directed to more advanced considerations – for example, Geddes (2017) and Henderson and Henderson (2004).

This book aims to provide a fresh perspective on the Picts who have often been marginalised in narratives concerning early medieval Britain and Ireland due to the paucity of evidence. The current pace of Pictish archaeology and scholarship in general is such that elements of this book may well already be out of date but it is important to take stock and provide a platform for future studies of the Picts and their legacy. The Picts and Pictland, so often left behind in broader narratives, can begin to take a worthy place at the heart of understanding a transformative period for European history when the kingdoms of medieval Europe began to take shape.

CHAPTER TWO

'The Smoke of Habitations'

Everyday Life in Pictland

> It is a sad, if somewhat surprising, fact that we cannot with confidence affix the label 'Pictish' to a single dwelling . . .
>
> Wainwright 1955, p. 87

It was still the case only a few years ago that we could count the number of Pictish dwellings on one or two hands at most but, thankfully, important progress is being made in illuminating the everyday lives of the Picts. In Atlantic Pictland in particular, substantial advances have been made in recent decades with major multi-period excavations of broch mounds and settlement agglomerations helping to illuminate the nature of first millennium AD settlement in the Northern and Western Isles (for example, Armit 1992, 73–86; Gilmour 2000, 34–106; Harding 2009, 171–99). In contrast, overviews of the Picts have tended not to dwell on the settlement record of eastern Scotland with its very limited evidence base (for example, Ritchie 1989; Foster 2014; Carver 1999). A review of Pictish archaeology in 2011 (Driscoll 2011, 257–64) highlighted the potential of the aerial record to help illuminate the settlement record of eastern Scotland but outlined how little we knew of the typical everyday settlement landscapes of this region. Since then, major publications on upland settlement in Highland Perthshire (Carver 2012; Strachan *et al.* 2019) and emerging evidence of the nature of Pictish vernacular architectural traditions in the eastern Lowlands (for example, Noble *et al.* 2020a, 327) have gone some way to alleviate the lacuna of knowledge regarding Pictish settlement in southern and northern Pictland. Nonetheless, our understanding of Pictish settlement remains significantly behind early medieval Ireland or England, for example, with over 40,000 ringfort settlements known in Ireland and hundreds if not thousands of settlement structures known from Anglo-Saxon England comprising halls, sunken-floored buildings and a whole range of different vernacular traditions (for example, Hamerow 1993, 2012; O'Sullivan 2008; O'Sullivan *et al.* 2014, 47–138; Carver 2019, 139–303). In comparison, in Pictland, we are still dealing with a settlement corpus of only a few dozen well-excavated

2.1 Main sites referenced in Chapter 2.

and dated settlement sequences (Figure 2.1). However, the evidence is growing and points to significant regional and localised variations in settlement form. To get at the heart of the diversity of Pictish lifeways and settlement traditions, we will embark on a regional tour of Pictish-era settlement.

Southern Pictish uplands

Pitcarmick-style dwellings

While there is a relative dearth of settlements in the eastern Lowlands, evidence from the 1980s onwards began to accumulate of a vibrant settlement tradition in the uplands (Figure 2.2). This began with detailed survey

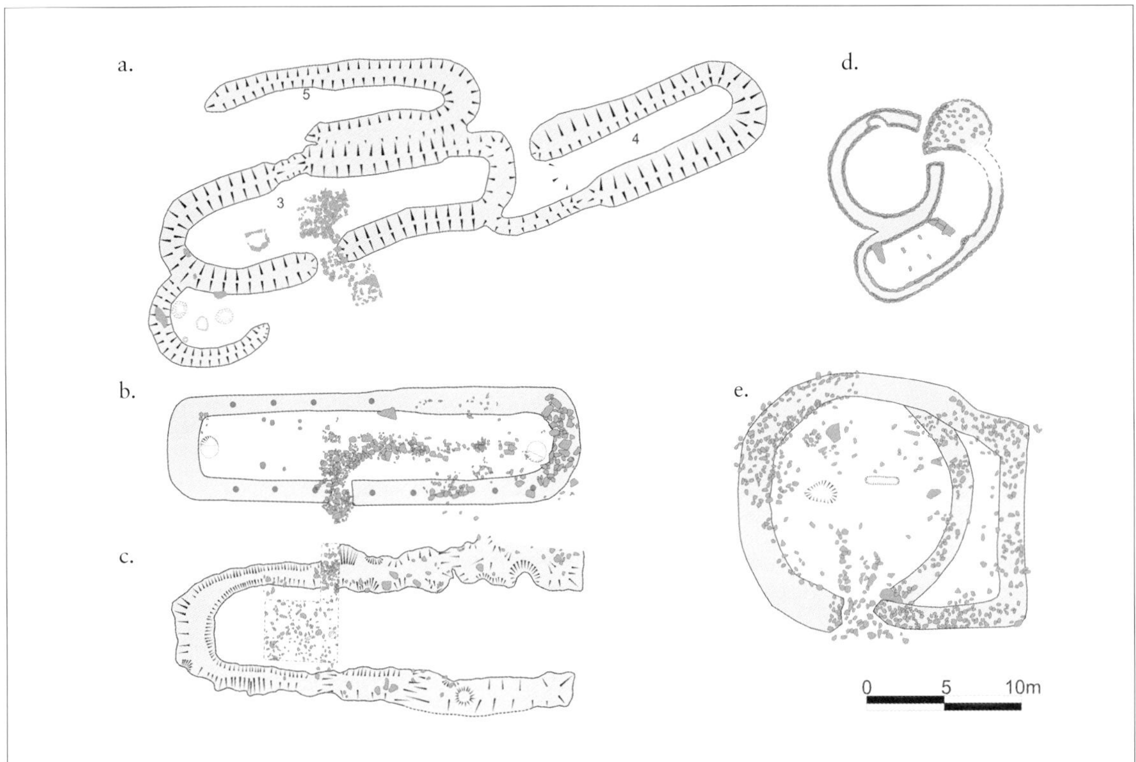

2.2 Pitcarmick-type and Pictish-era sub-rectangular structures from southern to Atlantic Pictland:
(a) Lair, Perthshire;
(b) Pitcarmick, Perthshire;
(c) Bunrannoch, Perthshire;
(d) Langwell, Caithness;
(e) Carn Dubh, Perthshire.

work in the 1980s by the Royal Commission on the Ancient and Historical Monuments of Scotland (RCAHMS) – now the Historic Environment Scotland (HES) survey team – in the Highlands of Perthshire that led to the recognition of a series of rectangular dwellings known as Pitcarmick-style structures. The survey work by the RCAHMS team located almost 50 of these structures (RCAHMS 1990, 12) and the distribution of these is now known to extend into the Angus glens. The RCAHMS survey work showed that these buildings range in length from 10m to 30m and are usually around 5m wide internally with rounded ends and bow-sided walls. The entrances to Pitcarmick houses are usually found on one of the long sides of each building providing direct access to what is likely to have been the main residential end of the building. Partially sunken floors have been identified in around half of all Pitcarmick-style buildings tending to occur in the eastern, often narrower, end of the buildings. Even prior to the excavation of these buildings, this phenomenon was linked to the possible stalling of animals in the opposite end of the buildings to the residential focus (RCAHMS 1990, 12).

Since the survey work of the 1980s, excavations at several sites have begun to flesh out the picture of what life must have been like in these upland dwellings. The most recent excavations have been at Lair, Glenshee,

Perthshire, where the early phases of the Pitcarmick-style longhouses have been dated to the 7th century and the site appears to have gone out of use around the 10th century AD (Strachan *et al.* 2019) (Figure 2.2a). This was therefore a longstanding and successful settlement. Environmental evidence from the site and the wider environs, combined with climate data, suggests Lair and perhaps other Pitcarmick-style settlements in the uplands of central Scotland may have been established in a period of climatic amelioration (Strachan *et al.* 2019, 140), which set the foundations for an expansion of settlement in the uplands.

At Lair, a number of Pictish period buildings were excavated. One, around 25m long internally and 5m wide, that was probably early in the sequence of structures on site, functioned as a byre house in its original incarnation and was perhaps used later as a storehouse (Strachan *et al.* 2019, 111). An adjacent building was much shorter, only around 13m long internally. With only an informal hearth, it may have been used for storage or solely for stalling animals (Strachan *et al.* 2019, 111). Three buildings formed another cluster (Figures 2.2a and 2.3). The largest was 20m long internally and the eastern half of the building had a sloping floor with a drain, with this end of the building interpreted as the byre end. The western end had a large central hearth and here finds of pottery, daub, stone, iron and bone suggest that this was the main living space for the building (Strachan *et al.* 2019, 112). This structure had a circular annexe attached to the south-west corner of the building (Figure 2.2a). Within the annexe, pits containing a broken whetstone and hammerscale were found suggesting that the annexe was used at least periodically for metalworking. Two adjacent buildings appeared to be later structures or outbuildings. Survey work suggests there were at least six other broadly contemporary buildings in the Lair landscape. All of these buildings were defined by turf walls, with cruck frames holding up thatched roofs.

The extent of excavation and the better representation of finds from Lair give glimpses of the activities carried out inside these upland settlements (Figure 2.3). Stone tools including what may have been a lamp suggest that the houses were illuminated, while whetstones indicate the sharpening of blades. Rotary quernstones tell of many hours spent processing plant material, probably grain. Meanwhile spindle whorls, including a decorated example, show that textile production and specifically the making of handspun textiles was carried out by occupants of the longhouses at Lair.

Elsewhere in highland Perthshire, longhouses have been excavated at Pitcarmick, the type-site. Two houses at Pitcarmick were investigated in the 1990s and shown to be broadly contemporary with the Lair examples, with the main phase of occupation dating from the 7th to 9th centuries AD (Carver *et al.* 2012). Two hearths, presumably from structures, were dated to the 5th to 6th centuries AD suggesting earlier Pictish activity in this

2.3 Reconstruction of the longhouse settlement at Lair, Glenshee. (© AOC Archaeology Ltd)

upland location. Like the Lair structures, the longhouses at Pitcarmick had turf walls, with hearths in the west end (Figure 2.2b). Areas of paving in the east end of each structure suggest one half of each building was used as a byre. It has been postulated that the houses at Pitcarmick could have held between 20 and 24 cattle in the eastern end, which suggests these were not marginal or poor settlements by any means (Figure 2.4).

Further into highland Perthshire, longhouse-style settlements have also been identified, most notably at Bunrannoch, by Kinloch Rannoch (Figure 2.2c). Here, a series of longhouses was originally located through survey work by Margaret Stewart who excavated one of these in 1961 showing that the longhouse wall consisted of a bank of turf and boulders revetted on the inside by wattle panels. Excavations in the early 2000s of two further longhouses at Bunrannoch produced similar results indicating two phases of wattle revetted turf and/or turf and stone walls (MacGregor 2010). These later excavations also showed evidence for internal features such as post-holes and pits confirming these were roofed buildings. The excavations in the 2000s obtained two radiocarbon dates, one from a wall layer and one from a pit in the interior for one of the Bunrannoch longhouses, indicating construction and occupation centred on the 8th and 9th centuries AD (MacGregor 2010, 407).

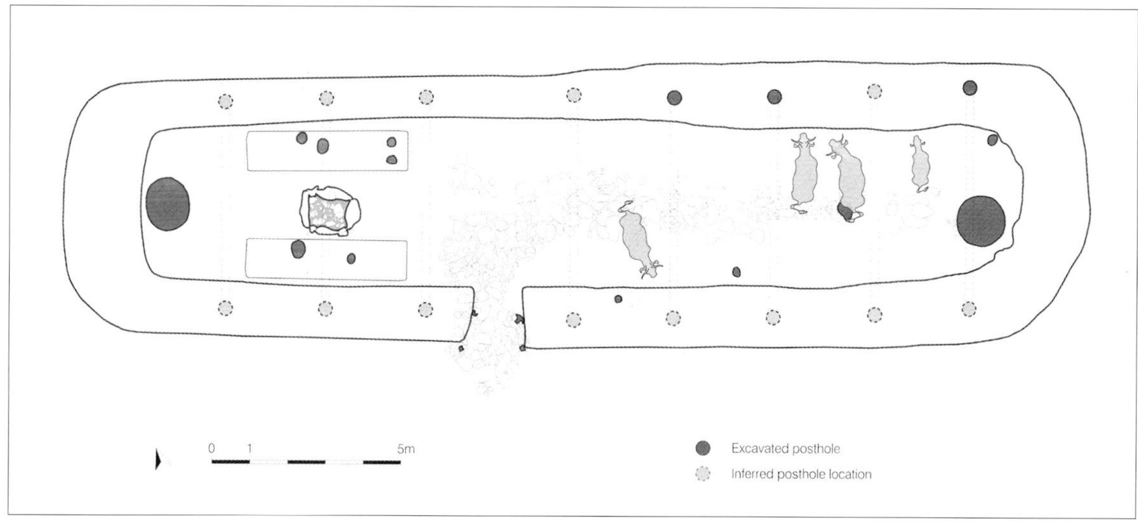

2.4 Schematic reconstruction plan of the Pitcarmick longhouse with residential area in western half of the building and cattle byre in eastern half. (© FAS Heritage)

Like some of the Pitcarmick and Lair structures, it looks like the Bunrannoch buildings may have been byre houses. Each of the Bunrannoch structures appears to have been open at the east end or had one gable wall built in less durable means. It has been suggested that the lack of a gable end wall may reflect the use of movable or dismantlable end walls to allow the movement in and out of cattle and the mucking out of the byre end, as attested in later historic rural buildings in Scotland. Over-wintering cattle in upland locations would have been important and it is possible that cattle were also brought indoors at other times for protection from cattle raiding, for milking and for the managing of breeding (Carver 2012, 194). As to function, given the marginal location of these settlements, it has been suggested these longhouses could have acted as shielings (for example, Alcock 2003, 265) – temporary residences used by farming groups who move to the uplands seasonally in order to obtain grazing for animals. However, pollen evidence from Lair indicates the cultivation of barley and perhaps other crops and the faunal record and botanical records from both Pitcarmick and Lair suggest a mixed farming economy, most likely focussed on year-round settlements. Origins for the byre-houses of Pitcarmick have been sought in European traditions (Carver 2012, 191–93) but the turf building form was clearly developing from at least the 5th to 6th centuries AD in Lowland Scotland and probably earlier.

Other building types were also constructed in the uplands of central Scotland. At Carn Dubh, Perthshire, a horseshoe-shaped building was constructed in the later first millennium AD (Rideout 1995) (Figure 2.2e). The horseshoe-shaped structure was a large building measuring around 15m by 12m internally. It was built over an earlier roundhouse and appears to have had a turf wall with a stone foundation. It had paving at the south-eastern entrance leading into the centre of the building and a hearth towards the back of the building. Few finds were located within but charred cereals were recovered from the floor layers. A radiocarbon date from charcoal from the hearth suggests occupation of the building during the 7th to 9th centuries AD. The form of the building is interesting for it resembles in plan at least the 'bag-shaped' buildings found at Portmahomack and the earlier horseshoe-shaped building from Rhynie (see below).

Homesteads?

Another feature of upland settlement in southern Pictland may have been the construction or at least reuse of some circular 'homesteads'. These homesteads were massive roundhouses – or more likely enclosures – extending up to 30m in diameter with monumental outer walls up to 4m thick (Stewart 1969; Taylor 1990). Many of these sites may be Iron Age in date and the most recent excavations at Black Spout, Perthshire, obtained Iron Age dating evidence (Strachan 2013). At Bunrannoch, one of the longhouses appears to partly overlie a homestead but excavation and radiocarbon dating of the homestead showed it was still in use in the early medieval period for metalworking (MacGregor 2010). A single radiocarbon date from a homestead at Litigan, Perthshire, suggests occupation (or re-occupation) in the late first millennium AD (Taylor 1990). At Aldclune, Perthshire, the latest roundhouse, enclosed by a double-ditched earthwork and a stone wall, was constructed around the 2nd to 3rd centuries AD but a silver penannular brooch from the site may suggest some form of activity in the site into the later first millennium AD (Hingley *et al.* 1997). Thus, some Perthshire homesteads show early medieval occupation potentially adding to the settlement variety in the southern Pictish uplands, but whether any were actually constructed in this period remains uncertain. Rectangular timber structures found at Logierait, Perthshire, add further diversity to upland Pictish settlement evidence (Ellis 2021).

Lowlands of the east

In the eastern Lowlands, major settlement changes occurred in the early centuries AD (Hunter 2007a, 43–44; Strachan *et al.* 2019, 143), with the large-scale abandonment of post-built roundhouses as the dominant settlement tradition – a tradition that had endured for more than 3,000 years from the Late Neolithic period onwards. Roundhouses were still built but in different ways with less in the way of earthfast timber posts acting as foundations. Knowledge of what replaced this roundhouse tradition in the eastern Lowlands is still very patchy. Given that Pitcarmick houses appear to have been year-round farmsteads supported by a mixed farming economy, similar versions of these buildings could have existed in the Lowlands. However, given that these were largely turf built with few earth-fast features and allowing for the patterns of land use in the Lowlands with much more intensive modern cultivation, any existing structures of this character may have been largely destroyed through later land-use practices. With the structures like those at Pitcarmick, Lair, Bunrannoch and Carn Dubh, few if any features would survive the impact of intensive ploughing. Around half of Pitcarmick-type structures have evidence of sunken floors, which could potentially partly survive below the ploughsoil in the Lowlands. There have been suggestions that such features are identifiable in the cropmark record. One possible example is a cropmark at Inchture, Perthshire, in southern Pictland, where aerial photography has identified the outlines of a possible building around 23m by 5m, marked by an outer enclosing line and a possible sunken floor in the east end of the building (Halliday 2019, 125). Other possible examples in the south include examples on the Inchtuthil plateau and at Inchcoonans, Balgarvie and Blairhall in Perth and Kinross, and Leuchars in Fife (Barclay and Maxwell 1998, 5; Halliday 2019, 125). The latter two are possibly associated with field systems that are also evident on aerial photographs, though their character and contemporaneity with any associated landscape features remain to be determined through future fieldwork.

These examples from the aerial record are intriguing but remain undated and poorly attested. Indeed, our knowledge of lowland settlement in both southern and northern Pictland continues to be very limited, with much of the lowland evidence appearing to be highly truncated. Isolated features and activity such as crop-drying kilns, the reuse of souterrains, areas of paving and working areas are known from the eastern Lowlands but such features rarely survive to any extent to reveal much in the way of detail to ascertain what these represent in terms of overall architectural form or the social or economic basis of these settlements (for example, Coleman and Hunter 2002; Dunwell and Ralston 2008, 135–36; Cook and Dunbar 2008, 149). There are also occasional truncated circles of postholes suggesting that roundhouse architecture may have endured into the later first millennium AD, though the examples are few in number (Dunbar 2012, 12; Cook 2016, 22).

Two sunken-floored or scooped structures from Easter Kinnear and Hawkhill, Fife, have been claimed to be Pictish in date (Driscoll 1997). These comprised oval to sub-rectangular scoops cut into the natural subsoil with a drystone retaining wall lining the scoop. One building had a paved floor. While structures such as these, with similar cropmarks evident in the aerial record, could fill a settlement gap in the Lowlands, the actual Pictish-era dates came from a series of amorphous features dug into the top of one building rather than the foundation elements of the building itself and therefore may represent reuse of an earlier structure. Indeed, a very similar building was dated at another site (also called Hawkhill but in Angus) to the last centuries BC and first centuries AD (Dunwell and Ralston 2008, 102–04). Thus, the dating for Easter Kinnear and Hawkhill structures and, by implication, other similar cropmark features needs further work to conclusively demonstrate their chronological position in the settlement of Lowland Pictland in the east.

Halls?

Really quite grand buildings may have existed in the Pictish Lowlands but again the nature of the evidence and lack of direct dating makes certainty as yet unachievable. The discovery of timber halls from elite settlements in Anglo-Saxon England and southern Scotland (for example, Hope-Taylor 1977; Kirby 2012; Blair 2018; Thomas 2018; Carver 2019, 155–63) have led to the search for such structures in Pictland. Possible examples of halls were identified in the cropmark record from the earliest aerial sorties of the Royal Commission, whose aerial programme began in earnest in 1976 (Maxwell 1976). Testing the possibility that Pictish elites may have adopted these fashions led to the excavations of the timber hall at Balbridie in Aberdeenshire (Reynolds 1980; Fairweather and Ralston 1993), which turned out to be thousands of years earlier, dating to the Early Neolithic. Other possible hall sites have been identified in the aerial record (for example, Maxwell 1987, 34), however, many of these, like Balbridie, have subsequently been shown to have very different origins with excavated examples at Claish, near Callander, Crathes, in Aberdeenshire, and Doon Hill, in East Lothian, conclusively dated to the Neolithic (Barclay *et al.* 2002; Murray *et al.* 2009; Ralston 2019).

One possible larger rectangular building is known from the Lowlands of eastern Scotland. At Newbarns, Angus, excavation by the University of Edinburgh in 1999 identified a sub-rectangular structure, straight-sided with rounded ends, that measured around 18m long and 6m wide (Dunwell and Ralston 2008, 138–40) (Figure 2.5c). The wall line of the building was defined by a shallow slot with the impressions of rounded and squared timbers evident at the base. External and internal posts may have formed the foundation of crucks and external buttresses. Newbarns could have been a high-status residence, given its size, but radiocarbon dates place it relatively late, spanning the 8th to 11th centuries AD, and neither finds nor additional internal features could be identified to further illuminate the character or function of the building. In terms of size and monumentality, the Newbarns building must have also been much slighter than a typical Anglo-Saxon hall. Since the Newbarns building shared morphological parallels, such as the rounded ends, with Pitcarmick-type buildings, it is

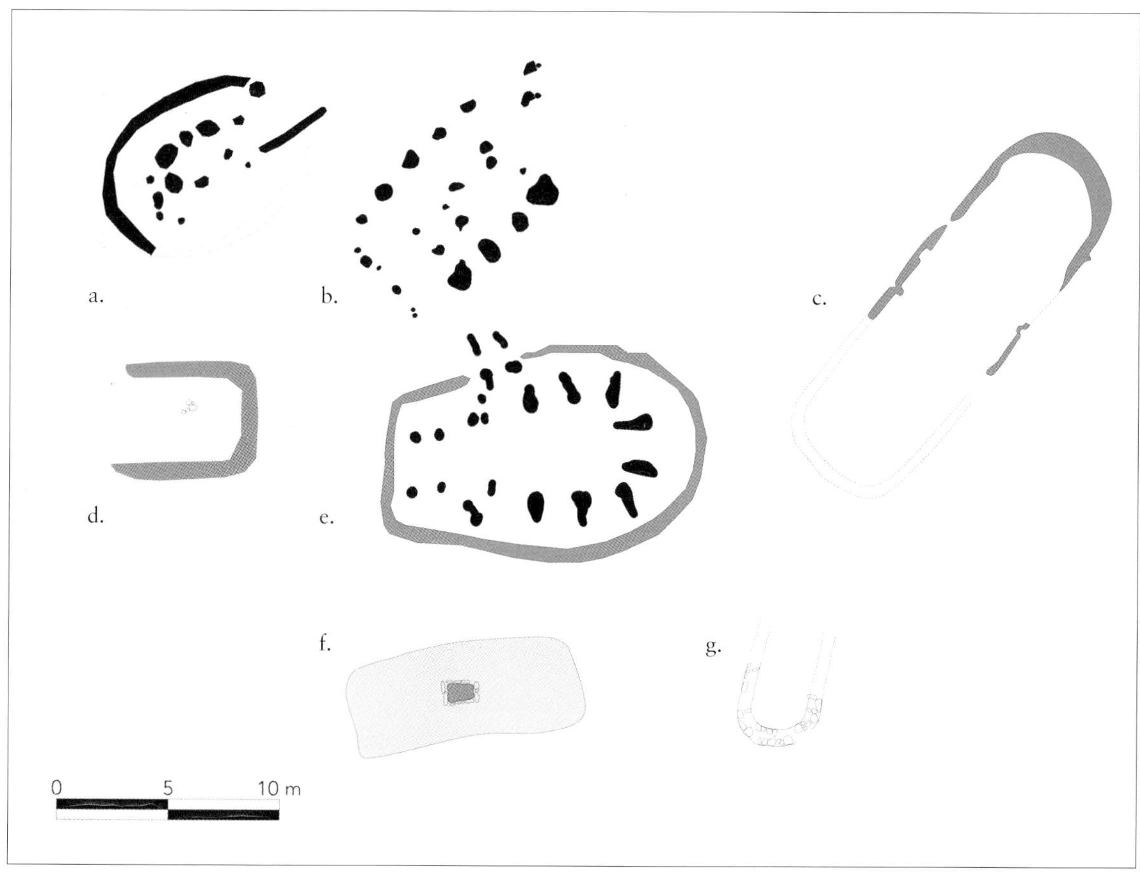

2.5 Lowland Pictish structures: (a) and (b) Rhynie, Aberdeenshire; (c) Newbarns, Angus; (d) Portknockie, Moray; (e) Portmahomack, Easter Ross; (f) Clatchard Craig, Fife; (g) Dunnicaer, Aberdeenshire.

possible that Newbarns was another potential Lowland equivalent of the Pitcarmick-style byre-houses (Dunwell and Ralston 2008, 140). Contemporary crop-processing pits were found to the west of the building but the evidence for the function and status of the Newbarns building is slim. Another 'hall-like' building was found at Callander Park, Falkirk, close to the Antonine Wall (Bailey 2006). The Callander Park building consisted of postholes and paving indicating a large building but again finds were few, meaning the function and status of this structure is difficult to assess.

Other large Pictish-era buildings may be identifiable in the cropmark record. Cropmarks from Lathrisk, Fife, near East Lomond fort (see Chapter 3), could represent hall-like buildings with at least five buildings evident averaging around 25m by 9m (Maxwell 1987, 33–34 and Figs 1–2). While these have been compared to Pitcarmick buildings (for example, Halliday 2019, 125), these examples do appear to be more complex with some having an annex or 'room' at one end of the building recalling the spatial layout and architecture of early medieval halls from Anglo-Saxon elite centres (Figure 2.6).

2.6 Cropmarks of at least five buildings at Lathrisk, Fife. (© Historic Environment Scotland)

Buildings within hillforts

A range of buildings have been found within enclosed settlements such as hillforts and promontory forts in both southern and northern Pictland. It is in these locations that the possibilities of retrieving Pictish period structural evidence may be greater, given that fort sites tend to lie at the margins of arable land and thus can retain better on-site preservation. However, this is not guaranteed and, even in the most unlikely of settings, modern agricultural processes have limited the evidence that can be retrieved. At Dunnicaer, Aberdeenshire, a series of buildings dating to the early Pictish period, was excavated on a sea stack from 2015–2017 (Noble *et al.* 2020a). The sea stack at Dunnicaer appears to be the sole stump left of what is likely to have been a much larger promontory fort destroyed by coastal erosion (see Chapter 3). Incredibly, even here, the fragile settlement remains have not escaped the impacts of later land use – in the 19th century, the top of the stack was cultivated by an enterprising local fisherman (Noble *et al.* 2020a, 283).

At Dunnicaer, the structures were built in ways that left little in the way of earthfast remains and, like at the upland sites of southern Pictland, such as Pitcarmick and Lair, the buildings must have been largely constructed using turf and other non-earthfast construction methods. From an early phase at Dunnicaer, a possible rectangular timber building was located but this was simply defined by a series of small, shallow postholes that would not have survived modern ploughing. Above, the floor layer of a later building with a central hearth fared better but the floor only survived in a hollow in the subsoil so the shape and character of the building is uncertain. The latest building detected on the stack survived the best. Here the stone footing of a turf-and-stone wall partly survived, defining a building that would have been up to 4m wide and at least 4.5m long but the eastern end of the building was unfortunately lost to erosion (Figure 2.5g). This building had replaced an earlier structure on the same footprint that had had a cobbled floor.

A number of other forts preserve buildings from the Pictish period. At a promontory fort in northern Pictland at Greencastle, Portknockie, Moray, excavation within the fort revealed a rectangular structure around 7m by 5.5m (Figure 2.5d), aligned east–west with an open or truncated west end (Ralston 1987, 20–21). Like the Dunnicaer buildings, few structural elements were identified with the structure comprising a low stone-faced wall with an organic fill, perhaps the footings of a turf wall. A probable post-pad was found towards the centre of the building. At Clatchard Craig, Fife, a hillfort in southern Pictland, excavations in the upper citadel revealed a floor layer and central hearth. Little structural detail survived, with no definite traces of an outer wall, but a pivot stone indicating a doorway and the extent of the floor layers would suggest a turf-walled rectangular building around 9m by 5m (Close-Brooks 1986, 145) (Figure 2.5f). Recent dating has demonstrated that this building is of the 7th century AD date (Noble *et al.* forthcoming). A large hearth was found in the upper citadel of the fort at the King's Seat in Stormont west of Dunkeld and was presumably part of a building similar to that at Clatchard Craig (see Chapter 3). Wattle floors were found at Dundurn – these could have presumably been enclosed by turf walls too (Alcock *et al.* 1989, 200–02).

Excavations at Burghead, Moray, a probable major power centre of Fortriu, have shown that the buildings there must have also used cruck frames or other non-earthfast structural means – for instance, postpads – for little survives other than floor layers, fortuitously preserved under layers of sand blow and modern overburden at this coastal site (see Chapter 3) (Colour Plate 8). The buildings at Burghead include rectangular and horseshoe-shaped buildings. One building had a suspended wooden floor and a stone-and-turf outer wall. There were also structures built up against the ramparts and a stone-walled rectangular building dating to the 7th to 8th centuries was found near the upper citadel entrance. This latter building must have been around 4.8m wide and perhaps around 10m long – a close

2.7 Traces of a large building at the Craw Stane complex, Rhynie, under excavation. The curving outer wall of the building can be seen cutting through the outer ditch of the enclosure complex to the right of the line of trowellers.

match for the building from Clatchard Craig.

In Aberdeenshire, early medieval settlement traces have been found in the enclosure complex at the Craw Stane, Rhynie (Figures 2.5a, b and 2.7). One post-built structure appears to have been rectangular or based on an internal setting of rectangular posts and another building was horseshoe shaped in outer form – like the later buildings at Portmahomack (see below). The rectangular building was at least 9m by 5m and the horseshoe-shaped building around 9m by 6m (Figures 2.5a, b). The latter had a shallow beam trench that may have been the foundation for an internal plank revetment for an outer turf wall. The floor layer of a highly truncated structure was also found outside of the complex. Settlement traces have also been found at a series of ringforts in Aberdeenshire – these include a building with a massive hearth at Cairnmore, traces of probable rectangular structures at Maiden Castle and a floor at Hill of Keir (Cook 2011a,b; Noble *et al.* 2020b) (Figure 2.8).

Buildings at ecclesiastical centres

In the Lowlands, the only other buildings identifiable have been found in an ecclesiastical context. While in a non-secular context, these buildings may provide clues as to the wider vernacular traditions of Pictland. The

2.8 Hill of Keir, Aberdeenshire – a circular ringfort-style enclosure with 7th–8th-century activity.

most complete groundplan of a building at Portmahomack, the major monastic site in northern Pictland (see Chapter 4), was Structure S1, a 'bag-shaped' (horseshoe-shaped) structure, with an entrance on the north-west side (Carver *et al.* 2016, 38) (Figure 2.5e). Although Structure S1 did utilise postholes, it is perhaps not that distinct from the tradition of largely non-earthfast components as is evident at sites such as Greencastle and Clatchard Craig, in that many of the postholes of the Portmahomack structure had flat stone slabs at the base forming post-pads (Carver *et al.* 2016, Illus. 5.9.9). The structural remains of S1 comprised an internal setting of posts and an outer wall line enclosing an interior of around 14m by 9m. The outer wall was interpreted as being constructed of turf perhaps lined with planks on the inside, with a roofed entrance passage giving access to the interior. A secondary phase of S1 at Portmahomack involved the addition of further posts within the interior, perhaps to support an upper level, and a flue was also added – argued to have been part of the conversion of the structure to a kiln barn – a building used for drying grain (Carver *et al.* 2016, 277). At least two other horseshoe-shaped buildings may have been present at Portmahomack but these were not nearly as well preserved.

Overall, the settlement evidence from the Lowlands of southern and northern Pictland is still slight but a number of Pictish forts and enclosures preserve structural evidence with all of the identifiable buildings tending to be of rectangular form with turf clearing forming an important construction material for the outer walls of these buildings. The buildings from Portmahomack show that turf was also a structural component in use in ecclesiastical settings, with the buildings here showing some similarities to buildings found at secular elite complexes such as Rhynie.

An urban-like settlement or a seasonal aggregation site of northern Pictland?

Given the very meagre settlement remains found in Pictland to date, we have potentially underestimated the scale of settlement (and society) in existence in first millennium AD eastern Scotland. There is some tantalising evidence for settlement centralisation in this period but whether this was part of year-round settlement or more specialised and perhaps seasonal occupation remains to be ascertained. New evidence has recently been uncovered of much larger settlement agglomerations than hitherto recognised at sites such as Tap o' Noth, Aberdeenshire. Conventional survey work had suggested a few hundred house platforms existed within a 16ha enclosure at Tap o' Noth (see Chapter 3). However, LiDAR surveys (essentially laser scanning from an aeroplane) and photogrammetry surveys (taking hundreds of photos from a drone and stitching them together to create a 3D model) have suggested that many more house platforms are contained within the lower fort – perhaps at least as many as 800 – making Tap o' Noth a hillfort with some of the densest concentrations of settlement remains known from northern Britain (Figure 2.9).

The houses inside appear to date from the Late Roman Iron Age (*c.*3rd century AD to the 6th century AD), though further excavations may provide a wider chronological range for the occupation of these platforms. The number of platforms on the site suggests an almost town-like population centre if even a small percentage of all the hut platforms were in contemporary use. While only a few of the platforms have been excavated to date, the mapping of the hut platforms suggests many, if not most, could be broadly contemporary as there are no clear examples of intercutting platforms and all are contained within the lower rampart. A series of trackways seems to service groups of platforms and suggests that these tracks are contemporary with the house platforms and relate to specific groups of buildings. Moreover, the fact that groups of platforms appear to be built on terraces suggests that large numbers of the platforms may have been laid out in an organised manner. There may have been a hierarchy to the settlement too, with groups of roundhouses ranging from around 5m in diameter to up to 11m. The smaller examples accord well with the average size of early medieval roundhouses identified in Ireland (around 4–7m in diameter) (Lynn 1994, 92; O'Sullivan 2008, 231), while the largest

2.9 Tap o' Noth – towards the centre of the photograph is a trench laid out to excavate one of the house platforms that lie below the Iron Age vitrified fort. This platform had Late Roman amphora sherds and a hearth of 5th–6th-century AD date.

platforms are equivalent in size to some of the largest known early medieval Irish roundhouse structures. The Irish law tract, *Críth Gablach*, for example, suggests that, at a royal ringfort, the roundhouse of the king should measure around 11m in diameter (Binchy 1979, 23) – around the size of the largest Tap o' Noth platforms.

The hillfort of Tap o' Noth and its extensive settlement remains stand overlooking an elite centre at Rhynie (see Chapter 3). Was this a major population centre, urban-like in form, that supported an early royal centre in the valley below or did Tap o' Noth have a more specialised role? Could it have been a site for seasonal or episodic gathering? Sites of assembly are thought to have played a crucial role in the structuring of early medieval societies across north-west Europe (for example, Pantos and Semple 2004; Iversen 2013, 5–6, 11; Semple and Sanmark 2013, 518; Semple *et al.* 2021). The limited historical sources suggest assembly sites were places of periodic gathering for law making, judgements and community decision making and could also have been associated with a whole range of social roles and purposes such as associated religious festivals, the conducting of trading through markets, horse racing, drinking and game playing and events of royal inauguration.

Unfortunately, in eastern Scotland, we know relatively little about assembly practices. While a tradition of popular courts existed in the later medieval period (O'Grady 2014), the existence of earlier places of assembly is difficult to establish. Elsewhere in Britain, the archaeological traces of assembly are overall slight, with most settings for assembly appearing to have been open air with little in the way of architectural elaboration and written sources providing few indications of formal arrangement, though an amphitheatre-style structure is known from the royal centre at Yeavering in Northumberland and may have been used during occasions of assembly (Hope-Taylor 1977, 119–22; Semple 2013, 90–91; Blair 2018, 105; Semple *et al.* 2020, 7, 14, 17). In Ireland, an *óenach* (assembly) was generally held on hills or mounds or at prehistoric hillforts (MacCotter 2008, 49–51). Various temporary structures were used at assemblies including huts, camps, terraces, enclosures and mounds or platforms (Bhreathnach 2014, 67–77). Assemblies of the highest level were generally held on royal land and called by a king (Jaski 2000, 192–93). None of this is at the scale and permanence of Tap o' Noth and activities such as horse racing and trading would have been difficult on a high steep site. Nonetheless, it could be that one facet of Tap o' Noth was as a major seasonal assembly site of a type and scale hitherto unknown – perhaps using the interior of the summit hillfort as a natural amphitheatre for events of assembly.

It is, however, also possible, given the well-built platforms, the huge investment in place and enclosing works, that Tap o' Noth was not a seasonal occupation site but a year-round settlement associated with a royal centre in the valley bottom (see Chapter 3). If this was the case and given its marginal siting and size, it must have been supported by food renders and tribute from a wider region. Hamlets and other forms of communal rural settlements are known from elsewhere in Europe, with Anglo-Saxon rural settlements, for example, often comprising clusters of timber buildings and *grubenhäuser* (sunken featured buildings) (for example, Hamerow 1993, 2012). In Ireland, settlement nucleation may have been a feature of the later early medieval period but evidence for settlement agglomeration really only emerges outside of ecclesiastical centres with the development of towns in the Viking Age at sites such as Dublin and Cork (O'Sullivan *et al.* 2014, 48). Thus, settlement agglomeration of the early medieval period, apart from towns like Lundenwic and Hamwic, before the Viking Age is not unknown but it is rare in Britain and Ireland. Overall, we have yet to fully digest what sites such as Tap o' Noth suggest for the character of society in Pictland around the middle of the first millennium AD but the identification of the date of this colossal hilltop settlement represents a major leap forward in Pictish studies.

Were there other major settlements (seasonally occupied or otherwise) matching the scale of the Tap o' Noth settlement in Pictland? While not as large as the Tap o' Noth fort, recent work at East Lomond fort in Fife, in southern Pictland, has identified an extensive enclosed settlement of the same date. At East Lomond, geophysical survey identified a lower annexe enclosure, defined by a stone wall that appears to form an annexe enclosure to a complex 'nuclear' fort. An early medieval date for the fort seems almost certain with the groundplan a good parallel for other complex early medieval forts, such as Dundurn and Dunadd, and there is a carving of a bull from the site that provides a good match for the bull carvings from Burghead and the Inverness area (see Chapter 3). The annexe enclosure at East Lomond loops off from the central fort complex on a low terrace that extends to the south of the fort and is around one hectare in extent (Figure 2.10). The geophysical survey identified numerous features inside and excavations by the enclosing wall have identified multiple hearths, paved surfaces and finds of Roman Iron Age to early medieval date including metalworking evidence and E ware, imported pottery from western France, along with radiocarbon dates extending from the 2nd to 7th centuries AD confirming Late Roman Iron Age and early medieval occupation. The annexe-enclosing wall itself has been dated to the 5th to 6th centuries AD. The remains at East Lomond suggest a similar density and complexity of settlement to that at Tap o' Noth, though not quite on the same scale. Other early medieval forts, such as the King's Seat, Perthshire, also have

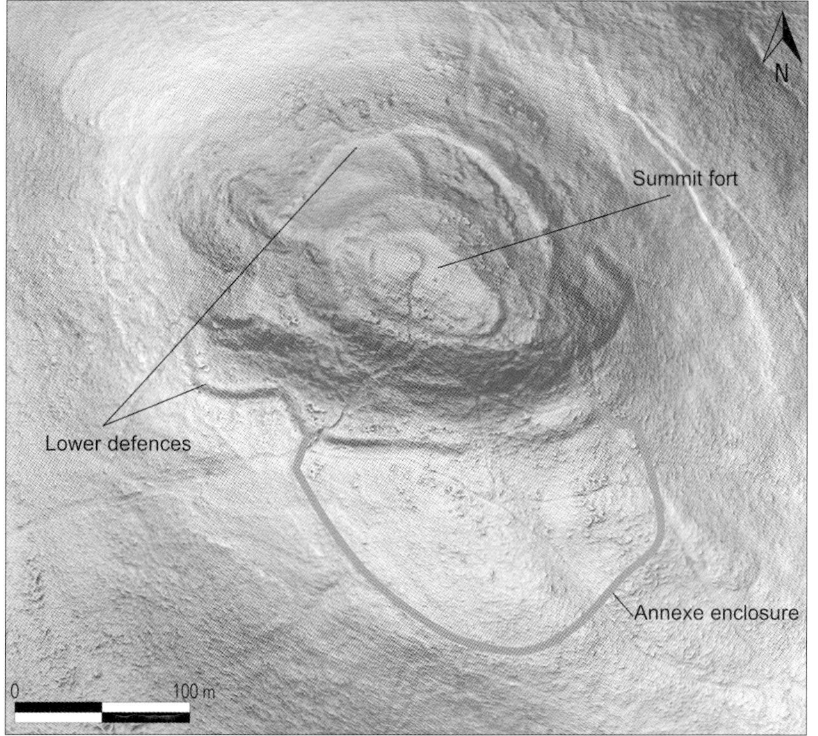

2.10 The complex defences of East Lomond hillfort in Fife. An extensive settlement has been identified on the shoulder of the hill below the nuclear fort within the bounds of an annexe enclosure.

large subsidiary enclosures attached to nuclear forts. It is possible that these large-scale settlements of the Late Antique period were widespread – a conclusion that would have been impossible to reach even a few years ago.

Atlantic Pictland

Caithness wags

Shifting focus to Atlantic Pictland, we find a relatively rich settlement record, though one that has rarely come from targeted excavation of Pictish period architecture but through incidental finds in the excavation of multi-period sites. In Caithness in the Highlands, in the Northern and Western Isles and in the Inner Hebrides, we can identify some of the same patterns as in northern and southern Pictland – such as a shift towards non-roundhouse forms during the first millennium AD – but also very different traditions of settlement architecture – such as cellular structures, figure-of-eight structures and a continuation or revival of monumental roundhouses, particularly in Shetland.

Starting with Caithness, a group of distinctive rectangular structures of first millennium AD date known as 'wags' are found mainly in the parish of Latheron. Wags are buildings with free-standing piers supporting a corbelled roof, perhaps helping span the roof in an area with an increasingly limited timber supply. At Wag of Forse, the site type, Alexander Curle originally identified both round and rectangular structures as wags (Curle 1912), though generally the longhouse form is what archaeologists think of when defining a wag today (Figures 2.11 and 2.12g). These rectangular structures occur in post-broch contexts at sites in Caithness with their stratigraphic position suggesting they date to the first millennium AD, though their exact chronology has never been fully established. Only three wag sites have been excavated: Wag of Forse, Yarrows and Langwell (Anderson 1891; Curle 1912; Curle 1948). Excavations by Curle at Wag of Forse identified two rectangular buildings and his excavations at Langwell (Figure 2.2d) identified a similar structure which appeared to be attached to a roundhouse, though the contemporaneity of these structures was not established (Curle 1941).

The lack of settlement debris from the excavated wags might suggest these were not domestic dwellings. Indeed, the long narrow galleried forms of the wag structures identified at Yarrows does not appear conducive to domestic routines and, in this case, the Yarrows structures may have been ancillary structures for stalling animals – a bit like the byres within Pitcarmick style structures (Anderson 1891). The monumentality of wags and the huge stone slabs used to build them would suggest a lot of care went into looking after cattle if this was the case. This is not improbable – the resources invested in these structures might have reflected the importance

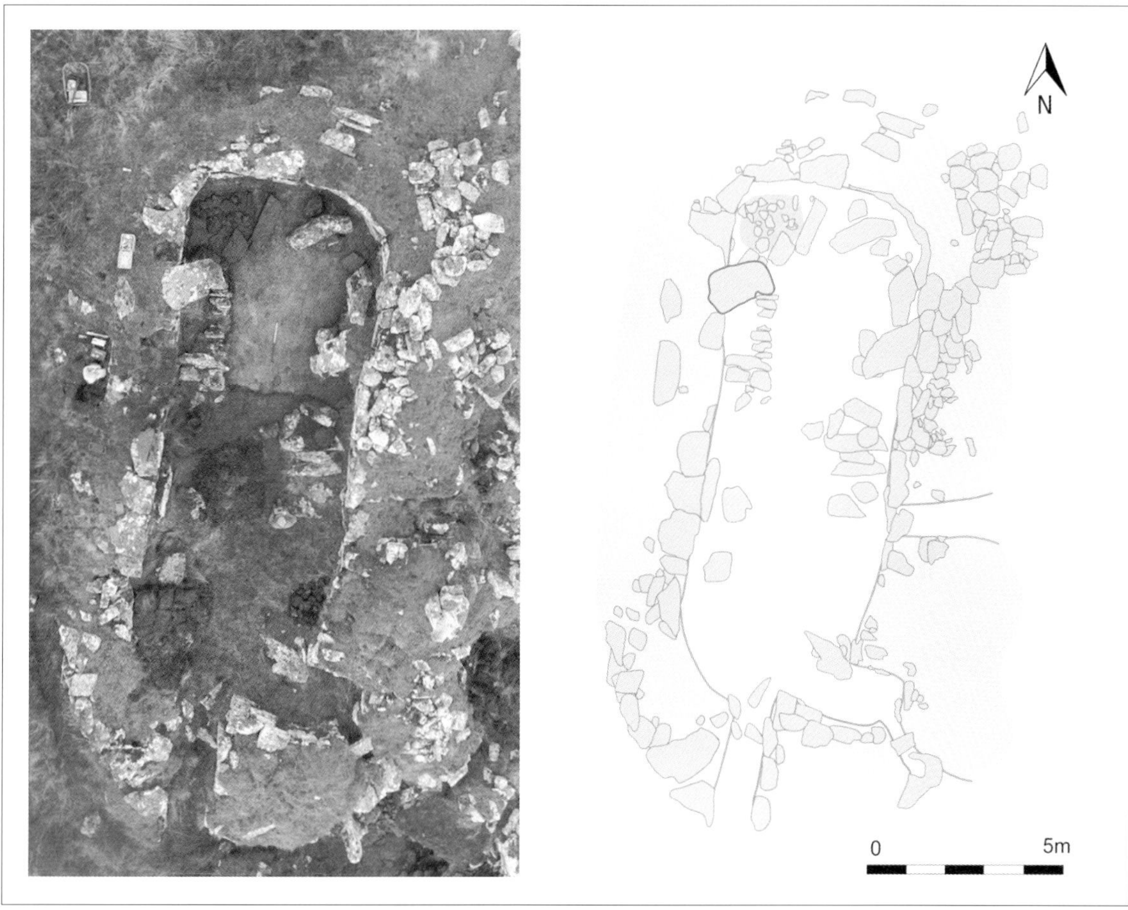

2.11 (Left) Aerial view of excavations underway in 2019 at one of the longhouses at Wag of Forse, Caithness. (Right) Plan of the rectangular building.

of cattle wealth to status and rank as well as to the agricultural economy in the early medieval period (see Kelly 1997, 27–29). However, other purposes might be sought for some of these wag structures. Given the grandeur of the Wag of Forse structures for example, these could have acted as communal buildings for a community – maybe a small version of a feasting or meeting hall – with the more everyday buildings, perhaps made of turf, that have not survived or have not yet been identified archaeologically.

Orkney

In Orkney as in Shetland and the Western Isles, there were traditions of cellular and figure-of-eight styles of architecture not yet attested in northern and southern Pictland. One of the most important sequences for establishing Pictish period architectural trends in Orkney is that from Howe, Stromness. Howe was a prominent hillock – called a *howe* (a 'mound') – on a farm overlooking the Bay of Ireland and Loch of Stenness in the western part of

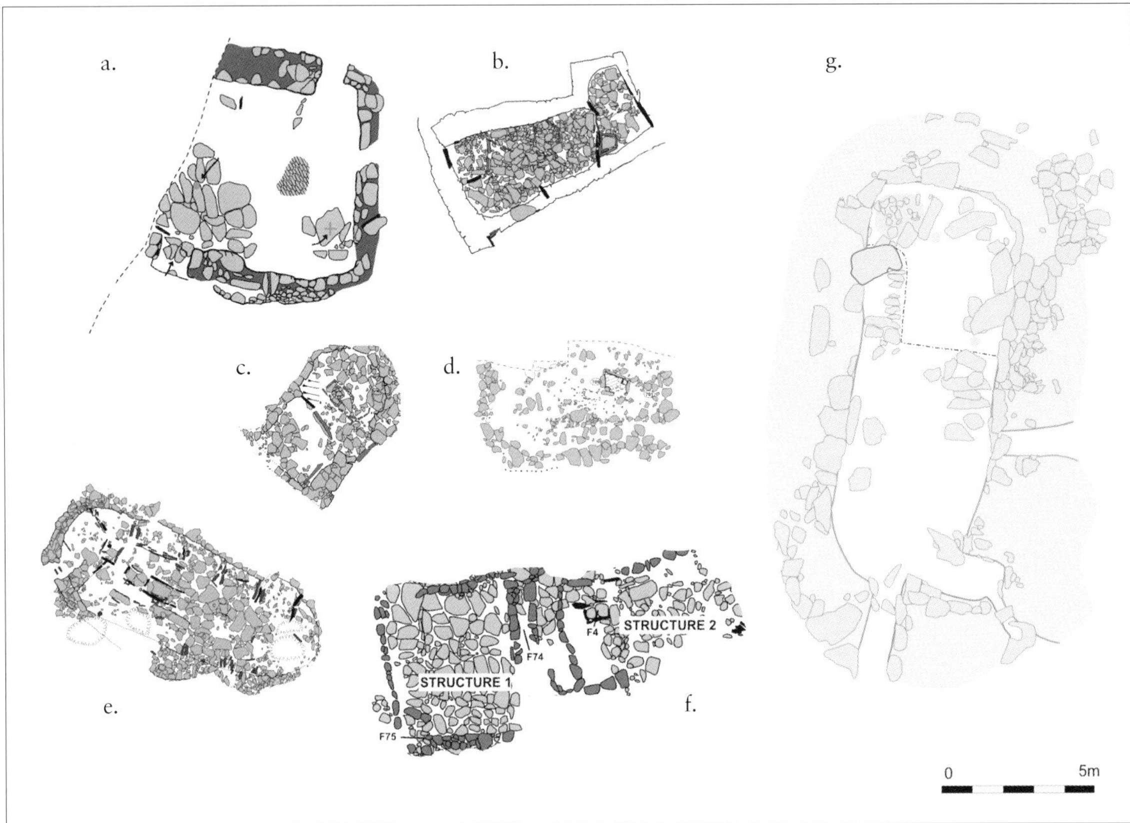

2.12 Comparative plan of rectangular structures in Atlantic Pictland:
(a) Buckquoy, Orkney;
(b) Howe, Orkney;
(c) Howe, Orkney;
(d) Dùn Mhùlan (Dun Vulan), South Uist;
(e) Howe, Orkney;
(f) Skaill, Orkney;
(g) Wag of Forse, Caithness.

Mainland Orkney. In the 1970s, the landowner declared his intentions to level the mound for agricultural purposes and government funding led to five seasons of rescue excavation from 1978–1982 giving an unusually detailed insight into a first millennium AD settlement sequence (Ballin Smith 1994). In the first millennium AD settlement phases, many of the buildings became more modest in terms of residential space than previous phases of settlement on site, but the Pictish-era buildings often combined a domestic focus with separate working yards, storage cells and other ancillary spaces.

At Howe, the later phases of occupation included Structure E, a small rectangular room with hearth and storage tank, and Structure W, a small 2m by 2m square structure with a central hearth, demonstrating that, like on the mainland, there was a shift towards rectilinear architectural forms. Some of the Howe buildings may have had specialised uses – for example, Structure W appears to have been used for ironworking at least in its latter stages and could have had more esoteric uses also (Ritchie 2003, 5) (see Chapter 4). Rectangular buildings were also a feature of the Howe sequence (Figure 2.12b), the most impressive of which was a stalled building (Figure 2.12e) – one of the most coherent and regular structures identified in the late phases of occupation. The stalled building was the largest of this phase of Howe and was sub-rectangular measuring around 10.5m by 4m internally. This building would have resembled the wags of Caithness, with upright panels dividing the interior into five stalls. A multi-cellular, 'shamrock'-style building was part of the latest phase of occupation with this phase dating to around the 6th century AD (see Shepherd in Ballin Smith 1994, 276; Ballin Smith 1994, 222–24). At Howe, mixed farming was the mainstay of the economy and, in the earlier phases of settlement, small-scale ironworking was carried out. Craftworking occurred throughout the history of the settlement with highly burnished pottery being made, and pins and toggles made from animal bone and antler, and querns, tools and pot lids from stone. The Howe community also had access to some of the finer things in life such as glass beads and decorative metalwork – some of the most decorative objects included zoomorphic penannular brooches and ring-headed pins.

Another important sequence in Orkney is that of Pool, Sanday (Hunter *et al.* 2007). Phases of settlement at Pool (Phase 5.1–5.2) included small square buildings such as Structure 16, probably an animal byre of some kind, and larger sub-rectangular buildings such as Structure 17 (Hunter *et al.* 2007, 81, 111). In the subsequent Phase 6, the settlement saw major expansion that included the construction of two figure-of-eight style buildings, with the smaller circular rooms attached to larger roundhouses. The figure-of-eight buildings were built with single skin walls being revetted into earlier midden deposits. Further additions occurred in the 5th to 6th centuries AD with the construction of a large rectangular building, Structure 23 (Figure 6.7) that measured at least 14m in length and around 3m in width. This appears to have been a roofed structure but it had no formal hearth within the area of excavation. It could have been a communal hall or gathering space and certainly this building appears to have had a central role in the settlement from this phase onwards. An upright stone orthostat within the western half of the Structure 23 had an ogham inscription carved on the stone while, further to the east, one of the paving slabs was found to have very simple Pictish symbol-style carvings on the underside of the stone (see Chapter 6). At its height, the settlement at Pool during the 5th to 6th centuries AD consisted of at least seven buildings, many of them conjoined by passageways and paved areas.

A further important sequence in Orkney is the Broch of Gurness (Hedges 1987, 69). Like Howe, the later phases at Gurness included the development of more rectilinear dwellings outside the broch entrance in the early centuries AD which, in turn, were replaced by a series of cellular buildings, including, like Howe, a shamrock-style building with an oval central room with a series of small cells opening from it (Figures 2.13 and 2.14a). A large rectangular building attached to the north-east side of the

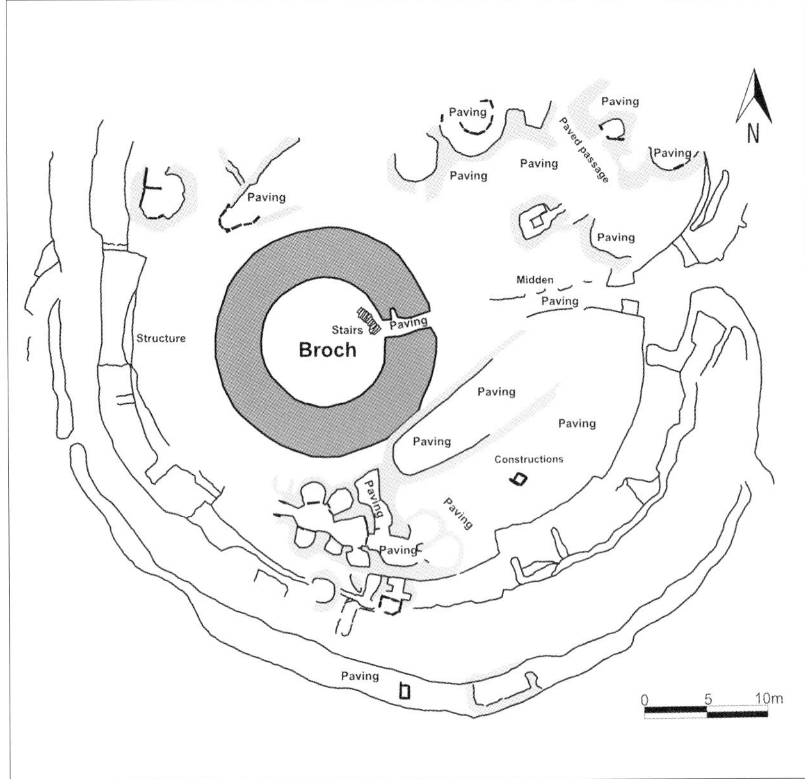

2.13 The Pictish period dwellings at Gurness, Orkney, included cellular and rectilinear buildings, centred around an Iron Age broch. (After Hedges 1987)

shamrock building may also belong to this phase too (Morris 2021, 568) (Figure 2.13).

The evidence from Pool, Howe and Gurness suggests experimentation with structural form in the Pictish period with rectilinear, round and cellular stykes all being deployed and a sequence from Buckquoy, Birsay, west Mainland, shows similar innovation in architectural form. At Buckquoy, small rectangular buildings with cells formed the first phase of settlement in the late 7th to early 8th centuries AD (Figure 2.14c) and these were replaced within a generation or so by a figure-of-eight building which was an impressive house measuring around 12m by 4m (Ritchie 1977) (Figure 2.15d). The latest phases at Buckquoy consisted of at least three rectangular buildings (Figure 2.12a), though only two of these survived in a good state of preservation. These latter buildings were assumed to be Norse for many decades but dating of occupation deposits within the building have suggested these were in fact of Pictish date.

Indeed, rectangular buildings are found widely across first millennium AD sites in Orkney. Recent excavations at The Cairns, South Ronaldsay, have identified two buildings that provide close parallels for the stalled building from the Howe and have been dated to the 3rd to 4th centuries

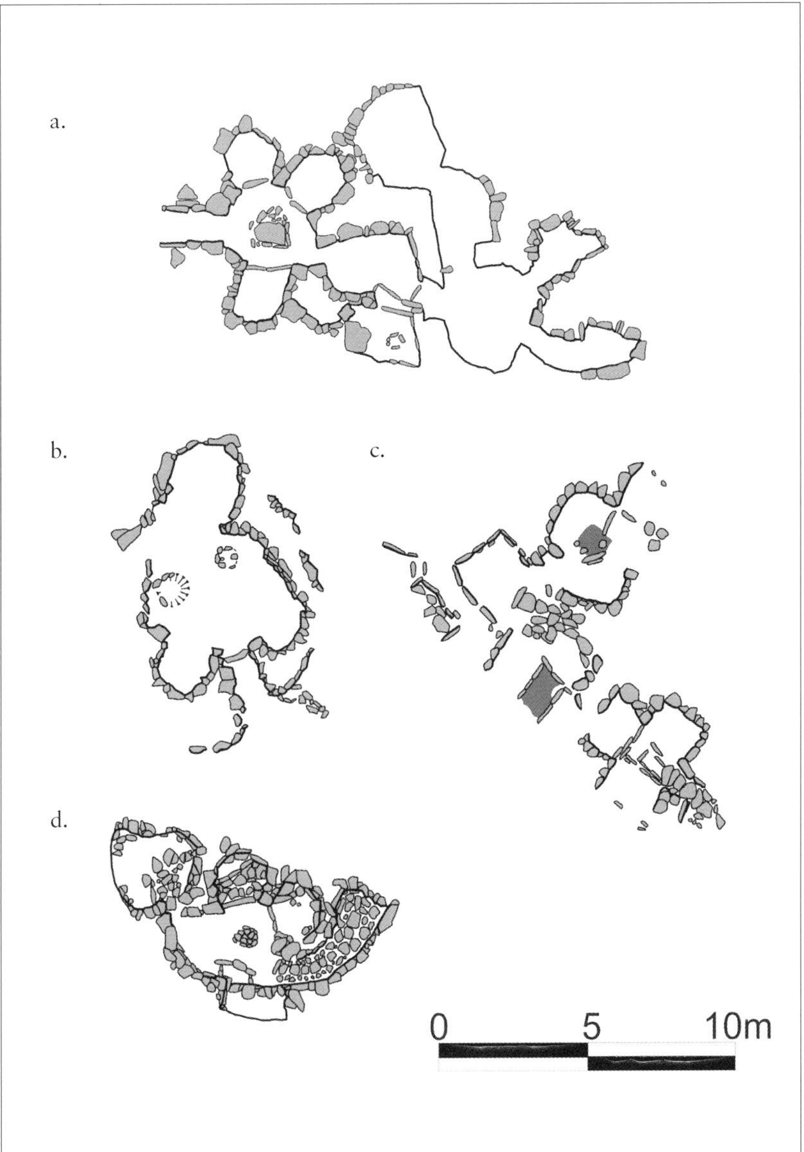

2.14 Comparative plan of cellular structures from Atlantic Pictland:
(a) Gurness, Orkney;
(b) Eilean Olabhat, North Uist;
(c) Buckquoy, Orkney;
(d) Loch na Beirghe, Lewis.
(After Gilmour 2000)

AD. Rectilinear structures have also been identified at Skaill, Deerness, in late phases of a multi-period settlement there (Figure 2.12f). These date from the 5th to 8th century AD and consisted of a series of rectilinear structures built in association with extensive areas of paving. These buildings had walls that were very slightly built with only single skin masonry revetments surviving to only a few courses high – like in upland southern Pictland, it may be that turf was a structural component of these buildings in Orkney.

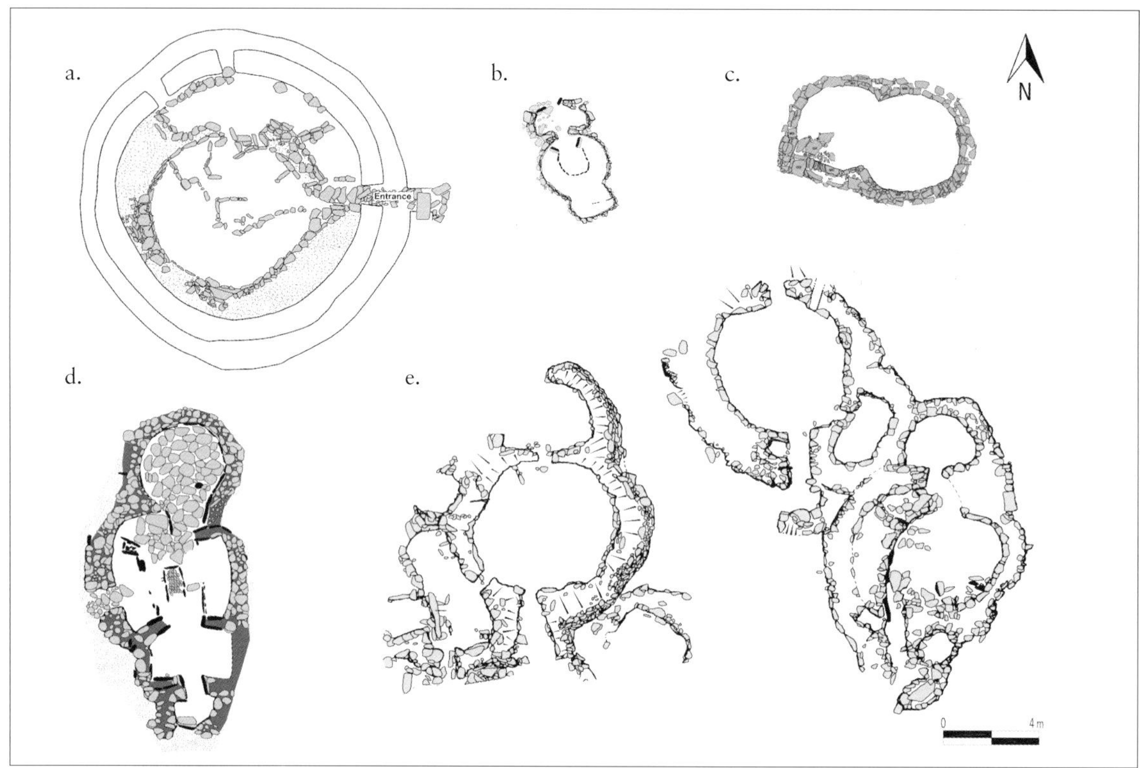

2.15 Comparative plan of figure-of-eight structures from Atlantic Pictland:
(a) Loch na Beirghe, Lewis;
(b) Scatness Structure 5, Shetland;
(c) Red Craig, Birsay, Orkney;
(d), Buckquoy Building 4, Orkney;
(e) Tràigh Bhòstadh, Lewis.

Shetland

In Shetland in the first half of the first millennium AD, we see similar traditions of cellular architecture to that in Orkney, along with the continuation of roundhouse forms with late forms of wheelhouse architecture (aisled roundhouses) being utilised in the second half of the first millennium AD. One of the most important sites for elucidating first millennium AD settlement transitions in Shetland is Scatness, near the southern tip of Mainland Shetland (Dockrill *et al.* 2010). Like Howe and Gurness in Orkney, the late Iron Age buildings at Scatness grew up around a broch tower which, by that point, had stood for centuries and reuse of this structure ensured that it remained at the heart of the early first millennium AD settlement. The early phases of the late Iron Age village at Scatness included an oval building, Structure 25, which has radiocarbon dates suggesting use from the 3rd to the 6th century AD. A cellular building, Structure 7, appears to be an early addition too, built inside the shell of the broch, with dates as early as the 6th century associated with activity inside the building. Structure 7 was particularly finely built with a horseshoe hearth at the centre of the multi-cellular building and its architectural form shares parallels with the shamrock building at Gurness.

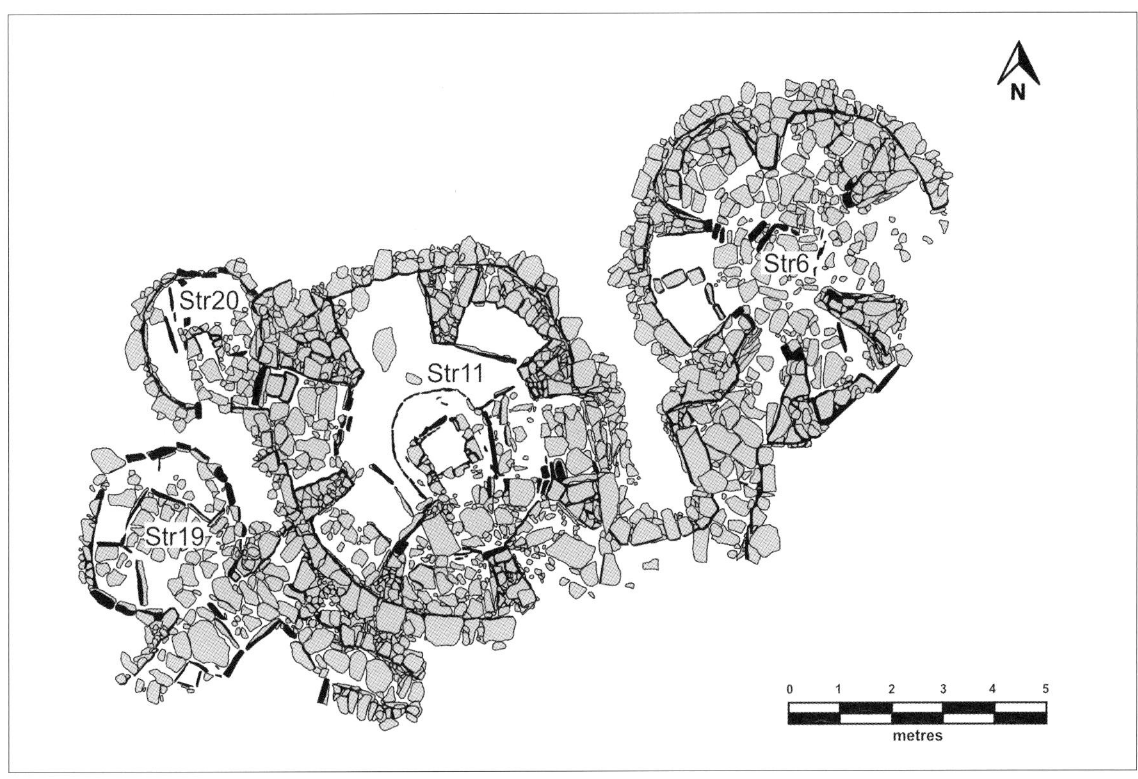

2.16 Plan of the wheelhouses at Scatness, Shetland. The circular form remained dominant in the far north of Atlantic Pictland. (After Dockrill *et al.* 2010)

Developments at Scatness in the 7th and 8th centuries AD included the construction and certainly use of monumental wheelhouses (Structures 6 and 11) (Figure 2.16) and possibly the construction and use of figure-of-eight buildings (Figure 2.15b). Other Pictish-era structures at Scatness were very small and it has been suggested that some of these buildings could have played specialised, even ritualised roles, due in part to their very small dimensions (Ritchie 2003, 5–7; Dockrill *et al.* 2010, 358; see also Chapter 4), but the use and construction of these could also mark developments towards the marking of more private and perhaps exclusive space within first millennium AD settlements as household groups perhaps became more hierarchical and diverse.

One of the most famous sites from the Northern Isles, Jarlshof, located on the south-west coast of Mainland Shetland, a stone's throw away from Scatness, was also occupied in the first millennium AD (Hamilton 1956). Intense storms in 1897 brought the ancient settlement of 'Jarlshof' (a name coined by Walter Scott for his novel *The Pirate*) to light. At Jarlshof, the late first millennium AD settlement, like that at Scatness, appears to have been dominated by impressive wheelhouse-style buildings that were built within an earlier courtyard attached to an Iron Age broch tower (Figure 2.17). At least three wheelhouses were constructed and a wheelhouse-style

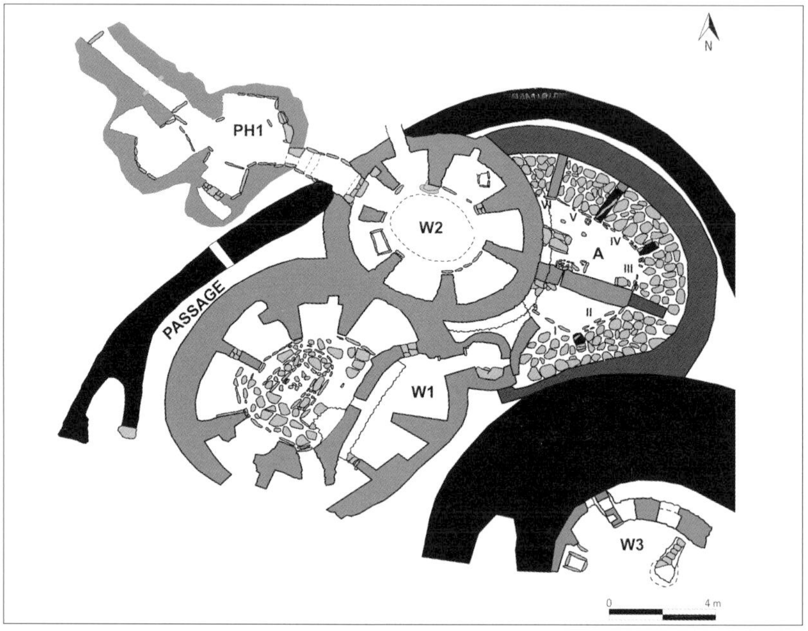

2.17 Plan of the wheelhouses built over the courtyard of an earlier broch at Jarlshof, Shetland. Cellular passage-houses – for example, PH1 – were added to the settlement in a late phase of occupation. (After Hamilton 1956)

building may have been inserted into the broch too. Late additions to the settlement at Jarlshof were the so-called passage-houses and other cellular types of building. Passage-house 1 (PH1) was added to one of the wheelhouses and shows a similar organisation of space to the shamrock-style structures from Gurness and Howe (Gilmour 2000, 60; Harding 2009, 181) (Figure 2.17). Based on the dating from Gurness, this might suggest that passage-house 1 may be no later than 6th century AD in date though, at Scatness, the wheelhouses and other structures remained in use in the 7th and 8th centuries AD and activity at Jarlshof appears to have continued into the late first millennium AD. Certainly, the wheelhouse styles at Jarlshof, with tapering piers and the U-shaped hearth in the largest wheelhouse, provide close parallels for the wheelhouses that were in occupation in the 7th to 8th centuries AD at Scatness (Dockrill *et al.* 2010, 356) and the passage-houses were in contemporary use, judging by the artefacts from both styles of building (Hamilton 1956, 83). Wheelhouse 2 at Jarlshof is arguably the best-preserved building of the Pictish period with the corbelled roof of the building and cells still partly in evidence (Figure 2.17). Corbelled roofs and the cellular forms of structures such as Wheelhouse 2 may have been solutions to the increasing scarcity of timber in the Northern Isles in the later first millennium AD. The interior of Wheelhouse 2 was around 7m in diameter with seven cells radiating from the central living space. Stone-built storage boxes were built into the floor of the dwelling. Finds from the settlement included abundant pottery, an ingot mould, painted pebbles, stone pot lids and lamps and carved bone objects.

Elsewhere in Shetland, a wheelhouse-style building may have been inserted into the broch interior at Scalloway judging by the presence of triangular piers of a first phase of a secondary occupation and rebuild in the broch interior (Sharples 1998, 43). This phase of reoccupation extended perhaps from the late 6th century through to the 8th century and finds from the broch include conical gaming pieces and part of an iron spear. The settlement at Scalloway also included cellular structures built outside the broch, including a possible shamrock-style building, House 1, along with a figure-of-eight building, House 9.

Overall, we can perhaps identify more localised patterns of architecture in Shetland than in other areas of Atlantic Pictland, with a continuation of the monumental roundhouse as one major element of settlement into the later first millennium AD. However, one structure from Scalloway, House 8 (Figure 2.12f), was a rectilinear building, showing that there was an awareness of wider trends and architectural traditions identifiable elsewhere in Pictland.

Western Isles

Settlement traditions in the Western Isles in the Pictish era followed similar patterns to other parts of Atlantic Pictland. Cellular forms of architecture appear to have been present from the early first millennium AD and partly replaced earlier roundhouse traditions (Armit 1992, 73–86; see also Gilmour 2000, 98–102). Few of the cellular settlements of the Western Isles are well dated but at Eilean Olabhat, North Uist, a cellular structure, broadly reminiscent of shamrock-style buildings from Gurness and other Northern Isles sites, was constructed around the middle of the first millennium AD (Armit 2008) (Figure 2.14b). This building was around 5m wide and 7.5m long and comprised a central sub-rectangular or oval space with three cells on the north, south-west and south-east sides of the central space. A late episode of use appears to have comprised a phase of bronze and silver working, represented by quantities of mould and crucible fragments. Substantial quantities of pottery were found in the same context suggesting some form of continuing domestic occupation of the building around the 5th to 6th century AD.

Like in the Northern Isles, brochs were reused in the Pictish period in the Western Isles. The most closely dated example is Loch na Beirghe, also known as Loch na Berie, on the west coast of Lewis, where a broch settlement was modified with a series of cellular structures inserted into the broch in *c.*300–600 AD (Harding and Gilmour 2000; Harding 2009, 176) (Figure 2.15a). The cellular phases of Loch na Beirghe show abundant evidence for metalworking with moulds for hand-pins, doorknob spear butts (a distinctive form of spear butt) and bronze pins in the earlier cellular levels dating to around the 4th century AD. A later structure resembling the Gurness shamrock building is likely to be of 5th century AD in date (Figure 2.14d). The latest phase at Loch na Beirghe was the figure-of-eight building occupying the broch interior (Figure 2.15a). Composite combs, penannular brooches and plain handmade pottery were amongst the finds from the interior of the latest building. In the Western Isles, figure-of-eight buildings have also been found at Great Bernera, Lewis, at Tràigh Bhòstadh where a least three figure-of-eight buildings were found at the site (Neighbour and Burgess 1996, 113–14) (Figure 2.15e). A sub-rectangular cell of House 1 at Tràigh Bhòstadh may have been used as a byre (Gilmour 2000, 105). The Tràigh Bhòstadh sequence appears to extend from the late 8th century through to second half of the 9th century.

Like Orkney and southern and northern Pictland, there were also buildings built in a rectangular fashion in the first millennium AD in the Western Isles. The most notable examples were found outside of the broch tower at Dùn Mhùlan (Dun Vulan), South Uist. The limits of these buildings were difficult to establish but are likely to have measured around 6–7m by 3m (Parker Pearson and Sharples 1999, 137) (Figure 2.12d). The stone elements of the walls of these buildings appear to have been the foundation and revetment for turf walls. The buildings had paved floors, drains and hearths and were associated with extensive midden deposits. From the floors, finds such as pottery and plant remains, including charred barley, suggest these were domestic buildings, though the earliest building, Building A, was interpreted as a possible barn, lean-to or outhouse. Building A has a radiocarbon date of the 3rd to the 4th century AD from a floor layer, while Buildings B and C have dates of the 5th to the 6th century AD.

Other duns and brochs were reused in Atlantic Pictland in the first millennium AD. In the Inner Hebrides, for example, there is a sherd of 7th-century E ware from Dùn Ardtreck on Skye (MacKie 2000), while at Dùn Beag, also on Skye, cellular structures may have been inserted into the broch and metalworking from the site includes ingot moulds and a mould that may have been for a doorknob spear butt (Gilmour 2000, 139–40). Finally, unusual sub-rectangular duns, such as Dùn Grugaig and Dùn Totaig both on Skye, may represent dun-like structures constructed anew in this period (Harding 2012, 168–69).

Settlement forms and long-term trajectories

While the evidence outlined above shows real diversity at both a regional and local level, the settlement architecture of Pictland does show important shared trends and trajectories across the wider region. One is the lesser visibility of settlement from around the 3rd century AD onwards, a phenomenon particularly affecting the lowland areas of northern and southern Pictland, where later land use has undoubtedly removed a large proportion of our settlement evidence. This is due in part to a shift towards using material such as turf and architectural traditions where earth-fast structural elements were less common (Ralston 1997, 24; Noble *et al.* 2020a, 320). This shift may have in part been due to the lesser availability of key materials such as timber but also appears to mark a change in vernacular form for even in the Northern Isles where walls had been commonly built in stone we see the construction of single-skinned walls that may have used material like turf or midden to insulate and support the stone components of walling. Given the problems for survival of these less robust forms of architecture we may not yet fully appreciate the range of buildings constructed in the first millennium AD, even in relatively well-explored regions. In the Northern and Western Isles it may be that the well-preserved stone-built buildings of this era may have only been one component of the settlement repertoire of the first millennium AD.

The trend towards rectangular architecture was particularly markedly felt in southern and northern Pictland, though this trend is found throughout Pictish areas (Figure 2.18). One factor in the adoption of the rectangular

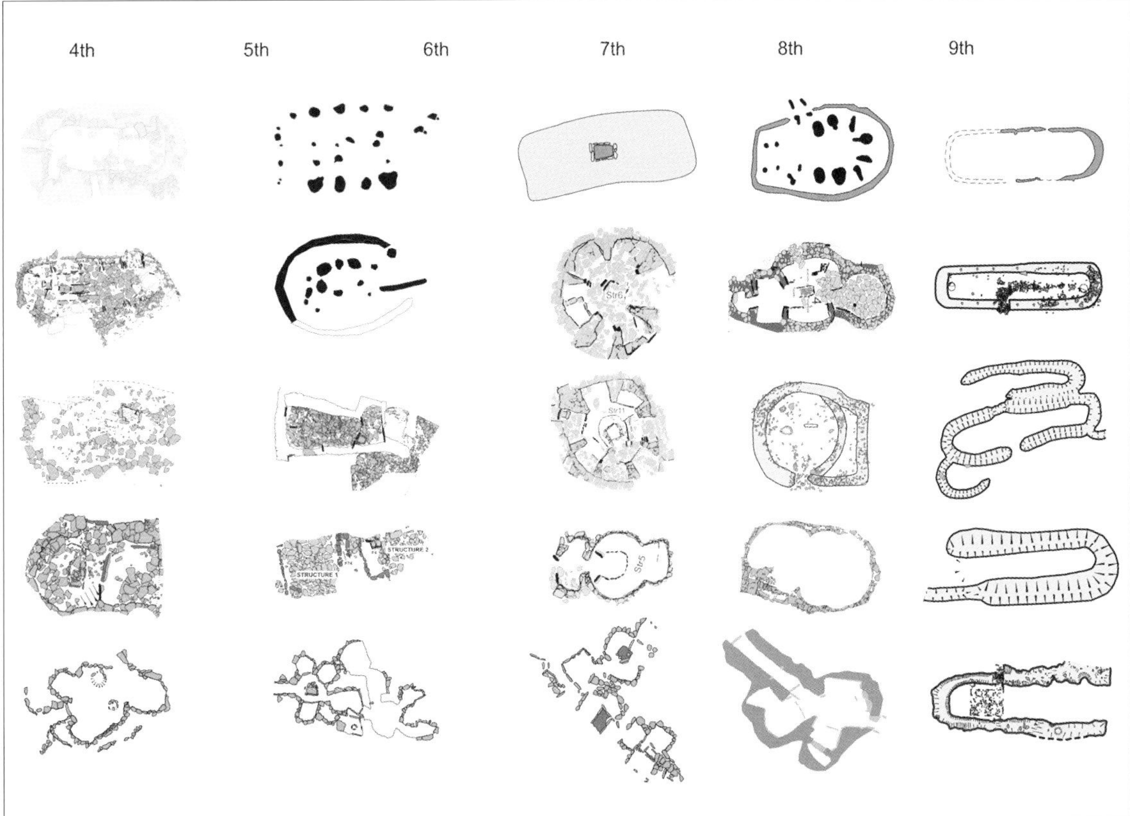

2.18 Settlement change through time in Pictland, based on direct dating and interpretation of sequences (not always well dated so dates are approximate). From the 3rd to 4th centuries, rectangular structures appear to emerge across Pictland with wags, turf-walled and stalled buildings possibly dating to this period. Cellular structures are also known, with this broad picture similar in the 5th and 6th centuries AD. In the later first millennium AD, wheelhouses in Shetland retain the circular form but, by the 9th century, the rectangular form, certainly in upland contexts in southern Pictland, was dominant.

form may have been contact with the Roman world (Noble *et al.* 2020a, 327). Locals serving in the Roman army or communities trading with the Roman military would have become aware of non-roundhouse forms of building and that may have given inspiration to local architectural innovators. The hierarchy of space and rank evident in Roman period buildings would have also been obvious and that hierarchical organisation of space and the *Romanitas* that came with it may have appealed to aspiring elites in the Late Roman Iron Age and early medieval period. Rectangular forms also allow for the easier subdivision and weighting of space, with differential access and deeper spatial layouts allowing clearer signalling and reinforcement of social differentiation – a factor that may have appealed to aspiring elites in the first millennium AD (see O'Sullivan *et al.* 2014, 93).

Other traditions emerged too in the Pictish era – in the north and west cellular forms (Figure 2.14) and figure-of-eight buildings (Figure 2.15) were new innovations after millennia of predominately roundhouse architectural traditions, though the roundhouse form did continue, particularly in Shetland. The figure-of-eight tradition is a particularly intriguing example of innovation and adoption for this architectural form shows connections to Ireland where figure-of-eight structures are also found (O'Sullivan *et al.* 2014, 91–92). The shared traditions between Atlantic Pictland and Ireland may represent Gaelic influence spreading northwards and eastwards, or the reiteration of long-standing connections in language and culture in these areas.

Indeed, while cultural connections across the Irish Sea may have been important, the adoption of this tradition may have had other motivations. Figure of eight structures with clear differences in the size and character of the rooms of these buildings may have been one means by which social differentiation was reflected and reinforced through architecture. Many of the cellular traditions of the north were smaller and less monumental than the Iron Age traditions of Atlantic roundhouses and broch towers that preceded them. While this could be seen as reflecting a worsening economic situation for these settlements and regions, other factors may also have been at play. The increasing diversity of architectural form could have enabled it to be more explicitly linked to the social standing and status of individuals or families, for example, with perhaps a hierarchy of structural types. At Scatness, for example, the principal dwellings in the 7th to 8th centuries AD may have been the elaborately constructed wheel-houses, but in the same phase there were much smaller roundhouses that could have been occupied by less wealthy, lower status families, or perhaps even slaves or labourers tied to the principal landholding family that owned the land at Scatness. Stone sculpture, such as the bear carving found in Structure 11 (Dockrill *et al.* 2010, 366), may have been another means of differentiating and signalling the social status of particular dwellings and their occupants.

Was there also a major centralisation of settlement in this period that could have also contributed to greater social inequality? The exact nature of what were obviously extensive settlements at Tap o' Noth and East Lomond around the middle of the first millennia AD is yet to be determined but, whether seasonal gathering sites or year-round permanent settlements, these speak of settlement organisation and agglomeration on a level not seen in northern Britain for many centuries previous and for many to follow. Our models of the scale and complexity of Pictish society may have to change in order to fully understand and interpret these developments. Other transitions speak of the vitality of settlement and the economy in this period – the settlement expansion in the central Highlands of southern Pictland in the 7th century are clear signs of the prosperity of the Pictish kingdoms, perhaps focussed on the southern territories. This could have been one development that helped set in train the increasing power of the southern Picts in the latter half of the first millennium AD, though we don't know whether or not similar settlement expansion was happening elsewhere. Overall, there are still many dimensions of settlement architecture that remain to be clarified for Pictland, but some of the wider trajectories and developments are beginning to become clearer.

The routines of everyday life

The houses described above would have been the venues for the everyday tasks of life that enabled and reproduced Pictish social and domestic life. Houses would have been places of care giving, sustenance, food preparation, play, places for sleep and shelter and socialisation. The archaeological evidence from Pictish-era houses provides some indication of the shorter- and longer-term routines of life, from everyday chores to more infrequent events such as episodes of construction. The building of houses would certainly have required a great investment in time, labour and resources and we can see evidence for intermittent repair and care through the relaying of house floors, the building and resurfacing of hearths and the addition of areas of paving or posts to support sagging roofs. Some sequences suggest rapid change – at Buckquoy cellular houses were replaced by a figure-of-eight structure and then by rectangular structures within a generation of one another. Other structures, such as the wheelhouses at Scatness and Jarlshof, appear to have been in use for centuries – generations of individuals were perhaps born, raised and died in a building that endured for hundreds of years, a testament in stone to the endurance of particular communities and lineages.

Lighting and maintaining the fire would have been one of the everyday routines at all of these Pictish-era settlements. The ubiquity of the fire and the resulting fumes are indicated in the 'Life of Findan', when the saint,

2.19 Dunnicaer – ashes from raking the fire of a Pictish-era building can be seen on the nearside of the hearth.

alone on Orkney in the 840s or 850s, sought high land so 'he could discover houses anywhere or the smoke of habitations' (Christiansen and Ó Nolan 1962, 151, 159). At Dunnicaer, one of the buildings had clear evidence for the raking and clearing of the ashes from a hearth in a building on the lower terrace of the sea stack (Figure 2.19). A knife sharpening stone was included in the make-up of the hearth surround – it is easy to imagine people sitting at this hearth, honing their blades and preparing a meal for the day. People would have, of course, slept in these buildings too – in the Northern Isles, the cells of some of the cellular buildings such as the shamrock building at Gurness may have been sleeping pods. These cells could have been closed off by hanging textiles or by wattle screens.

The preparation of food at these settlements is evidenced by the stone-saddle and rotary querns found in many of the houses described above. Grinding grain for flour must have been a laborious and repetitive routine. Textile manufacture is indicated by the presence of stone spindle whorls for spinning yarn. Evidence from elsewhere in the early medieval world suggests spinning was a task that women carried out – in some Anglo-Saxon cemeteries whorls have been found near the waists of female burials, perhaps suspended on belts (Strachan *et al.* 2019, 86). Gathering sheep wool and spinning yarn would have been an important job. The spinning of the whorl and spindle would have been a mesmeric task and one that literally created the fabric of life. Bone pins and weaving combs are other indicators of crafting and a Pictish cross-slab from Kirriemuir, Angus, appears to depict an upright warp-weighted loom (Foster 2014, 65). A beautiful woollen hood for a child, found in a bog in Orkney and preserved in the National Museum of Scotland, is testament to the skills of first millennium AD crafters (Clarke *et al.* 2012, 7) (Colour Plate 9).

Other tasks would have also kept the occupants of these dwellings busy. Firewood or other resources for heating and cooking would need to be gathered. Wood resources appear to have declined in availability in some locations such as Orkney in first millennium AD – at Howe, wood use became severely restricted in the late phases with increasing use of peat and perhaps turf as a fuel (Ballin Smith 1994, 134). Cutting peat may have been a communal task organised between separate households as occurred in more recent times. Clay for making pots would have had to have been gathered, with Pictish-era settlements in the Western Isles in particular maintaining a vibrant potting tradition throughout the first millennium AD. Elsewhere in Pictland, pottery, other than imports, is very rare but small assemblages have been found at Dunnicaer, Mither Tap and Rhynie. Cleaning would have been an everyday chore too – disappointingly for archaeologists most early medieval buildings appear to have been kept very tidy with few finds actually being discovered within the houses themselves – exterior middens (rubbish dumps) were maintained for disposing of the detritus of everyday life and, in many cases, middens would have been removed for manuring fields. At Deer Park Farms, County Antrim in Northern Ireland, exceptional preservation of early medieval houses provided evidence for human lice, human fleas and even intestinal parasites (O'Sullivan *et al.* 2014, 97) – a grim reminder of some of the more unpleasant realities of living in a pre-modern community. No such finds have been made in Pictland but coprolites (human stools) along with moss were found in waterlogged layers at Dundurn fort in midden layers around a stone water-filled tank (Alcock *et al.* 1989, 202), reminders of some of the other key routines of life!

Producing and maintaining tools for agricultural use, cooking and a range of everyday tasks were elements of the everyday for all settlements. The early to late first millennium AD settlement at Scatness appears to have been a relatively wealthy one with over 200 iron artefacts suggesting ready access to metals, with smithing residues suggestive of routine manufacturing and repair of tools (Dockrill *et al.* 2016, 345). At other sites, maintaining and procuring tools may have relied on contacts with other communities. At Howe, for example, ironworking was restricted to the early part of Phase 8 (Ballin Smith 1994, 233). The lack of production evidence in the later part of Phase 8 at Howe suggests iron tools and objects were sourced from other settlements. Iron blades were found in the Lair excavations and an unusual barrel padlock suggests that valuables were safely stored in one of the houses (Figure 2.20).

Houses and settlements would have also been the setting for the everyday playing out of social structure and hierarchy. The Irish law tract *Críth Gablach* emphasises the links between property and social status (O'Sullivan *et al.* 2014, 89) and it was probably similar in Pictland. Owning a

2.20 An unusual barrel padlock from one of the longhouses at Lair. This technology suggests the storing of valuables within the settlement. (© AOC Archaeology)

house or having the resources to build certain types of house would not have been the preserve of all. The practice of providing hospitality meant that the arena of the house would have at times been the central venue for the hosting of lords and retainers and the reproduction and negotiation of social identities of kinship, age and status (O'Sullivan *et al.* 2014, 79). Middling to higher status households were more than likely to have had servants or slaves and smaller ancillary buildings or rooms in Northern Isles settlements as attested at Scatness could have been spaces for lower status occupants, some tied to the land and their lord, others with a greater degree of freedom (as found elsewhere in early medieval Britain and Ireland – see, for example, Charles-Edwards 2000, 68–114). If contemporary societies and later medieval Scotland are anything to go by, individuals, households and perhaps sometimes whole settlements gave food renders of cattle, meat, grain, dairy produce and other items to their lord in return for protection.

It was the household too that may have been one basic unit for the mustering of the army of a polity (see Chapter 3), with a certain number of warriors obligated to serve a lord from each household. For Dál Riata, a probable 8th-century section of the text *Míniugud Senchasa Fher nAlban* (*Senchus*), shows that it was the household that formed the basis of the military levy (Dumville 2002). However, in eastern Scotland, by the 12th century, the davoch, a multi-settlement unit smaller than the parish, was the basis in Alba for army and labour service for the king, levied for him by the leader of each province, the *mormáer*, and the lesser nobles, the *toísig* (Ross 2015; A. Taylor 2016, 91–113). Moreover, in the 12th century, settlements also could provide *cáin* (an annual render to a lord) and *coinnmed* (hospitality to lords) which certainly reflect practices from the Gaelic period, if not earlier (Broun 2013; A. Taylor 2016, 84–91). It is likely that the *mormáer* and dabach were features of Pictland by 900, but had earlier antecedents (see Chapter 7). It is plausible, though not provable, that Pictish precursors of *cáin* and *coinnmed* existed too, though the nature of such renders could change significantly over time. Overall, while it is unclear how exactly obligations were met in Pictland, it is likely that individuals, households, settlements and local communities played important roles in relationships between clients on one side and their lords and kings on the other.

Age and gender would have been other categories of social differentiation that would have had fundamental effects on the lifeways and experiences of members of the household. We have virtually no direct evidence for Pictish legal practices but, in most comparable early medieval legal systems and in Scottish law after 1100, women and children had a restricted legal capacity. In early Irish law, children were legal dependants of their father and had limited status until they obtained an inheritance (Kelly 1988, 80–86) while, in later medieval Scotland, a noble son had a 'life-value' – used as a basis for legal participation and for determining the level of compensation – which was lower than but related to his father's position (Woolf 2007a, 346–48). In practice, unless a child's family was wealthy, they would need to work as much as possible. Women had a similarly lower honour-price, pegged at half that of a husband's in early Irish law (Kelly 1988, 11, see also 68–79), and, in later Scotland, their status and capacity declined on marriage (Ditchburn and MacDonald 2001, 130–32). In practice, while women played crucial roles, their status was determined in relation to men, only being able to gain a degree of formal power in exceptional circumstances, such as the deaths of many relatives or marriage to someone of lower status (Márkus 2017, 222–27).

Given that many legal concepts were shared between other Celtic-speaking societies in Wales and Ireland, it is likely that the Picts also inherited and applied many of the same ideas and practices from the ancient era (Márkus 2017, 189–91). Even if Pictish royal succession before the mid 8th century occasionally or always (which is very debateable) was through the female line, there is no evidence that this gave women in the royal dynasty an enhanced status, given that only the fathers of kings are mentioned (Márkus 2017, 216–19) and sources, such as the Irish chronicles, do not show that Pictish women played a direct role in politics. The 'Law of the Innocents' (Márkus 2008), promulgated in *c.*697 among the Picts as well as Gaels of Dál Riata and Ireland, protected monks, children and women from the effects of warfare because they were non-combatants.

Since potential participation in warfare was a key part of not just leadership but also society in general, it is likely that there was a pre-existing assumption in Pictland, as elsewhere in the Celtic-speaking world, that women would not be the heads of households, kindreds, communities or kingdoms, but we cannot rule out that they occasionally adopted these roles or had important influences in society outwith (or in defiance of) the formal legal arrangements.

Agriculture, landscape and travel

All settlements, no matter their status, would have been supported by an agricultural base with the annual cycles of production and consumption of domesticated animals and crops dominating the everyday routines in Pictland, as had been the case for thousands of years since the first introduction of agriculture over 4,000 years prior to the first mention of the Picts in Late Roman sources. The written evidence for diet in Pictland is meagre – there are references to cattle farming close to Loch Rannoch and (alongside game) in Lochaber in the Highlands in Adomnán's *Life of St Columba*, I.46 and II.37 (Sharpe, 1995, 148, 185–86), to catching salmon in the River Shiel in Moidart (II.19; Sharpe, 1995, 168) and the hunting of a boar on Skye (II.26; Sharpe, 1995, 175). There is also a reference, embedded in a poem in the tale *Scéla Cano Meic Gartnain*, to the ales of the Pictish plain of Circin tasting like wine (Evans, 2013, 19–20), a testament to arable farming and a vibrant drinking culture in southern Pictland (Figure 2.21). The Irish chronicles, which included a source kept at Iona from the late 6th century to at least *c.*AD 740, contain general items about cattle mortalities, plague, crop failures and the abundance of wild foods such as nuts, events and phenomena that are likely to have effected Pictland too (Peters 2016). Drawing on comparative evidence from Ireland would suggest that men and women and, indeed, children would have been involved in most agricultural tasks including ploughing, reaping and feeding and caring for animals (Kelly 1997, 448–52; O'Sullivan *et al.* 2014, 101).

The vibrancy of the agricultural economy undoubtedly fluctuated throughout the first millennium AD. In eastern Scotland, there is some evidence for a recession in the agricultural economy in the first half of the first millennium AD with a recovery and expansion sometime around the 7th century AD (Strachan *et al.* 2019, 142). This may mirror changes in England where, from the 7th to 9th centuries AD, there were major developments in the economy including an expansion in cereal agriculture and innovations in plough technology and an expansion in land use (Hamerow *et al.* 2020; McKerracher 2018). In Anglo-Saxon England, it has been suggested that increasing pressure on land or arable required animals to be brought in for overwintering, with increased archaeological evidence

2.21 (*Left*) A Pictish stone from Bullion, Angus, shows a warrior on horseback holding a shield in one hand and an enormous drinking horn in the other. Perhaps he was drinking ale from the Pictish plain of Circin. (© National Museums Scotland)

2.22 (*Above*) Drawing of the cart shown on a lost stone from Meigle, Perthshire. The cart is pulled by two horses with a driver and a canopied enclosure on the back with two passengers within.

for enclosures and droveways in the later first millennium AD (McKerracher 2018, 29–30). Such evidence is as of yet not forthcoming in Pictland but the emergence of the Pitcarmick-style longhouse with attached byres and greater use of upland landscapes could potentially be linked to similar developments.

In terms of arable crops, barley was the main arable crop type in Pictland, with both hulled and naked barley in use (for example, Ballin Smith 1994, 124), but oats and flax were also cultivated. Little in the way of the organisation of the agricultural landscape has been documented archaeologically but a series of field enclosures has recently been identified at Logierait, dating to the 7th to 9th centuries AD (Ellis 2021). Animal agriculture is likely to have had a central role in society judging by both the economic evidence and the frequency of depictions of animals, both domesticated and wild, on Pictish symbol stones and cross-slabs (Chapters 3 and 6). Cattle in particular may have been the basis of wealth, used in marriage alliances, food renders and as the equivalent of a currency (Kelly 1997, 27). Cattle are also one of the few domesticated animals to make a regular appearance in Pictish art. We lack large numbers of animal bone assemblages, given how few settlements have been identified, but, where preservation is good, cattle tend to dominate, particularly at the higher-status sites located within southern and northern Pictland. The character of kill patterns in the cattle bone assemblages suggests cattle were kept for dairying as well as meat.

Exploitation of non-domesticated plant sources is also in evidence in Pictish-era settlements. Remains of raspberries, hazelnuts and cherry stones were found at Dundurn, with black bearberry, crowberry and whortleberry or cowberry were discovered at Howe. Woodland would also have played a crucial role. Used for its resources in buildings, defences, tools and ships, it was also a location where pigs fed on nuts and a place for hunting (see *Life of Columba* II.3, II.26, II.37, II.45; Sharpe 1995, 155, 175, 185, 201; see also Chapter 3). In some regions, the majority of tree cover had been removed in prehistory, with only light woodland cover remaining (for example, Tipping 1994; Jones *et al.* 2020; Jones *et al.* 2021), but, in other areas, denser areas of woodland cover survived – for instance, those mentioned by Adomnán on Skye, in Moidart and Lochaber (II.26, II.37, II.45; Sharpe 1995, 175, 185, 201). There is some archaeological evidence for fishing but riverine and coastal fishing appears to have been the norm in the Pictish period rather than deeper sea fishing with isotopic analysis of Pictish-era individuals suggesting only minimal input of marine resources into the diet (Curtis-Summers *et al.* 2020). At Howe, cod and saithe were the main catch and, at Scatness, the occasional seal and whale bone turned up but this may have been opportunistic use of beached resources rather than active marine mammal hunting. Huge shell middens are known at the Sands of Forvie, Aberdeenshire, which appear to have resulted from the large-scale consumption of shellfish towards the end of the first millennium AD rather than being the result of using shellfish as bait (Noble *et al.* 2018b).

Moving around the landscape would have been by foot for most people. Ownership and riding of horses would have been the reserve of people of high rank (Kelly 1997, 89). A lost stone from Meigle depicted a two-wheeled carriage with a driver and two passengers protected by some form of roof or canopy to the vehicle (Figure 2.22). The carriage was pulled by two horses. Carriages require well-made roads or tracks. At Portmahomack, a roadway was found leading into the 8th-century monastery and a similar feature has been found at Fortingall, in Glen Lyon, Perthshire, at the entrance to the monastic vallum (see Chapter 4) but the extent of this kind of infrastructure in the Pictish landscape is uncertain – in southern Pictland, Roman roads may have been reused and repaired. The Irish law tracts associated major roads with kings and these were constructed to be wide enough so that two chariots 'could pass one another' (Kelly 1997, 391) but such features are rarely documented in the archaeological record.

Boats would have also been crucial for travel, not only on the western seaboard of Scotland, where the islands, sea lochs and the rugged and wooded nature of the land made sailing a necessity (Campbell 1999, 8–9)

2.23 Boats depicted in Pictland: (a) St Orland's Stone, Cossans, Angus; (b) Jonathan's Cave, East Wemyss, Fife.

but also inland for traversing rivers and lochs. Adomnán's *Life of Columba* provides abundant evidence of sailing on the west coast and north to Orkney (Sharpe 1995, 22–26, 30–32) but it also refers to the use of boats to cross rivers and lochs when travelling to Pictland up the Great Glen or from Argyll to southern Pictland (I.34, II.27, II.34; Sharpe 1995, 137, 175–76, 182–83). The existence of seagoing Pictish ships can be inferred from the *Life of St Columba* in II.42 (Sharpe, 1995, 196) and there are references to the use of sails on ships in the same source (for example, II.45; Sharpe 1995, 201–02), showing that sail technology was present in northern Britain in the early medieval period. Reference in the *Life of Columba* to single-person vessels, skin-lined boats and wooden ships again implies a range of craft capable of both inland and near-shore water travel as well as sailing longer distances (II.42, II.45; Sharpe 1995, 197, 201). Surprisingly, however, boats are rarely depicted on Pictish carved stones – the only examples being a small rowing boat with two rowers and four passengers shown on St Orland's Stone, a cross-slab at Cossans, Angus, and a boat carved on the walls of Jonathan's Cave, Wemyss, Fife (RCHAMS 2008, 50, 68) (Figure 2.23).

Conclusions

It is clear that there has been substantial progress since Wainwright lamented the lack of definite Pictish dwellings. Houses and settlements throughout Pictland have now been identified and dated, providing us with insights into the lives of ordinary people. Regarding architectural form, the picture emerging is one of diversity in the types of structures constructed in Pictland, not only between regions but also within localities, so there was no single characteristic Pictish tradition. However, the construction of rectangular structures is quite a striking feature of Pictland, notably appearing earlier than in Ireland which saw less in the way of direct Roman contact. In Pictland, closer contact with Roman areas of settlement and Roman lifeways to the south may have been one inspiration for this important architectural shift in Pictland. The adoption of rectangular architecture, alongside evidence for the clustering of buildings and variation in the size of structures, may indicate that social differentiation was increasingly marked through variation in the scale and form of architecture in this period. The evidence from the Northern Isles in particular may suggest more wealthy nobles and commoners living beside poorer, perhaps subordinate, members of the community in ancillary structures. In the eastern Lowlands of southern and northern Pictland, similar patterns may have been present, however, the use of non-earthfast wooden or turf structures for building means that settlement form and diversity remain a challenge to identify and interpret in these regions. There are still many parts of Pictland where further research, using careful analysis, will help to answer important questions raised by recent advances in understanding.

How quickly our evidence base can change is demonstrated by the recent discoveries at Tap o' Noth. It has generally been assumed that there was no major settlement nucleation in Scotland before the growth of towns in the 12th century but the unexpected dating of platform sites around Tap o' Noth to the 2nd to 6th centuries AD potentially transforms our understanding of the form, scale and character of Pictish society. If only a minority of the 800 or so platforms were houses occupied at any one time, that would still entail a large settlement of hundreds, drawing in people from a wide hinterland. If Tap o' Noth had an assembly function, then it could have brought people and communities together from a substantial region, ostensibly for common purposes but also resulting in increased social and economic interconnections. If this was a year-round settlement for even a small proportion of the house platforms, its marginal position suggests it was a settlement supported by a dependent community in the wider environs. In either scenario, the site clearly demonstrates a scale of organisation hitherto unknown in Pictland, in a period when, until recently, it had been thought that society had been small scale, relatively poor and in decline. As with Ireland, where development-led archaeology transformed the range and balance of known first-millennium settlement sites (O'Sullivan *et al.*, 2014), it is likely that more extensive excavation in Scotland will reveal a greater variety of settlement types, from individual houses to major centres like Tap o' Noth.

The discovery of buildings and settlements enables us to build up a picture of everyday life in a complex society, which depended upon local and distant relationships and contacts to extract, create, distribute and use the resources whose remains survive at archaeological sites. Houses were the centre of Pictish lifeways, being the setting for the routines of life and the stage on which the everyday iteration of social structure and status was played out. The domestic routines included everyday tasks of cooking, cleaning, tending to the fire and making and mending tools amongst many other activities. Archaeological excavation and analysis are powerful ways of revealing more about the everyday lives of the Picts when well-preserved settlements can be identified and carefully investigated.

At home, Pictish individuals would have had many obligations – to one another in the community, with unequal power relations likely to encompass both slave owning and different grades of the 'free' farmer, labourers and crafters, etc. Gender and age would have also been fundamental limiting factors on the level to which an individual could engage in everyday contexts and in the power politics of the era. How local society was organised is difficult to discern but it is likely that individual households and settlements strove to be self-sufficient, undertaking a mixture of arable and pastoral farming and utilising resources available in the landscape. People were also part of larger local networks of neighbours, kin and community, living in units like the later davoch, which provided mutual support and shared obligations. While we lack the detailed textual evidence of neighbouring societies, the 'Law of the Innocents' (Márkus 2008) does indicate that Pictland shared some general features with Gaelic society since integral to its operation were lords and kindreds which played key roles in an individual's life. We can strongly suspect that other aspects mentioned in the text, such as the existence of variation in compensation according to different ranks in society, including the concept of 'honour-price', as well as an implicitly limited role of women in political affairs, were as much part of Pictish society as in other contemporary early medieval societies and as it was in the post-1100 kingdom of the Scots. The legal and ideological context presented by such texts mirrors the material inequality shown by the variation in the houses and resources found in settlements, and the contrast between some dwellings and the archaeological evidence for the elite are explored in the next chapter. It is easy to dismiss the more modest and seemingly mundane evidence of everyday life but, in reality, it was the people's struggle not only to survive and prosper but also to provide food, labour and resources which underpinned the intrigue, success and splendour of the kings, nobles and leading churches that appear most prominently in our evidence for Pictland.

CHAPTER THREE

'And in thy Majesty Ride Prosperously'

Citadels, Kings and Warriors

Power ultimately flowed from the land (see Chapter 2) but Pictish kings could deploy material culture and architecture to underline their authority, with a number of dominant strategies of rulership identifiable. One important strand of Pictish rulership was the construction of fortified centres of power, the origins of which can now be traced back into the Late Roman Iron Age, the period when the Picts attacked the Roman Empire in episodes such as the 'Barbarian Conspiracy' of AD 367–368. Developments in the Roman Iron Age seem to have led to the emergence of a more militarised society, perhaps prompted by the proximity of the Roman army, which tried to exert control over these northern peoples through military intervention, gifts and bribes (Hunter 2007a, b). In the post-Roman period, the era of the fortified citadel really took off with fortified settlements dominating our knowledge of Pictish high-status sites. The construction of fortified settlements included coastal promontory forts, hillforts and lowland enclosures. We can also identify other forms of expressing rulership particularly from the 7th to 8th centuries AD onwards – stone carvings displaying the hunt, mounted warriors and weaponry and a greater use of Christian iconography. From excavations, we can also identify the importance of metalworking, the importation of exotic goods and feasting for creating bonds between a ruler and the ruled.

The received political narrative of first millennium in Europe has, until recently, been considered one in which polities outside the Roman Empire gradually coalesced as a result of the wealth which flowed from the imperial frontier through peaceful and forcible means such as raiding. Once the empire ceased to exist or reduced its contacts, it has been assumed that societies in regions like Britain faced crises, with collapsed economies able to support only small, impoverished polities in the 5th and 6th centuries AD (for example, Esmonde Cleary 1989; Fleming 2010). Much of the subsequent early medieval period was then regarded as characterised by economic recovery and more powerful, extensive kingships, until the Vikings produced another shock to the system. As will be seen, while it is clear that the Picts were fully integrated into European patterns of rulership, the discovery of Tap o' Noth, Rhynie, and other sites indicates that Pictland may have had a somewhat different trajectory, perhaps corresponding with recent arguments that have questioned the 'collapse' narrative of post-Roman Britain (for example, Dark 1994; Oosthuizen 2011).

Defending and administering the realm

One of the most significant developments in early medieval northern Britain was the re-emergence of fortified enclosures and settlements (Alcock 2003, 179–99). As in western England and Wales, the hillfort formed the most direct material manifestation of the power of potentates and their followers. In early medieval Pictland, a diverse range of enclosed architecture was involved in the developing frameworks of power and governance. These included 'nuclear' hillforts, smaller ringforts and coastal promontory forts, similar in form to those found elsewhere across early medieval Scotland (Lane and Campbell 2000; Alcock 2003, 179–99; Ralston 2004; Toolis and Bowles 2016). The emergence of these types of enclosure can now be traced back to the Late Roman Iron Age.

Early developments

One major breakthrough in Pictish studies in recent years has been the identification of defended settlements belonging to the Late Roman Iron Age and the 5th to 6th centuries AD which partly fill the gap in the archaeological record between the very visible settlement record of the early centuries AD and the occurrence of developed hillforts of the 7th century or later (Figure 3.1). One prime example is the site of Dunnicaer (Figure 3.2), nowadays a precipitous sea stack on the coast of Aberdeenshire, just south of the town of Stonehaven. In the 19th century, a group of youths found a low stone wall on the top of the stack and threw a number of carved stones into the sea (Thomson 1859, 70). These stones (Figure 3.3) were subsequently identified as Pictish symbol stones, with the Dunnicaer examples often mooted as early ones in the Pictish symbol tradition (for example, Alcock 1996, 2003, 372; Henderson and Henderson 2004, 171) – though a date earlier than the 6th century would not have been countenanced by many (Alcock 1996, 2–4; see also Chapter 6). Excavations from 2015–2017 identified that Dunnicaer contained the very substantially eroded remains of a promontory fort with a timber-laced rampart (Colour Plate 10) (Noble *et al.* 2020a). The fierce waves of the North Sea had penetrated bands of soft sandstone in the bedrock, cleaving chunks of the promontory off through time. All that was left of the fort was a short stretch of the timber-laced rampart – the wall identified by the youths – on the south side of the stack and the remains of multiple buildings inside,

3.1. Principal power centres and hoard sites referenced in Chapter 3.

most of them severely truncated by erosion and later activity.

The community at Dunnicaer was well connected and finds from the excavations included Roman Samian, coarse-ware pottery and glass (Figure 1.25; Colour Plate 7) – all rare imports this far north of the frontier. The most interesting Roman import was a sherd of a deep blue hemispherical Hofheim (the type site in Germany) cup, a find with few parallels – this may have been a diplomatic gift to the occupants of the fort or a precious treasure gained through raiding. Burnishing stones for metalworking, spindle whorls and quernstones suggest people lived in the fort for significant periods of time. Radiocarbon dating provided a firm chronology for occupation on the site with settlement throughout the Roman Iron Age

3.2 Dunnicaer as it survives today – battered and much reduced by the ferocity of the North Sea.

from the 2nd to late 4th centuries AD, with the symbol stones likely to have been from the rampart that was dated to the 3rd to 4th centuries AD (see Chapter 6).

What is particularly intriguing about Dunnicaer is just how unusual forts of this period are. Forts are a well-known element of the archaeology of the pre-Roman Iron Age and smaller numbers are known from the 5th to 6th centuries AD onwards but there are very few forts that date to the intervening period. Dunnicaer, at its height, falls in the period when the first references to the Picts emerge and seems to be a forerunner for the type of high-status defended settlement that became such a hallmark of Pictish elite society in the post-Roman period.

The Dunnicaer site and the society that created it may have contributed to the militarised elites that came to dominate in the Pictish period. The coastal location of Dunnicaer, with bays on either side of the fort, would make it an ideal staging post for sea raiding. The scale and reach of the raiding that the Picts were involved in during events such as the Barbarian Conspiracy of 367 suggests that these raids involved maritime attacks at a variety of scales, the likes of which could have been launched from promontory forts of the kind found along the east coasts of Aberdeenshire, Angus and Fife. Although supporting archaeological evidence has not been found,

3.3 (*Left*) Dunnicaer No. 1 Pictish symbol stone from Dunnicaer. (© University of Aberdeen Museums Service)

3.4 (*Right*) The Rhynie Man stone was ploughed up at Rhynie in 1978. He carries an axe over his shoulder and sports a fearsome grimace. (© Aberdeenshire Council Archaeology Service)

it is plausible that one aim of such raids was the seizure of slaves. The acquisition of slaves by the Picts, albeit via British raiders active in 5th-century Ireland, is indicated in Patrick's 'Letter to the Soldiers of Coroticus' (Hood 1978, 35–40, 55–59) and in the *Life of Columba*. In the latter example, the saint gently, on pain of death, persuades the Pictish wizard Broichan to free a Gaelic female slave. Certainly, by the 6th or 7th century, maritime power which had enabled such raids appears to have been an integral part of Pictish power with Adomnán's reference to a *regulus* of Orkney in King Bridei's court strongly suggestive of Pictish rulers having maritime networks of power that extended over significant parts of northern Scotland and the Isles (II.42; Anderson and Anderson 1991, 166–67). Dunnicaer was perhaps a prototype for the much larger promontory forts that appear to have developed from around the 7th century onwards such as Burghead and Green Castle, Portknockie, both in Moray, and just in the next bay along from Dunnicaer, at Dunnottar, Aberdeenshire.

Another series of early Pictish sites, also from Aberdeenshire, helps to further illuminate the Late Roman Iron Age and the early centuries of the post-Roman period. A series of forts is located in upper Strathbogie in the environs of the village of Rhynie in modern-day western Aberdeenshire.

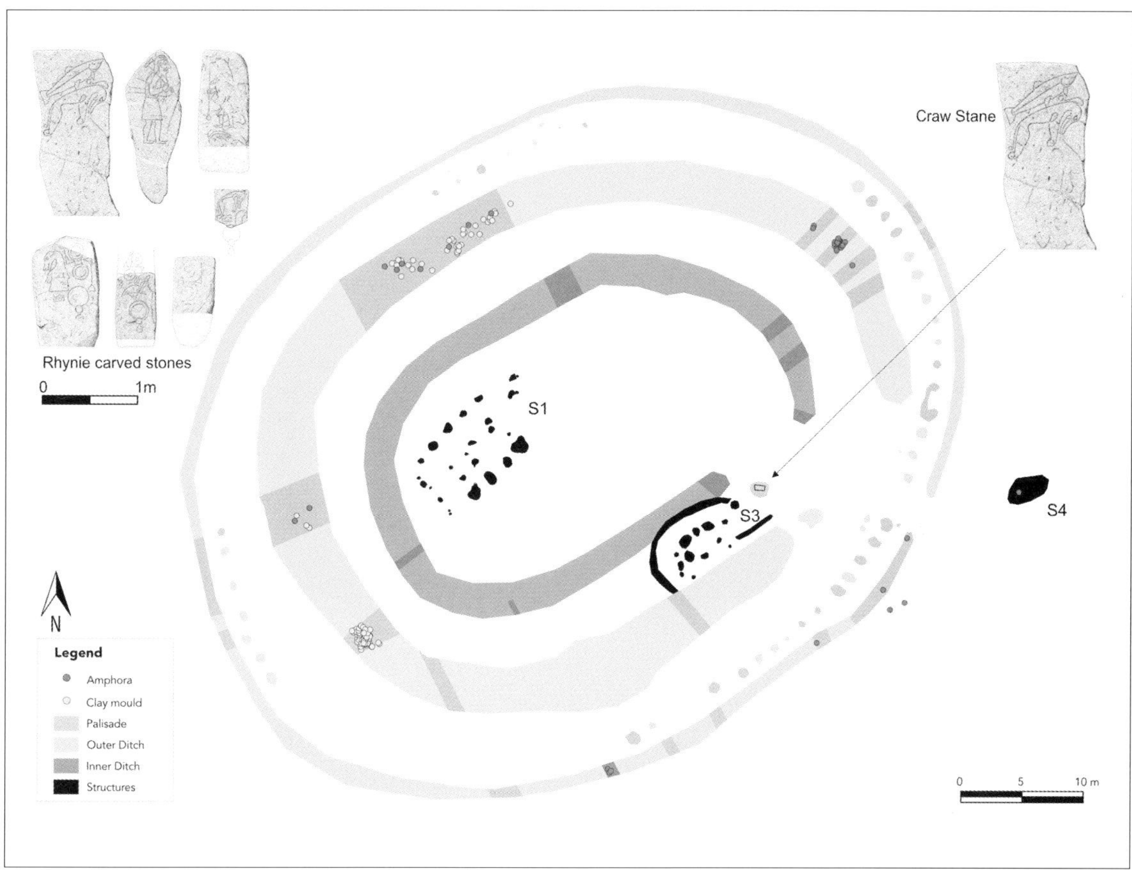

3.5 Plan of the enclosures and buildings identified at the Craw Stane complex, Rhynie, through excavation from 2011 to 2017. The early phase of the enclosure complex included ditches and ramparts, with a palisaded enclosure added later.

The name Rhynie includes the place-name element, **rīg*, 'king', and archaeological fieldwork suggests the Rhynie landscape was an elite Pictish centre from the 4th to 6th centuries AD (Noble *et al.* 2019b). Rhynie had long been known for its particular concentration of Pictish symbol stones when, in March 1978, farmer Kevin Alston ploughed up a spectacular stone known as the 'Rhynie Man' in a field on Barflat farm just to the south of the modern village (Figure 3.4). This was only a few metres from the Craw Stane, an in situ Pictish symbol stone (Colour Plate 11). In the summer of 1978, the council archaeologist Ian Shepherd took aerial photographs of a series of enclosures around the Craw Stane, indicating that there could be more to investigate.

Excavations around the Craw Stane from 2011 to 2017 found that the stone stood at the entranceway of a defended settlement which, in an early phase, comprised ditches and probably earthen banks surrounding a low glacial knoll (Noble *et al.* 2019b). In a later phase, an elaborate timber wall of oak posts and planks was built and inside there stood a series of buildings (Figure 3.5). The excavations revealed a rich material assemblage

3.6 (*Above*) Animal figurine mould from the outer ditch of the Craw Stane complex, showing the impression of a hound or wolf similar to those depicted on Pictish symbol stones.

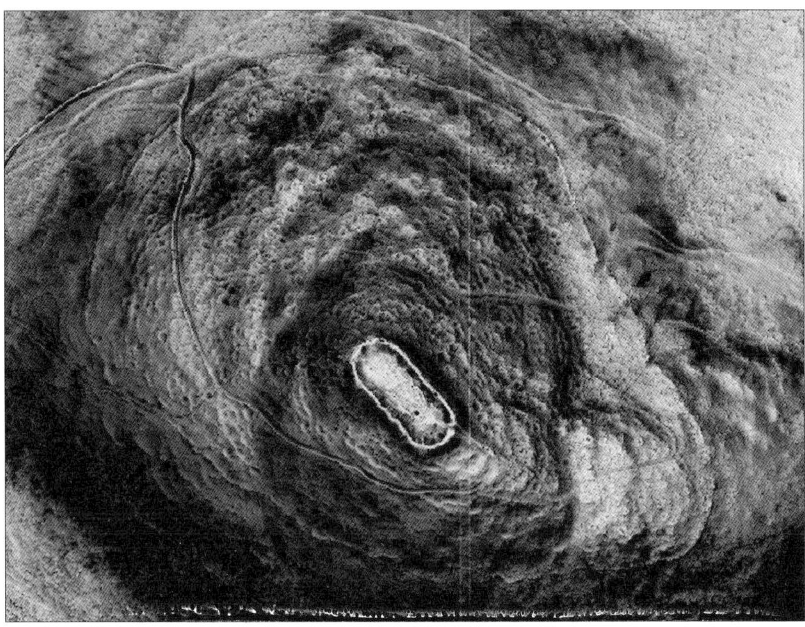

3.7 (*Right*) Tap o' Noth LiDAR survey showing over 800 house platforms enclosed within the lower fort on the hill. At the summit can be seen the remains of the Iron Age oblong fort.

including sherds of Late Roman wine amphorae imported from the eastern Mediterranean, sherds of glass drinking beakers from France and one of the largest ranges of metalworking production evidence known from early medieval Britain. The metalworking evidence included moulds and crucibles for making pins and brooches and even moulds for producing small animal figurines that would have resembled the animals carved on Pictish symbol stones (Figure 3.6). The material traces, of a character only found on the highest status sites in Britain and Ireland, and the place-name suggest that Upper Strathbogie valley contained an early Pictish royal power centre but it turns out the discoveries at the Craw Stane were only the tip of the iceberg.

Two other Pictish enclosed sites are now known in the valley. Cairnmore is a small ringfort that stands in an elevated position on hillslopes to the south-east of the Craw Stane complex, overlooking the southern and eastern routes into the valley. The fort is enclosed by the remains of two stone walls – the inner enclosing a small area of around 0.2ha in extent. The stone walls were flanked by a monumental series of timber posts that appears to have formed a post and plank revetment for the ramparts. Inside, a massive hearth from a central building was found and outside another building was located up against the outer stone wall. Radiocarbon dates show occupation spanned the 4th to 7th centuries AD. This may have been an elite settlement initially dependent on the royal centre in the valley below, but it continued in use after the Craw Stane complex had been abandoned.

To the north of Rhynie stands Tap o' Noth, one of the most spectacular forts in Scotland (Figure 3.7). The summit oblong fort is the second highest hillfort in Scotland and one of the best examples of a vitrified (heavily burnt) fort dating to the Iron Age. The summit fort lies above and within a massive stone bank or rampart that encloses around 16.75ha, one of the largest hillforts known in northern Britain. As noted in Chapter 2, excavations on the lower enclosure in 2019 showed that this impressively extensive enclosing wall was contemporary with Cairnmore and the Craw Stane complex, with the rampart constructed in the 5th to 6th centuries AD. Survey work also identified the 800 or so house platforms within the lower fort. Dates from a number of these platforms span the 3rd to 6th centuries AD and, along with the rampart date, show this settlement began to develop in the Late Roman Iron Age and reached its height in the 5th to 6th centuries AD.

Overall, the evidence from the Upper Strathbogie Valley, with the number and scale of sites in the valley, the material signatures of these sites and the place-name evidence, suggests that the valley was a multifunctional and polyfocal elite centre that emerged in the Late Roman Iron Age and endured for a number of centuries. By the second half of the 6th century, the Craw Stane complex and Tap o' Noth appear to have been largely abandoned – an elite focus appears to have moved elsewhere, leaving behind the very unusual material signatures of a multinoded early Pictish landscape of power.

In terms of the wider settlement pattern in Aberdeenshire in this period, a small handful of other sites shows that smaller ringfort-type settlements were found more widely in the north-east from the 5th to 6th centuries AD onwards. Maiden Castle on the slopes of Bennachie, Aberdeenshire, shows broad similarities to Cairnmore, comprising at least two successive enclosures – a thick stone-walled enclosure around 20m in internal diameter with perhaps successive phases of surrounding ramparts and ditches of 40m maximum in overall diameter (Cook 2011a, b). It is uncertain whether the stone-walled enclosure was roofed or perhaps simply enclosed internal buildings, traces of one of which has been identified. Test pits around the fortified site found evidence for unenclosed settlement around the enclosure. Dates from Maiden Castle suggest occupation first began in the 5th or 6th century AD and endured here into the 7th century AD. A much more complex fort on top of the nearby Mither Tap o' Bennachie, appears to have flourished from the 7th century onwards and may have been the successor to Maiden Castle (see below).

In nearby Angus, in southern Pictland, an enclosure measuring around 70m across at Balbinny, Aberlemno, has recently been dated to the 5th to the 6th century AD and may be another example of a small lowland enclosed settlement of the Late Antique period. We are, therefore, now finding evidence for the existence of a range of enclosed elite sites which demonstrate that there was considerable social stratification and a concentration of resources in Pictland beginning centuries before the 7th century when the Pictish over-kingship emerged or was consolidated.

The rise of the citadel lords

The most famous of the Pictish fortified enclosures are the hilltop sites often known as 'nuclear' hillforts, a defensive form with parallels in the Gaelic and Brittonic west and south. These forts appear to develop their most complex form from the 7th century AD onwards, the period in which the over-kings of Pictland strengthened their grip on rulership. A number of sites with nuclear forts show some sort of 5th to 6th century AD settlement evidence and thus these developed forts may have also sprung from earlier elite settlement forms. At their height, these sites were characterised by multiple enclosing elements that defined a hierarchical groundplan, with a central and higher enclosure and a series of lower enclosures radiating from a central nucleus. To date, these enclosure forms have only been found in northern and southern Pictland, with none yet identified in Atlantic Pictland. The most extensively investigated sites in southern Pictland are Dundurn in Perthshire and Clatchard Craig, Fife, and more recently the King's Seat, Perthshire; in northern Pictland, Mither Tap o' Bennachie, Aberdeenshire, has also been targeted for excavation.

Investigations at the hillfort at Dundurn, Perthshire, in 1976–77, were conducted as part of pioneering early-medieval scholar Leslie Alcock's long-term programme of excavating historically documented early medieval fortifications in western and northern Britain. His programme of work in Scotland began in 1973 and involved 'keyhole' excavation at sites that had references in the Irish annals or other contemporary sources (Alcock and Alcock 1990, 216). In Pictland, Dundurn is one of the few Pictish sites identified in early documents – the *Annals of Ulster* record a siege here in AD 682 (Mac Airt and Mac Niocaill 1983, 148) and the Alba king-list refers to Giric son of Dúngal, a late 9th-century ruler, dying at Dundurn (Anderson 2011, 267, 274, 283).

At Dundurn, Alcock's keyhole excavations revealed a prominent summit citadel enclosure with a series of lower enclosures on top of a craggy outcrop overlooking the upper Earn river valley (Alcock *et al.* 1989) (Figures 3.8 and 3.9c). Like the majority of early medieval forts in Scotland – Tap o' Noth aside! – the overall site was small – the outer terraces occupy an area covering 3ha in maximum extent but the defences may not all date to the same period. The summit citadel itself was only around 35m by 25m in diameter, with 4m thick timber-laced walls. Alcock suggested that the site may have originated as a palisaded enclosure in the 5th or 6th centuries AD, with the palisade subsequently replaced with a stone-built timber-laced

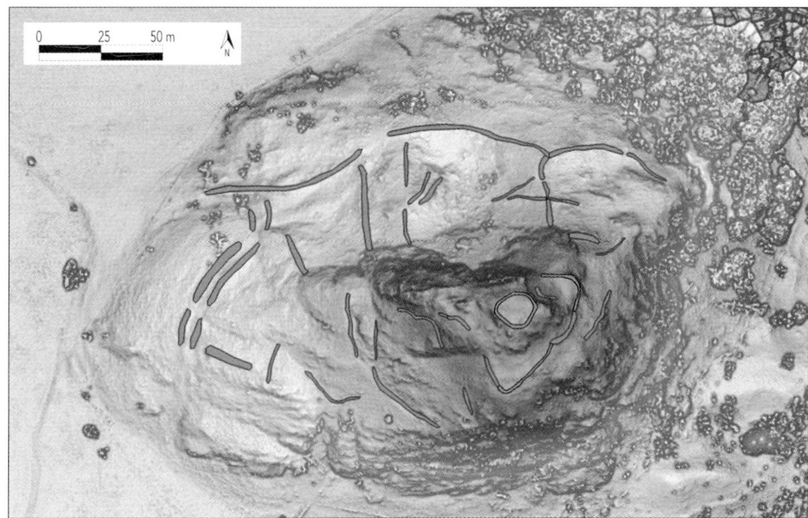

3.8 Dundurn hillfort – a 3D model based on drone photogrammetry. The plan shows the summit sub-circular dun-like enclosure and lower defences extending out from the summit.

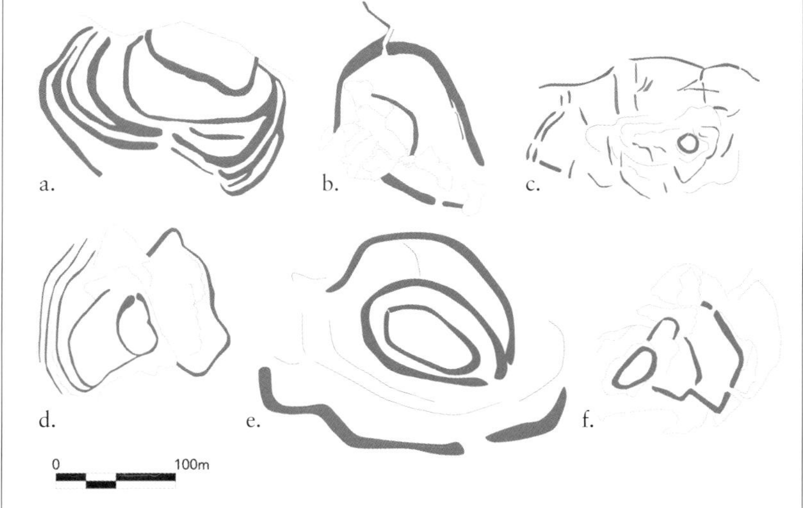

3.9 Comparative plans of a number of complex early medieval forts from Scotland: (a) Clatchard Craig, Fife; (b) Mither Tap, Aberdeenshire; (c) Dundurn, Perthshire; (d) King's Seat, Perthshire; (e) East Lomond, Fife; (f) Dunadd, Argyll.

summit citadel. Evidence of the primary palisade consisted of rock-cut grooves across the upper terrace as well as preserved timbers found in waterlogged deposits in a trench cut across the upper terrace defences. These timbers included a massive oak beam and thinner oak planks, some with evidence for wooden peg fasteners. The complex carpentry of this phase is reminiscent of the palisade at Rhynie that would have been broadly contemporary.

The wooden elements of the timber-laced rampart of the summit citadel that replaced the palisade at Dundurn had been secured using large iron nails or spikes up to 170mm long – over a hundred of these were found in Alcock's small trench over the summit enclosure. The front face of the rampart consisted of horizontal timbers laid in rock-cut grooves. In a later phase, the summit citadel was replaced by a more massive stone-built rampart after the original summit citadel had been destroyed by fire. Inside the fort, structural evidence and extensive midden deposits suggested intensive settlement of the fort interior. The evidence for material culture from Dundurn was limited due to the scale of excavation. However, one sherd of E ware from western France, another sherd of a vessel from the Rhineland and two sherds of imported glass indicate long-distance trade connections. Other finds, which included quernstones and whetstones, a glass boss, a spindle whorl, bone pins and a finely decorated leather shoe (Colour Plate 12), hint at both the everyday routines of its occupants and some of their fineries (Alcock *et al.* 1989, 214–21).

The most extensive excavations on a fort of the nuclear type in Pictland were conducted at Clatchard Craig in Fife, in advance of its destruction by quarrying (Close-Brooks 1986). Excavations carried out by Roy Ritchie in the early 1950s and by Richard Hope-Simpson in 1959 and 1960, showed that the hill had been enclosed by no less than seven individual defences but covering an area of less than 2ha (Figure 3.9a). The inner ramparts defined a sub-rectangular summit citadel. Below, two further ramparts enclosed an upper terrace, while a further series of ramparts seemingly reinforced the upper terrace enclosure. All of the inner ramparts showed evidence of timber lacing. Excavations in the interior of the fort revealed little apart from a hearth and floor surface in the upper terrace enclosure. Fine metalworking evidence was found in association with, and under the floor and hearth of, the building in the upper citadel, while ironworking took place in the upper terrace (Close-Brooks 1986, 146–47).

Recent higher precision dating has provided a much tighter sequence for Clatchard Craig than was available previously, with the new results suggesting the development and destruction of the fort covered a much shorter period centring on the first half of the 7th century AD, the entire sequence of construction to abandonment perhaps as short as a generation or two (Noble *et al.* forthcoming). The fort and its occupants may have had connections with nearby Abernethy, one of the most important ecclesiastical establishments of Pictland (see Chapter 4), with stone for one of the ramparts quarried from Carpow Roman fort which was on the later church estate, located by the Tay, north-east of Abernethy. Indeed, Abernethy may have been established in the same era as Clatchard Craig was constructed, both perhaps part of a major investment in both physical and spiritual protection by ambitious southern Pictish rulers. The excavations of Clatchard Craig also revealed dramatic evidence for the end of the fort – all three of the inner ramparts showed clear evidence for the destruction by fire. Radiocarbon dating suggests the site was abandoned in the period 640–670 AD. This was the period of Northumbrian hegemony over Pictland which probably focussed on the lands of southern Pictland and perhaps Fife in particular. This Northumbrian overlordship seems to have begun in the 650s and 660s under the rule of King Oswy. A Pictish rebellion was also ruthlessly suppressed by Oswy's son Ecgfrith in the 670s – it is possible that, in one of these events, Clatchard Craig was destroyed. The destruction of the fort would have been a powerful statement of dominance and power. Indeed, the repercussions of its destruction were such that the fort was never rebuilt.

A number of other complex multivallate forts have been excavated in recent years in Pictland. These include the King's Seat, Dunkeld – the latter place-name means 'fort of the Caledonians', suggesting the area was a pre-Pictish power centre (Figure 3.9d). The King's Seat is located on a craggy summit, a notable landmark on a bend of the River Tay and overlooking Dunkeld just to the west. The site is located in Stormont and is likely to have been a royal centre for the area. Its defences comprise an oval summit enclosure with a series of enclosures looping off from the summit. The summit enclosure measures 35m by 22m (0.06ha) located within a rampart that was around 4m thick. A lower enclosure wall loops off from the upper citadel to the west and a further, larger, enclosure or annexe extends to the east. A series of walls extends downslope further west. In the interior of the summit enclosure, a large hearth and postholes were found during excavations between 2017 and 2019. These features seem to have belonged to one large building – similar to that found in the summit citadel at Clatchard Craig (MacIver *et al.* 2019). In soil deposits around the hearth a large number of finds were identified including E-ware pottery, metal-working moulds of stone and clay, crucible fragments, glass beads, iron objects and spindle whorls. Further hearths were found in the lower enclosure on the west, along with more evidence for metalworking and additional sherds of E ware. While a precursor fort has not been found in the vicinity that may relate to the 'fort of the Caledonians', the King's Seat was clearly a significant citadel in the Pictish period, dominating an area associated with the powerful ancient Caledonians.

Another probable early medieval power centre in southern Pictland is the complex fort on East Lomond, Fife (Figure 3.9e). The summit fort comprises a sub-oval enclosure around 60m by 30m defended by two lower ramparts that encircle the hill. On the south-west are a massive rampart and ditch which appear to enclose a series of terraces on this side. This latter defence has a 2ha annexe enclosure appended on to the south (see Chapter 2). Two glass beads, a spindle whorl, an ingot mould and a slab bearing the incised outline of a bull have been found in the fort. An area for metalworking on one of the south-west terraces may be indicated by bloomery waste found during the course of a survey by RCAHMS in 1925. Recent survey and excavations have indicated occupation of the annexe

3.10 Aerial view of Mither Tap o' Bennachie hillfort. The defences of the fort were built around a prominent granite tor. Mither Tap may have been one of the main political centres of Ce in the 7th and 8th centuries AD.

enclosure in the 2nd to 7th centuries AD, with E-ware pottery and other finds suggesting this was a well-connected community of elevated status.

In northern Pictland, the only excavation at an early medieval hillfort of the complex citadel type has been at Mither Tap o' Bennachie in Aberdeenshire, one of the best-known hills in north-east Scotland (Figures 3.9b and 3.10). The fort lies on the eastern summit of the Bennachie hill range, sitting atop a craggy granitic tor known as Mither Tap (Atkinson 2006, 2007; RCAHMS 2007, 105–07). A Gaelic saga, *Orgain Benne Ce*, 'The Ravaging of Bennachie', is listed in a 10th-century document. Only the title survives but it implies that the site was known in the early medieval period and that stories of a catastrophic battle or siege at the site were perhaps retold in this tale (Dobbs 1949; Fraser 2009a, 109). The fort itself is defined by a lower stone wall, around 7–8m thick with an entrance on the eastern side. The upper citadel of the fort lies 30m further upslope and encloses a relatively small area of around 30m by 15m, with the rampart enclosing the area immediately south of the huge granite summit tor. Piles of rubble immediately downslope from the granite tor on the east, west and north sides suggest the summit may have also been enclosed with buildings on the very top of the tor. Excavations in 2019 revealed settlement platforms within the fort, evidence for metalworking, an elaborate well and extensive middens rich with animal bones within the interior (Figure

3.11 The extensive animal bone middens in the lower citadel of Mither Tap o' Bennachie – this is the jaw of a juvenile pig.

3.11; Colour Plate 17). Radiocarbon dating suggests the main phase of occupation was during the 7th and 8th centuries AD.

Other major hillforts in Pictland utilised the remains of Iron Age forts, such as Craig Phadrig, Inverness, where finds of E ware and a fragment of a mould for an escutcheon from a hanging bowl, plus a radiocarbon date from an occupation layer of the 5th to 6th century AD, all reveal an early medieval phase to the use of a fort originally constructed in the Iron Age (*c.*400–200 BC). Recent excavation at the site has also identified significant architectural refurbishment of the Iron Age oblong fort with a probable palisade slot dug into the remains of the vitrified ramparts. This phase of activity dates to the 5th to 6th centuries AD (Peteranna and Birch 2018). The size and form of this palisade is unknown but, if the foundation slot followed the outlines of the destroyed Iron Age rampart, it would have enclosed an area around 75m by 25m (0.18ha). Craig Phadrig is a strong contender – though not the only one – for the fort where Columba met King Bridei in the late 6th century, which Adomnán describes as being near where the River Ness met one end of Loch Ness (II.33, II.34; Sharpe 1995, 181–84).

Coastal promontory forts

As noted earlier, coastal promontory forts were a key early medieval high-status settlement type in Pictland. In the centuries after Dunnicaer was built, a series of Pictish-period promontory forts can be identified. The

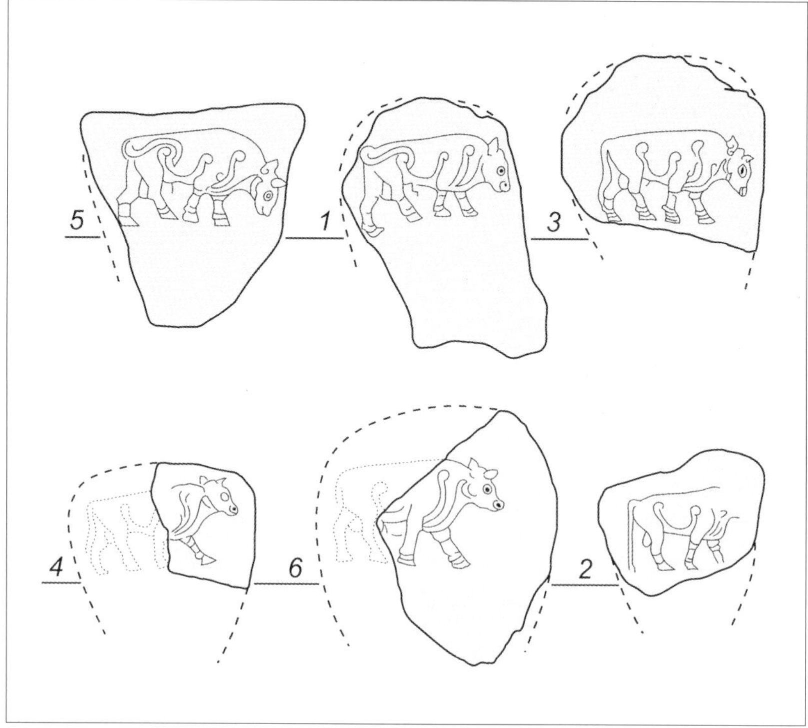

3.12 Drawing of the surviving Burghead bulls – only six survive today out of a total of 25–30 found in the early 19th century.

most sustained archaeological work has been along the Moray Firth coast of north-east Scotland where a number of sites show evidence of use or construction of defended promontory enclosures dating to the mid to late 1st millennium AD (Ralston 1980, 1987, 2004). The most spectacular example of these is undoubtedly Burghead, with its early medieval archaeology perhaps richer than any other site in Pictland. This is despite the fact that a large portion of the fort was destroyed in the early 19th century with the construction of a planned village and harbour built over part of the fort – a sad tale of destruction (Oram 2007) (Colour Plate 13). Only a few years after the start of the construction of the modern village, interested scholars reported significant finds from the fort. Professor John Stuart of the University of Aberdeen wrote in 1809 that the remains of the rampart, including many fragments of burnt timbers, could be identified and he reported on 'pieces of freestone' carrying the remains of carved figures, particularly that of a bull (as recorded by Pinkerton 1814, vi–viii) (Figures 3.12 and 3.13). Stuart recorded that the bull carvings numbered around 30, but only six survive today and four of these are only fragments (1867, 62). William Roy's military survey of the 18th century indicates a chapel around the entrance to the fort and it is from this area that the fragments of early Christian sculpture were found. These findings suggest an early Christian church and perhaps a graveyard were located at the main entry

3.13 Burghead bull held in Elgin Museum, Moray.

point to the fort or had been encompassed in the landward ramparts as the fort expanded. The sculptural fragments include part of a box shrine or altar and a cross-slab that has a depiction of a mounted Pictish warrior carrying a spear and shield.

Another spectacular find of the 19th-century discovery was the well of the fort. This was revealed in 1809 when a well shaft was sunk into the lower citadel of the fort in an area of particularly green and fertile grass, by residents who wanted a water supply for the modern village (Young 1890). Rock-cut steps leading down to an elaborately carved square well shaft, hewn from the bedrock were found (Figure 3.14). It is the largest and most elaborate well known from an early medieval fort in Britain and, at the time of discovery, was thought to be of Roman construction due to its elaborate nature. However, this appears to have been an integral part of the Pictish fort, incorporated into the landward defences.

A new programme of investigation at Burghead has been ongoing since 2015. Despite previous doubts about preservation in the fort interior, it has turned out that Burghead is remarkably well preserved – at least what is left of it. Floor layers of internal buildings are preserved under up to 1m of overburden from modern development and sand blow from the surrounding landscape. At least five early medieval buildings have been uncovered to date including large rectangular buildings in both citadels

3.14 (*Above*) The elaborate Burghead well with walkway around the central wall chamber. (© Joan Megson)

3.15 (*Right*) Part of an extensive activity area revealed during excavations in 2019 in the lower citadel of Burghead fort.

(Figure 3.15). Excavation at the seaward end of the upper citadel has also revealed exceptionally well-preserved stretches of the rampart that survive to around 3m in height. The rampart remains have revealed clear evidence for their destruction by fire. Finds from the excavations to date have included dress accessories, fragments of weaponry, iron tools, bone pins and metalworking evidence. From the floor layer and midden of one building came two coins of King Alfred. The coins had been pierced for wearing as jewellery. Over 80 radiocarbon dates have been obtained thus far from the excavations at Burghead showing that the site was occupied from at least the 6th century AD and was destroyed in the later 9th century or early 10th century AD. Evidence from the site suggests that Burghead must have been one of the principal centres of the northern Picts, located at the heart of Fortriu. The wide bay immediately west of the site may have also been one where boats could have been pulled up and where the naval power of the Picts could have been mustered (Shepherd 1993) (Colour Plate 14).

Pictish-era forts were also constructed at other points along the southern coast of the Moray Firth. At Portknockie, a smaller fort was constructed in the 7th century AD (Ralston 1980, 1987). It had timber-framed defences enclosing a relatively modest 0.3ha interior. Inside, one rectangular structure of probable 7th to 9th century date was located. Like the inland hillforts outlined above, promontory forts also reused Iron Age sites, as is evident at Cullykhan, Aberdeenshire, where Pictish period reuse included both occupation and refortification (Greig 1970, 1971).

On the coast to the south, a much larger promontory appears to have been defended in the Pictish period close to the location of the earlier fort at Dunnicaer. In the *Annals of Ulster*, sieges of Dunnottar are referred to in both AD 680 and 693 (Mac Airt and Mac Niocaill 1983, 146, 154; Fraser 2009a, 214). There are also references in the *Chronicle of the Kings of Alba* (CKA) to the killing of Donald son of Constantín (AD 889–900) by the 'heathen' at Dunnottar (Woolf 2007a, 123, 125), and to Æthelstan, king of the English, raiding with his land forces as far north as Dunnottar in 934 in the northern English *Historia Regum Anglorum* (Woolf 2007a, 161). Today Dunnottar is crowned by the remains of a spectacular 14th–17th-century castle (Figure 3.16). Unfortunately, a trench on the northern side of the promontory in 1984 failed to identify any early medieval deposits or defences (Alcock and Alcock 1992). It seems likely that any earlier deposits have been destroyed by the later castle. At 1ha, Dunnottar would be one of the larger early medieval fortified sites known in Scotland but what the character of the defences and settlement were like remains uncertain.

In Atlantic Pictland, no sites of the character of the nuclear forts or indeed promontory forts like Burghead or Dunnottar have been securely identified. The Brough of Birsay in Orkney may have been an elite centre of the Picts judging by the finds of metalworking moulds and crucibles for fine metalworking and a magnificent carved stone monument showing three warriors armed with spears and shields and four Pictish symbols above (Crawford 1987, 156; RCAHMS 2008, 114). Birsay became the

3.16 Dunnottar Castle – likely to be overlying a major Pictish settlement of the 7th to 9th centuries AD.

main centre for the Norse earldom of Orkney in later centuries, a role which may have been due to its elite status in the Pictish period (Crawford 1987, 156). Birsay is a large tidal islet with high cliffs around its western side – it may be that this naturally defensive position acted like the hill and promontory forts that were so popular further south. It is interesting to note that the adjacent promontory on Mainland at Buckquoy may have been demarcated by a ditch, though this feature is currently undated (Griffiths and Ovenden 2021, 533–42). Other sites in Orkney and Shetland, such as the Brough of Deerness, Mainland, Orkney, and Kaim of Isbister, Shetland, may have also been fortified settlements in the Pictish period, though only the former has occupation deposits directly dated to the Pictish era (Barrett and Slater 2009).

In the Western Isles, some of the duns may have been reused or even built in the later first millennium AD, though few sites have demonstrated this through well-dated sequences and very few coastal promontory forts or inland enclosures have been excavated in this region. In Caithness, it has recently been suggested that a fort recorded as being under siege in AD 679, Dún Baitte, might have been Dunbeath in Caithness (Grigg 2018, 42). However, this equation is very uncertain: the second element does not provide a clear match for the place-name, which incorporates Gaelic *beithe*, 'birch', but reinterpretation of this second element in the Gaelic-speaking era is possible (Simon Taylor personal comment). Dunbeath Castle is located on a distinctive coastal promontory overlooking the natural harbour at the Water of Dunbeath. Despite the uncertainty, Dunbeath would certainly make for an attractive location for a Pictish-period power centre but only excavation would reveal if there was occupation of this era there or at any nearby coastal promontories.

Later royal centres

Earlier references to centres of power for Pictland are dominated by references to defended, often hilltop, enclosures but, in the later 1st millennium AD, historical sources also refer to Lowland centres such as Forteviot and Scone. Stephen Driscoll (1998) has argued that the construction of such Lowland centres marked a development in the form and stability of kingship with the abandonment of the earlier fortified centres. However, as noted above, some sites, like Dundurn and Dunnottar, continue to be mentioned into the 9th and 10th centuries and the fewer references to fortified sites may simply be because our sources for Pictland become poorer from the mid 8th century onwards. It also perhaps reflects the limitations of our earlier sources – the evidence from Rhynie shows that non-hilltop elite centres were also a feature of the earlier Pictish period.

Nonetheless, there does appear to have been an escalation in the scale and complexity of later Lowland power centres and an increasing relationship with the Church with a notable juxtaposition between elite residences and important church buildings evident at a number of Lowland power centres. The later Lowland enclosures include relatively modest sized sites such as Upper Gothens, Perthshire (Barclay 2001), an enclosure around 62m in diameter, defined by a ditch and an internal palisade. Dating suggests this was in use between the 9th and 11th centuries AD (Figure 3.17). Inside the Upper Gothens enclosure, space was divided in two by a series of palisades that also provided an impressive entrance to the inner enclosure. A tinned iron buckle came from one posthole and the presence of slag suggested ironworking. The excavator interpreted the site as a high-status settlement, perhaps an estate centre of a lord (Barclay 2001, 43). In this case, no definite church site is known from the site or nearby but a cross-slab, found reused in Lethendy Castle, located around 2.5km to the west, could conceivably have been part of a nearby church.

What are likely to have been more regionally significant Lowland elite centres of the 9th century are documented at Forteviot, *Rathinveramon* and Meigle in southern Pictland. Forteviot is recorded as the *palatium* of Cináed son of Alpín (Kenneth mac Alpine), who died there in AD 858 (Anderson 2011, 250; Campbell and Driscoll 2020, 39). The site has an impressive collection of early medieval sculpture and an early Christian copper-alloy handbell – probably a recast of the original – is located in the parish church (Bourke 2020, 419–20; Campbell and Driscoll 2020, 122–28). The sculptural evidence from the vicinity includes the 'triumphalist' Dupplin or Constantine's Cross, a free-standing cross carved with a king

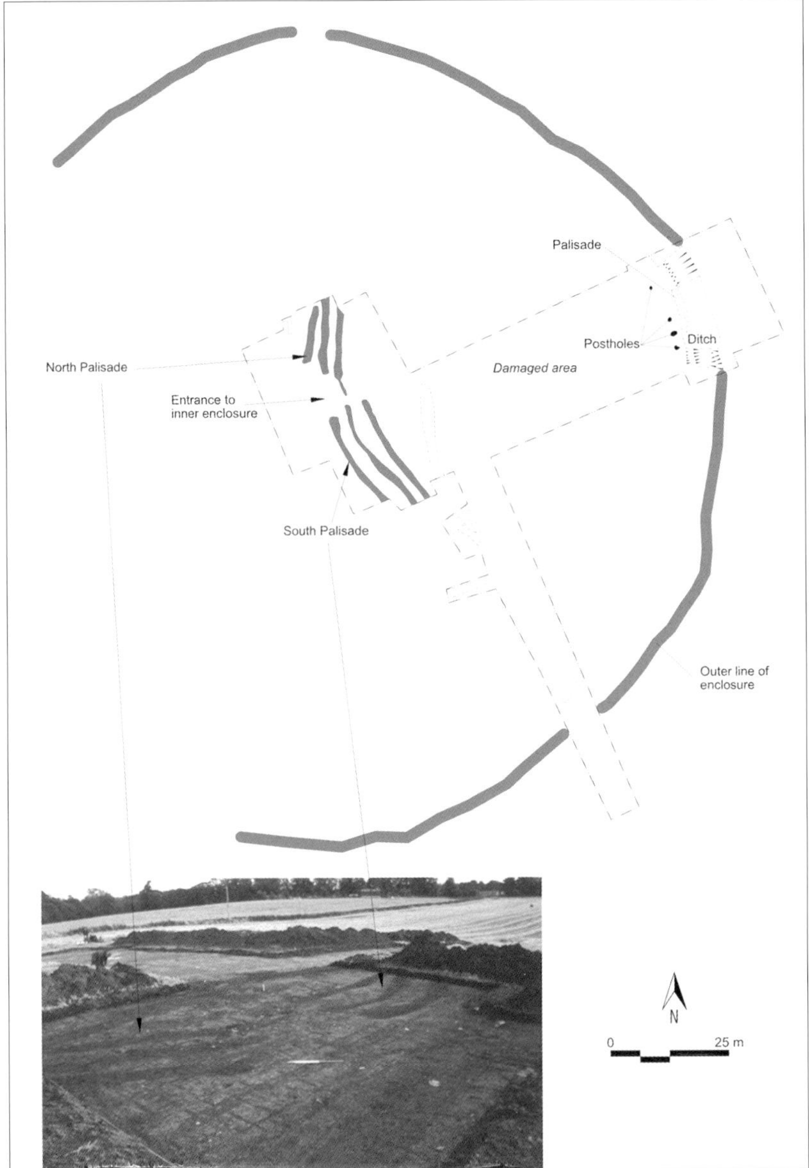

3.17 (*Right*) Upper Gothens, a lordly residence of the 9th to 11th centuries AD? The settlement comprised a circular enclosure with traces of internal divisions inside. (Drawing after Gordon Barclay 2001, photo © Gordon Barclay)

3.18 (*Opposite*) Dupplin or Constantine's Cross, Forteviot parish, Perthshire. The front and side face of the cross appear to show a hierarchy of warriors with:
(a) a mounted warrior, perhaps the important Pictish king Constantine himself;
(b) commanders on side of stone with impressive moustaches;
(c) younger foot soldiers.

on horseback, with his retinue depicted below (Henderson and Henderson 2004, 190; Campbell and Driscoll 2020, 149–58) (Figure 3.18). The cross is dedicated to Constantín I, a Pictish king who died in AD 820 (Forsyth 1995a). The cross has a huge socket stone that projects outwards from the front of the stone – this peculiar feature could have been used as a platform for proclamation (Goldberg 2012, 172; Campbell and Driscoll 2020, 155). The cross stood to the north of Forteviot on the Gask Ridge overlooking the village and parish church and on the later medieval parish boundary.

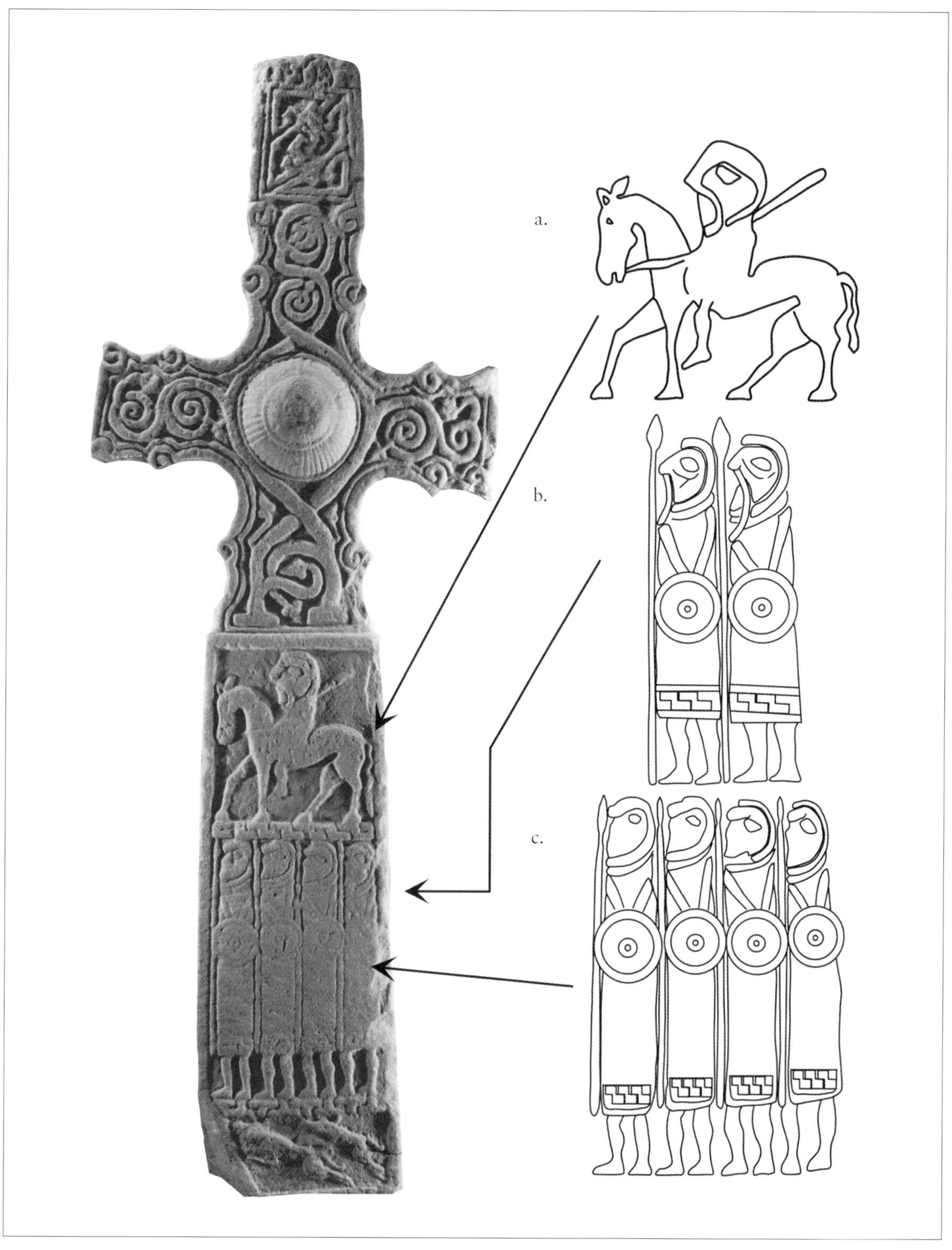
a.
b.
c.

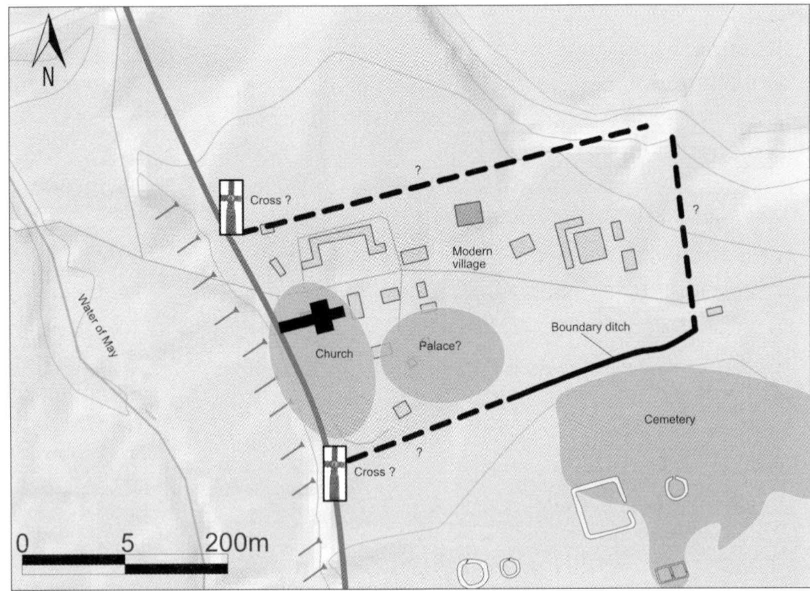

3.19 Plan of the main features of the royal centre at Forteviot around the modern village as identified by aerial photography and excavation. The boundary ditch may have cut off the promontory or could conceivably have enclosed a smaller rectangular area. A major cemetery was located to the south of the palace and church complex. The position of two crosses is speculative. (After Campbell *et al.* 2020, fig. 10.1)

Another cross, the Invermay Cross, stood to the south of the village and these two crosses may have framed and marked entry to the royal estate (Aitchison 2006, Fig. 17; Campbell and Driscoll 2020, 170) (Figure 3.19). Another impressive monument, the Forteviot Arch, must have come from an elaborate building found within the royal complex, probably a stone-built church (see Chapter 4). The royal complex appears to have been enclosed by a rectilinear enclosure, part of the boundary identified during excavations undertaken at the site from 2007 to 2011 (Figure 3.19). Given that relatively little of the complex has been uncovered, judging the extent of enclosure is difficult but the enclosure ditch, if it extended to encompass an area covered by the modern village and abutted the scarp edge of the Water of May, could have been around 6ha in extent.

To the south-east of the village, a large cemetery identified by aerial photography has been partly excavated. It included square and round barrows and flat graves and was centred around a square enclosure argued to have been modelled on Roman Iron Age shrines (Campbell *et al.* 2019, 91; Campbell and Driscoll 2020, 66; see also Chapter 5). Further burials were found near a prehistoric monument complex found directly south of the modern village. In an area just to the south of the parish church, further burials and possible traces of a wooden church of probable early medieval date have been identified. Unfortunately, no halls or other buildings that may have been part of the *palatium* have been located – these may lie under the modern village. Hence, what defined the *palatium* and its overall character is uncertain given that only parts of the site have been investigated and much of the earlier archaeology may have been destroyed. The complex may have been the setting for the royal court, perhaps housed in timber buildings, and a church building here would have helped legitimise the royal authority of the Forteviot rulers (Campbell *et al.* 2019, 98). The site could also have been primarily an ecclesiastical centre with a royal hall within its bounds (Woolf 2007a, 105, 313).

Rathinveramon – '*ráith* of the confluence/mouth of the Almond/*avon*' – is where King Domnall mac Alpín (858–862) is said to have died and King Constantín mac Cuilén was killed there in 997 according to the Scottish Regnal lists (Anderson 2011, 267, 74, 275, 283, 284). The *palatium* of *Cinnbelathoír* may have been the same site, since the *Chronicle of the Kings of Alba* locates the death of the same King Domnall there (Anderson 2011, 250). The name *Rathinveramon* indicates this *palatium* may have been near the mouth of the River Almond, a tributary of the Tay. At the confluence of the Almond and Tay lies Bertha Roman fort. The Roman fort was sub-rectangular and stood next to a ford and possibly a Roman bridge that spanned the Tay (Roy 1793). The fort is now ploughed flat but was upstanding in the 18th century. The Roman fort could well have been reused as the Pictish *palatium*.

Meigle is likely to have been another royal centre of the 9th century. The St Andrews Foundation Legend states that the account was written by a certain Cano son of Dubabrach in the *villa* of Meigle for King Uurad (*c.*839–842) (Taylor with Márkus 2009, 579). Meigle has one of the largest collections of Pictish sculpture known, including a series of cross-slabs (see Chapter 4). Like Forteviot, this may have been a royal centre with a church or perhaps Uurad had a royal hall within an ecclesiastical complex here (see Woolf 2007a, 105, 313).

Another interesting case is Scone, Perthshire, where later Scottish kings were inaugurated. In 905 or 906, we have our first reference to this site, in the *Chronicle of the Kings of Alba*, as the location for a meeting at the 'hill of belief' of Constantín, the king of Alba, and Cellach, the bishop of St Andrews, to decide the beliefs and laws of the Church (Anderson 2011, 251; Woolf 2007a, 134–38). While the description may have been altered later, the basic event – a meeting between king and leading clerics – seems likely to have happened. It indicates that seemingly wholly secular sites could have been the locations for important ecclesiastical events, underlining the intertwining of Christian and royal spheres (Driscoll 1998b, 170–73). Whether the famous 'Stone of Destiny', derived from local red sandstone (Hill 2003; Phillips *et al.* 2003), and the mound itself can be dated much earlier than the end of the Pictish era is unclear. Recent dating of ditch deposits associated with the mound produced later dates (O'Grady 2018), though it is plausible that Scone was already a significant Pictish assembly site of some kind.

Overall, our evidence for royal centres, skewed considerably by the survival of written evidence, shows that, by the mid 9th century, extensive Lowland elite centres, sometimes combining secular and Christian facets in more convenient locations for estates and controlling communication routes through important valleys, provided an important dimension of elite legitimation. Their prominence may have partly been at the expense of more defensive, hilltop locations – the citadels that were such an important feature of the earlier Pictish period – though some of these certainly endured into the late first millennium AD and even into the second millennium AD (for example, Peteranna and Birch 2018; Noble *et al.* 2020b, 192). Moreover, as outlined earlier, low-lying elite centres already existed as early as the 4th to 5th centuries AD as has recently been discovered at Rhynie. The 7th century does appear to be a key moment in the consolidation of the citadel lords for the prominence of complex hillforts in our albeit limited datasets in this century is notable. The 7th century may have been a particular period of military stress, in which nobles and kings devoted considerable resources to defence and the dominance of local landscapes. It is possible that the importance of hillforts declined in Pictland after Fortriu expanded its power as a result of the Battle of Nechtanesmere but forts like Dundurn, Dunnottar and Burghead either remained in use or were reused in the Viking Age, perhaps to deal with the Scandinavian threat. We therefore now have examples of a variety of sites in use over the entire duration of the early medieval period and examples in the Late Roman Iron Age. It is possible that elite centres at low and high elevations existed continually from the Late Roman period onwards, perhaps even in related complexes of multivalent sites, as found in the Rhynie landscape, with the balance between individual sites altering as the social, political and military context developed and changed.

Leadership and warriorhood

Like elsewhere in Europe, war and warfare were important underpinning elements of leadership in the Late Roman and early medieval periods in northern Britain. Elites were first and foremost leaders in war, with leadership in conflict one of the main qualities sought in aspiring rulers (Woolf 2007a, 26). Being a king gave an individual the right and ability to muster the realm's troops and lead them into battle (Alcock 2003, 31). Consequently, being a king was risky business. Leslie Alcock, examining the biographies of kings in Britain in the period of *c.*600–900 AD, worked out that around 30% died in battle, 6% were slain by contenders to the crown and 12% were assassinated by their own warband – so you had around a 50:50 chance of being violently killed as an early medieval ruler (Alcock 2003, 33).

In Anglo-Saxon England, from around the 5th century to the late 7th century, weaponry placed in burials was commonplace, with around one in five furnished male burials being accompanied by weapons (Härke 1990, 25). A martial ideology in early medieval English society is also known through Old English epic poetry such as *Beowulf* and *The Battle of Maldon* (Swanton 1978; Scragg 1991; Bazelmans 1999). In Ireland, there are few burials with weaponry but early medieval literature and law codes lauded the heroic behaviours of various warrior-leaders (Kinsella 1969; Kelly 1988, 19; Edel 2015). Closer to Pictland, the group of Welsh poems with origins in Scotland known as *Y Gododdin* praised the warriors of the Votadini polity centred on the Forth to Tyne area, a location just to the south of Pictland. The poems paint a picture of a life of feasting, plunder and heroic death (Clancy 1998, 46–78; Koch 1997).

Unfortunately, in Pictland, the historical sources are not as rich and nor is the burial record as illuminating as for areas such as Anglo-Saxon England. The early Roman sources describe the Picts and their forebears as attacking the Empire and the Roman military but rarely provide much detail, though Herodian stated that warriors of northern Britain fought naked and used narrow shields, a spear and a sword (Mann and Penman 1996, 43). Adomnán, in the *Life of Columba*, referred to an elderly pagan, Artbranan, who visited Skye to be baptised by the saint. Artbranan was called *primarius Geonae cohortis*, 'leader of the warband of the Pictish territory of Ce' (I.33; Sharpe 1995, 136–37 and n. 149). Evidence for the violence of later Pictish kings towards their rivals is preserved in the Irish annals for the 730s when Pictish leaders are recorded drowning their enemies, most notably in AD 739 when King Onuist son of Uurguist drowned Talorggan, son of Drostan, the king of Atholl. On his death in AD 761, the Anglo-Saxon *Continuatio Bedae*, stated that 'from the beginning of his reign right to the end he [Onuist] perpetuated bloody crimes, like a tyrannical slaughterer' (Forsyth 2000, 22; Fraser 2009a, 287–319). There are also references to sieges and battles at the fortified sites of Pictland highlighted earlier, adding to the impression of a violent age.

3.20 A silver sword pommel from Rhynie. The pommel does not have a perforation for fixing to the sword which indicates it is an unfinished item – so production of weaponry was occurring on site at the Craw Stane complex.

In the archaeological record, there are no warrior burials of the Pictish period – like Ireland and western Britain, burial was almost exclusively non-furnished. Weapons finds from Pictish sites are exceedingly rare too – amongst the slim number of finds are a sword hilt from Burghead, a sword or dagger pommel from Rhynie (Figure 3.20), sword chapes from the St Ninian's Isle hoard in Shetland and a few stray finds that may belong to this period (Clarke 2012, 78–79). What Pictland does have though is a rich pictorial tradition on stone (see Chapter 6) that references martial culture. In the early Pictish period, there are a small number of carvings of warriors, notably carvings from Tulloch, Perthshire; Collessie, Fife; and Rhynie (Figure 3.21). These stones show warriors in profile carrying spears and, in the case of the Collessie and Rhynie examples, also shields. The

3.21 The warrior carvings from Tulloch, Collessie and Rhynie. (© Andy Hickie) Image processing helps reveal the ghostly outlines of the warriors shown on these three standing stones. The outlines may have originally been painted. All three figures held spears with the Collessie and Rhynie warriors holding shields. Two symbols marked the identity of the Collessie warrior (centre).

type of spears that these warriors carry would suggest a date of 4th century to 6th century AD for the carvings for the warriors carry a distinctive type of weapon – a spear with a doorknob spear-butt. Moulds for these spear-butts are found in archaeological contexts of the 4th to 6th centuries AD date (Heald 2001). It is not certain whether these depictions were of actual people, mythical heroes or gods but the martial imagery is obvious. Across northern Europe, in the first millennium AD, sacral and martial imagery was used to underpin the new social and political hierarchies of the late Iron Age and early medieval periods (for example, Enright 1996; Ringtved 1999, 50; Hedeager 1999, 151; Price 2002). The warriors carved in stone appear to have been a Pictish expression of the martial ideology that was widespread across north-western Europe in the first millennium AD.

On later Pictish cross-slabs of likely 7th to 9th century date, armed figures became a common motif and are found on monuments from Fife in southern Pictland to Orkney in the Atlantic north. By the 9th century, the imagery of a warrior king had been infused with Christian and Imperial imagery (Henderson 1972, 158–60). On one cross-slab, we do not see merely mounted warriors but an entire battle scene. This is on a stone from Aberlemno, with the battle scene on the stone long connected to the most famous victory of the Picts – the Battle of Nechtanesmere of 685, when the Picts

3.22 The great battle scene on the back of the Aberlemno churchyard cross-slab and drawing of the detail of the battle. The image of the stone is based on a 3D model. (© Hamish Fenton)

gained victory over the Northumbrians (*HE* IV.26; Colgrave and Mynors 1969, 428–29) (Figure 3.22). '*Nectanesmere*' was how the battle was referred to in English sources. The *Annals of Ulster* record the battle thus:

> The battle of Dún Nechtain on the 20th of May, a Saturday, that is, in which Ecgfrith son of Oswiu, king of the English, having completed the fifteenth year of his reign, was slain with a great body of his soldiers (*AU* 686 [= AD 685])

Both the Anglo-Saxon and Irish annals entries refer to the battle location as containing the personal name Nechtan. Two locations have been proposed for the battle site – Dunnichen in Angus and Dunachton in Speyside (Woolf 2006). The traditional identification of the battle site is in Angus in southern Pictland just to the south of Aberlemno, where the cross-slab with the magnificent battle scene is located (Figure 3.22). Dunachton in the north has been proposed by Alex Woolf in his 2006 article in which he shifted Fortriu northwards and questioned the traditional location of the battle. One of the contributing factors in Woolf's shift of the battle site north was Bede's description of Ecgfrith being lured into '*angustias inaccessorum montium*', 'tight places amid inaccessible mountains', which describes the geography of the Speyside Dunachton better. However, Bede would have been around 12 when the event happened so we do not know to what extent his account was based on fact or was an exaggerated trope to explain the defeat of an Anglo-Saxon king. Indeed, the magnificent battle scene on the Aberlemno churchyard cross-slab still provides a compelling reason for locating the battle in Angus.

The Aberlemno churchyard stone itself is a huge block of sandstone standing some 2.3m tall. The stone has been carefully shaped with the cross on one face carved in bold relief, projecting around 0.1m from its background. On the opposing face of the stone are three rows of fighting figures displayed under two prominent Pictish symbols (see Chapter 6) (Figure 3.22). In the top row of the battle scene, we can see two mounted warriors, one chasing the other. The one being chased wears a helmet that closely resembles Anglo-Saxon-style helmets found at sites such as Coppergate in York (Addyman *et al.* 1982). The long-haired individual resembles the depiction of what we assume to be Picts on other Pictish cross-slabs. The long-haired rider brandishes a sword, while the helmeted warrior appears to have dropped his weapons while fleeing – if this stone was commemorating the Battle of Nechtanesmere, could this be the aftermath of the luring of Ecgfrith into an ambush? In the next row, the same helmeted warrior appears to have temporarily rallied or another warrior from the same warband has counter-attacked. He is repelled by rows of foot soldiers, standing three ranks deep in a schiltron-like defence. In the front is a commander with a sword and shield and behind is a warrior carrying a long spear or pike being thrust forwards in defence against the cavalry attack. A shield next to him may be from a warrior standing behind, providing protection for the pike wielder. At the back is a spearman carrying a shorter spear. In the final row, we see two mounted warriors confronting one another, perhaps the same two depicted on the first row, both now wielding spears and shields. On the right appears to be the culmination of the battle – the helmeted warrior, being pecked by a bird – the dead being the 'prey for ravens' as recorded in the *Gododdin* poems. The dead warrior is highly likely to have been a king for he wears both a helmet and a mail shirt – both weapons of war only owned by the very top tiers of early medieval elite society (Allen and Anderson 1903, 211; Alcock 2003, 171). This may be a depiction of the dead Ecgfrith, the defeated king of the Battle of Nechtanesmere, though there were other battles between the Picts and the Anglo-Saxons, including in 698 when a *dux* Berctred, son of the powerful Beornhaeth, himself called a *subregulus* by Stephen of Ripon, was killed in battle against the Picts (Fraser 2009a, 254). While we cannot conclusively link the stone to a commemoration of the Battle of Nechtanesmere, the monument certainly depicts a startling triumphalist scene on a cross-slab, showing the importance and prestige of successful leadership in warfare and the degree to which this kind of behaviour and triumphalism was accepted by the Church.

Another magnificent battle scene is depicted on Sueno's Stone in Moray (Figure 3.23). This is a later monument, perhaps dating to the 9th century. It stands 6.5m tall. Like the Aberlemno stone, there is a cross on one side with a scene below that appears to represent the anointing of Solomon as king, a biblical parallel perhaps for the inauguration of a contemporary ruler (Loggie 2020). On the panel below, there is a series of blade sharpening marks – while these could represent later reuse, intriguingly, similar marks have been identified on Irish monuments and have been suggested to represent events during rituals of lordship and perhaps inauguration (Newman 2009; see also Loggie 2020). On the back side of the monument, there are dozens of warriors posed in vibrant scenes of battle. These occur over four panels. The topmost panel has at least eight mounted and armed warriors processing to the right. In the panel below, the busiest scenes of battle are vividly portrayed (Figure 3.23). At the top stand five warriors looking out from the stone carrying swords and spears. Below, individuals are engaged in hand-to-hand combat with other warriors surrounding them. The centre of this panel has a vivid scene of decapitation centred around some sort of tower-like building, possibly the gatehouse of a fort. Headless corpses and severed heads are found around this building. Below are two pairs of warriors engaged in a swordfight, more severed heads, trumpeters and six mounted warriors who appear to be fleeing from a warband bearing swords and bows. The third panel down appears to show a bridge with decapitated prisoners lying prone below, while pairs of warriors fight each other. Finally, the lowest panel has a row of foot soldiers processing to the left.

It is hard to make sense of this melee but the martial imagery is incredibly explicit, as are the scenes of decapitation – the contemporary viewer would be left in no doubt of the military capabilities and power of the commissioner of this monument, nor of the retributions that would be enacted if that strength and authority was challenged. If the monument is of a 9th-century date, it could commemorate some of the battles between the Picts and the Vikings that occurred in the decades around the middle of the 9th century but could also record an internal conflict too (see Chapter 7). There are few parallels for the brutalist depictions of warfare on Sueno's Stone but a cross-slab from Dunkeld, a place that was raided twice in the 9th century by Vikings, also shows severed heads and decapitated individuals, along with mounted warriors (RCAHMS 1994, 89, 97).

The vibrant stone-carving tradition from Pictland gives some clues about

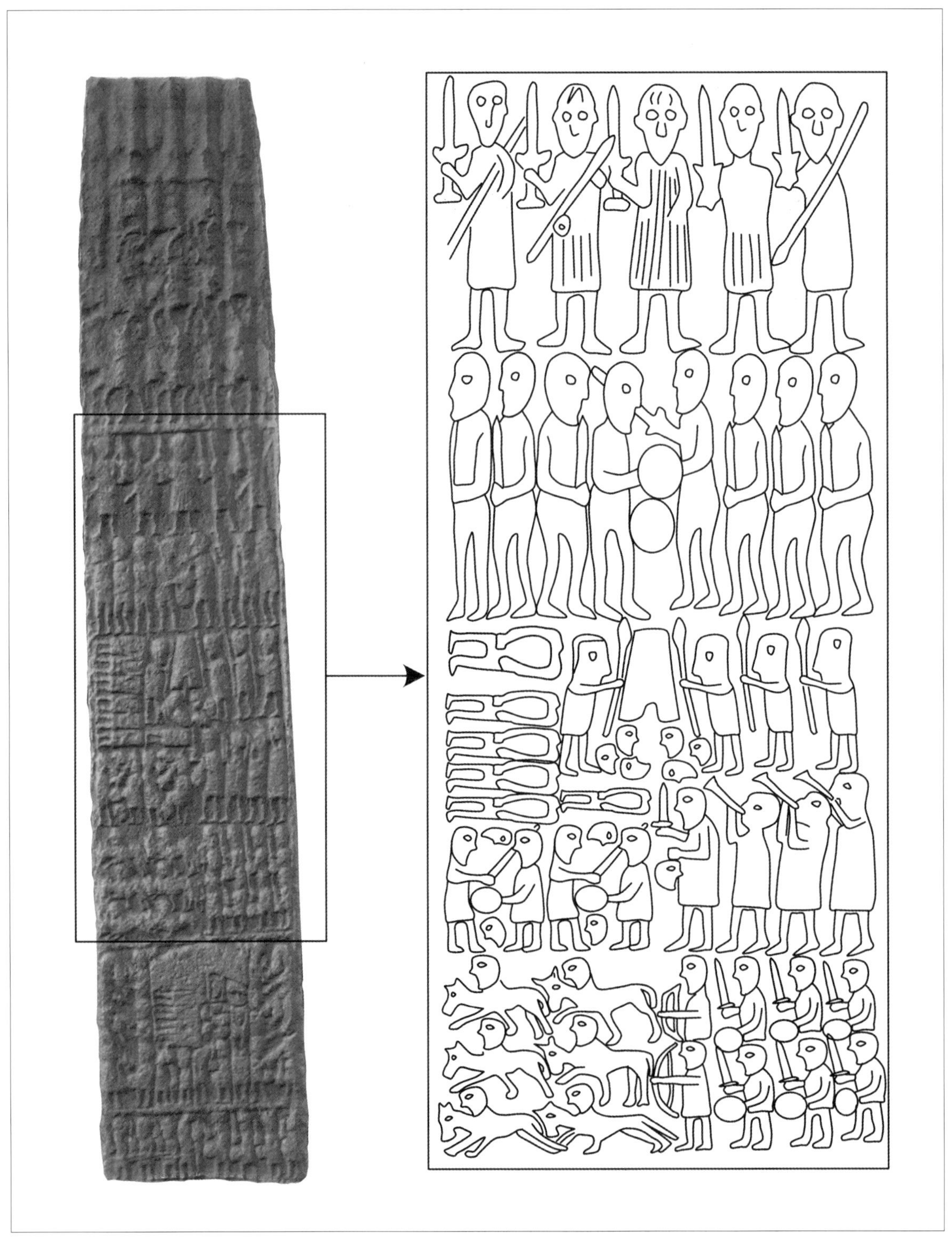

military organisation in Pictland. The presence of multiple armed riders on some stones suggests leaders were accompanied into battle by other mounted elites, perhaps the king's personal warband and bodyguard. However, the contemporary army muster for the Scots of Dál Riata, the *Míniugud Senchasa Fher nAlban* (*Senchus*), makes no mention of horses, though horsemen (*equites*) are mentioned in the *Life of Columba*, seemingly from Bridei's household. Mounted warriors are likely to have been the wealthier elite or various individuals linked to the king – for example, powerful clients, other nobles or even champions. The *Senchus* indicates that forces of over 2,000 soldiers could be mustered, suggesting that some battles were more than small-scale skirmishes and had perhaps had large numbers of soldiers on foot to accompany the armed warriors on horseback (Alcock 2003, 155). In 12th-century Scotia, kings could muster a much larger force, consisting of more of the general populace, for short periods – say, a month. Presumably this was more for defence rather than attack. Pictish-era stones show that foot soldiers were an important part of the warband, such as the phalanx of warriors on the Aberlemno churchyard stone, the ranks of foot soldiers on Sueno's Stone, the king's retinue on the Dupplin cross and the band of foot soldiers on an architectural fragment from Dull (Figure 3.24). The warriors on these stones may have included members of the general populace called up in times of great threat.

3.23 (*Opposite*) Sueno's Stone, Forres, Moray, showing the detail of the largest carved panel, depicting a huge battle in progress and the aftermath with decapitated warriors. The image of the stone is based on a 3D model. (© Hamish Fenton)

The most commonly depicted weapon borne by the warriors on the stones is the spear – they outnumber swords by at least 2:1 (Alcock 2003, 161–62). Some warriors are shown bearing shields, both large rectangular shields and also small one-handed bucklers used in hand-to-hand combat, paired with a spear or sword. Spears were also wielded and thrown by riders on horseback. Based on the Aberlemno cross-slab, Alcock has suggested that Pictish swords were short, around 0.5m long, much shorter than Anglo-Saxon swords, and similar to Irish swords (Alcock 2003, 163).

3.24 A war band shown on a sculptural fragment from Dull, Perthshire. (© Historic Environment Scotland)

They may have been intended as one-handed stabbing weapons rather than two-handed slashing weapons.

As well as land-based warfare, naval battles are also evident in the written sources. Gildas's references to raiding by the Scots and Picts on Roman Britain appear to have been via waterborne attacks. That the Picts could draw on a fleet at times of war is suggested by *AU* 682.4, which records that Orkney was ravaged by Bridei son of Beli. An entry in the 'Annals of Tigernach' for 729 also records the 'breaking' of 150 ships of the Picts at *Ross Cuissine*, perhaps Troup Head in Banffshire (Watson 1926, 507). Unfortunately, the form or sophistication of the Pictish vessels is not known. The large size of this fleet strongly implies it was setting out for raiding, conquest or to enforce tribute. What Pictish warships looked like is unknown. In the *Senchus* seven-bench ships with 14 oarsmen are referenced but this may be a standard measurement of military dues and both larger and smaller ships can be envisioned.

Hunting

One further marker of elite identity that appears to have been key to bolstering the strength and image of the Pictish nobility was the hunt. This appears to been particularly important in the late first millennium AD when hunting imagery is widely found on sculpture that likely dates to the 8th to the 9th century AD (Henderson and Henderson 2004, 124–29). Elsewhere in Europe, in the early medieval period, the hunt was a prominent ritual of royal authority and prestige, showing the king's prowess, and was an activity that asserted lordship over territory, as well as providing entertainment and sport (Goldberg 2020, 8). The prominence of the hunt in elite traditions goes back to at least the Roman period when hunting was an activity particularly associated with Roman militarised elites. Roman nobles of central and northern Europe hunted hares, wild boar, deer and foxes on foot and on horseback using nets, hunting dogs, spears and bows. These practices were also conducted by the barbarian kings of the Late Antique period and, like the Romans, hunting was used as a form of military training as well as being a prestige leisure activity. In Gaul, the Merovingians created the first royal forests around the 6th century and a whole range of specialised hunting dogs and hawks began to be bred more intensively from the early 8th century onwards (Goldberg 2020, 67). But it was with the Carolingians that hunting really began to be explicitly linked with royal rulership, property and power. Wild animals in royal forests became property of the crown and the right to hunt became by royal decree only. Charlemagne required his heirs to be trained in hunting 'in the manner of the Franks' as part of an activity that underpinned masculinity and nobility and provided essential skills and training (Goldberg 2020, 9, 158, 180).

In the first millennium AD, evidence for the importance of the hunt for elite identity is limited in Pictland. In a rare reference to the hunt, hunting dogs are said to have been chasing a boar in a dense forest on Skye in an episode in the *Life of Columba* (II.26; Sharpe 1995, 175). In Atlantic Pictland, there is interesting evidence for the decline of wild animals in the faunal record for certain sites. At Howe, Mainland, Orkney, for example, red deer were utilised less in the later Pictish phases than in earlier phases of the settlement with the percentage of red deer in the faunal assemblage declining from 18% to 4% (Ballin Smith 1994, 124). At another Orcadian site, Skaill, red deer also declined sharply in numbers in the Pictish phases (Buteux 1997, 54). It could be that wild animals were becoming less common, particularly in the island geography of Orkney, but it is also possible that access to animals such as deer were being restricted as hunting became a more overtly elite practice.

However, while the procurement of and provision for hunting dogs and horses were expensive and involved a pastime that was only accessible to the wealthiest, not all hunting events would have been restricted to the elite. There are other forms of hunting which are more accessible – trapping, for example, was an exercise carried out by commoners in Carolingian contexts (Goldberg 2020, 169). This was to increase the food supply and diversity for communities but it was also a practice that was designed to emulate elite lifestyles. Trapping is actually mentioned in the *Life of Columba* in reference to families on the poverty line. Adomnán recounts the story of Columba meeting a poor layman in the Lochaber area of the Great Glen who had been reduced to begging and could not feed his family. Columba sharpened and blessed a stick of wood for the man and instructed him to use it to trap game, which it miraculously did, catching a stag, hind and other game (II 37; Sharpe 1995, 185–87). Almost equally miraculously we have a Pictish trap preserved in the archaeological record in the collections of the University of Aberdeen. The wooden trap from the Moss of Auquharney in Aberdeenshire was found under almost 3m of peat during peat cutting in the spring of 1921 (Figure 3.25). The body of the trap is made from the trunk of an alder tree and it had a movable trapdoor made from birch and a 'bow' made of willow. The trap was designed to catch the leg of a passing deer or other wild animal. Radiocarbon dating shows the trap dates to around 550–650 AD.

On Pictish symbol stones, wild animals do occasionally appear (Figure 3.26) – there are, for example, wolves or what could be hunting dogs on stones from Newbigging, near Dundee, Leslie, Aberdeenshire, and Ardross, Highland (Alcock 2003, 416); boars on stones from Dores and Knocknagael, Highland; and deer on stones from Dunachton, Ardross and Grantown (RCAHMS 2008, 74, 86). There is also an unusual depiction of a bear from a stone found in a wheelhouse at Old Scatness in Shetland

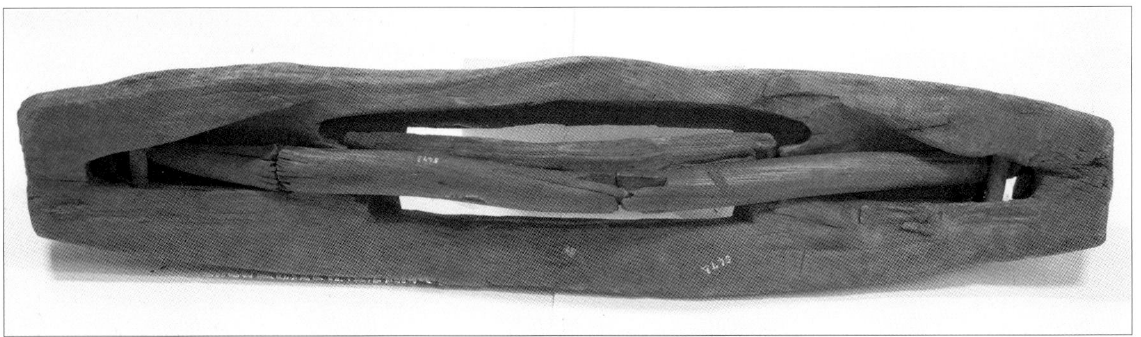

3.25 (*Top*) The Moss of Auquharney, Aberdeenshire, deer trap. The trap was designed to catch the foot of a deer and hold it in place inside its central chamber. © University of Aberdeen Museum Service)

3.26 (*Above*) Drawing of a small selection of wild animals shown on Pictish symbol stones: wild boar, wolf, stag and bear.

and, at the same site, a rudimentary but characterful depiction of a boar that was found used as a kerbstone of a hearth in another building (RCAHMS 2008, 234). Whether these animal carvings directly related to the prestige of hunting and status is uncertain – certainly it is unlikely that there were bears in Shetland by the first millennium AD but the accuracy of the representation suggests the artist may have seen a bear. It could have been a depiction of an animal encountered on a hunting trip to the Scottish mainland but we cannot rule out other meanings or inspirations for the portrayal – for example, that the bear was a general symbol for strength and power or that the image was copied from another object.

By the late first millennium AD, hunting certainly appears to have been an elite practice infused with the symbolism of rulership. Later traditions of Pictish sculpture regularly include hunt scenes on the back of cross-slabs. Animals associated with hunting are found on five times as many cross-slabs compared to symbol stones. It is a striking fact that this evidence for secular activity appears on monuments with crosses and other Christian symbolism, indicating a particularly close relationship between, and mutual acceptance of, the secular and ecclesiastical worlds – an acceptance that was generally rarely evident on sculpture in early medieval Britain and Ireland. On the later Pictish cross-slabs, we see stags, deer, what may be hares, boar and bears. There is no doubt about the status and role of the animals depicted – hunting dogs are shown pursuing magnificent stags, hunters lie in wait for their prey and very obvious depictions of elites on horseback are shown on the chase. While some of the hunt scenes may have had allegorical meanings, with potentially Christian messages and influences from Mediterranean, Continental art and ultimately Late Roman traditions (for example, Henderson and Henderson 2004, 125–29, 179; Clarke *et al.* 2012, 154–58), there can be little doubt that at least some of these scenes were based on a close depiction of contemporary hunts judging by the vibrancy, diversity and content of the scenes shown. The chase-style hunts are some of the most arresting and accomplished scenes carved on stone in early medieval Britain and Ireland. Chases of this nature would have required high levels of riding skill and the dogs would have undergone intensive training to be effective hunters. The dogs depicted appear to be lean dogs that pursued their quarry by keen senses and speed honed by selective breeding. The fierce hunting dogs are a clear marker of aristocratic power.

Different styles of hunting are also depicted. Hunting on foot with a spear is shown on the St Andrew's shrine and on cross-slabs at Nigg, Easter Ross, and Eassie, Angus. There are also depictions on four monuments – on cross-slabs at Shandwick, Easter Ross, Glenferness, Inverness-shire and St Vigeans, Angus, and on a lost architectural panel from Meigle, Perthshire – of individuals with crossbows and hooded shawls or cloaks – hunters clearly lying in wait to shoot boars or stags (Figure 3.27). As well as the horseback chase, there appear to be drive-style hunts where servants on foot drove game towards waiting mounted hunters who would then try to slay as many as they could. On Aberlemno 3 and Hilton of Cadboll, Easter Ross, we see two individuals standing near the mounted hunters blowing a long trumpet-like instrument (Colour Plate 15). Hunting horns like these would have been to scare game into the open, with different notes played to mark the progress of the hunt – to warn the hunters when game was in the open, when hounds should be untethered and when dogs should return to their owners. In the representations of the chase, we see groups of up to five riders, all of them well kitted out and resplendent on their rides, demonstrating this was a group activity likely to have been shared by a lord or king with their close retainers.

There are also depictions of hawking or falconry on Pictish-era stones – for example, on cross-slabs from Shandwick, Easter Ross; Fowlis Wester, Angus; Elgin, Moray; and on the St Andrew's shrine (Figure 3.27). Falconry appears to have become popular in the Late Antique period across Europe. In Anglo-Saxon England, there is a surviving 8th-century letter from King Ethelbert asking Bishop Boniface to send a pair of falcons from Frankia to Kent and the employment of hawkers by Anglo-Saxon kings is evidenced in 8th- and 9th-century charters, demonstrating that hawking was a common courtly activity in contemporary England (Oggins 2004, 38–39). In Pictland, the stones showing hawking – such as from Elgin and Shandwick – are likely to be 8th or early 9th century AD in date. Falconry and

3.27 Hunt scenes from Pictish cross-slabs:
(a) Nigg, Easter Ross – hunter on foot;
(b) St Vigeans, Angus – hunter with crossbow;
(c) Elgin, Moray – horse-rider with hawks.

hawking were particularly skilled hunting activities and were powerful symbols of intellect and mastery over nature (Goldberg 2020, 47, 151). In falconry, birds ascend and swoop on their prey, while hawks fly at lower altitudes and can hunt in more wooded terrain. Hunters using birds can go on foot or on horseback – on the Elgin and Fowlis Wester stones and the St Andrew's shrine, the hunter with a bird is shown on horseback while, on the Shandwick example, an individual on foot appears to hold a bird. Hawking and falconry targeted small mammals and birds, such as cranes, herons and ducks, and hares and squirrels. Bones of a goshawk were found in Phase 7–8 at Howe, Orkney, though whether this was a chance capture of a bird for consumption or a bird used in hawking is uncertain (Bramwell 1994, 155).

The regularity of the hunting scenes on Pictish cross-slabs makes it clear that hunting was a marker of elite activity and leadership in Pictland. Hunting was an activity that reinforced group identity and cooperation between a king and his nobles (Goldberg 2020, 89). On the Hilton of Cadboll stone, we also see a female rider showing that this elite activity also involved high-status women, perhaps a queen or high-born noble in this case (though see Clarke *et al.* 2012, 157–58) (Colour Plate 15). The use of hunting as a key emblem of kingship was very much following European trends – the 8th- and 9th-century depictions on Pictish-era stones are in the same chronological horizon as the rise to prominence of hunting as an expression of rulership in Frankia (Goldberg 2020; though see Clarke *et al.* 2012, 155–60, for alternative interpretations of the hunt scenes and the 'majestic riders'). Hunting may have been a prime activity for engaging other elites in events of hospitality and camaraderie. Some of the royal estates of Anglo-Saxon England were specifically placed to take advantage of prime hunting ground (Blair 2018, 106) – this could have been the case in Pictland too with early royal sites like Rhynie and later centres such as Dundurn located at the margins of the uplands. In events of hunting, elites would have been able to show off their bravery and skill. Hunting big game, wild boar in particular, was an inherently risky and dangerous activity that required a high level of weapons training and dexterity. The danger, skill and bravado involved in hunting meant that this was excellent experience for the battlefield. It was also a spectacle that could be observed by others as exciting events full of peril and jeopardy. The driving of animals towards the hunters or the soaring of a hawk or falcon to catch their prey would be events where elites could demonstrate their prowess and control of resources and indulge in activities that would enrapture the lords and allies that supported the incumbents of the current noble lineages.

Metalworking

In a non-monetary economy, the production, exchange and gifting of metalwork played an essential role in the early medieval economy and social structure in Pictland. The production and circulation of metalwork between a leader and his followers appears to have been another important means of cementing the relationships of hierarchy and subservience in the early medieval period – a king was the 'giver of rings' or the 'breaker of treasure' (Nicolay 2014, 6). The 'Law of the Innocents' of *c.*697, which was enforced in Pictland, stated (Márkus 2008, 21) that part of 'pledges' – objects handed over to guarantee the enforcement of legal cases or agreements (Kelly 1988, 164–67) – was to be in bronze or silver, indicating that metalwork could play a significant role in maintaining the peace. Many craftspeople themselves, particularly those who worked with precious metals and came from crafting families, were likely to have had a high status (Kelly 1988, 61–63; Heald 2010, 231; Clarke *et al.* 2012, 100; O'Sullivan *et al.* 2014, 215).

3.28 Drawing of images scratched into the whetstone from Portsoy, Aberdeenshire: (a) human head displayed on a sword or at base of a cross; (b) fish symbol; (c) tongs and crucible; (d) symbol; (e) human head.

Two carved stones from Pictland help to demonstrate the significance of metalworking. The first is the Portsoy whetstone which is a curious object, its rough and ready appearance perhaps belying its significance (Figure 3.28). The stone was found less than 5km from the major Pictish silver hoard from Gaulcross, Banffshire. The object is a small cylindrical stone of phyllite, carved with human heads on either end, one apparently displayed on the end of a sword, with carvings of a fish, crescents and tongs set between the heads. While not particularly finely made, the symbolism and form are redolent of power. A whetstone would be used for sharpening blades – though the Portsoy stone appears not to have been used in this way. Blades were the product of metalworking and were used in combat – the depiction of a human head pierced by a sword on the Portsoy stone is a reminder of the martial basis of power in the Pictish era. A more explicit reference to metalworking is the pair of tongs which appears to be plunging into a vessel of some kind, perhaps a bucket with water for quenching the hot metal objects grasped by the tongs.

A second carved stone that demonstrates the significance of metalworking is the Dunfallandy cross-slab from Perthshire (Figure 3.29). On the

3.29 The back of the cross-slab from Dunfallandy, Perthshire, showing two seated figures marked with symbols with a mounted figure 'labelled' with further symbols. Below are a hammer, anvil or crucible and tongs/pincers. (© Historic Environment Scotland)

back of the *c.*8th-century cross-slab is an elite figure on horseback, marked by two symbols (see Chapter 6). Below the rider are key mediums for underpinning rulership – the hammer, anvil and tongs that helped produce wealth. Tongs are also shown on other monuments such as the Pictish symbol stone from Abernethy. At Pictish power centres, metalworking production evidence is routinely found during excavation. At Clatchard Craig, the production evidence consisted of over 50 mould fragments, parts of tuyères (a clay nozzle through which air is forced into a furnace), a heating tray and a silver ingot, which were found in the upper citadel of the fort (Close-Brooks 1986, 145–46). In the lower citadel at Clatchard Craig, evidence for iron production was found and it would seem that the hierarchy of fort defences mirrored a hierarchy of production – fine metalworking in the upper citadel, blacksmithing in the lower fort enclosure. Intriguingly, the fine metalworking production at Clatchard Craig appears to pre-date the structure found in the upper citadel and perhaps dates to the construction of the defences. Was this an episode of production of fine brooches made for the clients who provided the labour to build the fort?

At the Rhynie Craw Stane complex, the focus of production appears to have been on elite markers of identity – handpins, brooches and other dress accessories. The exchange of these objects may have been a key means of signalling and reinforcing the social ties between a lord and his followers (Campbell 2007, 111). The presence of ingot moulds and the manufacturing evidence more generally show that the production, accumulation and use of wealth were important activities at this complex.

Hoards of metalwork are also occasionally found at sites in Pictland and these provide insights into the broad currency of metalwork objects in circulation. Two early Pictish hoards are known from Norrie's Law, Fife, and Gaulcross, Aberdeenshire (Figure 3.30). The Gaulcross hoard was discovered in 1838 at Ley Farm in a field that contained two stone circles of likely Bronze Age date. In 1837, the stone circles were ruthlessly removed in the agricultural improvement era. A hoard of silver was found during this process of destruction, seemingly in the ring cairn of one of the ancient stone circles (Stuart 1867, 74–75; Cramond 1887). A whole range of 'pins and brooches' was found but only three objects were retained from the original hoard. Research-led metal detecting in 2013 recovered more than 100 objects missed during the original discovery (Noble *et al.* 2016). The finds included Late Roman coins, fragments of pins and bracelets, the terminal of a large silver penannular brooch with twisted hoop band, a silver

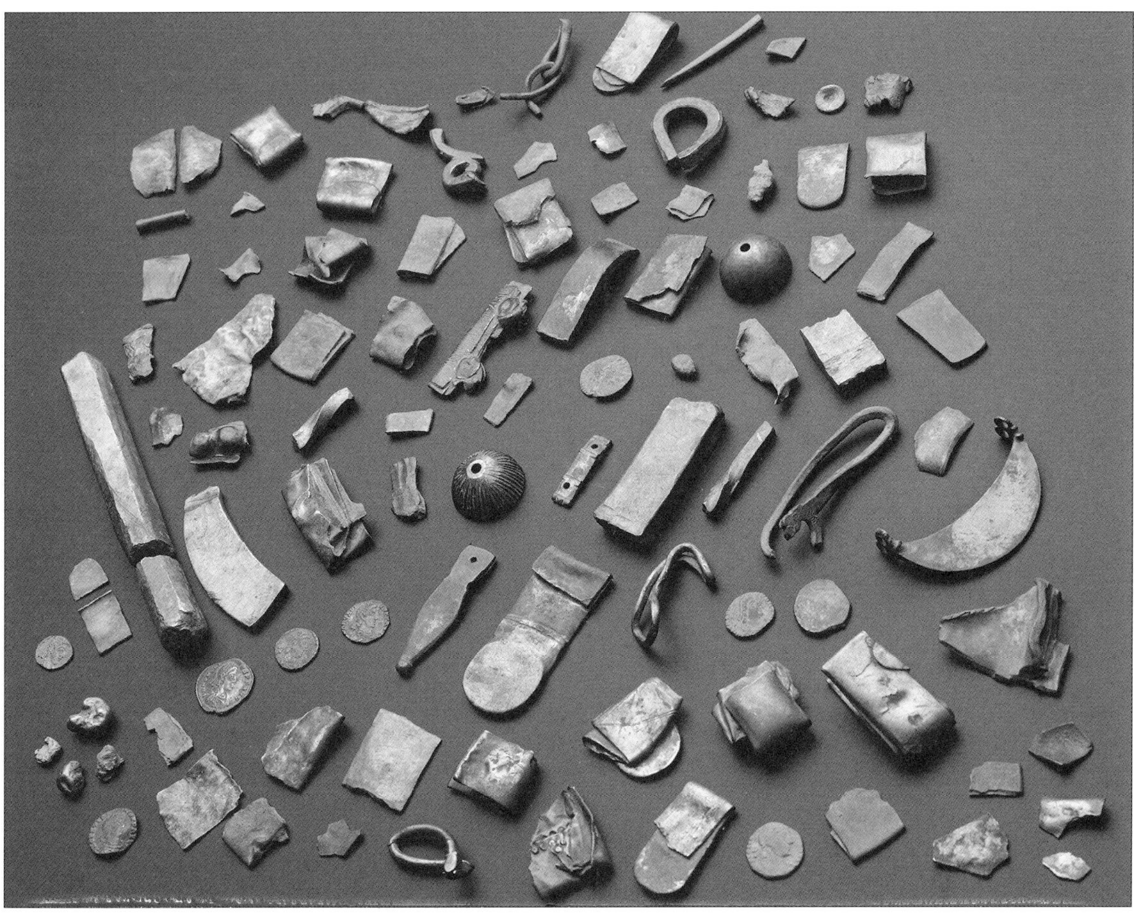

3.30 The Gaulcross hoard comprising Late Roman coins, military fittings, an ingot, bracelets and a whole host of objects in contemporary circulation in the 5th or 6th century AD. (© National Museums Scotland)

ingot, a lunate pendant, pieces of silver chain and two silver hemispheres (Figure 3.30).

The hoard from Norrie's Law, Fife, was found by a labourer digging for sand in 1819. Like Gaulcross, it was found in association with a prehistoric monument – in this case, at the base of a large prehistoric cairn. Over 12kg of silver is said to have been found but following its discovery much of it was immediately dispersed, sold and melted down (Graham-Campbell 1991). Around 170 pieces, mostly small fragments, have survived, but this represents only a small proportion of the original hoard. The surviving pieces include two hand-pins, a plaque decorated with Pictish symbols, two penannular brooches with twisted hoops, a complete spiral finger ring and fragments of others, chain fragments, decorated fittings and many fragments of bracelets. Roman coins, late 4th-century Roman siliquae, were also part of the original find (Goldberg and Blackwell 2013; Bland, Moorhead and Wilton 2013, 132).

Both the Gaulcross and Norrie's Law hoards may date to the 5th or 6th centuries AD (Noble *et al.* 2016). The earlier objects in these hoards have a Roman provenance and include fragments of vessels from Roman silver dining sets and objects with Late Roman military associations. It was the wealth of the Roman Empire that provided the source for the objects of status throughout the Pictish period with Roman silver melted down, diluted and recast over time until the Viking Age (Blackwell *et al.* 2017). The Roman objects may have originally come into native hands through looting, trade or bribes to local groups to keep the peace and perhaps even as military pay for those who went to serve in the Roman army (Hunter 2007a, b; Painter 2013, 230). In the post-Roman period, the silver was recycled and re-cast into high-status objects that underpinned the development of elite society. During the process of recycling, the Roman silver was remade into new objects but its origin may not have been entirely forgotten. Some of these later objects may have also directly referenced the Late Antique world, with items such as hand-pins showing the adaptation of Late Roman military styles both in terms of design and decorative techniques (Gavin 2013, 430; see also Youngs 2013, 415). Local symbols of power and status were also developed and deployed.

Why was this wealth hoarded, buried and never retrieved in the Pictish period? There could be fairly prosaic explanations behind their burial – perhaps they were the raw materials of a metalworker that were buried for safekeeping but never retrieved or perhaps they were the treasures of a powerful family (Collins 2013, 38; Painter 2013, 228; Rau 2013, 345). Certainly, items like silver hand-pins, bracelets and ingots found in the Gaulcross and Norrie's Law are uncommon finds – these were clearly high-status objects that would have belonged to some of the most powerful members or institutions of early medieval society (Youngs 2013, 421). Some hoards may never have been designed to be retrieved – these could have been sacrifices to the gods perhaps even a Christian god in a hybrid world of early Christianisation (see Chapter 4). It is interesting that both Norrie's Law and the Gaulcross hoards were buried next to ancient monuments – were these gifts to the past, to past lineages whose influence was being courted for future good fortune or simply locatable safe spots that had the bonus of being viewed as being protected by the ancestors? The appropriation of these ancient places may have been creative acts that aimed to link the society of the present directly with a deep ancestral past and places perhaps imbued with supernatural powers.

Power dressing

What we know about Pictish dress largely comes from what was carved on stones with the depictions of individuals likely to focus on the Pictish upper classes. We do not know much about the colours of clothes but it is likely that, as in Ireland, brighter coloured clothing was a marker of higher status, with purple clothing denoting a connection to royalty (Swift 2013, 21). In terms of types of clothing, thigh- to ankle-length tunics are shown on Pictish sculpture, some with elaborate hems, padding and other detailing. Hooded cloaks also appear on cross-slabs, though many of the cloak wearers may be clerics. A rare survival from the Pictish hillfort of Dundurn indicates the kind of leatherwork available to the Pictish elite (Alcock *et al.* 1989, 217, Illus. 16). This is a leather shoe fortuitously preserved in waterlogged layers at the fort (Colour Plate 12), made from one piece of leather and beautifully decorated with stamp designs all over the outer surface of it. A pair of shoes like this would have been an elite item of footwear, especially as replica versions suggest these were not the kind of shoes that could be worn for climbing hillforts – these were more like slippers (Hamish Findlay Lamley personal communication). These were for a high-status Pict at leisure time or for a person who could be borne up the hill by horse or cart.

In the archaeological record of Pictland, the most abundant power-dressing accessory was the penannular brooch. Brooches had been worn since the Iron Age, but became particularly common in areas beyond the frontier in the 3rd and 4th centuries AD (Kilbride-Jones 1980, 11; Youngs 1989a, 21; Blackwell *et al.* 2018, 108). The earlier forms of penannular brooches were thin bands of bronze or silver with zoomorphic (pseudo animal-ended) terminals, while later brooches had much larger flat panelled and highly decorated terminals and brooch pins. The skills of Pictish metal-workers were increasingly turned to producing beautiful and intricate metal-work objects that prominently displayed the wealth and connections of the wearer. Penannular brooches were found throughout Britain and Ireland with regional differences – an Irish law tract actually specifically refers to Pictish styles of brooches, calling these *catit* or *cartait* – a very rare survival of an actual Pictish word for an object or indeed a Pictish word of any form (Etchingham and Swift 2004, 38).

Penannular brooches were for fastening cloaks and other forms of dress – their use as cloak fasteners emulated Roman and latterly Byzantine styles (Whitfield 2004, 70). They were made up of two main parts, the brooch ring and the pin, and were fastened by the pin being pushed through a cloak and then the brooch ring swivelled so that the pin lay over the brooch ring, fastening it in place. In early medieval Ireland, brooches were worn by both sexes – men on the shoulder, women in the centre of the chest (Ó Floinn 1989, 89). In the earlier incarnation of the penannular brooch there may have been associations with the might of the Roman Empire and military success – in the 3rd to the 4th centuries AD, various forms of decorated brooch were used by the Romans to signal status and rank, particularly in the military (Whitfield 2004, 71, 73; Blackwell *et al.* 2017, 189). Individuals wearing brooches are shown on Pictish cross-slabs such as the mounted woman on the Hilton of Cadboll cross-slab who prominently displays a brooch on her chest and what may also be women on stones at Wester Denoon and Kirriemuir (RCAHMS 2008, 56, 62, 88). A brooch displayed on its own also appears to be depicted on the Brodie stone, Moray, located on the back of an impressive cross-slab between two fearsome fish monsters (RCAHMS 2008, 104).

Brooches were an enduring power symbol in Pictland and are found as single finds or within hoards from the Roman Iron Age to the 9th–10th centuries AD. Through time, some brooches became so large that they may have played specialised roles. The fanciest brooches could have played roles in inauguration as fasteners of regal cloaks, as dowries in marriage ceremonies or in ceremonial occasions such as major feasts and perhaps given as guarantees during pledges in bond making (Etchingham and Swift 2004, 33; Whitfield 2004, 96–99; Blackwell 2012, 15, 21–22; Grigg 2015, 68–72). Some may have also been relics held at major churches (Ó Floinn 1989, 89). The brooches, including designs such as the popular animal-headed terminals, perhaps gave protection (Blackwell 2012, 25). Whatever the case, we can see these brooches as important markers of individual status and identity with no two penannular brooches being the same.

Other elite dress accessories included hand-pins used for fastening cloaks and also perhaps used as hair accessories, as well as silver rings and bracelets as found in the Norrie's Law and Gaulcross hoards. The most spectacular status items, however, were undoubtedly silver chains (Colour Plate 16). Eleven silver chains are known – some from Pictland, in Aberdeenshire and Inverness-shire, but others cluster in areas such as the Lothians and the Borders – areas that are likely to have been part of the Brittonic kingdoms of southern Scotland. Despite this, the chains have often been termed Pictish due to the fact that two are decorated with Pictish symbols but it may simply be that the chains were of wider elite currency in early medieval Scotland. The chains are made up of pairs of solid silver loops with larger open-terminal rings used to fasten the chains. Each complete chain would have weighed several kilograms and used as much as eight times the silver as the fanciest of brooches (Blackwell *et al.* 2018, 95). They have been compared to later medieval regalia (Blackwell *et al.* 2018, 100) – they would certainly have been very uncomfortable and heavy to wear around the neck for any length of time. Two of the chains survive in what appears to be their original form and were too small to have been worn by adult men – if they were worn, they must have been by adolescents or women (Clarke *et al.* 2012, 185; Blackwell *et al.* 2018, 99). The chains could have also been used as diplomatic gifts, pledges or assurances or involved in processes such as hostaging or fostering (Clarke *et al.* 2012, 185). Some of the chains have similar silver compositions to Late Roman silver plate, suggesting that relatively pure Roman silver sources were used to create them. This fact, along with the use of enamelling has been used to suggest a relatively early date for the chains – perhaps 4th or 5th century AD (Blackwell *et al.* 2018, 102).

High-status feasting, drinking and gaming

Feasting and consumption is one further well-known way in which individuals and groups demonstrated power and influence in the Pictish period. Feasts occasion highly charged events of display which can be ritualised and imbued with socio-political, religious and economic dimensions (Mauss 2002, 49). In particular, events of feasting often involved very obvious displays of wealth and power (Russell 2012, 379). Feasting is also about forging bonds and a sense of group identity and it is these two strands that ensure feasting plays a central role in group formation, evolution and hierarchy (Enright 1996). During the Late Roman Iron Age in eastern Scotland, one important dimension of the Roman objects that circulated in native groups in Scotland was their association with feasting and drinking (Hunter 2007a). In the post-Roman period, feasting fulfilled the royal obligation of hospitality to a king's followers and brought an obligation to fight in the king's warband (Alcock 2003, 49). Consequently, great lengths were gone to in obtaining exotic foodstuffs and objects associated with feasting in a competitive system of hosting.

At centres of power, one diagnostic category of evidence that attests to the status of these places is access to Mediterranean and Continental objects (Campbell 2007). This included the importation of amphorae that held wine and oil, tableware and glass from the Mediterranean, and glass and pottery vessels and their contents from France. The focus of this trade was from the late 5th century to the 7th century AD. The best contextualised finds of imports in Pictland are from Rhynie. Here, around 90 sherds of amphorae from east Mediterranean sources have been found, representing at least four vessels – a small number but these were exceptionally rare exotic goods in this period (Campbell 2007, Table 19) (Figure 3.31). A sherd of tableware from North Africa has also been found, along with a handful of sherds of glass drinking vessels from the Mediterranean, western France and England. The number and range of imports suggest that Rhynie was a primary centre for redistribution in its region.

At Rhynie, Pictish rulers were drinking Mediterranean wine from fine glass drinking vessels of the kind described in the *Life of Columba*, II.33 (Sharpe 1995, 181), where an angel breaks the glass which the *magus*, Broichan, was holding in his hand for drinking while he was in the royal house of the Pictish king Bridei at his fortress by the River Ness. At the Craw Stane complex, the amphorae – principally their contents – and glass

3.31 Late Roman amphorae sherds from Rhynie. These unglamorous fragments give important clues about the character of activity at the Craw Stane complex, Rhynie. The amphorae vessels were probably for storing wine and came from the eastern Mediterranean.

vessels would have been precious objects. The feasting here was aimed at marking the supreme power of the hosts, the foodstuffs and objects at the feasts signifying the rarefied connections these individuals could secure to procure the fineries at the dinner table. Much smaller numbers of imports have been found elsewhere in Pictland – single sherds of 7th-century E ware from western France have been found at Dundurn, Craig Phadrig and Clatchard Craig and, more recently, sherds of E ware have been found at the King's Seat and East Lomond. These finds all occur at high-status defended settlements. From Atlantic Pictland, imported glass has been found at Brough of Birsay in Orkney and a single sherd of E ware has been identified from a dun at Dun Ardtreck on Skye (Campbell 2007, Table 19).

At feasting events, the telling of legends, the reciting of poems and tales and music may well have featured. Musical instruments are shown on Pictish cross-slabs such as on Lethendy, Perthshire, where figures playing a harp and pipes are shown, along with a drum in the background. However, whether this scene was based on contemporary Pictland, biblical imagery or copied from imported artefacts such as caskets or manuscripts is not certain, though the harp at least had become a popular instrument in Scotland by the late medieval period (Buckley 2005, 761–62, 769; Bannerman 2016). Game playing may have been an important part of major gatherings with shows of strength, horse racing and board gaming all possible entertainments for elites. Gaming appears to have been introduced to Britain in the Roman period (Hall and Forsyth 2011, 1326). In north-east Scotland, imported Romano-British glass gaming pieces have been found in a 2nd–3rd century AD grave at Tarland, Aberdeenshire (Hall 2007, 7). In the early medieval period, gaming objects are found throughout Pictland with gaming boards known from Buckquoy and Red Craig, Orkney, and gaming pieces from sites such as Scalloway in Shetland, Clatchard Craig in Fife, and Broch of Burrian, Orkney (Hall 2007,

Appendix). While probably not entirely restricted to elites, gaming was certainly part of elite culture and may have been an important part of learning strategy and a competitive test of intelligence for high-status adolescents and young adults (Hall 2007, 2, 28).

Conclusions

Until recently, Pictland was considered something of a material culture backwater, without considerable wealth or substantial settlements and centres, when compared to the rest of Britain. A decline in Roman objects and a reduction in other discovered remains found in Pictland from the 3rd century AD onwards (Hunter 2007a), combined with the end of Roman Britain and the lack of textual sources, until the late 6th century, led scholars to assume that the society was relatively poor and small scale until the rise of Fortriu in the late 7th century. In recent decades, the vibrancy of the later Pictish society, embodied in sculpture and metalwork and the power of the Pictish over-kingdom created by Fortriu, has been stressed. Moreover, the connections with neighbouring societies, including engagement with broader Christian and ancient models and concepts, in the period from the 7th to the 9th century, has rightly been highlighted. However, recent archaeological work is showing that this was not a sudden transformation but rather was a development from foundations established in the Late Roman Iron Age.

It is now clear that there were concentrations of wealth and power in Pictland before 600, as shown by sites like Burghead, Rhynie and Tap o' Noth. The appearance of Roman and Mediterranean imports at such locations and at smaller centres like Dunnicaer shows that the groups at these sites were part of long-reaching networks of communication and trade. The Picts at these centres were also manufacturing their own high-status objects, using wealth to redistribute, reinforce and enhance power structures. Some of the wealth of the Roman-era elite sites would have been derived from their hinterlands but, as with Scandinavia, it is possible – but still largely a theory to be tested further – that the presence of the nearby Roman Empire was an important factor in the Late Roman Iron Age. Trade and diplomatic relations with Roman Britain, mediated through the Roman army, may have played significant roles but the direct seizure of Roman goods and people through raiding could have been highly lucrative for the Picts. These expeditions may also have allowed some rulers and polities to build up substantial power bases at the expense of others, in an increasingly militaristic society. It can be speculated that the occupation of many fortifications in the 5th and 6th centuries was also partly a result of the instability and competition between members of the elite combined with the availability of greater resources as the spoils of Empire filtered into native hands.

It is uncertain whether there was a general reduction in trade and prosperity in Pictland after the 5th century to correspond with the wider economic contraction of the period around the Mediterranean and in Continental Europe (McCormick 2001). Certainly, sites like Rhynie and Tap o' Noth fell out of use but this did not happen till the 6th century and others, like Burghead, were created in the 6th century. In the 7th century, a new phase of fort construction began with the 'nuclear' citadel centres becoming key power centres, their similarity in form to Gaelic and British examples from northern Britain reflecting shared ideas of power, as well as political rivalries in the wider region.

The defeat of the Northumbrians by the kingdom of Fortriu at the Battle of Nechtanesmere in AD 685 ultimately seems to have resulted in – or continued – a further change in elite culture. While feasting, hunting and the distribution of precious metalwork, such as penannular brooches, continued to be features of elite society, the creation of a powerful, overarching kingdom of the Picts north of the Forth shifted the residences of the elite away from fortifications to some extent, to lower, more connected locations, such as Forteviot, partly inspired by English, Continental and Imperial models (Campbell and Driscoll 2020, 95, 168, 199). In addition, a new major element came to the fore, a more established, institutional and wealthy Christianity, which transformed society in multiple ways, to be discussed in the next chapter. One notable aspect of that Christian culture, which is very helpful to us, is the frequent depiction on sculpture of Pictish elite lay as well as clerical society, providing a fascinating window into Pictish ideals and practices.

Christianity was flexible enough not only to challenge but also to support secular ideals. For instance, the *Life of Columba*, I.37 (Sharpe 1995, 141), states that Psalm 44 (45 in the King James Bible) was sung by Columba and his monks outside of the fort of King Bridei, supposedly striking fear into the Picts, but much of the psalm is actually a statement glorifying kings while commenting on how they should rule (Grigg 2015, 111–13; Márkus 2017, 251–52). Its references to palaces, lavish clothes, to the success of the kingdom and to subjects praising the king, if he were Christian, would have appealed to Pictish rulers. Moreover, as this chapter has shown, lines, such as 'And in thy majesty ride prosperously because of truth and meekness and righteousness; and thy right hand shall teach thee terrible things', can be related to important facets of Pictish rule – the centrality of warfare, ensuring peace, maintaining control for prosperity; the importance of horses for hunting, warfare and travel; the significance of grandeur, in clothing, metalwork and bearing; and elite residences as emblems of success. Therefore, while there was significant change in the nature and display of power, there were also fundamental continuities in elite Pictish culture over centuries.

CHAPTER FOUR

'The Book of Life'

From Pagan Magi *to Early Medieval Saints*

Introduction

A major impact on all the societies of early medieval Britain and Ireland was caused by the adoption and consolidation of a new faith – Christianity. The practices of Christianity will have replaced those of an equally vibrant pre-existing belief system but the character of these pre-Christian world-views is difficult to reconstruct given how little detail of the pagan past was recorded in contemporary narratives. The adoption of Christianity would have certainly brought huge changes to Pictland. Connections to neighbouring polities – most notably the Gaelic west – and other areas of Europe would have become stronger through international Christian networks. Literacy and the use of Latin would have become more widespread and supporting the Church could have had significant implications for the redistribution of land and resources within a polity. Directly or indirectly, the Church also had an impact on society that extended far beyond matters of faith, affecting law, social customs, trade and kingship, as well as the movement of people and ideas.

There has perhaps been a tendency to downplay the impact of Christianity in Pictland, to regard Christianisation as quite a late development (for example, Hughes 1970; Carver 2016, 315–16). This has perhaps arisen due to the traditional paucity of evidence for the early Church in Pictland including a lack of identifiable early Christian church buildings and enclosures, as well as the dearth of historical information on the progress of conversion in Pictland. Nonetheless, we have perhaps underestimated the rapidity, extent and date of the adoption of Christianity among the Picts. Now, new multi- and inter-disciplinary perspectives are beginning to provide more robust pathways to understanding – from a greater appreciation of the roles that early Christian sculpture played in the practices of faith, to new archaeological information on the dating and character of early churches and enclosures, to studies of place-names and saints' dedications. Considering new information and previous knowledge in fresh ways is beginning to help us to understand the spread of Christianity in

Pictland more fully and to identify tentatively elements of pre-Christian religious practice.

Pre-Christian belief in northern Pictland

What came before Christianity in Pictland and how long did non-Christian practices endure after the initial conversions? It is tempting to look at the pantheon of Celtic gods and mythologies to reconstruct some elements of pre-Christian faith in Pictland but this can create generic and seemingly timeless narratives with little specificity for the region in question (Goldberg 2015, 212). In a general sense, it seems likely that belief in the pre-Christian period would have had a vernacular character – practised in the home and often locally and regionally specific with no book-based religion to dictate its character and use. Religion was lived with rituals and beliefs flowing from the everyday. There would have been beliefs and tales designed to explain the world around and there would have presumably been seasonal festivals and general practices that would have been shared. Some of these may have had a very practical basis (Williams 2003), focussed on the agricultural calendar, involving rites and practices designed to bring good fortune. These would have related to the necessities and routines of life – for example, food production, birth, death, marriage, procreation and rites of passage such as the taking of arms, along with ever-present conditions that framed the everyday such as the weather, aspects of the landscape, the sun and the moon. Rites that framed and justified social institutions and concepts regarding kindreds, kingships and hierarchies, as well as age and gender relations, are likely to have been other prominent elements of a pagan worldview.

In the late first millennium BC and earlier first millennium AD, classical writers, such as Caesar and Tacitus, provide hints of the potential structure and form of religion in northern Europe in a pre-Christian context. Religious specialists are referred to for areas further south such as Gaul, southern England and Wales, but the sources give little and at times conflicting detail (Fitzpatrick 2007, 290). According to classical writers such as Caesar, religious specialists with labels like 'druids' and 'seers' operated in these areas (Rankin 1987, 259–94). These figures met in sacred groves or other natural places and their importance was such that they were considered to belong to the elite class, often acting as intermediaries between rulers and the supernatural (Armit 2016, 103). Indeed, Gildas, writing in the first half of the 6th century, stated that, in the past, people in Britain 'heaped divine honours on mountains, hills, and rivers' but that they are 'now useful for human needs' (Winterbottom 1978, 17), indicating that their sacred dimension had restricted their exploitation.

In early Irish texts, there are also references to *druí*, 'druid', and *fili*, 'poet', which also has an etymology from an earlier word connoting seeing things or visions, indicating a likely ritual origin for this role, before the *fili* became Christianised and lost its more pagan elements (Kelly 1988, 43–49, 59–61; Charles-Edwards 2000, 189–99). Other figures, like the *gobae*, blacksmith, were associated with the supernatural (Carey 2019). Thus, there is evidence for pagan religious specialists in contemporary Ireland, though sacred attributes were perhaps attached more broadly to higher status individuals – lords, clerics, poets and perhaps some others – who constituted a *nemed* class (Kelly 1988, 9–10). *Nemed* is cognate with ancient Celtic *nemeton*, a term for a sacred site which appears in a place-name in northern Britain – *Medio Nemeton*, 'Middle *Nemeton*' – in the *Ravenna Cosmography*, an 8th-century or later text which used Roman sources (Rivet and Smith 1979, 185, 211). It is likely that the term *nemed* originally denoted those with access to the divine. Overall, the varied attributes and diversity of figures with a religious dimension in Ireland in the pre-Christian period is clear and, although there are difficulties in working back from later Christian evidence, the connections between status and the sacred are apparent.

For the Picts, some references to pagan belief are mentioned in Adomnán's *Life of Columba* but we have to remember that Adomnán was writing in a late 7th-century Christian milieu for a Christian audience which would have embraced tales of the inferiority of the pagan faith and the superior power of saints. Nevertheless, there may be echoes of truth in some of the depictions – and, in relation to the Picts, the *Life* was written *c.*697 AD – just over a century after some of the events portrayed. In these accounts, pagans are depicted as believing in multiple gods and spirits (II.11, II.32; cf. Sharpe 1995, 162, 179, 322–23). These gods and spirits could clearly be found to reside in a variety of locations such as wells and other landscape features. References to pagan holy wells are made but Columba blessed examples of these – it is clear that it was acceptable in early Christian practice for wells to continue to be venerated (Sharpe 1995, 323). In one encounter in Pictland, Columba went to a well that was 'worshipped as a god because the devil clouded their sense' (II.11). The water was thought to be poisonous and evil but Columba and his companions drank from the well and, from thenceforth, the water was a source of healing.

Deities were also associated with rivers. The two largest Aberdeenshire rivers, the Don and Dee, both appear in Ptolemy's *Geography*, written in the mid 2nd century AD, as *Dēoúana*, 'quintessentially divine one (female)', and *Dēoúa*, 'goddess', respectively, the use of the underlying ancient Indo-European divinity word for river names being 'a diagnostically Celtic cultural phenomenon' (Isaac 2005, 191–92). A later example may be found in the *Life of St Columba*, where a poor man in Lochaber put a stake in a river that Adomnán says 'in Latin may be called *Nigra Dea*', 'black goddess', probably the River Lochy (II.37; Anderson and Anderson 1991, 150–51). It is uncertain whether Adomnán was right to interpret the name *Loch dae* as '(shiny) black' plus 'goddess' (King 2005) but, given that in Gaelic *dae* could have meant a male 'god', it is perhaps significant that Adomnán clearly regarded it as plausible that a river in the Great Glen could be considered specifically not just divine but female.

In the *Life*, Columba has numerous encounters with pagan *magi* (II 33; Sharpe 1995, 334), designed to show the superiority of Christianity to paganism. However, given that there is contemporary evidence for the *druí* in Ireland and that Adomnán himself mentions a sorcerer and belief in witchcraft in Dál Riata (I.47, II.17; Sharpe 1995, 149, 167), the presence of such figures with perceived supernatural connections or powers at pagan Pictish as well as Gaelic royal courts would have been plausible to his readers (II.34; Sharpe 1995, 182–84). Columba battles with King Bridei's *magus* Broichan, who claims to be able to control the weather, in this case the wind and the mist. The pagan *magi* are of course depicted in a less than glowing light, painted as being malicious, taunting, controlled by the 'art of the devils' and the depictions are keen to show up the weakness of pagan gods in relation to the Christian God.

The archaeological record will often struggle to attest to the kind of practices and places of worship that are recorded by classical and early Christian writers – sacred groves, sacred wells or indeed the ability to control the weather and seasons are likely to leave little in the way of tangible traces for archaeologists to find! Some natural places do have potential for preserving evidence of pagan practices. Caves, for example, appear to have been important in the late Iron Age and early medieval periods. In the next chapter, we will see the role that caves appear to have had in relation to the transformation of the living and the dead – the scene of brutal and violent executions at the Sculptor's and Rosemarkie caves, for example (Figure 4.1) (see Chapter 5). That these were appropriate places for such acts may well have drawn on the specialness of these locations in a pagan – and perhaps even a Christian – context. Moreover, Sculptor's Cave, Covesea, in Moray, and the Wemyss Caves, in Fife, were decorated with Pictish symbols that may suggest that these were special places (Armit and Büster 2020, 259–60). The Sculptor's Cave was marked in distinct ways, including the deposition of Late Roman material, perhaps accompanying the bodies of the dead (see Chapter 5). At Rosemarkie, the violently killed Rosemarkie Man was buried next to food offerings and the cave was used for metalworking, itself a ritualised and almost magical process (Heald 2011, 231; Clarke *et al.* 2012, 100). Human remains in the form of 'bits' of the skeleton clearly had an active role in belief too. Armit and Ginn (2007) have shown that the deposition of human remains within settlement

4.1 Rosemarkie Cave, findspot of Rosemarkie Man – was this a ritualised space in the 5th to 6th centuries in northern Pictland? (© Rosemarkie Caves Project)

contexts continued in the Northern and Western Isles at least into the later first millennium AD, marking the foundation and perhaps cessation of settlements and phases of activity (Armit and Ginn 2007, 116). These acts may have conveyed the power of the ancestors or materialised the strength of a particular social group or demographic – for example, warriors. Most of the examples come from Atlantic Pictland due to the greater number of settlements excavated and the better bone survival. They include a skull fragment found in the drain of a building at Dùn Mhùlan (Dun Vulan) that has been interpreted as a foundation deposit for the structure (Parker Pearson and Sharples 1999, 137). At Buckquoy, a burial of a newborn infant was found in the north-east corner of one of the rectangular dwellings of probable 8th-century date (Ritchie 1977, 188). This could have been an expedient burial after a tragic event but the location appears very targeted and may represent the customary practices of an everyday folk belief that such remains could perhaps bring better luck to the community in the future, that the dead child had to be kept close to the family or perhaps that this burial marked important lifecycle events of the building and community that dwelt within (O'Sullivan *et al.* 2014, 98).

4.2 Metalworking tongs as found during excavation at Rhynie, placed in the deliberately backfilled posthole of the abandoned elite centre. See Figure 1.23 for the conserved tongs.

Offerings of animal bone are also found at sites too. At Rhynie, two postholes of the outer wooden palisade setting were deliberately backfilled with animal bone and, in one case, a pair of metalworking tongs was thrust into the upper fill of the removed post, accompanying the deposits of bone (Noble *et al.* 2019c, 77) (Figure 4.2). This appears to have been part of a ritualised closure of this elite centre around the middle of the 6th century AD. This could have been part of a structured and careful ending of an important pagan site in the face of a changing world – the abandonment of this centre broadly coincides with likely missionary and conversion activity in northern Pictland (Noble *et al.* 2019c, 83).

As highlighted above, one element of pagan practice may have been an interest in springs, wells and other water sources. Some Pictish forts had elaborate wells that seem to go beyond the practical needs for a water source. The well at Burghead, for example, is an incredibly complex feature. It has been interpreted as everything from a pagan water shrine or a place for ritualised drownings to a site for Christian baptism (Ritchie 1989, 15; Laing and Laing 1993, 23; Foster 2014, 44; Carver 1999, 30; Alcock 2003, 197; Oram 2007, 251–52). The well at Mither Tap too was a very elaborate affair with steps down to the well basin (Colour Plate 17). While these may have had ritualised roles, perhaps during seasonal festivals, the very practical function that these wells had in sustaining the community would have also entailed its central role in everyday life and cosmology (Bell 1992).

As well as natural features, were there also constructed spaces for pagan belief and ritual – an architecture of pre-Christian belief? Anna Ritchie was the first archaeologist to explore this, highlighting the presence of some unusual structures in first millennium AD settlements in Atlantic Pictland

(Ritchie 2003). These include a small circular structure (F13), around 2.1m in diameter at Skaill, Orkney, that had a cattle skull and other animal bones within it. This had been interpreted by the compiler of the report on Skaill (Buteux 1997, 48) as a 'shrine representing in miniature the house of the ancestors', his interpretation drawing on its unusual circular rather than cellular form. Another potential example was located at Scalloway, Shetland, where the final phase of occupation comprised a poorly made sub-square room in the broch, within the wall of which was found a human skull. This building appears to have been abandoned prior to the 8th century, with two cow legs placed as a closing deposit (Sharples 1998, 50).

At Pictish cemeteries in southern and northern Pictland, a series of large square enclosures have been interpreted as possible cult foci (Campbell *et al.* 2019, 90–91; Campbell and Driscoll 2020, 66), around which cemeteries grew (see also Chapter 5 and Blair 1995 for a discussion of square enclosures at Anglo-Saxon cemeteries). It is also possible that some of the buildings at elite centres, particularly in the earlier part of the first millennium AD, may have been the focus of pagan practices and belief – the horseshoe-shaped building at Rhynie found next to the Craw Stane is one potential example. Nonetheless, there are ambiguities about all these sites and their features and functions are potentially open to other interpretations.

Objects may have also been the focus of pagan beliefs. Bede wrote that people in times of plague would 'forget the sacred mysteries of the faith' and return to the use of idols and amulets (*HE* IV 27). One curious find type from Atlantic Pictland is painted pebbles (Colour Plate 18). Around 50 of these have been found on Iron Age and Pictish sites in the Northern Isles – they consist of white quartzite pebbles that have dots and curvilinear designs painted on the surface of the stone using soot (Brown and Reay 2015, 377–83). They have been interpreted as charm stones (Ritchie 1972, 299).

The use of a presumably quartz stone in healing is recorded in the *Life of Columba* – albeit, in this case, in a Christian context. Adomnán wrote that a small white stone taken from the River Ness was blessed by the saint and could then float in water which, when drunk, was used for healing by the pagan Pictish king Bridei (II 33; Sharpe 1995, 181–82). However, whenever a person was meant to die, the stone could not, miraculously, be found – as happened, in the end, to Bridei. It is highly unusual in hagiography for a blessed Christian object to work among pagans, even after the initial miracle, so this episode could reflect real cult practice relating to Columba (Sneddon 2018, 237–40). However, the idea of a disappearing – and presumably reappearing – object, combined with the pagan use of the pebble, make it likely that the tale supports various popular beliefs relating to such stones, but transformed them so that they supported the pre-eminence of Christianity over paganism.

Overall, there is, as yet, no neat package of material evidence that we can highlight to identify pagan objects or structures. It is clear that, prior to the wholesale adoption of Christianity, the material world of the Picts would have been constructed through the lens of a non-Christian ideology and, thus, the design of all material culture and architecture was influenced by a very different outlook. Identifying 'pagan shrines' or structures may continue to be difficult as non-book-based religions are unlikely to have the same formality of practices as that enshrined in the doctrines of the increasingly organised international structure of the Church, nor were their form and existence recorded in written sources. As ritual is likely to have been vernacular in character, the everyday world of the home and domestic life is perhaps one good place to start looking for indicators of the pre-Christian worldview.

One other important avenue for examining potential pagan practices and imagery is the rich corpus of stone sculpture from Pictland. At Burghead, only six bull carvings survive from the 19th-century find of 25–30 examples but their number and character have supplied a rich vein for interpreting their significance and the role of the fort (Oram 2007, 250). Foster (2014, 51) suggested the carvings represented elements of a pagan fertility cult, but they could be regarded more broadly as ritualised symbols of power and authority at a key fortified settlement of Pictland. The carving of a bull has also been found at East Lomond fort in Fife (RCAHMS 2008, 66), and similar carvings have also been discovered within the city boundary of Inverness, tentatively suggesting a possible cult and power centre located near the mouth of the River Ness (RCAHMS 2008, 84) (Figure 4.3).

Unusual carved stones at other sites can also perhaps give us insights into the character of pre-Christian belief. At Rhynie, the carving of the Rhynie Man has been linked with pagan animal sacrifice and the figure itself with pagan deities (Noble *et al.* 2013, 1147). The Rhynie Man carries an axe, with a very distinctive double-ended blade and extremely thin shaft. Its morphology is similar to the axe found in the Sutton Hoo Mound 1 ship burial (dated to the 7th century), which has been interpreted as an implement for sacrificing cattle (Dobat 2006). Dobat highlights comparative imagery and textual associations that suggest strong links between cattle, animal sacrifice and a cultic ritual role that supported the status and position of early Germanic kings and chieftains (Dobat 2006, 889; see also Henderson and Henderson 2004, 102). The abnormal facial features of the Rhynie Man may have intentionally created a 'shocking visage' designed to convey the otherworldly aspects of the figure and his actions (Aldhouse-Green 2004, 182). Indeed, a shamanic or mythological quality or role has been linked to other depictions of figures with exaggerated features or part-human, part-animal figures, such as the one at Mail and the two at Papil, both from Shetland (Turner 1994; Ritchie 2003, 4; Kilpatrick 2011)

4.3 The carving of a bullock from Inverness. (© Historic Environment Scotland)

(Colour Plate 19). It is hard to escape the conclusion that these were powerful figures in the pre-Christian ideology of northern Pictland and that they were depicted in the acts or preparation of rites associated with those ideological beliefs – though see discussion below. In other contexts, perhaps the Rhynie Man and the depiction of bulls at sites like Burghead referred to practices of sacrifice carried out at these elite centres. Given the evidence for feasting at elite centres (see Chapter 3), the sacrifices may have been conducted as part of feasts held during important social occasions. The bulls and the axe of Rhynie Man may therefore have symbolised the ruler's power, as well as possibly a connection with gods or mythologies. Potential parallels for such practices and symbolism can be found across early medieval Britain – Bede, in his *Ecclesiastical History* (*HE*), refers to the English pagan practice of sacrificing 'many oxen to devils' (*HE* I.30; Ritchie 2003, 3). Similarly, early medieval evidence for poleaxed bulls and cattle has been found at Irish royal sites, such as Lagore and Moynagh Lough, both County Meath (Hencken 1950; Bradley 2011). Could some of the Pictish symbol stones also have been direct conduits for pagan religion? Bede refers to gods made by people from wood or stone (*HE* III.22; Colgrave and Mynors 1969, 280–83), which would suggest that stone or wooden objects could themselves be seen as deities rather than merely symbolising or reflecting belief.

As in the Iron Age, we can consider the reuse of ancient sites as specialised locations for ritual practice as another potentially important dimension of belief – both in a pre-Christian setting and continuing in a Christian context (Hingley 1996). In southern Pictland, such appropriation was highlighted in the 1990s with Driscoll's work on Forteviot and Scone (for example, Driscoll 1998b, 2011) and this has been augmented by the new work at Forteviot through the University of Glasgow Strathearn Environs and Royal Forteviot (SERF) project (Campbell and Driscoll 2020). During excavations at the extensive prehistoric monument complex at Forteviot, numerous examples of early medieval interventions in the ancient sites were found (Campbell and Driscoll 2020, 91–93). This included the deposition of burnt material in Bronze Age cists and in the hollows of the postholes of a massive Late Neolithic timber enclosure. Giant pits had also been dug in the centre of at least two of the henge monuments (Campbell and Driscoll 2020, 82). A pit with cremated human remains was also found and dated to between the 7th and 9th centuries AD, a very late example of cremation. While much of this activity post-dated the 7th century and is unlikely to have been 'pagan' per se, it is suggestive of activity and perhaps ritualised activity that harked back to long-standing and traditional practices. The excavators have suggested that these activities could have been part of fire rituals to mark seasonal events such as harvest festivals (Campbell *et al.* 25–26) or funerary rituals (Campbell and Driscoll 2020, 92). The digging of giant pits in ancient monuments is harder to interpret – was this part of a search for relics or ritually charged ancient materials that could be reused in the funerary or kingship rituals at a major royal centre? Elsewhere in Pictland, early medieval interventions have also been found within other examples of prehistoric monuments. In Atlantic Pictland, a pit containing charred barley and a range of plant species, similar to many of the pits at Forteviot, was found at the centre of the Stones of Stenness, Orkney (Ritchie 1976, 44). This particular example dates to some time during the 5th to the 8th centuries AD. From Inverness-shire there are also mid- to late-first-millennium dates from a spread of charcoal and cremated bone associated with the central ring cairn of the Bronze Age cemetery of Balnuaran of Clava (Bradley 2000, 115). All of these events speak of an interest in the past that perhaps gives glimpses of the continuation or reassertion of everyday beliefs in the power of the landscape and the ancestors, even in the face of a fully Christian or Christianising context.

Early Christianity

The adoption of Christianity ultimately entailed a transformation of belief and culture, since the new religion involved accepting the teachings of the Bible, rendering Pictland ever more integrated into the wider world of

Christendom stretching to Africa and Asia. In the opinion of clerics like Adomnán embedded in this literate milieu, good Christians joined others who had gained salvation – a concept perhaps unknown in pagan times – whereas those who erred, like Feradach who, according to the *Life of Columba*, ordered the murder of the Pictish noble Taran, were excised from 'the Book of Life', not just killed by God for betraying St Columba but also carried off to hell (*VSC* II.23; Sharpe 1995, 172–73). The Bible was a heavenly publication but also had great power on Earth, its power enacted through saints, clerics and adherent Christians.

The conversion of the Picts has traditionally centred around two saints – Ninian and Columba. Bede records that Columba, an Irish saint of the late 6th century, had converted the northern Picts and that, at a much earlier date, St Ninian Christianised the southern Picts. Regarding Atlantic Pictland, in the *Life of Columba*, Orkney is mentioned as a destination for a certain Cormac who appears to have been seeking a place of retreat, though he returned to Iona several months after setting out (I.6, II.42; Sharpe 1995, 118, 196–98) – whether there was already a Church presence in the Northern Isles is uncertain but it may be that Cormac's journey was amongst the first journeys of Christians to the far north.

Ninian, as recorded by Bede, is often identified as 'the Apostle of the Southern Picts'. Bede says that Ninian was a Briton who trained in Rome and established an episcopal see at Whithorn in south-west Scotland, traditionally in the early 5th century. Dedications to St Ninian are indeed found throughout Scotland, most dating to the 12th century or later, when his cult became very popular. Clancy (2001), however, has made the case that Ninian was, in fact, Uinniau (St Finnian), with the attribution to Ninian deriving from scribal copying errors. We do not know for certain that Ninian was Uinniau but, if he was, the cult of Uinniau is confined to places like Kilwinning in south-west Scotland. His activity in Pictland may reflect later ideas or Northumbrian claims once they had conquered Galloway and taken over Whithorn. It is possible that there was an earlier foundation at Whithorn (Fraser 2009a, 88–90) since a Christian presence at Whithorn in the 5th century is attested by the Latinus stone. This is an 'unambiguously Christian' inscribed funerary monument of 5th century date displaying influence from the Late Roman and sub-Roman Church (Forsyth 2005, 115–17; Fraser 2009a, 88). A small number of similar stones can be found across southern Scotland, all south of the Forth (Forsyth 2005).

There is evidence that Christianity may have diffused to parts of Pictland from the Irish Sea area. St Patrick's letter to the soldiers of Coroticus (Hood 1978, 55–59) shows that Picts were buying Christian slaves seized in Ireland from the Christian leader Coroticus. This indicates some of the avenues by which that religion could have spread in Pictish society, especially as one of the key aims of missionaries, such as Palladius and Patrick, was to administer the faith to communities with Christians (Evans 2022, 316–17). In the same letter, Patrick refers to '*apostatae Picti*' (Hood 1978, 37, 58), implying that some Picts had experience of Christianity, though some had perhaps abandoned their faith – or, at least in the eyes of Patrick, they had (Fraser 2009a, 111–12). Overall, it does seem likely that there was Christianity in at least parts of Pictland in the 5th century, presumably more in southern Pictland than further north (Evans 2022, 317–18). While Bede's account may not be right in its specifics, he may have been broadly correct to state that the southern Picts received Christianity 'a long time before' the north, with the roots of this lying in contact with Romanised areas to the south and west.

In northern Pictland, following Bede, the Christian narrative has focussed on Columba. Columba, a member of the powerful Uí Néill dynasty of Ireland, came to western Scotland to establish a monastery on Iona in AD 563 which became a major centre of monastic life, devotion, learning and artistic excellence – one of the most influential Church sites of early medieval Britain and Ireland. Columban influence was far reaching, playing an important role in the conversion and the organisation of the Church among the Northumbrians as well as being a key influence in Pictland and Dál Riata. However, while Columba is credited by Bede (*HE*, III.3–4) with converting the northern Picts and Adomnán stated that the saint founded many Pictish monasteries (II.45), the process is likely to have been much more complex and drawn out than is perhaps credited (Clancy 2008a, 363; Fraser 2009a, 68–115).

The most complete analysis of the development of the influence of Columba and Iona has been provided by James Fraser (2009a), who has convincingly argued against focussing on the influence of Iona to the exclusion of other ecclesiastical establishments in the 7th century, while still recognising that it held a significant position. However, there are problems with some aspects of his depiction, in which he argues for a late-7th-century rise in Iona's fortunes, culminating in the monastery holding a dominating position in the Pictish Church from about 698, until the Easter and tonsure reforms of 716–17 prompted its demotion. One issue is whether Iona was ever the head of the Pictish Church. Iona was clearly influential, as is indicated by Adomnán's success with ensuring that the 'Law of the Innocents' of *c.*697 applied to Pictland, and the activities in the years following of Bishop Coeti and other Ionan clerics in Atholl and Fife. However, the only evidence for Iona's supremacy over the Pictish Church comes from Bede's statement written in 731 that Iona had, for a long time, controlled all the monasteries of Pictland, along with nearly all those of the northern Gaels, and supervised the general population (*HE* III.3; Colgrave and Mynors 1969, 220–21). If, as Fraser suggests (2009, 100), that idea came from a Columban source, it may represent wishful thinking or a dubious claim.

However, alternatively, it may reflect the viewpoint of those on the other ideological side of the events of 716–17 or Bede's own perception – influenced by knowledge of Iona's once-dominant role in Northumbria – with Iona's role presented as more anomalous, in order to stress the necessity for reform. Given that it is very unlikely that Iona was so dominant over the Church among the northern Gaels – presumably of Dál Riata and northern Ireland – we should assume that Bede was also exaggerating regarding the Picts.

Fraser also claims that Columba and his immediate successors were more successful in Atholl, Mar and possibly Strathspey than around the Great Glen where many of the Pictish episodes are located in Adomnán's *Life*. The implication is that Adomnán rewrote and created his text to depict Columba as more active at the centre of Fortriu's power in the north. However, apart from the statement, redated from *c.*600 to the 9th century (Bisagni 2019, 213–17) in *Amrae Coluimb Chille* that Columba was active around the Tay, there are surprisingly few Iona-related dedications in the south before the time of Adomnán, when a cluster of dedications to Iona clerics indicates intense activity in Atholl (Taylor 1997). Adomnán stated that there were Columban monasteries in Pictland (*VSC* II.46; Sharpe 1995, 203) but, unfortunately, he did not name any of them. Kinneddar is a plausible candidate but certainty is not currently possible and we cannot assume that Columba's actual life reflects where his cult or Iona were successful later. Nonetheless, there are a number of dedications to Columba in the north, which are admittedly undated and many are probably late – like those at Deer in Aberdeenshire, where the cult of Columba was probably added in the 12th century to St Drostan's because Columba was more prestigious (Taylor 1997, 46–50; Taylor 2000a). Some of these, as well as possible dedications to Columba's successors – such as Fergna (606/7–624/5) near Tomintoul, Banffshire, and at Pitlochry, Perthshire, and Cumméne (656/7–668/9) at Abertarff at the south-west end of Loch Ness (Taylor 1997, 56–59) – may relate to the spread of the Iona influence before Adomnán's abbacy (678–705). It is more plausible that Adomnán enhanced pre-existing episodes set around the Great Glen than relocated them there. Moreover, in an area which came under Fortriu's control after 685, Columban centres were probably established early at Inchmahome, on the Lake of Menteith (Stirling), and at Inchcolm, in the Firth of Forth (Taylor 2000a). Therefore, Iona's success in Pictland under Adomnán's leadership is likely to have been built upon firm foundations in both northern and southern Pictland, though he was operating in a diverse ecclesiastical environment.

The Columban community would have formed one part of a varied Pictish Church. By the 7th century, the Church was certainly firmly established in Pictland and there is no hint in sources such as Bede that there were any pagan Picts by the late 7th century. Dates for major church establishments are few and far between but the Pictish king-lists indicate that the foundation of the monastery of Abernethy in southern Pictland dates to the early 7th century (Fraser 2009a, 134) and the Irish chronicles *c.*623 include the death of a *Uineus*, abbot of Ner, which appears to have been an ecclesiastical establishment in Aberdeenshire located near Fetternear (Clancy 2008a, 367–71). Another monastery, at Applecross in the north-west, was founded by Máel Ruba, a monk from the community at Bangor in County Down, Ireland, in 672 (*AU* 673.5; Mac Niocaill and Mac Airt 1983, 142). It became a significant centre and Máel Ruba's cult spread, probably centuries later, in northern Scotland.

In terms of the conversion process itself, kings and other members of the elite must have had an important role in Christianisation, giving land for establishing ecclesiastical centres, protecting missionaries and providing wealth for Church activity including conversion missions. Irish figures tend to get most of the credit for the conversion process but more local clergy and saints, some at least of Pictish descent, as well as Britons, are likely to have had strong roles in the conversion of Pictland, though many of them may have been trained in the west (Clancy 2008, 387).

Local dedications in north-east Scotland include saints, such as Drostan, Talorcan and Gartnait, while, in Perthshire and Fife, localised cults of saints such as St Serf are identifiable – for example, at Dunning and Culross. Moreover, Ternan (Torannán in Ireland), a Pict who travelled to Ireland, has dedications at Banchory-Ternan on Deeside and Arbuthnott in the Mearns and may have been significant in the area slightly later, in the early 8th century (Clancy 2009, 24–26; Plumb 2020, 106–14). In the far north, dedications suggest that Christian clergy from Fortriu and Ce may have been key figures in the conversion of Atlantic Pictland. For example, Drostan and Fergus, important saints in north-east Scotland, also have dedications in Caithness – these may indicate missions from north-east Scotland to northern Scotland in the 7th or 8th century (Clancy 2008a, 384). Likewise, it has been suggested that Curetán was responsible for the spread of Christianity in the Northern Isles, with dedications such as St Boniface on Papa Westray – Boniface appears to have been another name for Curetán (Veitch 1997, 638). However, the date of these dedications is uncertain and Christian practices and figures emanating directly from the Gaelic Church are also likely in Atlantic Pictland, if the attempted travels north to Orkney and beyond of Cormac ua Liatháin are indicative. Gaelic conversion is particularly plausible in areas like the northern Hebrides and the north-western seaboard, which were accessible from Dál Riata. This potential is indicated by episodes in the *Life of Columba* describing visits to Skye and the north-western seaboard, as well as the martyrdom of Donnán on Eigg in *c.*617, according to the Irish chronicles. We might further expect that the bishopric founded on Lismore in Loch Linnhe by

Lugaid, alternatively known as Moluag, (d. *c.*594) would also have been significant in the Christianisation of nearby Pictish lands but, similarly, there is no concrete proof to confirm these probabilities.

The Archaeology of the early Church

The archaeology of the early Church in Pictland has been traditionally difficult to identify with few stone buildings and little to rival Anglo-Saxon England or Ireland in terms of surviving churches (for example, Foster 2015). Nonetheless, significant progress has been made in recent years in identifying early Christian sites using archaeological approaches. In northern Pictland, the progress has been particularly dramatic through the work of the University of York's project at the Pictish monastery of Portmahomack, Easter Ross, which has revealed the development – and demise – of a monastic settlement through the course of the later first millennium AD. Advances have also been made at other sites in the north, such as Kinneddar (Noble *et al.* 2019b), while, in southern Pictland, geophysical survey and excavation have begun to characterise and date the development of vallum boundaries that enclosed the sacred space of early Christian ecclesiastical centres (for example, O'Grady 2011). The next section of this chapter will set out the evidence we have for the early Christian Church in Pictland, starting in the south and moving northwards, perhaps broadly mirroring the conversion process that brought Christianity to Pictland (Figure 4.4).

The early Church in southern Pictland

St Andrews and Abernethy

Undoubtedly, two of the most important churches of southern Pictland were those at Abernethy and St Andrews and, unusually, we have origin legends for both preserved in medieval documents. Abernethy is dedicated to the Irish saint, Brigit of Kildare, now, along with Columba and Patrick, one of Ireland's patron saints. The shorter Pictish king-lists refer to the King Nechtan son of Uerp as Abernethy's founder. He is likely to be the Nechtan *nepos* – 'grandson' or 'descendant' – of Uerp, of the early 7th century in the longer king-lists, or a relative (Fraser 2009, 134). From the environs, there is a Pictish symbol stone of probable 7th century date and nine fragments of early Christian sculpture including cross-slab fragments, slabs with relief crosses, a fragment of an ogham-inscribed stone that may have been part of a recumbent monument and a number of fragments of free-standing crosses (Proudfoot 1997).

A fragment of an early medieval cross-slab is also known from Carpow, just under 2km to the north-east of Abernethy (Proudfoot 1997, 53–54, 61).

4.4. Major ecclesiastical sites referred to in Chapter 4.

Marjorie Anderson linked this monument with one of the boundary stones, Cairfuill, recorded in the Abernethy foundation legend probably from the late 9th century (Anderson 1980, 92), though Simon Taylor (2005, 16) has suggested that this monument may have been the more impressive Mugdrum Cross, found a little further to the east. The Pictish symbol stone from Abernethy is now displayed on the wall of only one of two Irish-style round towers known from Scotland, located at the heart of the town of Abernethy at the edge of the modern churchyard. Little is known about the archaeology of any early Christian establishment at Abernethy but excavations in 2006 near the round tower revealed a boundary wall and perhaps the wall of a structure, the former dated to the late 9th or 10th century AD (Fyles 2008). The boundary wall was argued to have been an internal division within an early Christian vallum at Abernethy.

Two versions of a foundation legend survive for St Andrews, written down in the 12th century (Broun 2000b; Taylor 2000b). These record that 'King Hungus' founded the site. Hungus is likely to have been the powerful 8th-century King Onuist son of Uurguist (reigned 732–761) (Fraser 2009a, 318) since the earliest contemporary reference to St Andrews is in the Irish annals which record the death of Abbot Túathalán in 747 at *Cinrigh Monai* (*Kinrymont*) during Onuist's reign (Taylor with Márkus, 405–11). *Kinrymont* was the older name for St Andrews, meaning 'end or head of the king's upland or muir', indicating its strong royal connections (Taylor with Márkus 2009, 411, 478). From at least the 10th century, St Andrews was a site of pilgrimage for the cult of St Andrew and an increasingly important episcopal centre, with sources referring to its bishops rather than an abbot, though a monastic dimension continued into the 12th century (Taylor with Márkus 2009, 405–07). A 10th-century king of Alba, Constantín mac Áeda, retired to St Andrews in the 940s (Taylor with Márkus 2009, 406).

Over 80 pieces of early medieval sculpture come from St Andrews

4.5 The front panel of the St Andrew's shrine showing, on the right, David rending the jaws of the lion and, on the left, a magnificent hunt scene. This monument may have held the corporeal relics of the local saint, Regulus or Rule. (From Thomas 1971, p. 156) (© Historic Environment Scotland)

cathedral and environs – by far the biggest assemblage of early Christian sculpture in Pictland, a rival to the collections of Iona and exceeding that of the great Northumbrian monasteries, such as Lindisfarne and Monkwearmouth (Geddes forthcoming). The majority appears to date to the 8th and 9th centuries AD and includes over 50 highly accomplished grave-markers, at least two and probably as many as four free-standing crosses, a house-shaped shrine, a cross base, recumbent grave-markers and the magnificent St Andrew's shrine (Figure 4.5) – often called the St Andrew's sarcophagus but more properly a shrine (Thomas 1971, 156–57; 1998, 84–96). Like those at Abernethy, some of the crosses may have functioned as boundary markers, with the St Andrews Foundation Legend B referring to 12 crosses that marked the precinct of St Andrews (Taylor with Márkus 2009, 578). In the sculptural repertoire, figurative or animal carvings are rare, with the emphasis being on key pattern, interlace and bold depictions of the cross. The group of 50 grave-markers in St Andrews style are very similar, suggesting they perhaps covered the graves of important monks of the *familia* of St Andrews (Geddes forthcoming). The stones have been mainly found in the cathedral grounds following the discovery of the St Andrew's shrine in 1833 (Hall 1995, Illus. 1; Foster 1998b, Fig. 9) (Figure 4.6). To the east of the cathedral, excavations in 1860 and consolidation in the 1950s of the foundations of St Mary's, Kirkhill, revealed further stones including free-standing cross fragments (Hall 1995, 23; Foster 1998b, 45). St Mary's was associated with a *Céli Dé*, 'Servants of God', community in the 12th century (Taylor with Márkus 2009, 417, 491–92). Over 70 and perhaps as many as 300 or more burials from St Mary's were found during excavations in the 1980s (Rains and Hall 1997, 8–9). Dated examples centre on the 7th to 10th centuries AD (Rains and Hall 1997, Table 1). A further burial area has been located in the grounds of St Leonard's School, around 200m south-west of the cathedral, and this is where the house-shaped shrine was recovered (Foster 1998, 48). House shrines of this type were for important saints or patrons of the Church and its location away from the cathedral, along with the evidence from St Mary's, suggests a polyfocal establishment with perhaps multiple churches, burial grounds and associated monuments. St Andrews Foundation Account B refers to seven churches and a royal nunnery being founded at St Andrews, though this may reflect later rather than Pictish perceptions (Taylor with Márkus 2009, 579).

Whether the ecclesiastical foundation at St Andrews was enclosed by a monastic vallum is uncertain but the area defined by the modern streets of the town, South Road and the Pends – the line of a 14th- to 16th-century enclosure wall – could have marked the extent of an earlier enclosure of around 4.5ha in extent (Hall 2005, Illus. 1) (Figure 4.6). This line incorporates almost all the early medieval carved stone findspots, bar the example from St Leonard's School. However, the enclosure could have been

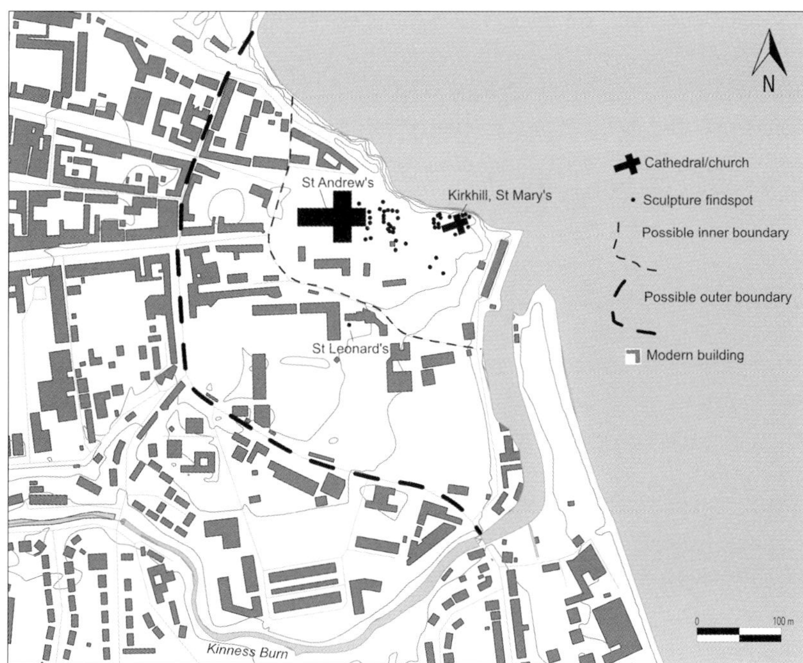

4.6 St Andrews – the present cathedral and modern town layout showing the findspots of early medieval sculpture, the position of Kirkhill and the projected lines of two possible outer enclosure boundaries. (Base map © Crown Copyright/database right 2021. An Ordnance Survey/EDINA supplied service)

bigger for Abbey Walk, around 200m out from the Pends, follows a very similar line and could mark the limits of an earlier outer enclosure boundary (Alcock 1988b, 331). This would have enclosed an area of around 14ha.

Atholl and Stormont

Moving into Highland Perthshire, at the Pictish territory of Atholl and the area further down the Tay later called Stormont, there was a series of major churches, the most important of which appears to have been Dunkeld. According to the shorter Pictish king-lists, which survive in a 13th century version, the church at Dunkeld was built during the reign of Constantín son of Uurguist (*c.*788–820) and the reference to a 'Túathal son of Artgus, chief bishop (*prím-epscop*) of Fortriu and abbot of Dunkeld' dying in 865 (*AU* 865.6) indicates that the leading cleric of Pictland also held this abbacy at that point (Anderson 2011, 169; Woolf 2007a, 65). A portion of the relics of Columba was brought to the church from Iona in *c.*AD849 and the church may have been rebuilt at this time (Woolf 2007a, 98–99). Appropriately, the dedication of the church was to Columba.

Little is known of the form of the early phases of this ecclesiastical centre or its landscape. The current cathedral was not begun until around the 13th century (RCAHMS 1994, 124) but a geophysical survey in 2019 located traces of a ditch encircling the site of the later cathedral. Excavation recovered charred material from the base of the ditch that dated to the 9th

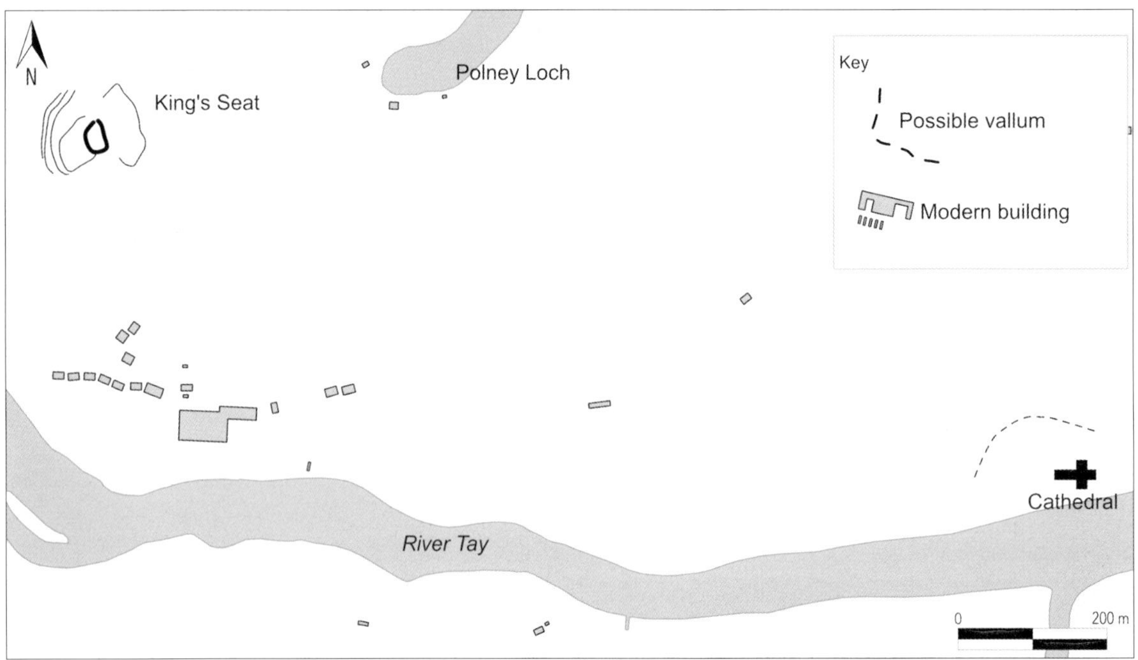

4.7 Illustrative map showing position of Dunkeld Cathedral on the River Tay with 9th- to 10th-century enclosure ditch identified in geophysical survey. The King's Seat hillfort is around 2km to the west. (Base map © Crown Copyright/database right 2021. An Ordnance Survey/EDINA supplied service)

to 10th century AD. This feature may be a vallum enclosure surrounding the ecclesiastical centre (O'Driscoll and Noble 2019, 7–8). The full extent and line of this vallum is difficult to establish, but may have enclosed an area of around 8–10ha (Figure 4.7). Sculpture from Dunkeld includes a fragment of a cross-slab, another unusual, very tall and very plain cross-slab and a spectacular cross-slab fragment which features both religious figures and brutal images of combat and beheadings (Henderson and Henderson 2004, 244, n. 71). One further unusual monument is a very large, roughly triangular block of stone which has, on one face, an incised depiction of a man on horseback carrying a spear and drinking from a horn and, on the top, a sunken equal-armed cross with expanded terminals (Figure 4.8). This has been described as an architectural fragment but, given the cross on top, other roles could be suggested such as a very tall foot support for an abbot's chair or even an inauguration stone (Clarke 2012, 109). A bronze handbell from Little Dunkeld, just across the Tay, may have come from the early medieval church of Dunkeld (Bourke 1983, 467; Bourke 2020, 148).

Upriver from Dunkeld, Fortingall, in Glen Lyon, appears to have been another major early Christian establishment in a valley in the centre of upland Perthshire. The site sits beside the River Lyon in Atholl, close to the heart of a network of upland routes connecting the lower Tay basin with routeways westward, as well as north and south through the Highlands (see Haldane 1973, 112). Fortingall church is dedicated to Coeti, a

4.8 Details from a triangular block of stone from Dunkeld carved on the front with a mounted figure carrying a spear and drinking from a horn. A small equal-armed cross is on the top of the stone. (© Historic Environment Scotland)

bishop of Iona who died in 712, and is located within a notable concentration of Coeti dedications in Glen Lyon and the upper Tay valley suggestive of a local cult (Robertson 1997, 135–36). Surrounding the modern churchyard, aerial photography has revealed two rectilinear enclosures extending towards the floodplain to the south and abutting the hills above Fortingall to the north, enclosing an area of around 4ha in extent (Figure 4.9d). Excavations in 2011 indicated that the ditches were part of an early Christian ecclesiastical enclosure (O'Grady 2011). The outer ditch was flanked by a thick stone-faced bank. Dates of the 7th century AD were obtained from charred material in the ditch and a burnt layer in the bank make-up produced dates from the 9th to the 10th centuries AD. A roadway was found entering the site on the south with a 6th-century Anglo-Saxon type of bead found in the road make-up. Geophysical survey suggested the presence of buildings inside the enclosure and traces of metalworking were found in the excavations. This adds to an already impressive repertoire of early medieval finds from Fortingall that include a copper-alloy coated iron handbell (Bourke 1983, 467; Bourke 2020, 380) and a rich assemblage of sculpture (Robertson 1997). The sculpture assemblage consists of around a dozen pieces including richly decorated cross-slabs, simple cross-incised stones and a recumbent cross-slab with three ring-headed crosses that bears close resemblance to a very similar monument from St Andrews. The cross-slabs are likely to date to the 8th to 9th centuries AD (Robertson 1997, 143). A massive stone font also comes from the site.

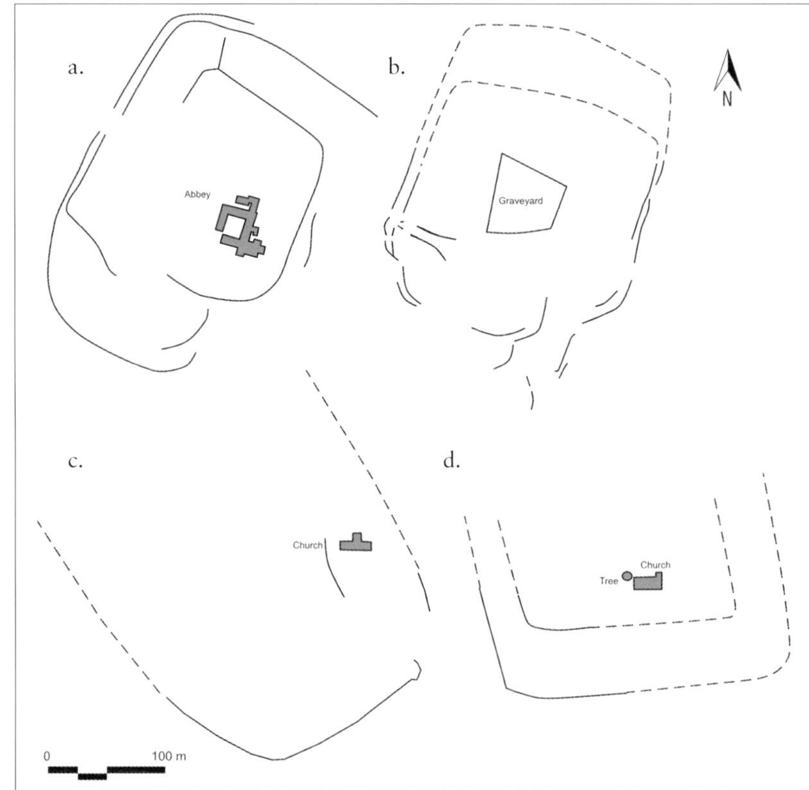

4.9 Plans of vallum enclosures at churches in Pictland compared:
(a) Iona, Argyll;
(b) Kinneddar, Moray;
(c) Portmahomack, Easter Ross;
(d) Fortingall, Perthshire.

Nearby, Dull, in the Tay valley to the east, is likely to have been an important early Christian site too. The church there was dedicated to Adomnán, ninth abbot of Iona, author of *Life of Saint Columba* and contemporary of Coeti (Will *et al.* 2003, 57), with again a notable concentration of Adomnán dedications in the area. Dull was described as a monastic settlement in the 12th century and is recorded as a royal thanage in the 13th century (MacDonald and Laing 1970, 129, 132; O'Grady 2008, 293). The early medieval sculpture from the site includes a decorated panel with warriors (see Chapter 2), five recumbent cross-slabs, a name inscribed stone, the socket of a free-standing cross or cross-slab, four undecorated free-standing crosses and a large stone font (Will *et al.* 2003, 59). The name stone is likely to date to the early 8th century (Will *et al.* 2003, 69) and the other monuments are of probable 8th- to 9th-century date. Further west up Glen Lyon and along the north shore of Loch Tay, there are further cross-marked stones and handbells associated with the small chapel sites known as Cladh-Bhranno and Balnahanaid (Bourke 1983, 467; Robertson 1997, 135; Bourke 2020, 378–80; Busset and Evemalm-Graham 2020, 63). It is clear that considerable resources were expended at these church centres. Also, as Simon Taylor (1997, 60–61) states, the dedications to

4.10 The modern church of St Vigeans atop a great glacial mound. Over 30 sculptured monuments including numerous cross-slabs, a house shrine, recumbent grave-markers and a free-standing cross, all likely to be of 8th- to 9th-century date, are known from St Vigeans. (© Jane Geddes)

Adomnán and Coeti indicate that there was considerable Ionan influence in the late 7th and early 8th centuries in this area, which is possibly also reflected in the existence of *cill* names in Atholl (Taylor 1996, 101–03, 106; though see cautions on dating in Clancy 2011, 364–68).

Another important church site in Atholl may have been Logierait. A 12th-century charter lists three *cill*-name chapels as belonging to Logierait which, in the 12th century, was *Logie Mahedd*, a place-name which includes an affectionate form of the name Coeti. Taylor states (1996, 102) that Logierait was 'the chief church of Atholl', based on its location next to the secular centre of Rait. Rait in the later Middle Ages was the judicial centre for the earldom, though its status in the Pictish period is not clear. From Logierait there are two cross-slabs (Mack 1997, 49–50), one with a large mounted figure, the other with two horseback riders and Pictish symbols.

Angus – the great mound of St Vigeans

St Vigeans church dramatically sits atop a steep glacial knoll with the modern graveyard populating the steep slopes of this impressive mound in eastern Angus (Geddes 2017, 19) (Figure 4.10). The quantity and quality of sculpture suggest an important early Christian centre here. The church is dedicated to the Irish saint Féchín (d. 665), though the place-name preserves a Pictish version of the name (Taylor 2017, 39). The sculptural assemblage includes over 30 monuments and fragments including numerous cross-slabs, a house-shaped shrine, recumbent grave-markers and a free-standing cross, all likely to be of 8th- to 9th-century date. The house-shaped shrine may have been for relics of St Féchín himself (Geddes 2017, 143–45). There are also architectural fragments suggestive of a stone church and fragments of church furniture (Geddes 2018, 65, 84). The imagery on the stones includes a wonderful mix of tonsured clerics, sinners and secular figures, providing statements about the power of the church, the secular elite and the salvation that Christ could bring. One cross-slab has an inscription on the side that includes the name Drosten, the name of both Pictish kings and a saint, along with two other probable names that also appear among Pictish royal names (Clancy 2017, 115–17). The stone may be recording royal patronage of the monument or the commemoration of kings and possibly a saint or a combination.

Churches at southern Pictish power centres

The royal palace complex at Forteviot (see Chapter 3) clearly had an important church. The Forteviot arch, a magnificent piece of 9th-century sculpture, is likely to have been part of an elaborately carved doorway or chancel arch of a major church building (Hall *et al.* 2020, 137) (Figure 4.11). That church is likely to have been located where the present parish church in the modern village of Forteviot is situated. Excavations only 20m away to the south of the church have located dug graves and a possible beam slot from a building (Campbell and Driscoll 2020, 101). The beam slot could have been the foundation for an earlier wooden church, a shrine or some sort of building associated with the ecclesiastical centre but the dating for this feature and the associated burials is unclear (Campbell and Driscoll 2020, 122, 202). A cast copper alloy handbell from the church is likely to be a recasting of an original of 9th- or 10th-century AD date (Campbell and Driscoll 2020, 123). As well as the arch, there is an important assemblage of early Christian sculpture from Forteviot that included at least four major free-standing crosses, including the Dupplin or Constantine's Cross (Figure 3.18). The number of monuments is only matched by major monastic sites (Campbell and Driscoll 2020, 165). However, it is more likely that Forteviot was mainly a secular power centre with an important royal church rather than a monastic site (Campbell and Driscoll 2020, 203; see also Chapter 3), though the latter is possible too (Woolf 2007a, 95, 313).

As outlined in Chapter 3, Meigle was also a 9th-century royal centre but, judging by the sculptural assemblage that includes a range of cross-slabs, grave-markers and architectural fragments, the site had an important church here too. The assemblage is similar in size and range to that at St Vigeans. However, the stones at Meigle have much less in the way of overt biblical imagery, with more of a focus on the secular elite befitting of its role as an elite residence (Geddes 2017, 156–57; see also Chapter 3). Other

4.11 The Forteviot arch, a magnificent piece of 9th-century sculpture likely to have been part of an elaborately carved doorway or chancel arch of a major church building. (© National Museums Scotland)

elite settlements may have had churches located nearby. At Mare's Craig, a few hundred metres east of Clatchard Craig hillfort, an early Christian handbell was recovered and what appears to have been a series of long cists was found, along with masonry that could be the remains of a later church building (Watson 1929, 149–51; Stevenson 1952, 111; Close-Brooks 1986, 179). This could have been a chapel associated with the probable royal fort at Clatchard Craig. Likewise at Dundurn, in the Lowlands below the fort, a small chapel site known as St Fillan's is located (Alcock *et al.* 1989, 196). This is defined by a circular graveyard that may be indicative of an early date and one incised cross-slab of early medieval date has been found in the grounds of the church.

The early Church in northern Pictland

Major Church sites of Fortriu

Rosemarkie, on the Black Isle in Easter Ross, may have been the main ecclesiastical centre of Fortriu (Woolf 2007b, 56). By the end of the Middle Ages, the body of Moluag of Lismore, an important Gaelic saint, was believed to lie at Rosemarkie (MacDonald 1994, 28–29) but this place's principal association was with Curetán, one of the guarantors of the 'Law of the Innocents' in AD 697 (Woolf 2007a, 315) and a probable bishop of Fortriu (Veitch 1997, 637; Woolf 2007a, 311; Noble and Evans 2019, 148). The area around Rosemarkie is significantly built up, making identification of any kind of enclosing vallum – if one existed – difficult.

Nonetheless, from the site, a large body of early Christian sculpture of a sufficiently diverse character survives to suggest that a very important early church existed here. The sculptural assemblage includes a magnificent cross-slab boldly decorated with key pattern and vine scroll (Henderson and Henderson 2004, 66). There are also some large decorated panels that may be from shrines or could have been mounted on the walls of the church. The collection also includes what may be other architectural fragments from a stone-built church such as an equal-armed cross on a small boulder that may have been placed on the wall behind an altar (Henderson and Henderson 2004, 211). This substantial sculptural corpus combines with the textual evidence to indicate that Rosemarkie was, at least for a while, likely to have been the pre-eminent ecclesiastical centre in all of Pictland. Its dedication to St Peter may have proclaimed its superiority over *Cennríg-monaid* (dedicated to St Andrew) founded in Fife in the 8th century, since a similar pattern of Peter and Andrew dedications can be found earlier in the Anglo-Saxon Church in Kent and Northumbria (Fraser 2009b).

In the agricultural heartlands of Moray stood another key ecclesiastical centre of Fortriu at Kinneddar, near Lossiemouth. During the later medieval period, Kinneddar was one of the seats of the bishops of Moray (Dransart 2016, 59). Earlier origins to the site are suggested by an extensive collection of early medieval sculpture and its dedication to or establishment by Gartnait, a royal name in the Pictish king-lists (Clancy 2008a, 378). The place-name Kinneddar derives from Gaelic *cenn*, 'head, end' – perhaps a promontory or a chief place – and *foither*, probably derived from a Pictish word referring to a district or region, and together may mean 'end of the *foithir* (district)' (Taylor 2011, 107; Taylor with Márkus 2012, 325, 376–78). It may have been the main ecclesiastical centre for a territory that included the major fort at Burghead (Noble *et al.* 2019b, 140). The sculptural evidence from the site includes fragments of a Pictish symbol stone, composite shrine slabs, cross-slabs and freestanding cross fragments. One fragment of a shrine shows David wrenching apart the jaws of a lion and is a close parallel for the St Andrews sarcophagus. Geophysical survey and excavation have shown that an impressive vallum enclosed around 8.6ha. Its rectilinear plan and subdivisions display some striking resemblances to the vallum of Iona. Excavations have revealed that the vallum enclosure was created during the 7th or early 8th centuries and was maintained into the 12th century or later. Kinneddar stood on a raised ridge of land at the edge of the former sea loch of Loch Spynie and would have been part of a large peninsula that included the location of Burghead fort, nearly cut off by the sea loch and areas of wetland (Armit and Büster 2020, Illus. 7.2).

The most intensively investigated early Christian establishment in Pictland is Portmahomack on the Tarbat peninsula, located north of Rosemarkie. The place-name Portmahomack includes the name Mo Cholmóc,

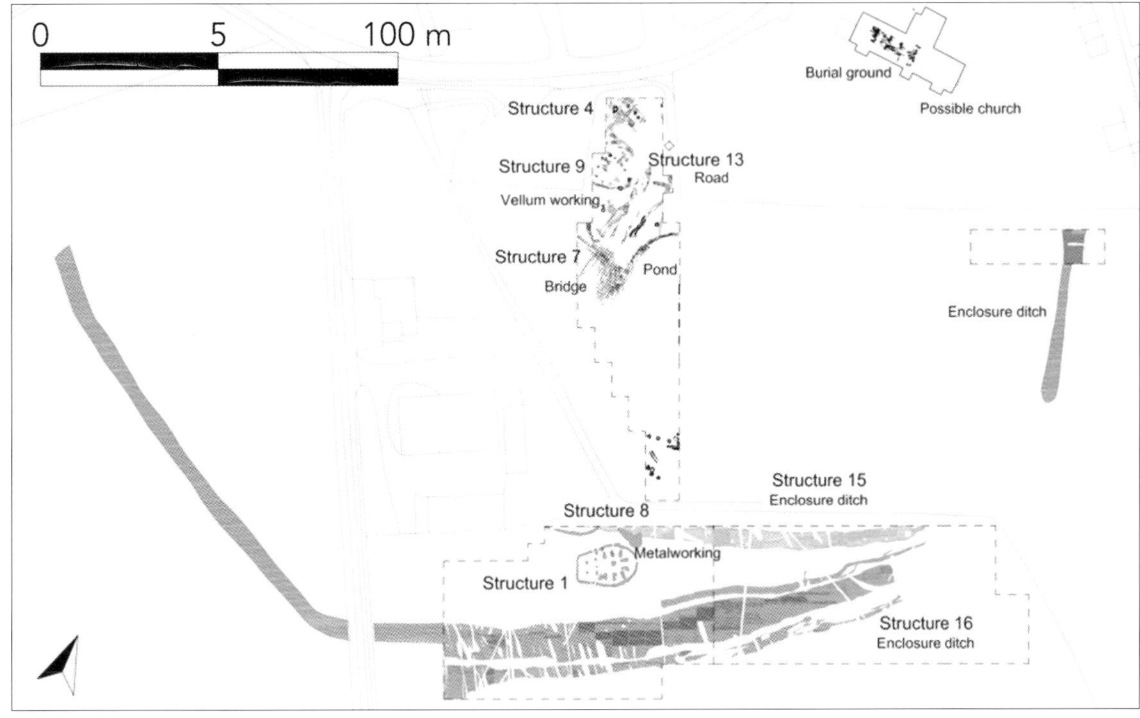

4.12 Plan of the monastic vallum and settlement features identified during University of York excavations at Portmahomack. (© FAS Heritage / University of York)

which may reflect a dedication to St Colmán (Ó Riain 2011, 463; Macquarrie 2012, 336–37; Stokes 1905, 76; Carver *et al.* 2016, 337). At Portmahomack, the early church was enclosed by a vallum enclosure which can be traced surrounding the modern churchyard. The visible area enclosed by the vallum could have been around 12ha if it went all the way to the beach to the north of the church, but the exact line of enclosure is uncertain (Figures 4.9c and 4.12). The site has been interpreted as originating as an elite settlement in the 5th to 7th centuries AD based on a small number of structural remains and finds, some early cist burials and the possible presence of a barrow cemetery (Carver *et al.* 2016, 89). The monastic settlement began sometime between the late 7th and the early 8th centuries AD. Within the vallum, on either side of a road heading towards the church, evidence for craftworking was found with the production of precious metalwork, glass and vellum being undertaken to the south of the church. The vellum working evidence is particularly striking showing the production of illuminated books was occurring at Portmahomack during the life of the monastery. Large timber buildings were also identified – timber and turf-built 'bag-shaped' buildings – that were associated with metalworking as well as the storage and processing of cereal. There was also evidence for the management of water with a dam, bridge and pool and other structural remains associated with a densely populated site. During the excavations hundreds of fragments of sculpture were found with different types of monument identifiable (Figure 4.13). These included simple cross-marked stones, grave-markers, a sarcophagus lid, elements of a possible composite shrine and fragments of four monumental cross-slabs. There are also architectural fragments of a likely 8th-century date that are strongly suggestive of a stone church (Figure 4.14). The most impressive of these is a corbel with a human head fashioned in the round and a possible fragment of a roof finial (Carver *et al.* 2016, 149–54). The east wall of the crypt of the later church may have also incorporated fragments of an earlier church wall of 8th-century date (Carver *et al.* 2016, 169–78).

In the far north-west of the mainland is Applecross, on the Atlantic coast of Wester Ross, founded in AD 672 by Máel Ruba (*AU* 673.5; Mac Niocaill and Mac Airt 1983, 142), a monk from the prominent Irish monastery of Bangor, County Down, in Northern Ireland. His death and those of the abbots that followed him are recorded through to the 9th century in the Irish annals showing that this Irish connection remained strong (Fisher 2001, 87). The site is located in a sheltered, fertile valley of the Inner Sound, looking over to Skye and Raasay. At Applecross today, the ruins of the 19th-century parish church stand within a modern burial

4.13 The calf stone, one of many pieces of sculpture found during excavations at Portmahomack. (© FAS Heritage / University of York)

4.14 Roof finial from probable Pictish-period stone church at Portmahomack. (© FAS Heritage / University of York)

ground but the bounds of the earlier foundation are perhaps hinted at by an earthwork identifiable in the earlier 20th century that defined a large curvilinear enclosure measuring around 190m by 150m (Thomas 1971, 41, Fig. 15). Within the grounds of the church stands a 2.6m tall, plain, cross-slab. A much more impressively decorated cross-slab is represented by a series of richly decorated fragments (Thickpenny 2019). This latter example has knotwork and interlace designs strongly reminiscent of monuments from the Tarbat peninsula and from Rosemarkie, and analysis of the carving technique by Thickpenny has suggested that monuments from Applecross, Rosemarkie and Nigg were carved by the same hand or same workshop. The monument does have some differences, however, for it also resembles 'Irish-style' free-standing crosses with its pierced ring more akin to western traditions of carving than that found in eastern Pictland (Fisher 2001, 88).

Smaller Church establishments of Fortriu and Ce

More modest church establishments are also evident in northern Pictland. At Parc-an-caipel, Congash, Inverness-shire, the footings of a rectangular

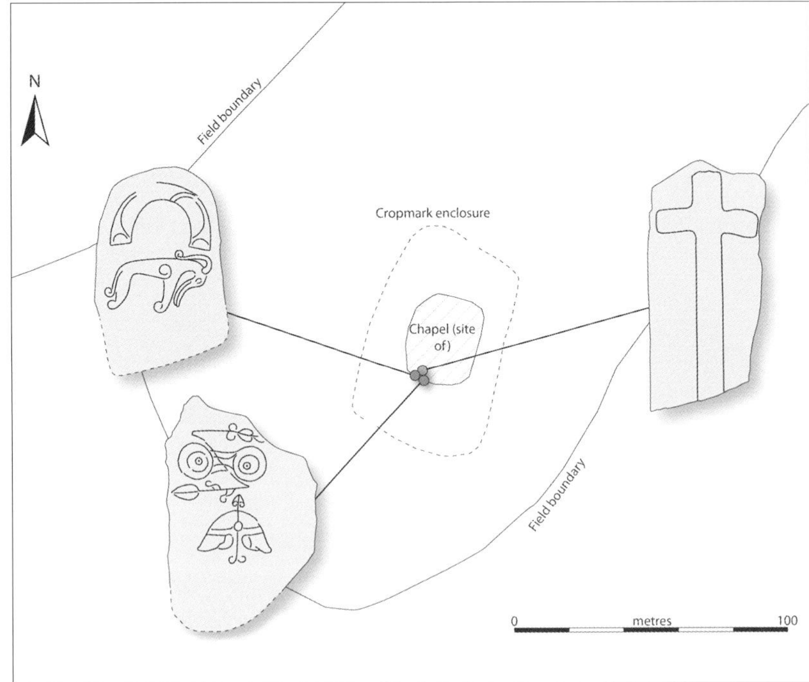

4.15 A probable chapel site lies within a rectangular enclosure identified by aerial photography at Parc-an-caipel, Congash, Inverness-shire. Two Pictish symbol stones and a cross-marked stone have been found here.

building, a probable early chapel, lie within a sub-rectangular or square enclosure which in turn lies within a rectangular enclosure around 96m NE–SW by 67m NW–SE with two entrances on the shorter sides of the enclosure (NMRS NJ02NE 1) (Figure 4.15). Two Pictish symbol stones flank an entrance to the banked enclosure on the south-west side and a cross-slab has been located near the entranceway. The enclosures, sculpture and place-name are strongly suggestive of some form of early Christian establishment.

In Aberdeenshire, no major sites of the scale of Portmahomack or Kinneddar are known but two references to the early Christian centre at a place called *Nér* in *c.*623 and 678 may relate to Fetternear, in Aberdeenshire, and specifically to a site called Abersnithock, where a chapel dedicated to St Finnan was (Clancy 2008, 367–71). A large concentration of early Christian sculpture in Aberdeenshire at Tullich is indicative of another early church site. Tullich was associated with St Nathalan, whose relics were kept there and were said to heal the sick into recent times. Nathalan is probably the same Pictish saint as the Nechtan in the name Abersnithock (Clancy 2008a, 368 n. 5, 371). Recent survey and excavation have identified two different enclosing features around the modern church, the inner measuring around 58m by 55m and an outer at least 95m by 64m. The monuments from the site include a Pictish symbol stone and 16 incised crosses. These monuments may have demarcated entrances or areas of special sanctity within the relatively modestly sized ecclesiastical enclosure (Geddes *et al.* 2015, 261).

An early church at Burghead

Like southern Pictland, there is evidence for the close juxtaposition between the Church and places of power in northern Pictland. The impressive Pictish fort at Burghead preserves important, albeit fragmentary, examples of early Christian sculpture. These monuments appear to be associated with an early chapel near to the entrance of the fort (Oram 2007, 256). The chapel at Burghead and a nearby well are dedicated to St Aethan. The sculpture from Burghead includes fragments bearing interlace and key-pattern that may be from a cross-slab or series of cross-slabs, a slotted corner slab and a fragment of a panel with a carving of a stag being brought down by hounds (Henderson and Henderson 2004, 203). The latter two fragments suggest the presence of composite shrine monuments of the type found at nearby Kinneddar (Thomas 1971, 152). There is also a fragment from a small cross-slab with a relief-carved cross on the front and a mounted warrior on the back from Burghead. The chapel site at the entrance to the fort may have been associated with a cemetery but a further cemetery was also located outside of the ramparts on the seaward end of the fort (MacDonald 1862, 358).

Atlantic Pictland

As discussed earlier, we know very little about the arrival and development of early Christianity in Atlantic Pictland, though it is clear that the Church became firmly established before the Viking Age. The first documented bishopric for the Northern Isles was based at Birsay on the north-west coast of Mainland Orkney, where the later Earls of Orkney maintained a residence from the 11th to the 17th centuries AD (Crawford 1987, 155). The church on the Brough of Birsay is dedicated to St Peter, which may – very tentatively – be linked to the move in the 8th century by King Nechtan towards Rome's doctrine on the tonsure and dating Easter, and potentially also the reformist stress on the cult of St Peter (see Lamb 1998). Notably, as well as Orkney, there is a distinct concentration of Peter dedications in Moray, suggesting a possible direct link between the church of Orkney and that of 8th century Fortriu, though none of the church dedications in Fortriu or the Northern Isles can be closely dated (Stanton 2018, 18, Fig. 6).

The early excavations on the Brough of Birsay found traces of a possible earlier church under the 12th-century chapel foundation consisting of a stretch of wall and possible early graves and this and its island setting contributed to its interpretation as an eremitic monastic settlement (Radford

1959, 18). However, more-recent findings have put greater weight on the Pictish phases belonging to a high-status secular settlement and the findings at the church and their date have also been questioned, with the putative early graves possibly being later in date rather than contemporary with the Pictish metalworking and other finds (Ritchie 1989, 53; Morris 1995, 287; 2021, 567–69, 577; see also Curle 1982, 93–95). There are two cross-incised stones from the Brough and a portable cross-slab (Scott and Ritchie 2014, Illus. 7, Illus. 10), suggestive of some form of early Christian focus here, though none of the monuments are clearly early or particularly helpful in judging what was on the islet in the Pictish period. The presence of an iron handbell from the 'lower Norse horizon' and one from the vicinity of a long cist cemetery on the adjacent mainland at Saevar Howe is also strongly suggestive of one or more important churches in the Birsay area in the later centuries of the first millennium AD (Bourke 1983, 467; Bourke 2020, 376–77). However, a church serving a secular elite residence would not be unusual as noted above (see also Chapter 3), and the magnificent sculptured stone showing three warriors with at least four symbols from Brough of Birsay may have been a secular demonstration of power for there is no evidence that it had a cross on the other side. The potentially similar chiefly residence at Brough of Deerness may have had a chapel associated with the Pictish as well as the later Norse phases, though that is by no means certain (Morris and Emery 1986; Barrett and Slater 2009, 92).

Other forms of early Christian site may also be identifiable in the Northern Isles. Raymond Lamb has suggested that some isolated stack sites may have been eremitic retreats or small monasteries (Lamb 1973, 78–82) established to create 'deserts in the ocean' where religious ideals could be focussed on to the exclusion of the everyday world. However, it seems more likely that in many cases that these were elite residences, northern versions of the fortified promontories and other enclosed settlements found further south (see Chapter 3; Barrett and Slater 2009, 85). Other early Christian sites on Orkney are suggested by sculptural remains (Scott and Ritchie 2014). St Boniface, Papa Westray, has a small assemblage of monuments including a cross-slab with Pictish symbols and two further cross-slabs, and a particularly fine altar frontal of probable 8th- or 9th-century date comes from a chapel site on Flotta. The find of a lightly incised cross with an ogham inscription and an iron handbell from the Broch of Burrian are curious finds from the post-broch settlement – was this a private chapel in an elite settlement or was there a chapel site here of uncertain character (MacGregor 1974, 96)? A cross-slab from Appiehouse, a recent find, may have come from a chapel site at Colli Ness, reputed site of a long cist cemetery (Scott and Ritchie 2014, 181). One interesting feature of the Orcadian evidence is its lack of composite shrines in contrast to the relatively abundant evidence from Shetland (Scott and Ritchie 2014, 193).

4.16 Altar frontal from Papil, Shetland, showing crozier-bearing monks, a figure on horseback and a walking figure with a book satchel at the back of the procession. (© Shetland Amenity Trust)

Moving further north, Shetland has a number of fragments of composite stone shrines, particularly from St Ninian's Isle and from Papil, West Burra (Scott and Ritchie 2009) (Figure 4.16). These shrines are likely to have been used to hold the relics of saints and may have also acted as the altar in smaller churches, though it has also been suggested that some of these types of monument found elsewhere in Pictland were not shrines at all but parts of screens and other church architectural fittings (Clarke *et al.* 2012, 45, 95). The large panel from Papil shows a procession – perhaps on pilgrimage – of monks with croziers, accompanying a figure on horseback – perhaps a secular elite or a saint. The panel is part of at least three shrines – if that is what they are – from Papil and there is also an impressive and perhaps early form of cross-slab from Papil too, showing four monks with croziers, two of which carry book satchels, standing underneath a circular cross-head. Below are the two 'bird-men' discussed earlier with a human head between their beaks. They carry axes over their shoulders like Rhynie Man but, rather than being emblematic of pagan belief and elite power, the fact that the Papil individuals were on a Christian cross-slab may indicate syncretic beliefs or the use of these images to castigate pagan practices (Kilpatrick 2011).

The Christian site at St Ninian's Isle, Mainland Shetland, is set on a

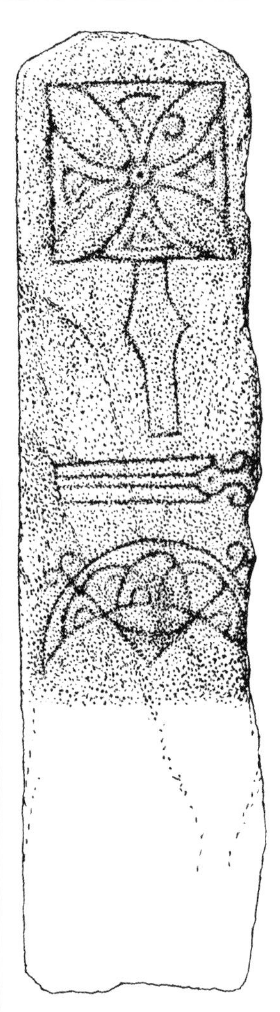

4.17 The Raasay cross has a cross of arcs within a square frame, with a chi-rho scroll attached to the right-hand side of the upper arm of the cross. Beneath are two Pictish symbols – a tuning fork and a crescent and V-rod. (© Historic Environment Scotland)

small projecting islet, linked to the mainland by a spectacular sand bar. Excavations in the 1950s found traces of an early chapel, of probable 7th- to 9th-century AD date, below the ruins of later church buildings (Barrowman 2011, 35–41, 197–99). The famous St Ninian's Isle hoard of silver vessels, brooches and pieces of weaponry appears to have come from the floor of a phase of this building (Barrowman 2011, 201–03). A cemetery of long cists and dug graves was associated with the early church at St Ninian's, along with fragments of at least two composite shrines, ten cross-marked slabs, an ogham stone, a cruciform-shaped stone and a recumbent grave-marker. The burials date from around the 7th century to the 11th or 12th century AD, with east–west (E–W) burial dating from the 7th to 10th centuries AD suggesting the continuity of this religious foundation and its cemetery from the Pictish into what is usually regarded as the Scandinavian era (Barrowman 2011, 199; see also Chapter 7).

Like elsewhere in Pictland, churches may have been found at secular power centres too. At Cunningsburgh, in the east Mainland of Shetland, there is a fragment of a double-disc carving, likely to have been part of a cross-slab, and another fragment with relief carving and an ogham inscription that may well have been part of a second cross-slab. The place-name Cunningsburgh probably derives from Old Norse *konungsborg*, 'king's fort', and the sculpture findspots come from Mail cemetery adjacent to a possible broch or dun site on a small, now tidal, islet (Noble *et al.* 2019, 86).

In the Western Isles and northern parts of the Inner Hebrides – Skye, Raasay, Eigg, Rum, Canna, Muck – where Pictish influence is likely, there is relatively little in the way of evidence for the early Church. The sculptural evidence from these areas is particularly thin showing little in the way of major investment in monumental carving. There is a small collection of early Christian sculpture from Kildonan, Eigg, where Donnán was martyred in AD *c.*617, that includes two cross-slabs and four probable grave-markers (Fisher 2001, 92–95). Whether Eigg was part of Pictland or part of the Pictish church is a moot point but the sculpture is reminiscent of Pictish traditions. One cross-slab, which may reuse an earlier monument (Gondek and Jeffrey 2003), has a ring-headed cross with knotwork and key pattern with a hunt scene on the back of the kind found widely in northern and southern Pictland (see Chapter 3). What may be a relatively early cross-bearing monument from Raasay incorporates both Pictish symbols and an incised cross of arcs with a Christogram in a square frame, the symbols and cross carved in a similar style, perhaps by the same craftsperson (Henderson and Henderson 2004, 62) (Figure 4.17). In a similar tradition, at Pabbay, on Barra, in the Western Isles, a simple incised Latin cross appears above two symbols (Fisher 2001, 106). Other than these isolated examples of modestly ambitious carving, most of the Western Isles and northern Inner Hebridean early Christian sculpture consists of simple cross-incised monuments and other probable forms of small grave-markers. Overall, little of the investment in sculpture seen so vividly on mainland Pictland is found in the western parts of Atlantic Pictland and nor does the investment in early Christian monuments in this area match that found in the Northern Isles.

The character and development of Christianity in Pictland

As outlined in this chapter, tracing the character of pagan belief in Pictland is not an easy task but there may have been some overlap in practices and traditions even in a Christian milieu. Conversion brought an end to the major practices of paganism but it seems likely that some pre-Christian beliefs continued as part of everyday folk beliefs and rituals and in modified Christianised forms. In early medieval Gaelic manuscripts, the existence of pagan charms alongside Christian texts indicates that a surprising degree of acceptance was possible, even among the learned clergy (Carey 2019, 1–27). While Adomnán was hostile to paganism, the *Life of Columba* does provide examples of pagan sites being blessed by Columba and becoming early Christian locations, suggesting that some of the early Christian sites attested by archaeology may have had origins as sites of pagan significance. Fortingall is a possible candidate for a site in Pictland that was both a pre-Christian and Christian sacred site. Within the churchyard stands the Fortingall Yew, Scotland's oldest tree, which is thought to be two to three thousand years old. It was customary in later centuries to light the Beltane fire at the base of the tree and it has been suggested that this was originally a sacred tree of the Iron Age (Watson 1926, 248, 352; Robertson 1997, 136). Nearby place-names such as Tullochville and Coshieville – including Gaelic *bile*, 'sacred tree' – and Duneaves – incorporating *neimheadh*, from *nemeton*, 'sacred place' – are further suggestive of a sacred landscape surrounding this stretch of the River Lyon (Watson 1926, 244–50, 314; Robertson 1997, 136), though the word could also be used for Christian places (Taylor with Márkus 2012, 452–55). If the yew was an Iron Age sacred tree, then it is likely to have retained significance in a Christianised, early medieval context, given the importance of totemic or sacred trees in contemporary Ireland (Lucas 1963; Kelly 1997, 387–88). Edwina Proudfoot has suggested that Abernethy too might have been a pre-Christian site of significance (Proudfoot 1997, 61). She suggests an unusual stone with carved human heads from Abernethy may have been part of a pre-Christian religious complex (Figure 4.18), the location of which may have been one motivation for the establishment of a Christian focus at Abernethy. However, not all sites associated with pagan worship will have been embraced in the Christian faith, since missionary activity elsewhere in

4.18 Carved stone with four human heads from Abernethy. (Courtesy of and © Perth Museum and Art Gallery, Perth & Kinross)

Europe could also be violent, with the deliberate destruction and forcible removal of venues and objects of pagan veneration (Fletcher 1997, 44–55).

Regarding the era for the conversion of Pictland, a 5th-century date for at least some sort of Christian community in Pictland, probably in the south, seems likely. The presence of established Christianity in Gaelic Argyll by the time of Columba's arrival in 563 and evidence of Christian inscribed stones found in small numbers from Dumfries and Galloway, the Borders and Lothian (Forsyth 2005, Fig. 8.1) make some sort of Christian community in southern Pictland in the 5th century probable. The broad narrative of conversion happening from south to north as suggested by Bede also seems likely, perhaps reflected in traditions such as the long cist cemetery having a greater impact on southern Pictland than in the north (see Chapter 5). Adomnán's *Life of St Columba* suggests that Gaelic ecclesiastical figures were also trying to garner influence among Pictish elites in northern Pictland by the late 6th century. The evidence from the Northern Isles suggests the early Church may have had important connections with that of Fortriu (Veitch 1997), indicating Christian missions to the far north had, at least partly, sprung from northern Pictland, but earlier and competing Christianising missions may have emanated from the west as well as the south.

Influence on the Church also came from Northumbria. In the 710s, the Pictish king Nechtan wrote to Abbot Ceolfrith of Northumbria to ask advice on changing the observance of Easter from the Columban to Roman practice and for architects to help build him a church in stone (Fraser

Colour Plate 1. Dice tower from Vettweiß-Froitzheim, with the inscription 'PICTOS VICTOS HOSTIS DELETA LUDITE SECURI' ('The Picts are beaten, the enemy annihilated, let us play without a care') and 'VTERE FELIX VIVAS' ('Good luck, live well') on the other sides. © Jurgen Vogel, LVR-Landesmuseum Bonn.

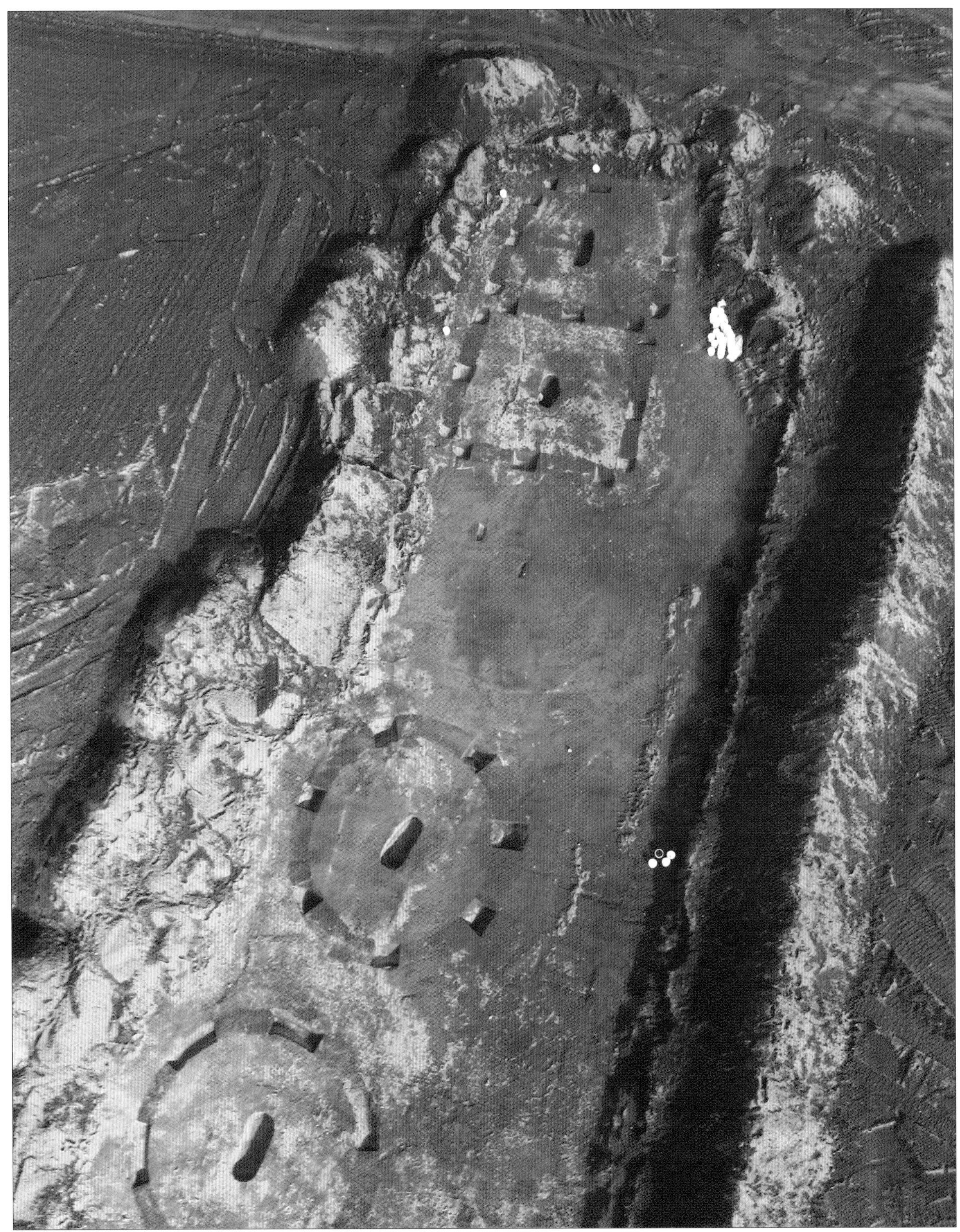

Colour Plate 2. Bankhead, Perthshire: barrow cemetery under excavation. © AOC Archaeology.

Colour Plate 3. Norrie's Law plaque with symbols. © National Museums Scotland.

Colour Plate 4. Mould for a penannular brooch from the Brough of Birsay, Orkney. © National Museums Scotland.

Colour Plate 5. Penannular brooch from Clunie, Perthshire. The brooch features gold filigree designs creating spiral and zoomorphic decoration focused on the terminals of the brooch. © National Museums Scotland.

Colour Plate 6. The hoard from St Ninian's Isle, Shetland, comprising 28 silver and silver-gilt objects including bowls, brooches and sword fittings. © National Museums Scotland.

Colour Plate 7. Roman glass – these sherds do not look like much, but they were from very unusual Roman glass vessels acquired and used by occupants of the Pictish promontory fort at Dunnicaer.

Colour Plate 8. One end of a 9th-century building under excavation at Burghead, Moray. The hearth of the building is located near the large measuring scale.

Colour Plate 9. (*Left*) Woollen hooded shawl with a knotted fringe, found in a moss in St Andrews Parish, Orkney. Dated to the 3rd to 7th century AD. © National Museums Scotland.

Colour Plate 10. (*Below*) Reconstruction of the promontory fort and settlement of Dunnicaer. © Alice Watterson, Kieran Baxter and Kieran Duncan.

Colour Plate 11. The Craw Stane, Rhynie, with Tap o' Noth hillfort in the background. © Cathy MacIver. The Craw Stane stood at the entrance to the high-status 4th–6th century AD enclosure complex.

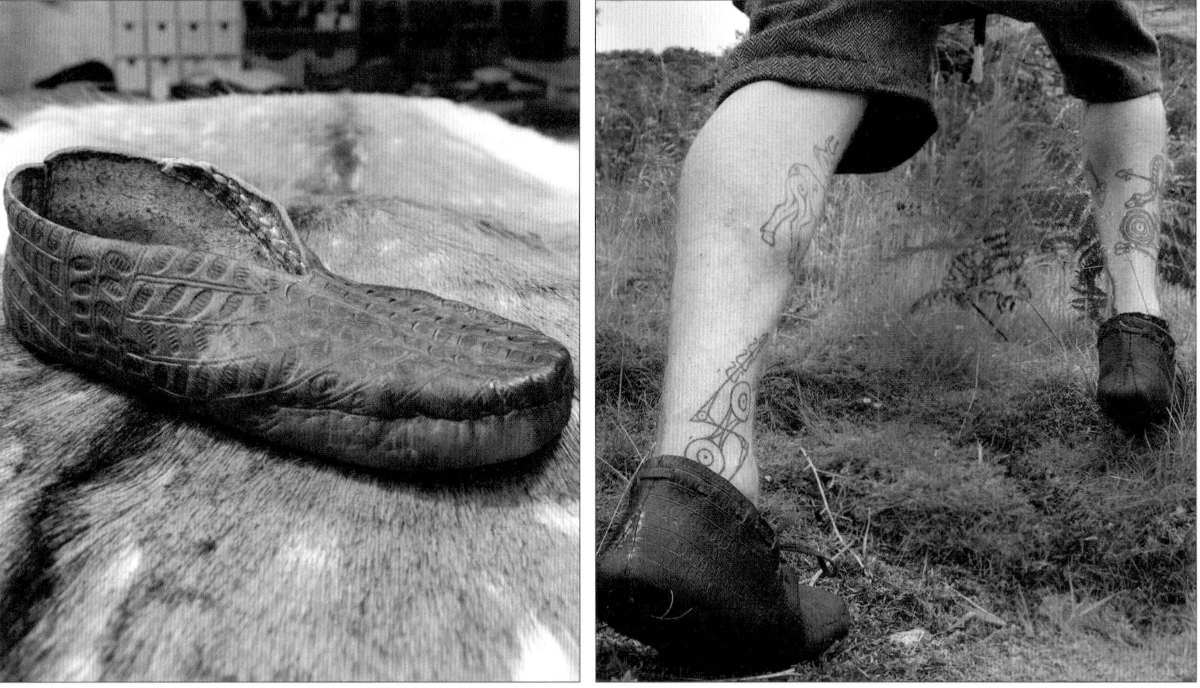

Colour Plate 12. Recreation of the Dundurn leather shoe by leatherworker Hamish Lamley: (*left*) on show in Hamish's workshop; (*right*) the modern Dundurn-style shoes in action at Dundurn hillfort. © Hamish Lamley, Pictavia Leather.

Colour Plate 13. Aerial image showing the surviving parts of the ramparts and settlement at Burghead, Moray, located at the end of the promontory. The modern town destroyed around half of the fort.

Colour Plate 14. 3D reconstruction of the fort at Burghead. Upper fort on right, lower citadel on left, landward ramparts with church in background. The wide bay to the west (right of image) may have been used for landing boats. A cemetery was located on the seaward side of the fort, outside of the ramparts. © Alice Watterson, Kieran Baxter and Kieran Duncan.

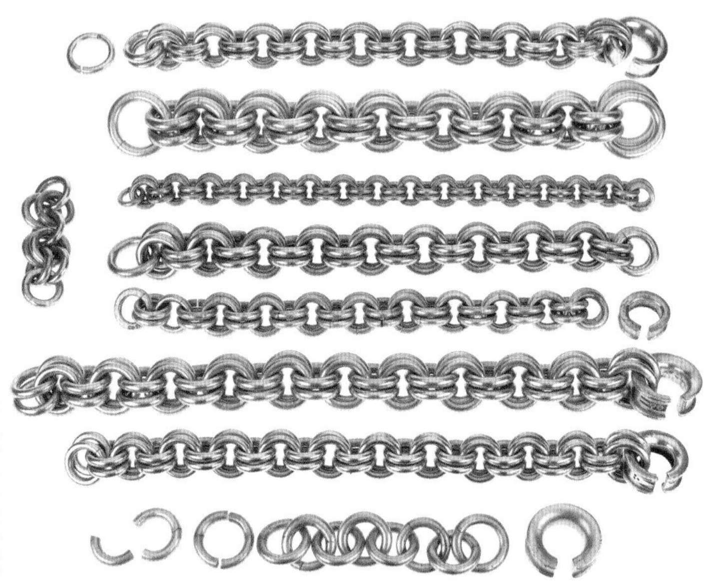

Colour Plate 15. (*Above*) In the centre of the Hilton of Cadboll stone, deer are shown being chased by hunting dogs and two armed horseriders. Above this, a third mounted person is shown sitting side-saddle with a fourth rider behind. To the right are two trumpeters blowing long horns. © National Museums Scotland.

Colour Plate 16. (*Above right*) Silver chains from early medieval Scotland. Two of the chains have Pictish symbols on the terminal rings, the designs inlaid with red enamel. © National Museums Scotland.

Colour Plate 17. (*Right*) The well at Mither Tap o' Bennachie with carefully constructed steps down to the well shaft.

Colour Plate 18. (*Above*) Painted pebbles found in first millennium AD settlements in Shetland. © Shetland Amenity Trust.

Colour Plate 19. (*Right*) The cross-slab from Papil, Shetland, and inset showing detail of the axe-bearing part-animal, part-human figures. © National Museums Scotland.

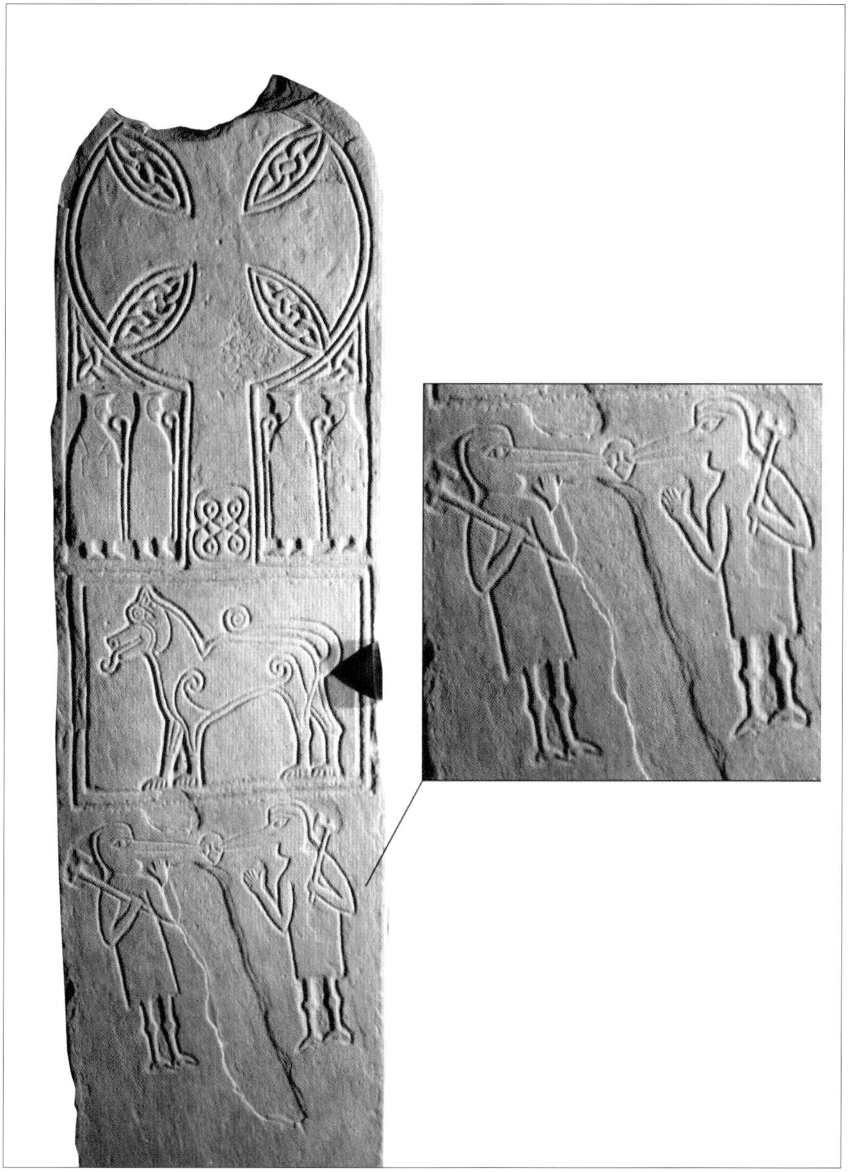

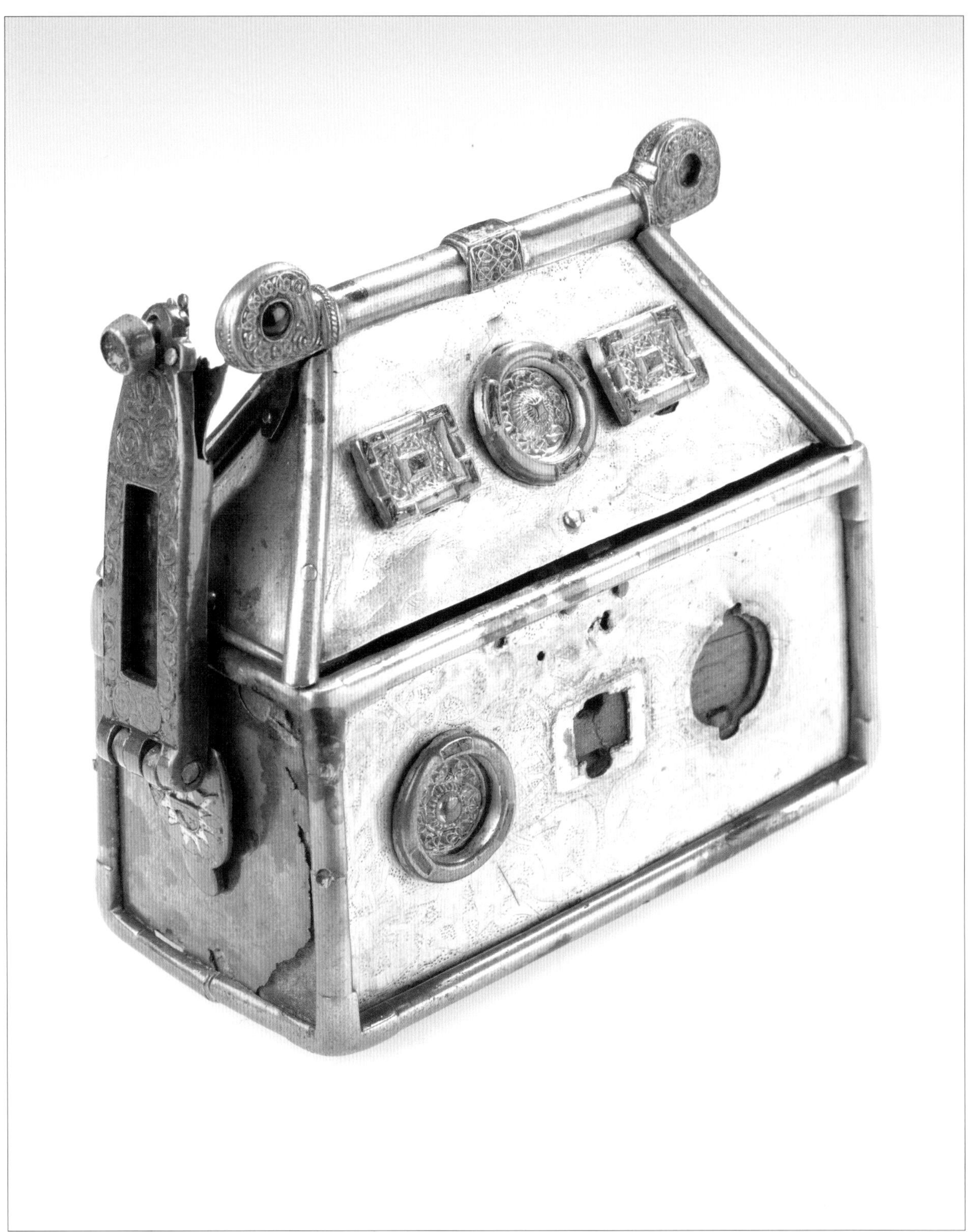

Colour Plate 20. The Monymusk reliquary consists of a small wooden box encased within silver and bronze plates with decorative mounts. This may have held the relics of an important saint. © National Museums Scotland.

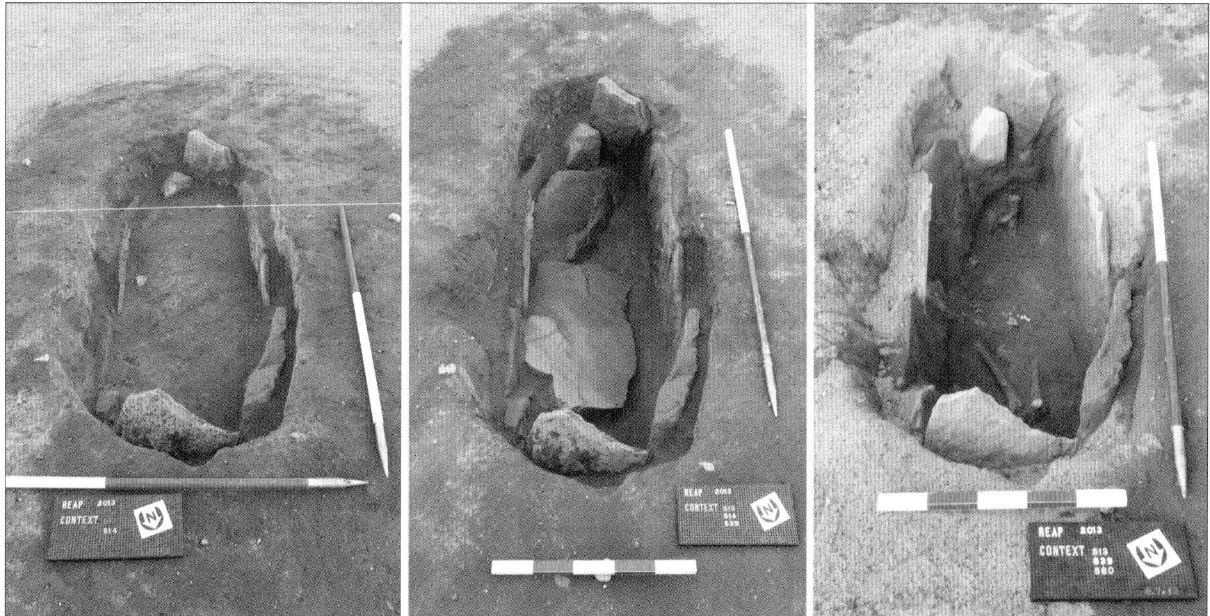

Colour Plate 21. Stages of excavation of the long cist at Rhynie containing the partially preserved remains of a young adult.

Colour Plate 22. The skeleton of the 'Rosemarkie Man' (Rosemarkie, Highland) showing the unusual posture the body was laid out in. © Rosemarkie Cave Project.

Colour Plate 23. (*Above*) Carving of a bear found in the floor layers of the wheelhouse, Structure 11, Scatness, Shetland. © Shetland Amenity Trust.

Colour Plate 24. (*Right*) Chain from Parkhill, Aberdeenshire, made of double rings of silver with a penannular terminal ring chip carved with symbols also found on Pictish symbol stones. © National Museums Scotland.

2009a, 276). Bede reports that Pictland was reformed and placed under the direction of the Apostle Peter. In AD 717, the Iona *familia* was expelled from Pictland – perhaps a further attempt by Nechtan to secure more control over the Church and to install native bishops and clergy who were more loyal to him, with the support of his powerful Anglo-Saxon neighbours to the south (Fraser 2009a, 280; Woolf 2013, 5). Indeed, we can assume that interaction with the Anglo-Saxon Church was more substantial than our written sources demonstrate, since political dominance over at least some of the Picts in the 7th century was accompanied by Northumbrian bishops such as Wilfrid gaining ecclesiastical jurisdiction over the Picts and, in 681, a bishop of the Picts was established at Abercorn, just south of the Forth (Fraser 2009a, 195–97, 213). It is unlikely that the journey of St Cuthbert, then Prior of Melrose, to the Pictish *Niudwari* in Fife at some point from 664 to the mid–late 670s was the only direct contact of that period (Evans forthcoming). It is likely that the fact that King Aldfrith of Northumbria (685–705) had previously been a monk of Iona and that Adomnán visited Northumbria in the late 680s to recover captives would have also helped the exchange of ecclesiastical ideas between the northern English and the Picts, even if there were political tensions, especially since one of the key Columban routes to Northumbria passed through Pictland.

We can assume that direct contacts continued after the early 8th century as is indicated by the appearance of the names of the Pictish kings in the Durham *Liber Vitae*, 'Book of Life': *Unust* – probably Onuist son of Uurguist, 732–761; *Custantin* – Constantín son of Uurguist, *c.*788–820, immediately following Charlemagne; and *Uoenan* – Unen son of Unuist, 836/837–839 (Forsyth 2000, 25). Since this was a list, originally kept at Lindisfarne, of those to be prayed for by the clergy so the subject could go to heaven more quickly, it reflects those revered by the monastic community or who had donated to the foundation. The latter scenario is perhaps more likely in the case of Onuist, described as a 'despotic butcher' in the Northumbrian *Continuatio Bedae* chronicle (Fraser 2009, 287) but it is significant that, in all these cases, Pictish kings valued the Northumbrian Church into the 9th century.

How quickly the Church and the Christian faith took hold is uncertain but, as noted above, there is no indication in any of our 7th-century sources that the Picts were pagan and the archaeology from sites, such as Portmahomack, Kinneddar and Fortingall, suggests major ecclesiastical establishments were emerging or being consolidated in this period. Clancy has suggested that the early establishments were small churches that initially served restricted territories defined by the geography and structure of secular land divisions and polities (2008, 392). However, it should be acknowledged that the near-total lack of references to Pictish ecclesiastics before the late 7th century means that the names of important early Church figures of the conversion period, perhaps before many of the more substantial Church buildings and institutions were established, are lost to us, making it difficult to link dedications and churches to the early processes of Christianisation.

In northern Pictland, the historical sources hint at the pre-eminence of Rosemarkie as a major centre of religion in the north – at least during the episcopate of Bishop Curetán at the end of the 7th century. At Rosemarkie, the sculptural assemblage is one of the richest of Pictland, though excavation at Portmahomack, a site with no early references, shows what archaeology can bring to the table in terms of tracing the development and spread of Christianity and identifying major centres without early historical records. In southern Pictland, Dunkeld was clearly a very significant Christian centre in the 9th century and, while the sculptural assemblage here is quite modest, it does include some unusual monuments that hint at the significance of this site. Bishops of St Andrews are mentioned from *c.*900 onwards and this site has the richest sculptural assemblage outwith Iona in early medieval Scotland.

Given the limited evidence for Pictland, it is difficult to establish how the Pictish Church operated. In Ireland, there were monasteries with monks and nuns living a life of contemplation, labour and scholarship generally separate from the rest of society under the leadership of an abbot or abbess. Bishops, usually one for each local kingdom, were in charge of Christianity among the general populace, with priests active at local churches, though the extent to which most people experienced Mass or were taught about the religion would have varied considerably. In practice, the secular Church and the monasteries were closely connected – some bishops would have been based at monasteries and some bishops may have formerly been monks (Etchingham 1999). Monasteries had significant landholdings, wealth and influence on political affairs. With some variation, the organisation and importance of the Church in Ireland seems to have been generally the same as throughout early medieval Britain. Indeed, the Church had influences that spread beyond the boundaries of individual polities (Charles-Edwards 2000). In western Scotland for instance, Iona was a monastery but it not only had subordinate monasteries in Ireland, Dál Riata, Pictland – though, apart from Dunkeld, these have not been identified – and in Northumbria, it also appointed bishops like Coeti (d. 712), who was venerated in Perthshire in southern Pictland (Taylor 1997, 60–61). Among the Northumbrians, many of the early bishops were Iona appointments or were former monks like Cuthbert (d. 687) and some, like Wilfrid (d. 707) and Ceolfrith (d. 716), abbot of Monkwearmouth-Jarrow (Bede's monastery), had been born into relatively privileged families before becoming monks and then bishops. There was, therefore, a close relationship between the Church and the wider lay world. In Pictland, the evidence is limited but Pictish bishops are directly referred to in contemporary sources associated with major social and political developments – Bishop Curetán was one of the guarantors of the 'Law of the Innocents' in about AD 697 (Woolf 2007a, 315), for example.

In terms of organisation of the Church, episcopal organisation may have broadly mirrored the structure of the Pictish kingdom and would have changed as the polities of Pictland took shape. In the later medieval period, northern and eastern Scotland was controlled by bishoprics centred in Strathearn and Menteith (at Dunblane), Fife (St Andrews), Perthshire (Dunkeld), Angus (Brechin), Aberdeenshire (Mortlach then Old Aberdeen), Moray (Birnie, Kinneddar and Spynie and finally Elgin from the 1220s), Ross (Rosemarkie), Caithness (based at Halkirk then Dornoch) and Orkney (Birsay then Kirkwall) (McNeil and MacQueen 1996, 335; Evans 2014, 51). The specifics of the ecclesiastical structure of the Church in Pictland is unclear, other than to say there is likely to have been at least two bishoprics, one in the south and one in the north (Fraser 2009, 257–59; Woolf 2007b, 316). The death of Túathal, chief bishop of Fortriu and Abbot of Dunkeld, is referenced in the *Annals of Ulster* in an entry for 865 (Woolf 2007a, 56), while Bishop Curetán is likely to have been based at Rosemarkie (Veitch 1997, 637). Bishops being located at monastic locations is plausible elsewhere. An obituary notice of Tuathalán, Abbot of St Andrews, is recorded in AD 747 but, from the 10th century onwards, it is only bishops of this centre who are mentioned in the sources, though the existence of a *Céli Dé* community in the 12th century indicates the continuation of a monastic dimension (Taylor with Márkus 2009, 405–16). We might also suspect that Pictish bishops resided for periods at the important ecclesiastical centre at Kinneddar since, in the 12th century, it was a seat of the bishops of Moray.

Below the level of the bishop in the early medieval Pictish Church would have been clergy who administered at a local level to the community to some extent. The parish system in Scotland did not develop till the 12th century but must have been based on pre-existing secular land units and Church divisions. For example, the substantial landholdings of the monastery at Abernethy on the south side of the River Earn and the Tay estuary were divided by the 13th century into parishes, each centred on a former chapel or subordinate church, such as the potentially Pictish church of Exmagirdle, Perthshire, whose place-name includes the early ecclesiastical element *eglēs*, 'church' (Rogers 1992, 216–32, Barrow 2003, 42, 272; Taylor with Márkus 2012, 365). Elsewhere, some dioceses, especially Dunkeld and St Andrews, not only consist of blocks of parishes but also detached parishes, scattered in a wider region (see McNeill and MacQueen 1996, 348–49, 353).

We can suspect that these detached parishes may represent monastic and episcopal lands or jurisdictions, some located along useful transit routes. For instance, the parish of Ardersier was in the region of Moray but actually part of the diocese of Ross, conveniently directly across the Moray Firth from Rosemarkie (and Fortrose), the seat of the bishops of Ross (Taylor forthcoming), so the bishops could control both sides of a ferry crossing. Similarly, a remarkable string of detached parishes in Dunkeld diocese and Columban dedications to Columba and his successor Baithéne, from Inchmahome (Stirling Council), Inchcolm in the Forth and then into the Borders, reflects the route from Iona to Lindisfarne, which would have been important in the 7th century, when the Columban community played a significant role in the Northumbrian kingdom. It seems likely, therefore, that later medieval bishoprics sometimes reflected much earlier ecclesiastical territories, consisting of smaller, local areas, connected to monasteries and larger church establishments.

Church units would have defined particular Church communities each with property and responsibilities. However, caution is needed in assuming that we can extrapolate back from the 12th to the 9th centuries or even earlier or that later divisions reflect much earlier secular units; in Abernethy's territory, Exmagirdle, for example, only just survived to become a parish due to grants in the early 13th century to Lindores Abbey (*Lindores Cartulary*, nos. 42–48, 68, 70–72; Dowden 1903, 43–52, 74–79). Later parishes might cut across earlier units, which is understandable if secular and ecclesiastical lordships altered in extent as kindreds, lords and Church institutions dominated different areas over time. However, there are hints of these earlier local divisions, not only in place-names, dedications and diocesan affiliations, but also through the presence of Pictish churches (and associated graveyards), and the location of early medieval carved stones on or near the later parish boundaries (RCAHMS 2007, 118–19, 124, 128; Forsyth 2008b, 407, 409).

Through time, changes in Christian belief and organisation happened as society developed and altered. New ascetic movements emerged with the *Céli Dé* forming and their influence spreading in the late 8th century, for example. The *Céli Dé* – also now known as the 'Culdees' – were hard-line ascetics, practising extreme abstinence. A movement for the reform of monastic life which originated in Ireland, the rapidity of its expansion and significance is unknown but it spread to more institutions in eastern Scotland than it ever did in Ireland (Clancy 1996, 112; Woolf 2007a, 314–15).

Other changes include greater alignment of Church and kingship. From the 8th century onwards, a greater presence or juxtaposition between Church and secular elite residences is seen at sites such as Forteviot, Meigle and Burghead. In the Viking Age, the Church perhaps lost some of its wealth with the appropriation of its lands in the face of a rapidly changing and deteriorating political context with the arrival of Viking raiders and settlers in the west, north and east (Woolf 2007a, 316), though certain Church sites, such as Dunkeld and Abernethy, appear to have continued and to even have witnessed significant investment (Maldonado 2021, 178–85).

Royal patronage was undoubtedly key to the development of many ecclesiastical centres and the spread of Christianity more generally. Different kings are likely to have had their favoured church locations and patronised and established anew foundations of their choosing. The surviving foundation legends for both St Andrews and Abernethy emphasise particular Pictish kings in the origin of these major ecclesiastical centres, though a desire for prestige and patronage may have influenced their choices of patron. A 12th-century text described an earlier grant to St Andrews of lands in east Fife called *Cursus Apri*, the 'Boar's Raik' – a name that Watson associated with a mythological boar hunt and Taylor with a tribal emblem and possible earthworks in the area (Watson 1926, 397–98; Taylor with Márkus 2009, 420–23) – but another possibility is that this had been partly royal hunting ground (see Chapter 3). The sculptural evidence is once again an important clue to patronage. The repeated use of David imagery at sites such as St Andrews, Forteviot, Kinneddar and Kincardine in Ross and Cromarty, for example, has been used to suggest royal patronage at these establishments, since the image of David, the great Old Testament king, was employed to highlight the imperial pretensions of the powerful Pictish kings of the 8th and 9th centuries AD (Fraser 2009a, 360) (Figure 4.19). The lesser investment in elaborate cross-slabs and associated monuments we see in some areas, such as the Western Isles and Aberdeenshire, could also be due to less significant royal activity and influence over these areas (Henderson 1971), though it could also be that patronage was simply invested in different mediums and venues in different regions. Church furnishings are also likely to have been the subject of royal patronage – the 15 handbells that survive in areas of Pictland at sites such as Little Dunkeld and Forteviot are obvious examples of elite resource investment in the fittings of major churches (Bourke 1983, 467; Bourke 2020, 146–48, maps 7–8).

4.19 On one side of the Dupplin Cross there is a seated figure playing a magnificent harp – this is most likely a representation of the Old Testament King David. (© Historic Environment Scotland)

There are also juxtapositions between certain high-status secular sites and important Church estates. The fort at Clatchard Craig may have been connected to Abernethy for it used stone from Carpow Roman fort, the Roman fortification lying within the later boundaries of Abernethy's core territory (Noble *et al.* forthcoming; see also Chapter 3), suggesting elite interests in both the monastery and the fort. The location of Kinneddar and its proximity to Burghead suggests links here too. The King's Seat overlooking Dunkeld is another obvious example of the juxtaposition of an elite secular site and major Church establishment. Logierait by the confluence of the Tay and Tummel may have benefitted from being close to Rait, if that later medieval centre of Atholl has Pictish origins, and near to Fortingall and Dull, at the confluence of the Tay and the Lyon, is the striking hillfort of Caisteal Mac Tuathal. The place-name of this latter fort has been suggested to be connected to Túathal, bishop of Fortriu and Abbot of Dunkeld, whose death is recorded in the Irish annals in 865 AD, though this identification is very tentative given that the name seems to refer simply to the descendants of someone called Túathal. Nonetheless, the fort is morphologically similar to the King's Seat, Dunkeld (see Chapter 3), and is an excellent candidate for an early medieval fort whose occupants perhaps patronised the ecclesiastical establishments at Dull, Fortingall and maybe even Dunkeld.

As well as the larger, royally endowed Church centres, there would have been a patchwork of ecclesiastical sites of different sizes and forms (Clancy 2008a, 391). Here smaller assemblages of early Christian sculpture than that found at the larger centres may provide an important correlate for sites below the top tier of the major ecclesiastical centres. Parc-an-caipel, in Inverness-shire, and Tullich, Aberdeenshire, may be examples of important but smaller-scale Church establishments. The occurrence of small numbers of cross-marked slabs and the relatively modest character of the carving at sites such as Congash and Tullich may indicate the more localised networks of early Christian sites, with smaller establishments perhaps part of an expansion of pastoral services that may have occurred from leading churches in the later 7th and 8th centuries AD (Clancy 2008a, 392). These smaller establishments may have been funded by means other than royal endowment. Notes in the Book of Deer, for example, depict a Pictish mormáer of Buchan as the donor of lands at Aberdour and Deer for the foundation of the church, with later grants in the Gaelic period also largely coming from local figures rather than the king (Forsyth *et al.* 2008, 137; Broun 2008, 355–56). Other forms of more specialised early Christian locales are likely to have existed too – the Caiplie Caves in Fife, full of rudimentary Christian crosses on the walls, may have been eremitic retreats and sites of pilgrimage (Fisher 2001, 61) (Figure 4.20).

What was the character of the churches at the smaller and larger ecclesiastical centres? It seems likely, as in Ireland, that the earliest churches were mostly built of wood (O'Sullivan *et al.* 2014, 152; Ó Carragáin 2010, 15). At the Isle of May, timber phases may have been under the 10th-century stone phase (James and Yeoman 2008, 177) but unfortunately no early Christian site in Pictland has seen the level of investigation needed to identify what may be relatively ephemeral and modestly sized early church groundplans (Foster 2015, 74). Nechtan's request for stone masons from Northumbria implies stone churches from at least the early 8th century AD and the architectural sculpture from sites such as Meigle, Dull, Forteviot, Portma-

4.20 Incised crosses at Caiplie Caves, Fife, may represent the use of the cave by early medieval hermits. (© Historic Environment Scotland)

homack and Rosemarkie of a probable 8th- to 9th-century date suggests an ambitious era of church building with perhaps relatively large stone-built churches in the later Pictish period (see also Henderson and Henderson 2004, 205–13; Clarke *et al.* 2012, 97). The presence of probable altar screens and other church fittings gives clues about the internal furnishings but unfortunately few pieces of church metalwork exist other than the handbells (Bourke 1983, 2020, 146–48; Clarke *et al.* 2012, 45, 97; Henderson and Henderson 2004, 181). Handbells would have been used for ringing the monastic hours and during a whole range of religious ceremonies such as at funerals, processions and calls to prayer (Bourke 2020, 154–223). One other rare survivor of church metalwork in Pictland is the Monymusk Reliquary, a 'house-' or more appropriately a 'church-shaped' reliquary (Blackwell 2012, 35) (Colour Plate 20). These have traditionally been identified as portable reliquary containers but they could have also been containers for the Eucharist kept at important churches (Blackwell 2012, 38).

In Pictland, it is the sculpture once again that gives us the most vivid insights presently available into the world of these early ecclesiastical centres. The presence of composite shrines at major ecclesiastical sites suggests that these may have held the relics of saints, kept at the more important establishments, some becoming the most sacred relics within Church centres that became famous destinations for pilgrimage and healing (Blackwell 2012, 43). Perhaps the most impressive and distinctive early Christian monuments of the Picts were the magnificent cross-slabs. These normally included a cross on one side and on the back they could include hunt scenes (see Chapter 3), biblical imagery and Pictish symbols (see Chapter 6).

These monuments were carved using the motifs of the Insular art style incorporating design elements found across Britain and Ireland – including spirals and trumpet-shaped scrolls, interlace, key, knot and fret pattern, zoomorphic motifs and vine scrolls (Henderson and Henderson 2004, 15). These stones show influences through the international network of the Church, from Rome, Constantinople and the wider European Church, reflecting connections that would have brought books, metalwork and objects and materials for the Christian faith to Pictland. The most magnificent examples of Pictish cross-slabs resemble the all-over patterned 'carpet pages' of Insular manuscripts such as the Book of Durrow and the Book of Kells (Henderson and Henderson 2004, 31–57, 66) (Figure 4.21), and this would be especially the case if the cross-slabs were painted. The principal function of these cross-slabs was to prominently display the Christian cross but a whole range of other motifs were included, including a stunning array of animals inspired by native, classical and Mediterranean sources.

Biblical imagery centred around motifs showing the servants of God – from the Apostles to the 'Desert Fathers' Anthony and Paul, to the contemporary clerics who communicated the word of God. Rarer depictions include crucifixion scenes, images of the Trinity and the Virgin Mary. More subtle Christian messages may include the vine-scroll used on a number of cross-slabs – this may have symbolised wine and by implication the blood of Christ. Sacred numerology also appears to have been a feature with decorated bosses on some crosses, for example, totalling 12 in number to symbolise the apostles perhaps and other decorative motifs numbering three or seven, for example, may have represented the Trinity and the seven days of creation respectively. More direct images appear to have represented judgement and damnation (Henderson and Henderson 2004, 138–57) (Figure 4.22). Less obviously, Christian-aligned scenes or characters may have referred to folklore, mythology and legends of the Picts (Henderson and Henderson 2004, 137; Kilpatrick 2011) and, as noted in Chapter 3, these stones are also an important source for the everyday life and ideologies of the Pictish elite.

The cross-slabs erected at important Church sites and in the wider landscape were huge investments in resources, labour and craft and speak of high-status patronage being concentrated at particular sites in the later first millennium AD (see Gondek 2006). In a church setting, some of these stones marked the sacred geography of a holy place and others might have been associated with specific saints or events in the life of that saint, acting as the focus for prayer, teaching and the practice of Mass (Henderson and Henderson 2004, 138–40, 161, 180–81; Clarke *et al.* 2012, 33, 172). The outer boundaries of ecclesiastical centres are likely to have been marked by monuments too. The property notes in the Book of Deer and both the Abernethy and St Andrews foundation legends suggest that stones may

4.21 The cross-slab from Nigg. At the top, the two figures bowing are the Desert Fathers Anthony and Paul. A raven is flying in between them to miraculously deliver bread. The bread represents the celebration of Mass which, in turn, represents the body of Christ in the Eucharist. (© Historic Environment Scotland)

4.22 Meigle 26 shows a monster chasing a human – the torment of the damned. (© Historic Environment Scotland)

have been used as estate boundaries of early churches (Forsyth 2008a, 406; Taylor 2005, 16; Taylor with Márkus 2009, 578).

The churches at major centres appear, in many cases, to have been enclosed by banks and ditches. The early 8th-century Gaelic collection of canon law, the *Collectio Canonum Hibernensis*, states a holy place should be surrounded by two or three enclosures of increasing sacredness (O'Sullivan *et al.* 2014, 145). These boundaries also had a legal role in marking zones of sanctuary and quite possibly a practical function too in terms of defining areas of working, animal keeping, industry and other activities, within the inner bounds of the monastery enclosures. Large enclosures have been confirmed at sites including Portmahomack, Kinneddar and Fortingall, though complete groundplans are not known at any Pictish site as of yet. The enclosures at Kinneddar and Fortingall and, at a smaller scale, Tullich and Congash suggest at least two enclosures at each of these sites – one marking the immediate area around each church and a larger outer enclosure. At Portmahomack, the outer enclosure appears to have enclosed different zones of activity with an industrial quarter found to the south of the church and the main burial ground around the church itself (Carver *et al.* 2016, 194). In Ireland, ecclesiastical sites tend to have two enclosing boundaries, very occasionally three, and these also show evidence of zoning of activities with craftworking often confined to the outer enclosures (O'Sullivan *et al.* 2014, 147).

In Ireland, there tend to be direct correlations with the size of vallum enclosures and the importance of particular church sites (O'Sullivan *et al.* 2014, 147) and the same is likely in Pictland. The vallum at Fortingall may have been around 4ha, while that at Kinneddar was at least 8ha, St Andrews could have been even larger but this has yet to be confirmed. The shape of the Pictish vallum enclosures thus far identified are interesting for they are rectilinear in shape rather than the common circular form found in Ireland. The rectilinear form is found at Iona and may have provided the template for some sites in Pictland (Campbell and Maldonado 2020, 61–63). The dating evidence from Kinneddar and Fortingall suggests some of these large vallum enclosures may be as early as the 7th century AD – broadly contemporary with the vallum of Iona – and these may well have replaced more modest and earlier enclosures.

The extent of the enclosures of some of these Pictish ecclesiastical centres – along with the archaeological evidence for sites such as Portmahomack as major centres of production and, presumably, exchange – brings to the fore the important role these sites may have played as major population centres and nodes in commercial trade, as well as religious and perhaps secular administration. Unsurprisingly, given the scale of these ecclesiastical centres, there has been a long-running debate about the potential proto-urban role of large monastic sites in Ireland and elsewhere. The idea of 'monastic towns' was developed by Doherty (1985) who suggested that some of the most influential sites were large religio-economic complexes incorporating social, religious, administrative and commercial functions. This has been widely debated (for example, Etchingham 1999; Graham 1987; Swift 1998; Valante 1998; O' Sullivan *et al.* 2014, 175–78) but there is no doubting the scale of some of these centres, nor the resources they were able to draw upon to create the monumental sculpture and rich metalwork produced at these sites. These must have been centres that inspired cultural and economic innovation (Woolf 2013, 13; see also Maldonado 2021). In Ireland, contemporary major Church sites such as Clonmacnoise were central sites of consumption and resource use – analysis of faunal remains, for example, suggest that Clonmacnoise by the River Shannon in the Viking Age was a commercial hub on a par with the major trading settlement of Dublin (O'Sullivan *et al.* 2014, 177). Similarly, on the Continent, some monasteries also had substantial related trading settlements and were producing large quantities of goods for trade (Henning 2009).

In Pictland, apart from Portmahomack, few sites have been excavated on any scale and we have few extensively excavated secular settlements of elite status or otherwise to compare to them, but it is certainly the case that the ecclesiastical enclosures at a number of Pictish sites represent the largest enclosed settlements thus far identified in Pictland. Kinneddar at over 8ha in extent – almost double the size of the contemporary secular centre at Burghead – is only exceeded in size by the earlier hillfort at Tap o' Noth (see Chapter 3). The construction of these enclosures speaks of the ability of these sites to draw on wealth and a large contributing population. The later situation of some centres may give us clues that these were not just Church settlements in their earlier incarnations. St Andrews, for example, is referenced as an important trading centre in an 11th century Gaelic poem, many years prior to St Andrews becoming a burgh (Taylor with Márkus 2009, 410).

Conclusions

Overall, we can identify widespread evidence for the early Church in Pictland, most certainly from the 7th century, but there were Christian communities in Pictland in the 6th century and quite probably the 5th century too. Major ecclesiastical centres with core territories hectares in extent were developing from the 7th and 8th centuries onwards, becoming the largest enclosed settlements known in Pictland in the later first millennium AD. The Church and its establishments would have undoubtedly brought many changes. Early Christianity required religious specialists – priests – and often involved monks, nuns and a hierarchy of abbots, bishops and other administrators, in what gradually became highly formalised structures focussed, ideally, on glorifying God and promoting and maintaining correct Christian practices and beliefs, while punishing sinful behaviour. The Church became an integral part of wider public life, increasingly shaping social structure and secular politics. Indeed, the Church may have played an active role in the consolidation of the kingdoms of Pictland and the power of the over-kingship of Fortriu (Fraser 2009a, 259; Foster 2014, 123; Grigg 2015), though clerical wealth, power and ideology could also act as a check on royal ambitions. The adoption of the Christian faith allowed the Picts to engage with international networks, placing Pictland at the north-western edge of the European Christian Church network.

The archaeological record is also beginning to illuminate some of the practices and places related to pre-Christian belief, some of which may have remained a part of everyday beliefs even in the face of a predominantly Christian social framework. Thus, wells could be sacred in both a pagan and Christian context and stones could be charms or the focus of healing but this hybridisation of pagan, Christian and everyday belief is not unusual across Europe in the first millennium AD. Pictland did not remain more pagan than anywhere else in Britain and Ireland once conversion became widespread. The new religion was here to stay and permeated all facets of Pictish life, part of a key turning point in Scottish history.

CHAPTER FIVE

'Performing the Sorrowful Funeral Rites'

Ways of Death and Burial

Death is a crucial time of personal and social stress, when the living mourn the departed, perform rituals to commence the journey of the dead in the afterlife and look to the future of an irrevocably altered community. A sense of this can be gained from an episode in Adomnán's *Life of Columba*, in which a boy in a newly converted Pictish household suddenly dies (II.32; Sharpe 1995, 179–80). There is immediate ideological conflict since the *magi* attacked the parents, claiming that their gods were stronger than the Christian deity. However, Columba comes to the family's house, where the child's parents were 'performing the sorrowful funeral rites' and consoles them, before visiting the dead boy lying indoors in a temporary resting place (Anderson and Anderson 1991, 138, 140; authors' own translation). A tearful Columba prays to Christ and the boy is raised from the dead, mourning becomes rejoicing and the pagan *magi* are thwarted – Christianity is vindicated. This is not a contemporary or unbiased account but it evokes effectively the reality of grief for loved ones, the existence of rituals for the dead and how death could also be a focal point of social and ideological tension. Unfortunately, what it does not provide is an account of the final funeral rites, in which the deceased are laid to rest, but archaeology is increasingly demonstrating that burial practices underwent dynamic change in the Pictish period.

The development of cemeteries for the dead in Pictland around the middle of the first millennium AD was a dramatic innovation in the ideology of death and the afterlife in north-east Scotland. Set against the very sparse background of the funerary traditions of the Iron Age, the flourishing of major long cist and barrow cemeteries in the 5th to the 7th centuries AD marks a period in which the dead became much more visible in the region's landscapes. The most common new monumental burial form of this era consisted of square and round barrows or cairns built over extended inhumations. A tradition of long cist or dug grave cemeteries also proliferated, particularly in southern Pictland. By the 8th century, burial practice appears to have become more closely associated with the Church and focussed on ecclesiastical establishments, though only small numbers of churchyard cemeteries have been excavated from this period due to the continuing use of many Christian sites to the present day. The broad patterns of Pictish mortuary traditions, with field and monumental cemeteries of the 5th to 7th centuries AD being replaced with a shift to church burial from the 8th century, mirrors trends in burial forms across Britain and Ireland in the first millennium AD.

The characterisation of Pictish ways of death was slow to be established. In Wainwright's classic 1955 edited volume, *The Problem of the Picts*, no clear examples of Pictish cemeteries or burials could be identified (Wainwright 1955b, 94–96). But, only a year after this publication, the first long cist cemeteries of southern Pictland were discussed by Audrey Henshall, including examples in Fife, Angus and Perthshire (Henshall 1956, 265–70, Appendix II). Illumination of the monumental cemeteries of Pictland followed in the coming decades with further synthesis and excavations of long cist burials in association with square and round cairns or barrows at cemeteries such as Lundin Links, Fife, and Redcastle, Angus (Ashmore 1980; Close-Brooks 1984; Greig *et al.* 2000; Alexander 2005). Today, many examples of Pictish monumental cemeteries are known as cropmarks through the identification of dozens of square and round barrow cemeteries during aerial survey programmes by the Royal Commission for Ancient and Historical Monuments of Scotland and local government archaeology teams (Maxwell 1978; Mitchell and Noble 2017; Mitchell 2020) (Figure 5.1). However, excavation of these cemeteries has generally been quite limited and often the acidic soils of much of Scotland limit the recovery of human remains and reduce the chances of even accurately dating these forms of burial (Mitchell *et al.* 2020). Nonetheless, we have today a much clearer understanding of the forms of burial that characterised funerary traditions in Pictland, though we still have a much more limited dataset than early medieval Ireland or England, for example.

Iron Age precursors

While there is an increasingly recognised funerary record from the 5th to 7th centuries AD, what marks the preceding Iron Age traditions of mortuary activity is its relative sparsity. After the urnfield cemeteries of the Bronze Age, there was little in the way of a standardised burial type till the long cist and monumental cemeteries flourished from the 5th century AD onwards (for example, Armit 2016, 116–22; Ashmore 1980, 2003, 35). Prior to the early medieval period, the most common way of treating the dead seems to be largely archaeologically invisible – whether this was excarnation or the disposal of bodies in the sea, in caves or other natural places, or other means is not clear (Armit 2016, 117). Examples of cemeteries of simple dug graves are known in Scotland from the Early Iron Age, at sites

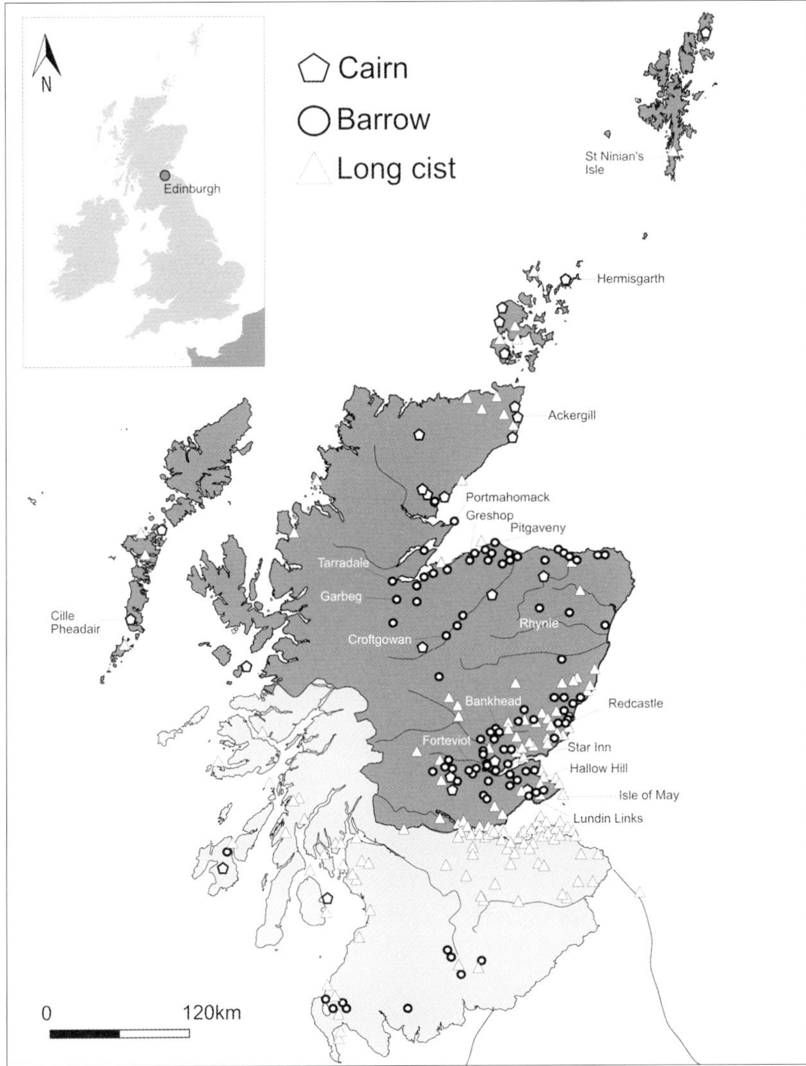

5.1 The distribution of probable early medieval square and round barrows, cairns and long cists, with major sites mentioned in Chapter 5 highlighted. (After Maldonado 2013 and Mitchell 2020)

such as Broxmouth and Dryburn Bridge, both in East Lothian, and there are rare examples of burials with weaponry from eastern Scotland dating to the early centuries AD (Armit 2016, 116–22) but, overall, the numbers of burials are small and the patterns are difficult to discern. Cemeteries with more than a handful of burials are also very rare, though there are more unusual burial contexts such as the Knowe of Skea, Westray, Orkney, where dozens of adult, child and neonate burials have been found at a coastal promontory (Gooney 2015). Human remains in the form of isolated skeletal parts such as fragments of skull or long bones are routinely found at Iron Age settlements and this is a tradition that continued into the mid to late first millennium AD (Armit and Ginn 2007). However, this practice cannot be seen as a standardised burial rite or simply as a step in the process of mortuary activity – rather, human remains appear to have been used in quite complex ritualised and totemic ways.

There are Roman Iron Age burial practices that have some resemblance to the traditions which became dominant from the 5th century AD onwards, including burials in cists and under barrows and cairns. These include cists from An Corran, Boreray, Outer Hebrides, and a large annular ditched barrow from the Inchtuthil plateau in Perthshire that covered a boulder constructed cist and other examples of cist burials from the same era are known from Dundee to Shetland (Carter and Fraser 1996; Badcock and Downes 2000; MacGregor 2004; Sheridan 2004, 176; Brady *et al.* 2007; Winlow and Cook 2010). A few cist burials are also known from the 3rd to 4th centuries AD, such as Northton, Harris, and Balnabruach, Easter Ross (Tucker and Armit 2009, 216; Carver *et al.* 2016, 101), and a cemetery from Galson, Lewis, has dates that span the 1st to the 6th centuries AD, though this site is not fully published (Neighbour *et al.* 2000).

Thus, there are broad similarities between examples of burials found in the early centuries AD and the long cist and monumental barrows of the 5th century AD onwards but the Iron Age inheritance is not entirely clear as these Roman Iron Age monuments are few and far between and dating using higher precision methods has tended to push the date of monuments later (Mitchell 2020, 305). Looking at the earlier examples in detail also highlights differences from the traditions of the 5th century AD or later. Where cairns or barrows are present, these can be quite rudimentary – as at Sands of Breckon, Shetland – or of uncertain form – for example, Loch Borallie, Sutherland (Carter and Fraser 1996; MacGregor 2004). There are also variations on the extended burial form with flexed examples, crouched individuals and burials with heads at the east end (Loch Borallie) and a N–S orientation for the double burial at Balnabruach rather than the much more standard W–E orientation found in the vast majority of early medieval long cists and barrows and cairns. Thus, while there are burials that broadly match the long cist and monumental traditions that swept across Pictland in the 5th and 6th centuries AD, few provide exact parallels and nor is there evidence for widespread and inter-regional traditions prior to that date.

The dead made visible – early medieval burial traditions

From the 5th century onwards, there is undoubtedly a step change in the evidence for burial with long cist cemeteries and monumental cemeteries emerging on a widespread scale in the post-Roman period. From Shetland to the Firth of Forth, very similar burial monuments were constructed suggesting strong links between the dispersed communities of Pictland

(Ashmore 1980; 2003; Maldonado 2013; Mitchell and Noble 2017) (Figure 5.1). These burial forms represent the largest and most visible cemeteries of the dead since the Bronze Age and will be considered first.

Monumental cemeteries

In Pictland, the most characteristic and impressive burial tradition was the construction of square and round barrows (earthen construction) and cairns (stone construction) that covered single or, more rarely, multiple inhumations. The square and round cairns and barrows have frequently been identified as a distinctive Pictish burial tradition but, while there is a distinct concentration of square monuments in particular within Pictland, similar cemetery and burial types have been identified in Dumfries and Galloway, and also in Wales and England, and there are broadly similar monuments in Ireland too (Ashmore 1980; Close-Brooks 1984; Cowley 1996; Longley 2009, 113–15; O'Brien 1999; 2009, 148; 2020, 82–93) (Figure 5.1). Thus, the monumental cemeteries located in Pictland were identifiable as part of broader British and Irish traditions but do have a distinct regional flavour and concentration.

Monumental cemeteries in Pictland varied in size, form and construction methods but certain shared traits and trends appear across all cemeteries. Where upstanding examples survive, they are generally low and flat topped, surrounded by a stone kerb or a ditch or both and occasionally an outer bank. The ditched examples vary, with some bounded by a continuous ditch and others with interrupted ditches and, in some cases, stone boulders or slabs are located at the corners of the enclosing elements. Particular materials seem to have been significant such as white quartz and sand for the grave fill, suggesting care and symbolism behind monument creation (Maldonado 2013, 18). The majority of barrows cover single graves but cairns have also been shown to cover groups of individuals, as at Lundin Links, Fife, and Ackergill, Caithness.

In all areas of Pictland, most cemeteries contain six or fewer monuments (Winlow 2011, 341; Mitchell and Noble 2019) but larger examples are known. The largest cemeteries in northern Pictland are Garbeg and Croftgowan (Figure 5.2), both in Inverness-shire, and Tarradale, Ross and Cromarty, that all have upwards of 25 barrows. In the south, large cemeteries include Star Inn Farm, Dundee and Lundin Links, Fife (Greig *et al.* 2000; Mitchell 2020, 224). Dispersed clusters within a wider landscape are also known, with groups at times separated by watercourses or other natural features as found on the Lunan Water, Angus, where cemeteries at Invergighty Cottage, Hatton Mill and Boysack are found on both sides of the river within a few hundred metres of one another. In Atlantic Pictland, on the Northern and Western Isles, square and round cairns are known,

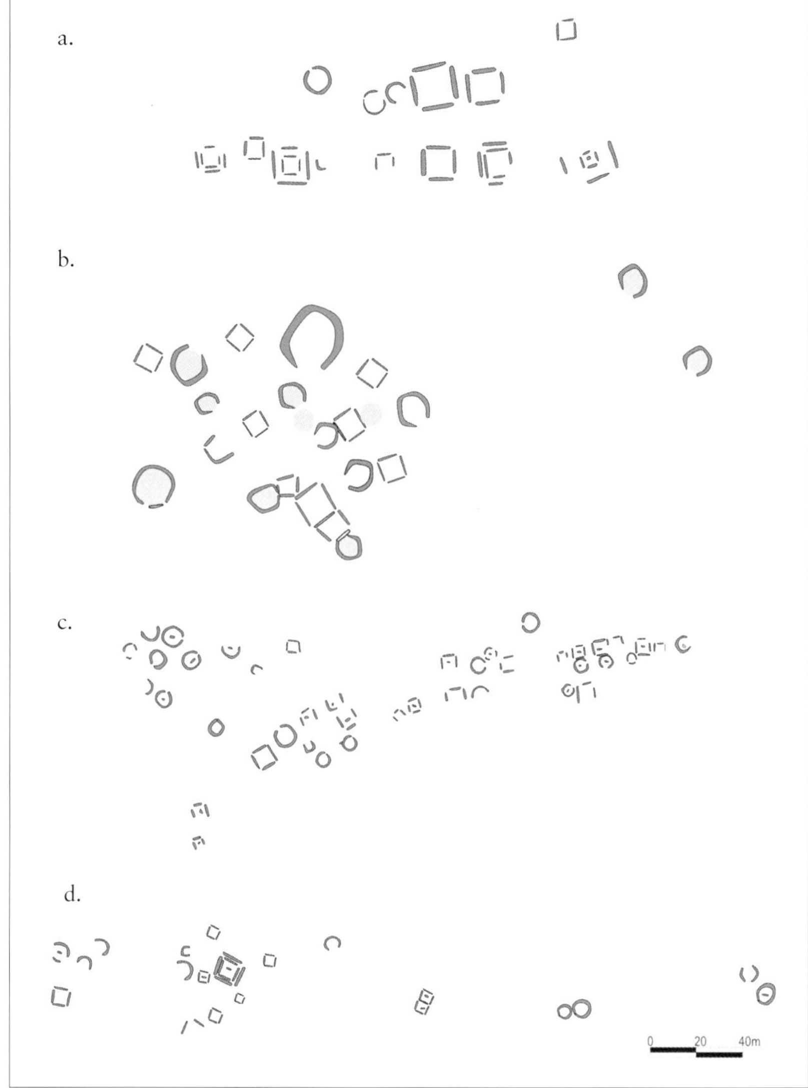

5.2 Examples of barrow cemeteries identified from the air or upstanding:
(a) Pitgaveny, Moray;
(b) the upstanding cemetery at Garbeg, Highland;
(c) Croftgowan, Moray;
(d) Star Inn Farm, Dundee.
(After Mitchell 2020)

generally in small numbers, but larger cemeteries are found on Orkney at Hermisgarth on Sanday and on the island of Hoy (Mitchell 2020, 258–60).

The largest cemetery that still survives upstanding is Garbeg, Inverness-shire, where around 26 upstanding barrows have been recorded – 14 square or sub-rectangular and 10 circular (Wedderburn and Grime 1984) (Figure 5.2). There are also upstanding barrows at Whitebridge, Brin School, Croftgowan and Pityoulish (all Inverness-shire) (Rae and Rae 1953; Stevenson 1984; Alexander 2000). These cemeteries contain both square and circular mounds up to 10m in diameter. Cairn cemeteries are also known at sites

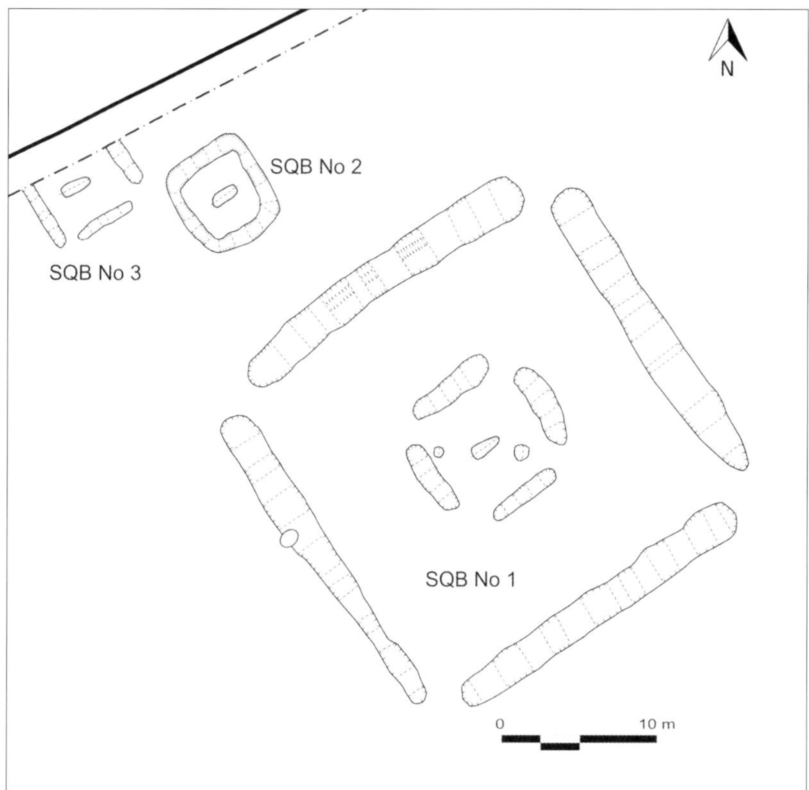

5.3 Plan of three barrows excavated at Greshop, Moray. One of the barrows (SQB 1) appears to have been enlarged to make it a monumental burial mound. (After Mitchell *et al.* 2020)

from Fife to Caithness but stone cairn monuments are concentrated in the Highlands and Islands (Figure 5.1). This may be a relic of survival for Lundin Links, Fife, and sites such as Tillytarmont, Aberdeenshire (Woodham 1975), show that cairns as well as barrows were constructed in the Lowlands but the levels of survival make the ratios uncertain. In the Lowlands, the vast majority of monuments survive as cropmarks, and the process of destruction may have occurred relatively late in many cases. The barrows at Bankhead of Kinloch, Perthshire, for example, appear to have survived as upstanding monuments until the 19th century but the barrows had been removed by the time of the excavation of the graves and surrounding ditches (Mitchell *et al.* 2020, 31).

The barrows and cairns at individual cemeteries tend to average between 4m and 12m in maximum extent. Yet some sites in eastern Scotland contain barrows that are much larger than the norm, including examples of square and round barrows up to 25m across. Examples of cemeteries in northern Pictland with large barrows include Greshop and Pitgaveny, both in Moray (Figures 5.2 and 5.3), and Hills of Boyndie, Aberdeenshire. In southern Pictland, large barrows are known at Invergighty Cottage, Angus, Star Inn Farm, Dundee (Figure 5.2), Hall Hole, Perthshire, and Kettlebridge, Fife.

In some cases, oversized square monuments appear to have been enlargements or elaborations of smaller monuments, most notably at northern Pictish examples such as Greshop and Pitgaveny. Tarradale, Inverness-shire, also has larger circular barrows of 20m in diameter but the dating of these elements of the cemetery is uncertain. As well as numbers of monuments, the larger cemeteries have other characteristics that stand out. They tend to have more variety in their size, shape and architectural construction, which could be suggestive of their importance and longevity.

The barrow and cairn tradition of Pictland can be paralleled with similar traditions of monumentalised graves across Britain and Ireland. In Ireland, as in Pictland, cemeteries were established in the 5th to 6th centuries AD, likewise marking a distinct change from the sparser burial evidence of the Iron Age (O'Brien 2009, 136–38; 2020, 45–46, 49). Some very large enclosed cemeteries were created in Ireland, including the construction of settlement cemeteries that could reach hectares in extent (O'Sullivan *et al.* 2014, 283–99), but, in Ireland, the focus on monumentalising individual barrows and graves of individuals was a much rarer practice. Nonetheless, there are examples in Ireland of cemeteries that appear to cluster around what may be founder barrows or graves. A very small number were furnished with grave goods, such as neck or toe rings, and these tend to be associated with barrow traditions, though of differing forms to those found in Pictland (O'Brien 2009, 142–43; O'Sullivan *et al.* 2014, 293; Bhreathnach 2014, 125–26). In Wales, the most typical burials from the 5th century onwards were east–west orientated and unenclosed but ditched barrow graves are also known, including square enclosures that were probably barrows (Longley 2009, 113). References in the praise poem *Englynion y Beddau*, 'The Stanzas of the Graves', suggest that, by the 9th or 10th centuries, burials in mounds were associated with prestigious, heroic, elite figures of the past (Longley 2009, 115). The Pictish monumental cemeteries also emerged in the same horizon as a barrow building tradition in Anglo-Saxon England that began with relatively modest monuments and culminated in the elaborate princely burials of the late 6th and 7th centuries AD (Carver 2005; Dickinson 2011, 230; Geake 1992; Welch 2011, 269; Scull 2009, 277). In Anglo-Saxon England, the building of mounds has been connected with the emergence of powerful hereditary aristocracies (Carver 2002, 136).

In Pictland, the small number of mounds or cairns at most sites suggests that the monumentalisation of burials was not a common rite and is likely to have been an elite practice, commemorating select individuals. In Pictland, there are generally no grave goods distinguishing individual burials. Nonetheless, monuments were made more prominent through the scale of the mounds or cairns constructed. Like in the early Anglo-Saxon barrow tradition, it is the investment in construction, time and material that at least partly appears to have reflected wealth, status or significance of those interred and/or those who were orchestrating the burial rite (Scull 2009, 277). A notable and excavated example of one of these enlarged Pictish barrows was found at Greshop, Moray, where the largest monument was initially a relatively modest square barrow around 10m across. This barrow was in turn enclosed by a set of additional ditches creating a monument 28m across (Mitchell *et al.* 2020, 26). The other barrows discovered at the site measured 7m or 8m across but the enlargement of the one example greatly increased the size differential between these monuments. Thus, from the outset or through time, one of the monuments at Greshop was made to stand out through a greater investment in labour and was more monumental in form. Once complete, it was around four times the size of the other barrows in the cemetery.

While individuals buried in certain enlarged barrows may have been particularly influential in life, what perhaps mattered more was the ways in which the living community manipulated the status of the dead and the architecture of the cemetery for their own needs (Barrett 1994, 51; Ó Corráin 1998). The aggrandisement of particular barrows and cemeteries was an act that would have been socially and politically charged. The elaboration or enlargement of existing barrows may have happened during the creation of other monuments or as part of other important social events, perhaps when social relations were being established, reworked or maintained. In this respect, social status was not simply reflected in architecture of this kind – it was actively forged and manipulated through the creation of cemeteries (Williams 2007; Maldonado 2013, 8).

As well as barrow enlargement, there is another interesting phenomenon found in Pictish barrow cemeteries – the conjoining of barrows or cairns to create elaborate linked monuments. This is found widely at northern Pictish barrow cemeteries such as Tarradale, Croftgowan and Pitgaveny (Figure 5.2a) and at southern Pictish cemeteries such as Forteviot and Sherrifton, Perthshire, and Boysack, Angus. Cairns were also conjoined at cemeteries such as Lundin Links in Fife (Figure 5.4). At Pitgaveny, the barrows were arranged in two main rows, with the southern row having at least seven conjoined barrows. Each mound or cairn constructed altered the form of the landscape through a process of accretion, each adding to an evolving narrative that embodied the community of both the living and dead (Barrett 1994, 113, 123; Bradley 2007, 165).

The conjoining and elaboration of certain barrows may be part of the same phenomenon. Both developments suggest the importance of particular members of society and imply that the creation of lineages or dynasties of the dead, whether real or fictive, may have comprised an important element in the establishment and maintenance of cemeteries (Williams 2007). As well as following wider trends across Britain and Ireland, the occurrence

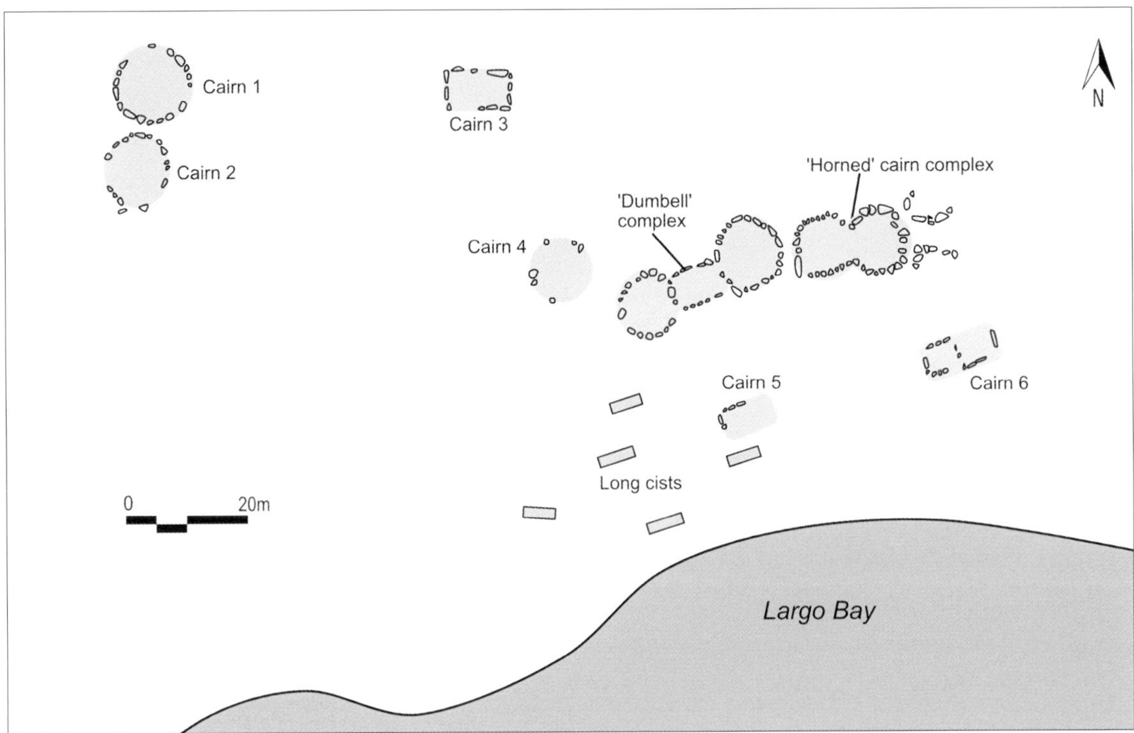

5.4 Plan of the cemetery at Lundin Links, Fife. (After Greig *et al.* 2000)

of these cemeteries, from the 5th to the 7th centuries AD, may mark the critical period in Pictland in which lineage, territoriality and claims to land and ancestry became emphasised in consolidating regional hegemonies.

Overall, the monumental cemeteries indicate sweeping changes to mortuary practice and the visibility of the dead in the landscapes of the living in Pictland from the 5th century AD. Some cemeteries could reach quite impressive extents with 30 barrows or more, but these must have only covered the graves of a very select portion of the community. While there are many commonalities in these monumental cemeteries in southern, northern and Atlantic Pictland, each cemetery was unique and each has an important story to tell.

Ways of death in southern Pictland

In order to assess the diversity of Pictish burial practices we can consider evidence from some of the sites of monumental cemeteries that have been excavated, taking in to account some of the issues of preservation and recovery that can limit interpretation. Undoubtedly the best attested Pictish cemetery is that at Lundin Links, Fife, discovered within a series of coastal dunes near the village of Lower Largo in southern Pictland (Greig *et al.* 2000) (Figures 5.4 and 5.5). Rescue excavations followed storm erosion

5.5 Lundin Links under excavation in the 1960s. (Lundin Links archive, courtesy of Moira Greig)

in the mid 1960s and six round cairns, four rectilinear cairns and six other cists containing a total of 24 inhumations were found. The cairns included unusual monuments such as the so-called 'dumbbell complex' that consisted of two round cairns joined by an oval setting of stones and the 'horned cairn complex' comprising a number of sub-circular cairns and linking structures. These two latter monuments were notable for containing multiple inhumations in single cairns – a relatively unusual aspect of Pictish inhumation practices. Radiocarbon dates from the skeletons centre on the 5th and 6th centuries AD (Greig *et al.* 2000, 611). Over 20 individuals were identified from the excavations in the 1960s with more of the burials female than male, with all six individuals from the horned cairn complex identified as female, four with congenital skeletal traits that suggests they may have been a family group (Smart and Campbell-Wilson 2000, 601; Lorimer 2000, 603–04).

Another important excavation of a Pictish cemetery is that at Redcastle, Angus, the existence of which was revealed by aerial photography (Alexander 2005) (Figure 5.6). A total of 16 graves were excavated at the cemetery which comprised five square barrows, two round barrows and nine unenclosed graves – though some of these may have originally been covered with barrows. Cropmarks of further barrows outwith the excavation area suggest that the cemetery was larger than revealed by excavation alone.

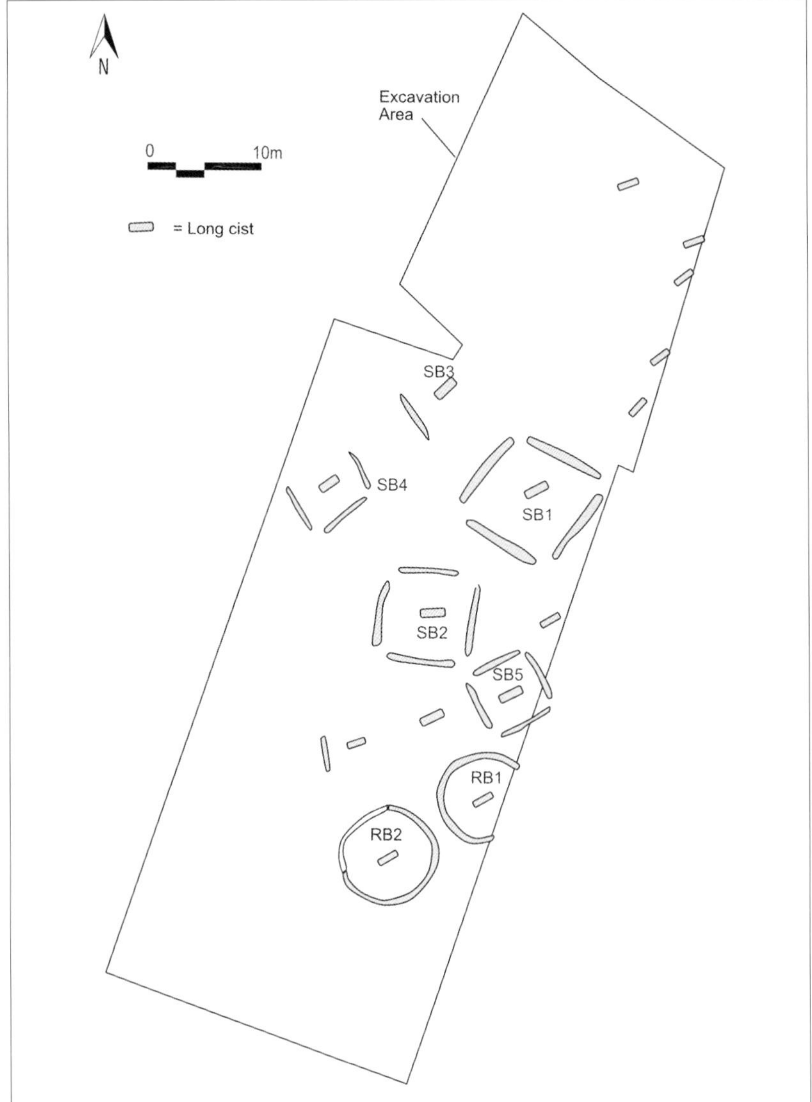

5.6 The cemetery at Redcastle, Angus, consisted of a mix of round and square barrows along with a series of unenclosed graves. (After Alexander 2005)

Preservation of the human remains therein was variable and the radiocarbon dating showed a spread of dates indicating activity spanning the 3rd to 9th centuries AD, but more recent re-analysis of the dating and new, more accurate, radiocarbon dates suggest cemetery use was restricted to between the 5th and 7th centuries AD (Mitchell 2020). Bone preservation at Redcastle was poor but all of the individuals appeared to be adult (Sinfield 2005, 103).

The 5th- to 8th-century cemetery at the southern Pictish royal centre of Forteviot (see Chapter 3) comprised at least 10 square barrows and three or four round barrows and at least 40 dug graves, all identified from crop-

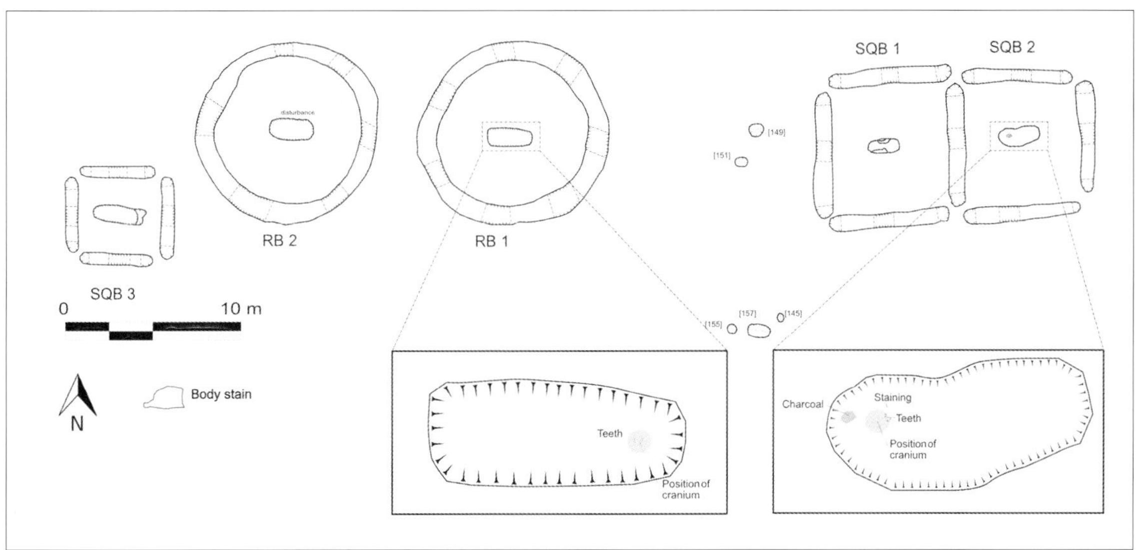

5.7 The Pictish cemetery at Bankhead, Perthshire. Two round barrows, a square barrow and two conjoined square barrows made up the small cemetery. Only fragmentary human remains survived in the acidic soils. (After Mitchell *et al.* 2020)

marks, spread over a distance of some 800m. Excavations of two pairs of conjoined square barrows showed that each had initially comprised a single barrow that had been modified with the construction of an additional barrow on the east, perhaps suggesting a familial relationship between individuals buried in each pair of monuments (Campbell et al. 2019, 88). Intriguing architectural detail was also found comprising posthole settings around the graves of one pair of conjoined barrows that may have been supports for some form of raised mortuary house above the burials or perhaps a temporary structure used in the interment ceremonies. In the western part of the complex, one of the most intriguing features was a large square enclosure about 30m across, around which many of the early medieval barrows clustered. This enclosure was very regularly made and it has been suggested it could have performed a cult function – perhaps a sanctuary site or an assembly place (Campbell *et al.* 2019, 90–91; Campbell and Driscoll 2020, 66; see also Chapter 4).

Cemeteries could also be relatively modest, as was that found at Bankhead, Perthshire, during development-led excavations (Mitchell *et al.* 2020) (Figure 5.7). Here the cemetery only consisted of five barrows. The barrows were positioned to respect each other, with the graves – all containing adults – on the same ENE–WSW alignment located in the approximate centre of the barrows. Like the two conjoined pairs at Forteviot, the western barrow at Bankhead appears to have been constructed first, with the eastern barrow added later. The conjoined square barrows each enclosed a single grave but the acidic soils had removed most of the evidence for burial apart from a body stain, skull fragments and some teeth in the western grave. Similar fragmentary remains were found in the other square barrow. The

5.8 Rhynie square barrows under excavation – see Figure 5.9 for plan.

shared alignments and the small number of barrows along with radiocarbon dating suggest the cemetery was a short-lived example, and dating also suggests that both square and round barrows were in contemporary use.

Dealing with death in northern and Atlantic Pictland

There have been much fewer excavations in more northerly areas of Pictland but slowly some cemeteries in this region have begun to be revealed in more detail. Excavations in 2013–2014 demonstrated that the early Pictish elite centre at Rhynie had a contemporary cemetery located at what is today the outskirts of the modern village (Figures 5.8 and 5.9; Colour Plate 21). In 1836, two of the symbol stones found in the village of Rhynie (stones 2 and 3) were removed during the construction of a turnpike road and a 'quantity' of human bones was found near the stones. Antiquarian reports and local newspapers also record the discovery of E–W oriented long cist burials (Henderson 1907, 163). One of the Pictish carvings, the warrior with a spear, is said to have been found in association with a cairn

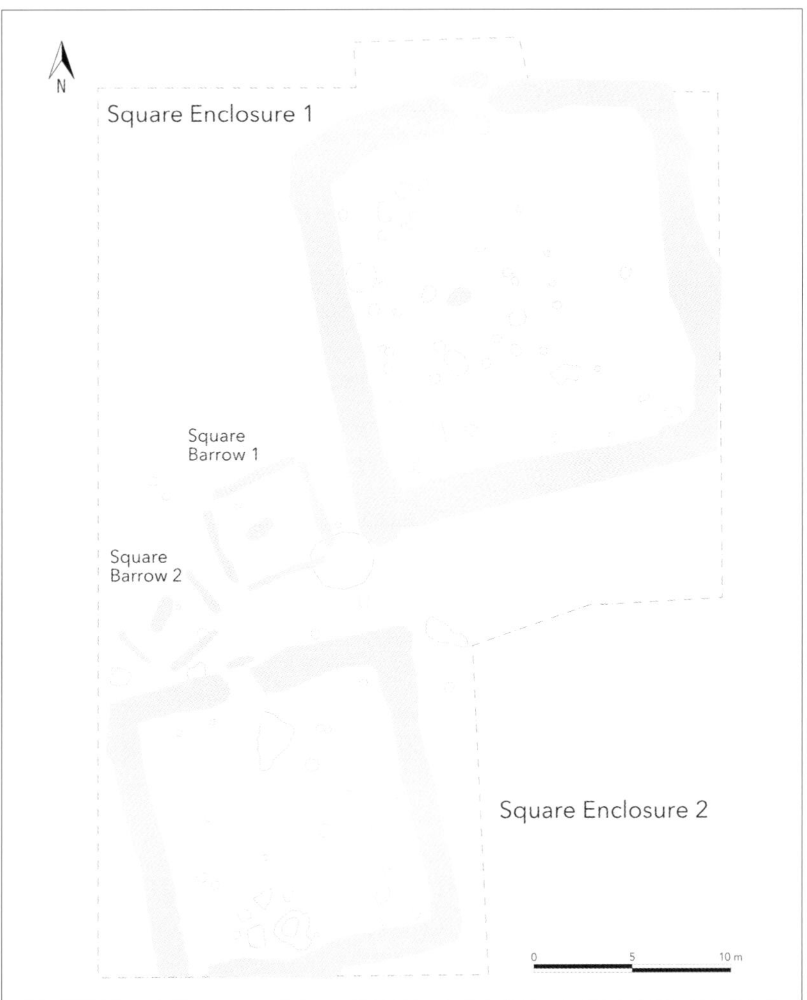

5.9 Two small square barrows and two much larger square enclosures were excavated at Rhynie, Aberdeenshire.

near the south side of the present village (Logan 1829, 56) and nearby, in the 1990s, aerial photography revealed two large square enclosures beside the previously located symbol stone findspots and burials. These were around 16–20m across with peculiar short segments of ditch at the entranceways to the interiors. Nothing was found to illuminate the function of the larger enclosures but they are reminiscent of the square enclosure found at Forteviot – the enclosures could have had similar cult associations or may have been a location for important gatherings associated with funerary ceremonies at the cemetery. Immediately adjacent to these enclosures at Rhynie, two square barrows were also identified – one a well-built stone cist that preserved the skeleton of the Pict interred. The burial was probably that of a woman but the preservation is such that certainty is not possible. The individual was found with their legs close together – they may have

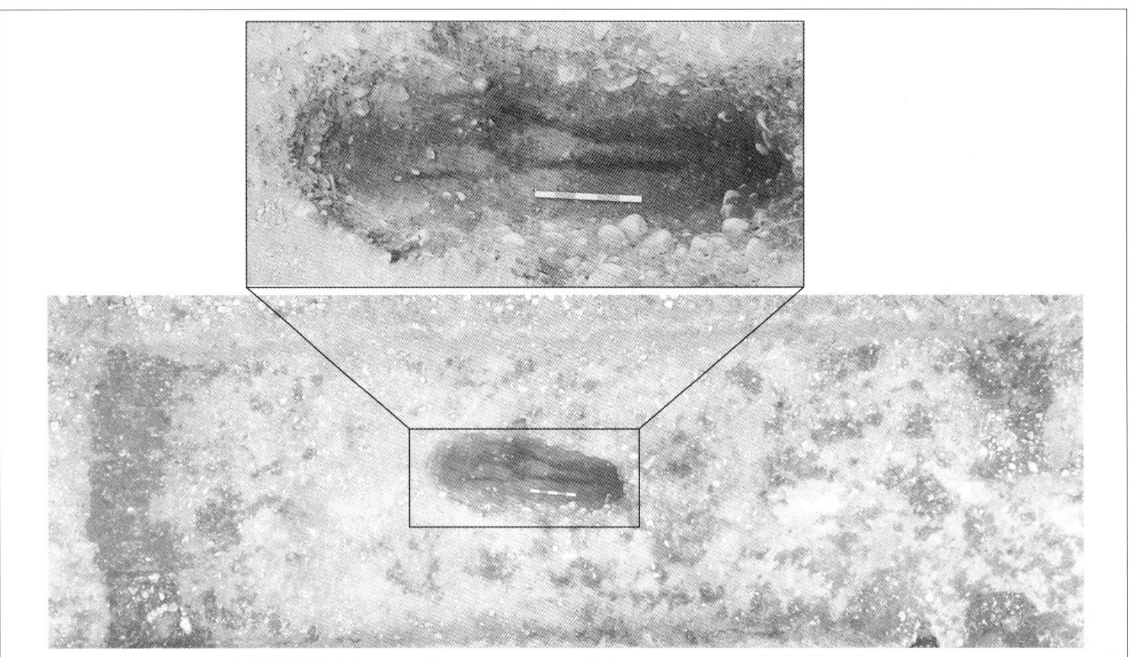

5.10 One of the circular barrows at Croftgowan under excavation in 2021 showing the body stain of the individual interred in the central grave.

been wrapped in a shroud or other funerary dress. This burial was contemporary with the 5th to 6th century phases of the Craw Stane complex.

The most recently excavated Pictish cemetery is that of Croftgowan, Inverness-shire – the largest Pictish cemetery known with over 40 barrows identified (Mitchell and Noble 2017, 14, Fig. 8; Mitchell 2020, 111–15). Unfortunately, destruction of what appears to have been largely an upstanding cemetery took place around 1800 and the outcome of this destructive process is marked on the Ordnance Survey First Edition map for the area as 'Site of Tumuli "Human remains, Sword Blades, Buckles, & c found here ad 1800"'. Excavations in 2021 targeted a number of barrows to test the preservation of the cemetery. Despite the harsh gravel soils, human remains were identified in three barrows – two round barrows and one square. In one of the round barrows, the soil impression of the skeleton was found with the enamel caps of the individual's teeth and fragments of skull found at the south-west of the grave (Figure 5.10). In the largest trench excavated, it was shown that a round barrow replaced two conjoined square barrows, providing an unusual insight into the sequence of barrow construction and the relative dating of examples of square and round barrows.

What would have been one of the more spectacular Pictish cemeteries was located on a terrace overlooking the Beauly Firth at Tarradale (Mitchell and Noble 2017, 15; Birch and Noble 2019). This cemetery is now only visible from the air from a plane or drone in the right conditions. The ceme-

5.11 The Tarradale, Highland, Pictish cemetery under excavation during 2019. The outlines of square and round barrows can be seen in the trenches. (© Andy Hickie / Tarradale Through Time project)

tery was located on an area of gravel terraces, now undulating fields, a few hundred metres from the Beauly Firth. The cemetery would have been virtually enclosed by water, with the firth, a stream course and boggy land to the north-west creating an 'island' of the dead. The cemetery comprised over 30 barrows, at least 23 circular – the largest up to 14m in diameter – and at least eight square barrows ranging in size from around 6–7m across to over 30m. The square barrows included both continuous ditched monuments and causewayed examples. Excavations in 2019 by the Tarradale Through Time project, a community initiative, confirmed the groundplan of a large part of the cemetery through trial trenching (Figure 5.11). The excavations found barrows clustered close together and uncovered barrows and unenclosed graves not evident on aerial photographs, suggesting the cemetery was even more extensive than hitherto identified. In some parts of the cemetery, monuments were so tightly packed together they must have been near contemporaries of one another and may have been built over a short space of time. In general, barrows appear to have enclosed single inhumations. Only a few examples of barrows preserved evidence

5.12 Tarradale log burial showing the cut for the log coffin and detail of the body stain in the grave, outlining the skull and torso of the interred. (© Tarradale Through Time project)

of those interred. Traces of a log coffin were located off centre of a round barrow. The shadow of the decayed timber was apparent during excavation, as was the shadowy decayed body of the individual interred, turned to a stain in the acidic soil (Figure 5.12).

Moving further north into Atlantic Pictland, few cemeteries have seen detailed excavation. Ackergill, Caithness, is one of the most intriguing examples but it was not served well by excavation prior to modern methods and partial destruction of the ridge upon which some of the burial monuments would have stood. Square and round cairns were identified in the early-20th-century excavations by Edwards and Barry (Barry 1902; Edwards 1926, 1927; see Ritchie 2011, 127) on a long natural ridge of sand close to the shore of Sinclair's Bay, Caithness. The cemetery at Ackergill appears to have consisted of a minimum of nine rectangular or square kerbed cairns, four or five circular kerbed cairns and three long cists without cairns (Ritchie 2011, 133). Two Pictish symbol stones are known from Ackergill, one found in the 19th century on the ridge where the cists were later found and one during Edward's excavations in 1925, found near the head end of a disturbed long cist. The burial monuments included a round kerbed cairn that covered an unusual oval drystone chamber that housed four inhumations. Towards the centre of the ridge a further series of square and rectangular cairns and isolated long cists was identified. The cairns were kerbed and, in some cases, had standing stones at the corners and midway along the longer sides of the rectangular examples. Unfortunately, the dating of the monuments at Ackergill is uncertain – the skeletons from Barry and Edwards's excavations are lost, though recent dating of a skull from the mound in the National Museum of Scotland collections has indicated a 5th- to 6th-century AD date for at least one individual (Sheridan *et al.* 2019) and a long bone recovered after disturbance to the mound in the early 2000s has been dated to the mid 3rd to late 5th centuries AD (Hunter Blair 2004, 82).

Another example from Atlantic Pictland is a single square cairn excavated at Cille Pheadair in South Uist which was discovered during the excavation of a Norse settlement in 1998 (Parker Pearson *et al.* 2018). The cairn was defined by a kerb of upright stones and was a small example, only around 2.5m across. The central long cist contained the skeleton of an adult female laid on her side. The body had been repositioned after some degradation had taken place, with some of the finger bones left in the original location and the sternum missing. This burial had originally been dated to the mid 7th to late 8th centuries AD, making this potentially one of the latest examples of the monument-building tradition, but a more recent higher-precision date suggests the interment occurred in the 5th or 6th century AD (Mitchell *et al.* forthcoming), but this is still important evidence for burial in cairns in the Hebrides of the kind found on the mainland to the east.

Long cist cemeteries and related traditions

Long cist cemeteries represent another important Pictish burial tradition with wider currency across early medieval Britain and Ireland (Figure 5.1). Long cist cemeteries are particularly common in southern Pictland with over 90 examples known in Tayside and Fife alone (Winlow 2011, 344). In northern Pictland and Atlantic Pictland, they are not widely known. It is uncertain whether the lack of long cist cemeteries in the north may represent a real difference in the burial traditions of these areas or simply the difficulties of detecting these through aerial photography and the fewer opportunities for their discovery in the form of large-scale infrastructure developments in less densely populated landscapes.

In Tayside and Fife, over half of the identified long cist cemeteries contain fewer than five graves (Winlow 2011, 344–46). This is comparable to the size of the average monumental cemetery. There were, however, much larger long cist cemeteries. The most notable example is Hallow Hill, Fife, where at least 150 inhumations have been excavated, but the cemetery may have held as many as 400 to 500 burials (Proudfoot 1996, 415) (Figure 5.13). The cemetery at Hallow Hill was first excavated in 1861 when 20 cists were revealed. Then, in the 1970s, an extensive campaign of excavations was undertaken after part of the cemetery was disturbed by a housing development (Proudfoot 1996). Hallow Hill, the name of the area today, is located to the west of St Andrews and is a locally prominent low hill situated at the confluence of the Cairnsmill and Kinness burns before the

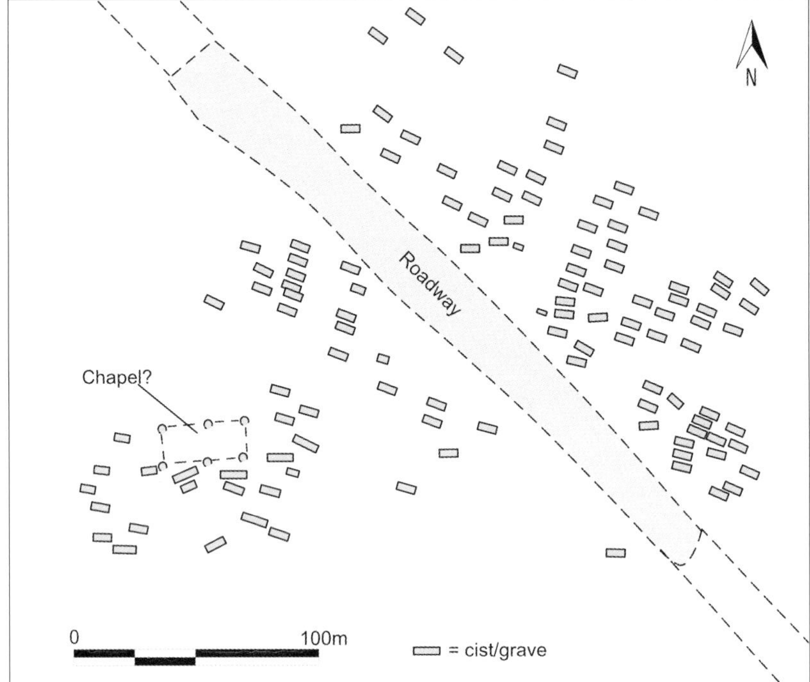

5.13 Hallow Hill, Fife. The long cists were found adjacent to an old roadway. A possible chapel site was found in the western part of the cemetery. (After Proudfoot 1996)

Kinness flows east to St Andrews Cathedral. The early name for Hallow Hill was *Eglesnamin*, first recorded in 1140 in a grant by the bishop of St Andrews to the newly founded St Andrews Priory (Taylor with Márkus 2009, 466–67, 473; Proudfoot 1996, 391–98). The *eglēs* place-name element derives from Latin *ecclesia*, indicating that there was a church here associated with an early Christian community (Barrow 1983; Taylor with Márkus 2012, 365).

Through the centre of the cemetery at Hallow Hill was a cobbled road that was up to 4m wide and on either side of this road were the burials. Over 145 burials were uncovered, the majority in long cists with 10 dug graves and 13 boulder-edged graves. The graves were found in regular rows and the cemetery shows a clear uniformity to the spacing of the graves implying that they were marked above ground and their positions respected. All of these burials were single inhumations with the exception of Cist 48, which held two individuals in sequential deposits (a male with a prone female added above), and Cist 54, which was a double-level cist with two individuals, the lower being the burial of a child. Within the cemetery, the graves appear to have been clustered with the more unusual styles of burial – the boulder-edged and dug graves – mainly on the south-west of the cemetery. The clustering of graves may highlight that, while these were communal burial areas, they were perhaps the focus for different communities and that the grouping of burials in certain cemetery locations may have been important indicators of factors such as identity, affiliation, social differentiation and status.

Nearly all of the burials were in a general E–W alignment with the heads of the individuals at the west end. The bodies were laid in an extended position, some having their arms crossed over their chests. In contrast to the monumental cemeteries, both adults and children, some just a few weeks old, were buried at Hallow Hill. A small number of individuals showed evidence for trauma including a young male in his twenties who died from a severe fracture to the skull (Young 1996, 430). The cists were carefully constructed in the majority of cases, with particular attention taken over the head end of the cist from where construction of the grave proceeded. The stones of the head end were closely fitted and similarly the best quality stones on the floors of the cists tended to be at the west or head end too. The majority of the graves were unfurnished but two graves were found to contain Roman objects that included a glass cup, a sherd of Samian ware, a finger ring, a brooch, a seal box, a silver bracelet fragment, an iron blade and a range of natural objects including a painted white quartz pebble. If these were contemporary with the other interments, the objects deposited with these individuals must have been family heirlooms for some of them would have been centuries old when deposited with the two child burials. The Roman objects, such as the seal box, would have been unusual and this suggests they were perhaps exclusive hand-me-downs in a high-status family. Both of the furnished graves along with a dug grave (Grave 119) may have been covered by small cairns. The original dating with large error margins suggested a 6th-to-9th-century span for the cemetery but the majority of burials appear to be of a 7th- or early 8th-century date.

Another example of a long cist cemetery in southern Pictland was excavated more recently at Lochhead Quarry, Auchterforfar, Angus, following its discovery during quarrying activities. Twenty cists were found but it is likely the cemetery was larger. Most of the cists contained intact human remains and the individuals probably included both children and adults based on the size of some of the cists. Of the 17 adults identified, five were thought to be male and eight female (Dunbar and Maldonado 2012). Radiocarbon dating of the cemetery suggests it dated to between the 5th and early 7th centuries AD.

Warriorhood and violent ways of death

Many of the deaths outlined above would have been in the household surrounded by family members. Other deaths would have been bloody and brutal in a society where warfare was regular and warriorhood part of ideology and worldview. In certain parts of Britain, weaponry was regularly deposited with the dead as part of the warrior culture and ideology that infused early medieval life. This was particularly so in Anglo-Saxon England where weaponry in graves is a regular occurrence (for example, Härke 1990, 22–25; Härke 2001, 2014; Hines and Bayliss 2013; see also Chapter 3). While there are no known examples of weaponry in burials from Pictland – and grave goods are extremely rare more generally – the warrior sculptures described in Chapter 3 do share interesting juxtapositions with likely contemporary cemeteries. At Rhynie, as noted above, the carving of the warrior was found in association with a stone cairn at the northern end of the likely cemetery distribution. The warrior carving at Newton of Collessie in Fife was also found in close proximity to a series of burial monuments. Immediately adjacent to the Collessie stone is a number of barrows identified by aerial photography and geophysical survey. The complex of monuments includes a massive square barrow, measuring around 23m across, with the morphology of the feature and associated monuments being characteristic of the Pictish monumental cemeteries outlined above, with the square barrow being one of the largest yet identified (Ashmore 1980; Winlow 2011, 341; Mitchell and Noble 2017, 12, 27) (Figure 5.14). Under a kilometre to the east is a further barrow cemetery at Melville House, again of early medieval morphology, consisting of ten square and circular barrows of more modest and more typical dimensions – 6.5–10.5m across. The third warrior carving known at Tulloch may have also been found within a cemetery context (Hall *et al.* 2020, 135). It could be that the stones depicted individuals buried in the cemeteries with which these stones appear to have been associated.

Depictions of the human form are exceedingly rare prior to the Roman period. The very act of carving these figures in stone, a tradition that was largely without precedent in eastern Scotland, must have been a significant and powerful statement in itself underlining the significance of these rare depictions. It has been suggested by previous commentators that the Collessie

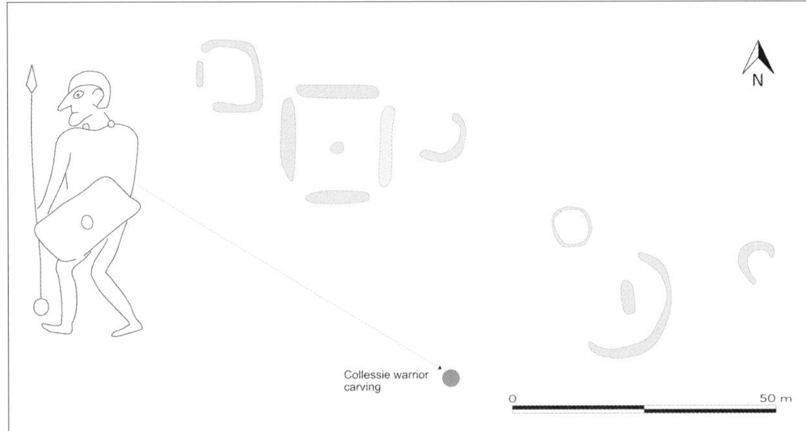

5.14 Plan of the barrow cemetery identified by aerial photography located adjacent to the Collessie warrior stone in Fife.

figure may be a warrior-god (for example, Mack 2007, 164) and, certainly, the very small number of these sculptures suggests they were only carved in very special circumstances and the similarity in pose and weaponry might point to a more universal figure such as a god or mythical/semi-mythical figure (Hall *et al.* 2020, 138). Either way, these carvings and their juxtaposition speak of a warrior ethos that permeated both life and death.

While there are no burials with weaponry there are a number of Pictish period skeletons that show evidence of violent deaths. At Lundin Links, the skeleton of a male aged 40–50, buried in the westernmost cairn of the 'dumb-bell complex', shows evidence of decapitation in the form of three sharp-force injuries to the back of the skull which removed part of this individual's skull cap (Boyle 2020, 249–50). Similarly, a skull from Lundin Links, presumably from the cemetery, appears to have met a violent death with evidence of decapitation too (Boyle 2020, 247–50). Hasty burial after an episode of conflict could also explain the unusual triple burial found in what appears to have been a recut waste pit at Hawkhill in Angus dating to the 7th or 8th century AD (Rees 2009).

Two cave contexts give insight into further violent deaths – Covesea in Moray and Rosemarkie Caves on the Black Isle, Highlands. The Sculptor's Cave, Covesea, has numerous Pictish symbols carved on the cave walls. This cave is cut off at high tide and is difficult to access – a liminal space at the edge of land and sea (Armit and Büster 2020, 3). The cave was a place for the deposition of human remains in the Late Bronze Age and during the Roman Iron Age a number of individuals appear to have been placed in the cave with projecting ring-headed pins, amber and glass beads and pierced Roman coins, suggesting that individuals were interred in their finery (Armit and Büster 2020, 256). A number of individuals appear to have been less well treated – during the 1920s excavations of the cave, a number of human neck vertebrae showing sharp force trauma were found in the cave deposits. Up to nine individuals appear to have been decapitated with a sword or an axe within the cave interior (Armit and Büster 2020, 198–99). The blows came to the back of the neck and, in some cases, multiple blows – up to 11 – were needed to sever the head from the body. These blows appear to have been administered when the victims were kneeling suggesting these were executions. The dating of the vertebrae suggests that the killing of these individuals was a single event or a series of events closely related in time and that this took place in the 3rd or early 4th century AD – in the period in which the first references to the Picts emerge. These individuals could have been from a rival lineage who were publicly and brutally killed in episodes of conflict in the tumultuous centuries of the Late Roman Iron Age (Armit and Büster 2020, 254–55).

A slightly later but equally startling insight into violence and death has been found in a cave near Rosemarkie on the Black Isle in Easter Ross.

5.15 Rosemarkie Man, Rosemarkie, Highland, reconstruction of face using the profile of the skull from the burial. (© Chris Rynn, Centre for Anatomy and Human Identification, University of Dundee)

Rosemarkie Man was located in a dark alcove of the cave and found during excavations in 2018 (Birch 2018) (Colour Plate 22). The burial was of a young man (Figure 5.15) who had suffered severe trauma to the head from multiple blows that represent deliberate overkill – this individual's death was literally a bloody spectacle. A series of radiocarbon dates from bones of Rosemarkie Man himself and from the animal bone offerings have indicated that his death occurred between the first half of the 5th century and the first half of the 6th century AD. The individual was buried in a striking pose – his legs splayed with stones weighing down the limbs. The character of the burial is similar to some deviant-type burials known from elsewhere in Europe. However, there are hints this may have been a ritualised death, perhaps even a high-status one. Animal bone appears to have been used as offerings around the head end and the cave was used for metalworking (see Chapter 4). The individual also consumed a high protein diet through his life and was very well nourished and well built. Was this person a victim of a ritualised execution, perhaps of a rival elite, the practice echoing the grisly events that occurred at the Sculptor's Cave a number of generations previously?

Church burial

By the end of the first millennium AD, the Church began to influence burial location and manner more strongly. In Ireland, it was in the 7th century that the Church sought to establish consecrated Christian burial grounds with the aim of attracting patronage from wealthy families (O'Brien 2009; O'Sullivan *et al.* 2014, 303) and, in the same century, in Pictland, we see the waning of the importance of monumental cemeteries and evidence for the use of churchyard cemeteries. The establishment of churchyard cemeteries reflected the rise of the cult of saints and the desire on behalf of the converted community to be buried near the relics of important saintly figures. Few early medieval churchyard cemeteries are known from Pictland due, in the main, to the lack of excavation at what can often still be functioning burial grounds at churches that have endured for a thousand years or more. Three examples of probable church cemeteries can be highlighted to explore some of the likely characteristic elements of churchyard burial in Pictland.

Isle of May

The Isle of May, a small island just over 1.5km long, is located off the south-east coast of Fife at the mouth of the Forth. This was a pilgrimage site in later medieval Scotland, the pilgrims coming to see the shrine of St Adrian. 'St Adrian' appears to be a corruption of the early medieval Ethernan or Itarnan, a saint recorded as dying among the Picts in the *Annals of*

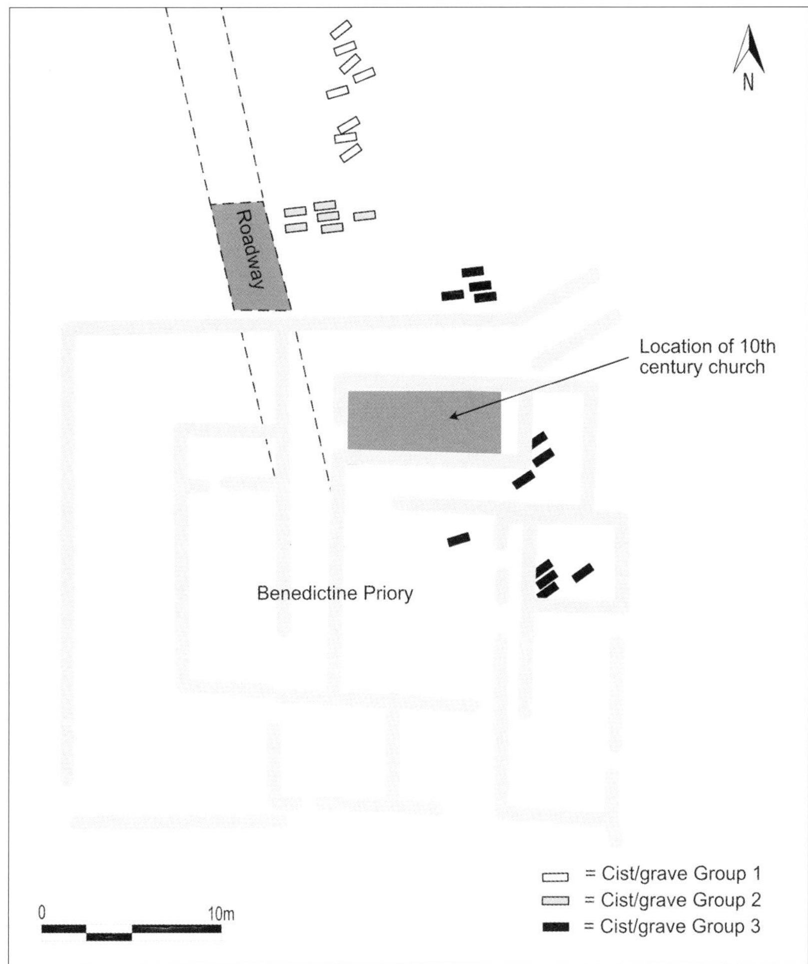

5.16 Isle of May, Fife, dedicated to Ethernan or Itarnan, a saint recorded as dying among the Picts in the *Annals of Ulster* in the year 668 or 669. Excavations here have recorded an extensive long cist cemetery. (After James and Yeoman 2008)

Ulster 669.2 (AD 668 or 869) (Mac Niocaill and Mac Airt 1983, 138). Dedications to Ethernan appear across eastern Scotland but there is a distinct concentration in Fife, including on the adjacent mainland at Kilrenny where a number of cross-slab monuments stood and numerous crosses were incised on the walls of the nearby Caiplie Caves (also the location of a long cist cemetery), located in the same parish (James and Yeoman 2008, 3). Excavations on the Isle of May from 1992–97 revealed burials dating from the late 6th century onwards and evidence of a stone church that dated from the 10th century, which may have replaced one or more earlier wooden churches (James and Yeoman 2008, 173–77). Around 50 graves of early medieval date were found, mainly to the north of the church on a raised beach that appears to have been built up and revetted with walling as early as the 5th to 6th century AD (Figure 5.16). As far as can be established – only parts of the site were excavated – the early burials were organised in three groups to the east of a roadway that perhaps led to the church buildings or settlement the graves were associated with. The burials included long cist graves, stone or pebble-lined graves and dug graves. Some of the later burials were marked with large flat sandstone slabs and many burials had white quartz pebbles included in the grave fills (see Chapter 4 for a discussion of charm stones). All individuals had their heads to the west. The northernmost burials appear to have contained some of the earliest interments with graves dating to between the 6th and 8th centuries AD. These interments were laid out in two parallel rows running N–S. Every identifiable burial in this group was male. Graves to the south in the other two groups were dated from the 7th to 11th or 12th centuries AD. Group 3 burials at the southern end of the cemetery were located around the later priory chapter house and cloister and the site of the earliest stone church and consisted solely of dug graves. In the latter two groups, the graves were again laid out in rows but contained a more mixed population, though almost all of the directly dated individuals were male once more. Indeed, for the cemetery as a whole, only two possible female burials were directly dated to prior to the 11th to 12th century (James and Yeoman 2008, 33, Illus. 4.17), the results strongly suggestive of a monastic community in the early phases of the site. Like the field cemeteries, individuals buried in ecclesiastical contexts were not free from violence and trauma. An individual from Isle of May, in one of the 6th to 7th century cists, survived a sharp force trauma to the head but another was not so lucky, dying from fatal sword blows to the head (Boyle 2020, 252–53).

Portmahomack

As outlined in Chapter 4, the evidence from Portmahomack gives us the best baseline for considering the early Church of northern Pictland. A cemetery, in association with a wealthy settlement at Portmahomack, appears to have been established during the 5th to 7th centuries AD (Carver *et al.* 2016, 103–04). From the monastic settlement, 58 burials were identified in the nave of the modern church, with some dating to the late 7th and 8th centuries and others to the 9th to 11th centuries (Carver *et al.* 2016, 106–22, Table 5.2.1). The majority belonged to the earlier period. These were orientated W–E and included dug graves and graves with stones around the head – termed 'head-box' and 'head-support' burials. They were organised in a series of rows, seemingly aligned on a probable early church to the east. The later burials were placed in the same rows as the earlier interments suggesting continuity in grave organisation over many centuries. Small cross-slabs appear to have marked at least some of the burials and a number of individuals may have been buried in shrouds. Like the Isle of May, the vast majority of the burials – 93% – were of mature males, which

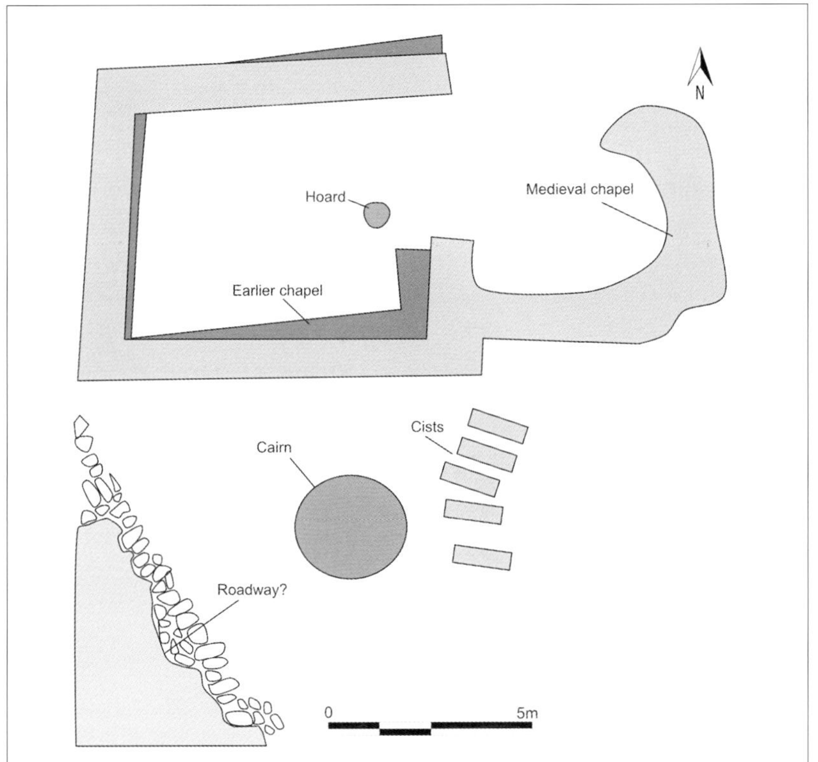

5.17 St Ninian's Isle, Shetland. The long cist and cairn cemetery was found next to an early chapel possibly dating to the 7th to 9th century AD. The famous St Ninian's Isle hoard was found within the chapel site. (After Barrowman 2011)

again is strongly indicative of a monastic population. Isotopic analysis suggests that the few individuals who were not local came from more westerly areas and some perhaps had more exotic origins too (Carver *et al.* 2016, Table 5.2.23). At Portmahomack, individuals showing evidence of trauma were found throughout the cemetery and included an adult male who had blade marks on the back of his skull that showed no signs of healing, evidence that this violent attack was the cause of death (Carver *et al.* 2016, 119).

St Ninian's Isle

St Ninian's Isle is most famous for the hoard of early medieval silver found during excavations in 1958 (Small *et al.* 1973) (Colour Plate 6). The hoard, which included silver bowls, spoons, brooches and items of weaponry, was found within the remains of a pre-11th-century chapel with an associated long cist cemetery. The dating of the early church is uncertain but may have been built between the late 7th and late 9th centuries AD (see Chapter 4), while the cemetery began sometime in the late 7th or early 8th century AD (Barrowman 2011, 197). The burials consisted of short cists, long cists and cairns (Figure 5.17). The short cists are intriguing – they could be pre-Christian burials on the site, with the only dated example, a burial of a flexed female lying prone and aligned N–S, being the earliest dated burial at St Ninian's Isle (Barrowman 2011, 80, 192). Other short cists contained cremation urns, burnt and charred bone and seashells, though this material is now lost and the date of each uncertain. A group of four of the short cists – including the dated burial – was covered by a small cairn. Many of the short cist burials were accompanied by quartz pebbles, as were many of the later long cists. The earliest dated long cists belonged to the 8th or 9th century AD. The cemetery and church were furnished with stone sculpture including cross-incised stones, an ogham stone and multiple composite shrine posts. Some of the long cists were marked at the head end by cross-incised stones (Barrowman 2011, 194). Burial at the site continued into the 9th century and a group of infant burials dates to the 10th century. The later medieval church was built over the top of the earlier establishment and remained in use till the 19th century, and it was only due to the removal of thousands of later interments that the early medieval phases of St Ninian's Isle were reached – an undertaking only likely to be carried out in a development-led context today.

Changing ideologies of death – and belief?

As is evident from the barrow cemeteries, long cist cemeteries and the burials at churches, extensive W–E burial – with the head at the west end – is found widely in eastern Scotland from around the 5th century AD onwards. W–E burial is a tradition also found widely in western Britain and in Ireland from the same chronological horizon. This arrangement had become widespread across Western Europe by the middle of the 1st millennium AD and Pictish traditions seem to fit this more general shift in European mortuary practices (for example, Halsall 2012, 15; Hines and Bayliss 2013, 553). It is a tradition often directly equated with Christian burial – in Christian tradition, when rising on the day of judgement, the body of the deceased is thought to rise to face Christ in the east (Rahtz 1978, 3–4). Charles Thomas, in his influential work in the 1970s, linked W–E cemeteries directly with Christianity, assuming these were early manifestations of Christian practice (Thomas 1971, 50). Thomas categorised long cist cemeteries as developed or undeveloped depending on the presence or absence of associated church buildings or other religious structures, but both types of cemetery he explicitly linked with early Christianity and the Christianisation process. This has been debated however. In Ireland, O'Brien has sought the origins of this practice in Late Roman burial and has questioned the association with Christianity (O'Brien 2020, 49). In contrast, Gleeson sees this practice as very much a 5th-century innovation in Ireland and one explicitly linked to a Christianising context (Gleeson 2017, 308).

He points to the clustering of W–E burials in landscapes with early *domnach* – meaning 'the Lord's place' – church establishments. The *domnach* churches in Ireland are likely to be 7th century or earlier based on the founders' floruits and nomenclature (Gleeson 2017, 289). In Wales, W–E burial has been routinely linked to a Christian context (for example, Dark 2000, 117; Seaman 2006) and a 5th-century horizon for the emergence of these cemeteries seems to broadly correlate with the dating from Ireland. But doubts have also been cast on a direct link between Christianisation and W–E burial (for example, Seaman 2014, 11), with the lack of Church control over burial prior to the 7th century highlighted along with the diverse relations and ideologies that may be expressed in burial.

In Scotland, interpretation has also varied with W–E burial and long cist cemeteries in particular directly linked with Christianisation in early scholarship (for example, Henshall 1956; Thomas 1971, 50; Alcock 2003, 64; though see Fraser 2009a, 71, 83–92). Orientation, lack of grave goods and, in a small number of cases in southern Scotland, their juxtaposition with Latin inscribed memorial stones as found in the Lothians, for example, on the other side of the Forth at the Catstane, Midlothian, have been highlighted as markers of the adoption of Christianity (Cowie 1978, 169–71). However, more recent studies have moved away from directly linking Christianity to burial rites (see Maldonado 2013, 3; 2016, 42), arguing that it is impossible to read belief from burial rite alone and that these burials had more to do with individual and group concerns about family, lineage, status and landownership. The occurrence of cist burial in an Iron Age context is also highlighted as evidence of some limited continuity between Roman Iron Age practices.

However, it is difficult to trace a coherent line from the much more prevalent 5th-century traditions of Pictland back to the Iron Age examples. Overall, like Ireland, the adoption of W–E burial on a large scale seems to be a notable phenomenon that really took hold in the 5th century. The change is such that it seems unlikely that the impetus was solely about changing individual or family concerns alone. Rather, this seems to be a response to fundamental shifts in worldview, of which the adoption of Christianity and the following of wider European trends seem a likely source or, at the very least, an inspiration. That is not to say that every individual in a long cist was a Christian nor that pagans and Christians could not be buried side-by-side in a similar manner, but it does seem likely that Christianity was an influence on the adoption of this style of burial. Here, the apparent paucity of long cist burial in northern or Atlantic Pictland may be relevant given the suspected time lag in the adoption of Christianity in the north compared to the south (see Chapter 4) – it could be that the long cist cemetery style of burial in particular was, indeed, more closely linked to Christian communities or communities at least in closer contact with late- and post-Roman trends found to the south, west and east. Certainly, it is notable that the place-name element *eglēs*, 'church', among the northern Britons and southern Picts, corresponds roughly to the core area in Scotland where long cist cemeteries have been found (Barrow 1983, esp. 4). Both distributions point to a period of strong British and southern influence on Pictish Christianity, when concepts were shared across the Firth of Forth, a context most plausible in the period before the mid 7th century, when Britons were most involved in the Irish Church, though dynastic connections between Strathclyde and Fortriu, in the late 7th century, might have enabled British influence to continue a bit later in Pictland (Barrow 1983; Dumville 1993, 133–45).

By the 7th century, there is little question that most – if not all – cemeteries are likely to have been Christian and it is interesting to note the fall-off in the tradition of monumental barrows and cairns in the early 7th century. In Anglo-Saxon England, the practice of monumental and furnished burial appears to have been abandoned in the face of a strengthening Christian faith, for recent Bayesian modelling of radiocarbon dates has suggested a strong correlation between the cessation of elaborate furnished and monumentalised burial and the consolidation of the early Church in Anglo-Saxon England in the third quarter of the 7th century AD (Hines and Bayliss 2013, 553). The ostentatious and very visible form of the barrow and cairn monuments of Pictland suggests that it was issues surrounding lineage, status and claims to land that were foremost amongst the communities who constructed these, rather than religious belief, but we cannot rule out that some of these also covered the burials of Christians, particularly in southern Pictland. Christian acceptance of such burials is indicated in the *Life of Columba* (I.33; Sharpe 1995, 136–37) which tells of an elderly warband leader from Ce called Artbranan who came by boat to Columba on Skye for conversion to Christianity and baptism – his need for an interpreter was further evidence that he was Pictish. After baptism, Artbranan died and was buried under a cairn, 'still visible there today', while the stream he was baptised in was called 'the water of Artbranan' by local people, indicating how cairns and other features could become part of a Christian landscape.

The irregular and modest 5th- to 7th-century long cist burials from Auchterforfar seem like particularly good candidates for cemetery practices and burial traditions directly influenced by Christian practices and lifeways and there seems little doubt that 7th-century long cist cemeteries such as Hallow Hill and the long cist and dug graves of the Isle of May that appear to start in the late 6th or more likely 7th century were Christian (Fraser 2009a, 90). The number of burials at Hallow Hill and the early place-name *Eglesnamin* suggest that this was a cemetery where burial was perhaps more accessible to a wider, largely Christian, community than the elite burials of the monumental cemeteries. That the Isle of May was the cemetery of an early Church establishment is also difficult to dispute given the male dominated profile of its early phases. Thus, while certainty is not possible, it does seem likely that the broad and widespread shift to W–E burial took place in a Christianising context and that, by the late 7th century, the Church was having much more influence over burial rites, with cemeteries moving to churchyard contexts. At the same time, elite practice shifted to other forms of expression and away from the construction of large burial monuments.

Conclusions

In the 5th and 6th centuries AD, monumental traditions emerged alongside long cist cemeteries and related traditions and the emergence of both can be related to new beliefs and ideologies – most prominently Christianity. The new traditions may have also drawn upon developing conceptions of group cohesion, lineage and status as the Pictish kingdoms took shape. With regards to social status, it cannot be coincidence that these formal cemeteries emerged in an era in which there may have been an increased emphasis on the importance of select families and particular status groups as the institutions of kingship and lordship began to consolidate. Monument building and the creation of new forms of mortuary practice often occur at horizons of social change and centralisation during transitional periods in the establishment of elites. Emulation, competition and a desire for power within an emerging early medieval society may have been strong motivating factors in the construction of monumental cemeteries in Pictland. Such was the power of this strategy that similar monuments were constructed from southern to Atlantic Pictland – these monuments thus speak of the developing bonds and links between regions that underpinned the development and expansion of the Pictish identity in northern Britain. Overlapping with the monumental traditions and ultimately superseding them was a non-monumental practice of long cist burial. This practice is likely to have been more directly influenced by Christian practices and was a tradition found in both field cemeteries and at churchyards, the latter of which is likely to have formed the dominant burial locale from the 7th century AD onwards. Investment in burial traditions became less from the 7th century and it may be that Christian practices, with elite expressions increasingly focussing on elaborate cross-slabs and other – not necessarily Christian – elite ways of displaying or using wealth, diverted elite investment and competition away from burial by the end of the 7th century as the Christian religion firmly took hold in Pictland.

CHAPTER SIX

'Marking the Sign'

Symbols of Identity

The most iconic element of the archaeological record for the Picts is the symbol tradition, most commonly found today carved on stones. The symbol stones have long been identified as Pictish because their distribution closely matches the extent of the Pictish kingdoms as reconstructed from historical sources and place-names (for example, Stuart 1867, 3; Allen and Anderson 1903, cix; Wainwright 1955b, 43; see also Chapter 1) (Figure 6.1). The symbol tradition includes a distinctive group of symbols – some abstract, others naturalistic. The latter includes the striking animal designs and objects such as mirrors and combs (Henderson and Henderson 2004, 167) (Figures 6.2 and 6.3). The abstract designs include symbols that have been given names such as the 'double disc' or the 'crescent and V-rod' to describe forms that have no obvious counterparts in what we know about the everyday world of the Picts (Figure 6.4). There are over 200 carved stones with these symbols known from eastern and northern Scotland (RCAHMS 2008). Approximately two-thirds are incised on boulders and unmodified standing stones and the other third are symbol-bearing cross-slabs, many of them finely carved in relief, with the stones shaped to display the Christian cross, the symbols and occasionally biblical scenes and other figurative depictions (see Chapter 4). The symbols also occasionally appear on cave walls as well as on metalwork, bone and other portable objects. Around 30 symbols appear regularly on the stones but other symbols are unique or appear only a handful of times (Samson 1992, 37; Forsyth 1997, 87). There have been repeated attempts to decipher the meaning of the symbols since the 19th century, with wide-ranging interpretations, including that they were icons of pagan or Christian religion to symbols of rank or tribal identity, memorials to the dead and countless 'fringe' ideas and speculation. Cracking the code has been a pastime of many interested in the Picts and their symbols.

A history of symbolism

The symbols are so connected to the Picts that it is worth tracking the origins of this association and outlining previous ideas on their potential

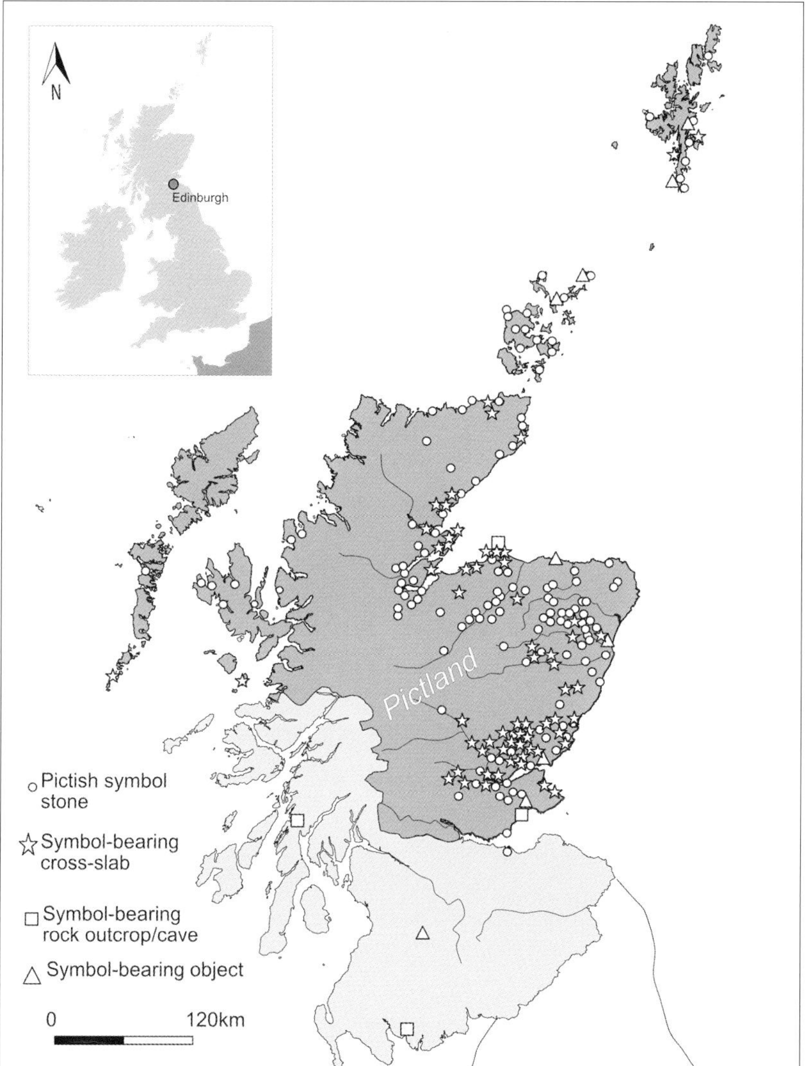

6.1 Distribution of symbol-bearing stones and objects.

meaning and purpose. Those familiar with the historiography may want to move onto the next section but it is worth exploring the development of scholarship on the tradition. The first concerted interest in the Pictish symbol stones can be traced back to the antiquaries and travellers of the 18th century – figures such as Alexander Gordon, Charles Cordiner and, the most famous of the three, Thomas Pennant (Henderson 1993). The first linkages between carved stones in eastern Scotland and the Picts came in the 19th century. Pinkerton, in his 1814 edition of his *An Enquiry Into the History of Scotland*, noted a concentration of stones in Angus 'the centre of the Pikish (*sic*) dominions' (Isabel Henderson personal comment). The first detailed national consideration of the stones came in 1856 and

6.2 (*Above*) A range of animals shown on Pictish symbol stones. The animals depicted include domesticated animals but the focus was on animals from the wild.

6.3 (*Right*) Pictish beasts – a fantastical creature commonly depicted on Pictish symbol stones and on cross-slabs. This selection is a range of beasts appearing on various Aberdeenshire monuments showing both variety and consistency in size, convention and style.

6.4 (*Opposite*) A selection of abstract symbols along with mirrors and combs drawn from the corpus from Aberdeenshire illustrating a variety of symbol types and form:
(a) crescent and V-rods;
(b) double discs and Z-rods;
(c) discs/triple discs;
(d) arches; (e) mirror cases;
(f) tuning forks, pincers, shears and others;
(g) S-shapes, rectangles and notched rectangles;
(h) combs;
(i) mirrors.

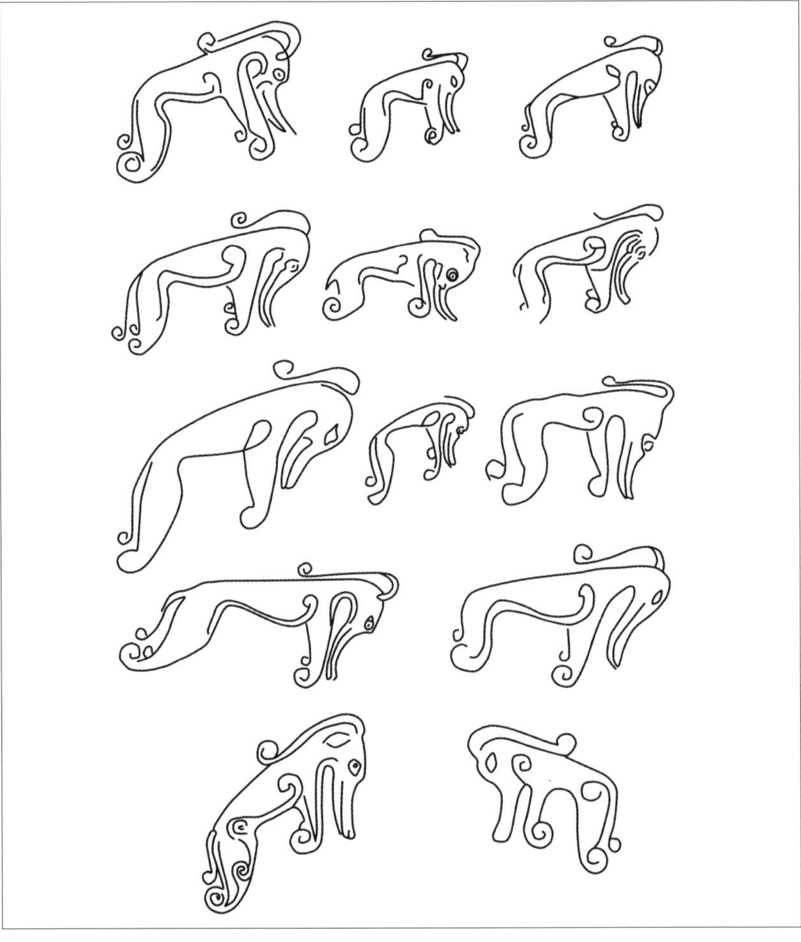

a)
b)
c)
d)
e)
f)
g)
h)
i)

6.5 The Rossie cross-slab (Perthshire) as depicted in John Stuart's *Sculptured Stones of Scotland*.

1867 with John Stuart's two-volume *Sculptured Stones of Scotland* (Figure 6.5). In his second volume, Stuart explicitly linked the stones with the Picts:

> The result of wider investigation and further thought has led me to believe that the peculiar symbols on the Scotch pillar-stones are to be ascribed to the Pictish people of Alba, and were used by them, mainly on their tombs, as marks of personal distinction, such as family descent, tribal rank, or official dignity. The peculiar symbols described . . . are found almost solely on the monuments of that part of Scotland lying to the north of the Forth; and we learn from

> the venerable historian of the Angles, that in the beginning of the eighth century the inhabitants of this country, known as Pictavia, and Alba, were the Picts, whose southern boundary was the Firth of Forth.
>
> Stuart 1867, 3

In these sentences, Stuart made an explicit connection between the distribution of the stones and Pictish territory and also made a tentative interpretation of the monuments as markers of identity, mainly used in a sepulchral context.

A full catalogue of the early medieval carved stones of Scotland came in 1903 with the herculean effort of J. Romilly Allen, an engineer by training who, under the direction of the Society of Antiquaries of Scotland and funded by benefactors to the society, recorded around 500 monuments by train, boat and on foot over the course of two years (Allen and Anderson 1903). The volume was published with Dr Joseph Anderson, Keeper of the National Museum of Scotland, who wrote its introduction. Anderson and Allen, following Stuart, identified the monuments of eastern Scotland as belonging to the Picts, even though Anderson had not explicitly done so in his earlier 1879 and 1880 Rhind Lectures, *Scotland in Early Christian Times*. Clearly Allen's extensive catalogue and distribution of monuments had persuaded Anderson of the Pictish attribution (Allen and Anderson 1903, cx; Henderson 1993, 23). As noted in Chapter 1, Allen and Anderson also created an enduring classificatory scheme for the stones:

> Class I – Monuments with incised symbols only
> Class II – Monuments with symbols and Celtic ornament carved in relief
> Class III – Monuments with Celtic ornament in relief, but without the symbols of the other two classes.
>
> Allen and Anderson 1903, xi

Allen and Anderson saw these categories as overlapping in time but also broadly sequential. Function and meaning was little remarked upon, other than to argue that the symbols could not have been distinctly pagan for they appeared on Christian monuments too (Allen and Anderson 1903, xxxix, cxi–cxii, 108). With regards to origins, Allen's gargantuan task of mapping all the extant monuments allowed them to note that the greatest prevalence of the symbol stones was in northern Pictland and specifically in Aberdeenshire, where they saw the origins of the system to lie (Allen and Anderson 1903, civ–cix).

Allen and Anderson's work proved so impressive that it was a generation before scholars attempted to tackle the subject again (Henderson 1993,

32). In 1940, Cecil L. Curle produced the first wide-ranging art-historical review of the whole corpus since Allen and Anderson, though her efforts were largely focussed on assessing the chronology of the monuments through art-historical methods. Curle said little about function other than questioning the funerary associations (Curle 1940, 65).

Francis Diack's work was completed in 1922 but was not published till 1944. Diack followed Allen and Anderson in their classification scheme and in seeing Aberdeenshire as the area of origin but he diverged significantly on chronology and function. He argued that the symbols had a long history before they appeared on monuments and pointed to the classical references to the Picts being tattooed:

> When these facts are brought together, the true nature of these sculptured symbols seems, in my opinion, to leap to the eye. They are simply the tattoo-designs belonging to each individual and varying according to what he was, repeated on his stone.
>
> Diack 1944, 28

Diack's idea was that this was a tradition that had its origins in another medium – the earliest forms being tattoos – and was only later transferred to stone (see Chapter 1 for Herodian comments on Britons and tattooing). Diack suggested that the symbols represented different ranks and classes of Picts, with the abstract symbols originally based on designs that were more representative in nature – notched rectangles being chariots, for example (Diack 1944, 53). The form of these, Diack argued, had debased through time and had become purely abstract by the time the designs were first carved on field monuments. To Diack, the symbols were markers of the elite, each symbol relating to categories of lordship and rank: kings, sub-kings, *magi* and landholders (Diack 1944, 68, 73). Diack suggested that the animal figures could have been cult symbols relating to pagan belief. He also explored the possible linguistic syntax of the symbols, examining positioning and the sequence of symbols. Diack's work was quite extraordinary for the time and echoes of his ideas can be found in many subsequent interpretations.

In the 1950s, Robert Stevenson wrote the chapter on Pictish art in Wainwright's *The Problem of the Picts* (1955). He analysed the art-historical parallels for curvilinear and animal designs in relation to the symbol stones and came to the conclusion that Pictish symbols were heavily influenced by Anglo-Saxon metalwork and illuminated manuscripts (1971, 1993; see Henderson and Henderson 2004, 31), with the animal symbols, for example, a response to the animals of Northumbrian and Irish Gospel books. With regards to the abstract symbols, one of Stevenson's prominent ideas was that of the declining symbol, perhaps drawing on Diack's work, suggesting that symbols had been created by a 'master' carver and that over time these designs tended to simplify or break down (for example, Stevenson 1955, 102–03), ideas that influenced subsequent work by other scholars (for example, Henderson 1958, 50; 1967, 110).

Isabel Henderson tackled the symbols in a series of publications from the late 1950s onwards (for example, 1958, 1967, 1971). Her first paper questioned Anderson's 'unavoidable conclusion' that the symbol stones originated in Aberdeenshire, instead suggesting the Moray Firth area as the main innovating region (Henderson 1958, 57). In Henderson's later work, the interpretation of their function fluctuated with individual and group identity and boundary markers being cited as possible uses (1967, 1971).

In the 1960s, Charles Thomas, like Diack before him, suggested that tattooing may have been the earliest form of the system (Thomas 1961). Thomas developed his ideas in a 1963 paper, sticking broadly with the same chronology, but he elaborated his ideas on function a great deal. He argued that the symbols were not simply artistic motifs but 'primitive pictograms' that conveyed simple messages. These messages, he argued, used a particular syntax and ordering and the symbols were likely to have represented particular objects or classes of data (1963, 74). He noted the use of pairs as the most common form of deployment and suggested that each stone was conveying a simple message – most commonly, a memorial to the dead that may have included references to that person's status and kin. Specific symbols, Thomas suggested, may have been associated with particular ranks – for example, the double disc denoting the grade of king (Thomas 1963, 78, 81). Other symbols may have had religious or talismanic meanings.

In the 1980s, new ideas emerged. Jackson, in a radical interpretation, saw the symbols as public statements of marriage alliances between matrilineal clans (Jackson 1984, 24–26). The common pairing of symbols was the basis of this interpretation, with each symbol of the pair argued to represent a family group and the mirror and comb symbol, where present, indicating the bride wealth or dowry that went with the marriage (Jackson 1984, 88). Driscoll (1988) took a very different tack, linking symbol stones to elite expressions, inheritance and administration. A funerary context was favoured with expressions of societal position and landownership key – the erection of memorials legitimising positions of authority and descent through the dead and the ancestors (Driscoll 1988, 228). Laing and Laing concentrated on dating rather than function but their interpretations favoured a funerary role (for example, Laing and Laing 1984, 1993).

In the 1990s and 2000s, a new favoured interpretation emerged – that the symbols were a limited representation of the Pictish language, most likely a naming tradition. This was an interpretation first made in an innovative article by Ross Samson in 1992. Samson suggested that the specific 'meaning' of individual symbols was not recoverable as they never meant to directly symbolise an object or even a concept. Rather, these performed a function that was more similar to that of a letter, a syllable or a word. Samson pointed to the pairing of symbols and it was this combination he saw as being key, suggesting the symbols were expressing names or parts of names, which gave the full identity of an individual through combination. He argued that the most frequent symbol pairs represented the commonest Pictish names, pointing to the fact that, in contemporary Anglo-Saxon England, many personal names were dithematic – that is, they were made up of two elements, with each element normally – but not always – a single syllable. While the range of individual symbols was limited, the combination of symbols to make names was key – thus the crescent and V-rod followed by a double disc and Z-rod had a different meaning from the same symbols in reverse order (Samson 1992, 49). Nearly all of the common symbols are abstract, but less common and representational symbols such as the animal carvings could have also been names, Samson suggested – for example, the animals found on stones such as representations of a pig or boar, hound, deer and horse are found as personal names in contemporary Ireland and perhaps explains why some animals can appear both singly and in combination – a bear could be a name in its own but might also be a name element (Samson 1992, 55–56). Samson pointed to potential qualifiers of names. The mirror and comb, for example, nearly always appear at the end of a symbol chain in an auxiliary position – if we assume they are read from top to bottom – and could have been, Samson proposed, used to denote a female name. If that was the case, then Samson notes between a fifth and a quarter of individuals recorded were women (Samson 1992, 59). It may, of course, be an assumption that the mirror and comb equal female (as Samson discussed; see also Alcock 2003, 374). It could have done the exact opposite or may have indicated something entirely different – for example, rank or another social distinction of some kind, or that the person was deceased. The important thing to note is that the mirror and comb appear to have added extra information – it expressed something in addition to the name, meaning the messages could have greater complexity, though still limited in scope.

In 1997, Katherine Forsyth built on Samson's analysis by developing new perspectives through a comparison of the symbol system to an Irish system of writing – ogham. She supported Samson's overall thesis (Forsyth 1997b, 87). For Forsyth, it was a system akin to other forms of inscriptions which suggested that it must have been invented at a single point in time and this would explain why it remained very similar across at least four or five centuries of use. Forsyth examined the depiction of individual symbols and noted that elements, such as notches on crescents and double discs and the application of V- or Z-rods, could be other forms of modifiers to the identities being expressed – these small variations would allow for a greater number of names, identities or messages to be represented. Forsyth agreed that it was likely that the meaning of the individual symbols could only be derived in relation to the rest of the system and, given that the semantic range must have been so limited, it 'is hard to imagine that it is anything other than a personal identification: "(here lies) A", "(this belongs to) A", "(this was erected by) A", "(pray for) A, A"' (Forsyth 1997b, 94). Forsyth's comparison of ogham and symbol tradition highlighted the very similar contexts in which both are found – in caves, on slabs at settlement sites, in burial contexts and on domestic objects – again suggesting that the two systems conveyed similar messages and purposes in very similar contexts (Forsyth 1997b, 91).

The naming tradition interpretation was a fresh new perspective and the idea that the symbols represent names or identities of some kind has been widely referenced in most recent literature. Alcock (1996, 2), in an article on the earliest Pictish carvings, agreed that the symbols may have represented elements in two- or three-element names but also suggested titles as a possibility. Alcock proposed that the system was developed to 'make public and permanent statements which could be understood throughout Pictland'. Alcock proposed that the system was likely to have been created within the context of increasing political centralisation and it would probably have been regularised by a high authority, a king, and even identified a potential candidate – Bridei son of Maelcon (*c.*556–584), the same king Henderson had identified in 1958. Alcock's 2003 book, *Kings and Warriors, Craftsmen and Priests in Northern Britain* AD *550–850*, covered similar ideas – that the symbols generally represented names and perhaps lineages but that these monuments may have also asserted claims to land (Alcock 2003, 364, 372–75).

Looking at more recent approaches that have attempted to interpret the symbols, the Hendersons, in *The Art of the Picts*, proposed that the symbols could have been visual projections of power and protection – much like the role the Christian cross performed on later monuments, often in tandem with symbols. Next to these carved stones, they suggested, the exercise of authority could be carried out – pledges made, protection guaranteed, land rights agreed and renders collected (Henderson and Henderson 2004, 171–72).

Other recent interpretive approaches have included that of Clarke, who focussed on the 'multiple lives' of stones, pointing to examples that had been reused through time. He suggested that the symbols had a life independent of the stones – that is, they may have been found on other media and had a long evolution. He suggested that the deployment of symbols on standing stones was a specific reaction to the process of Christianisation in Pictland. Clarke posited that the Pictish symbol stones were intended to evoke the past – deliberately reusing or imitating prehistoric standing stones at a time of social stress brought on by changes and challenges to traditional ways (Clarke 2007, 35). The symbols were said to reflect important social memories and ways of life under threat and the deployment of what may have been a tradition of some age by this stage on stones was to restate important community messages through the deployment on monuments that reified the past.

In the 2010s, statistical analysis was brought to bear on the problem. Rob Lee, Philip Jonathan and Pauline Ziman used statistics and information theory to follow up on the idea of the symbols being part of a system for displaying limited messages reflecting language (Lee 2010 and Lee *et al.* 2010). Through the use of a mathematical model that discriminated between random characters, repetitive symbols – for example, heraldry or Morse code – words, syllables and letters, they found a correlation between the Pictish symbol system and that of syllables and words. They again favoured a naming tradition as the most likely interpretation of the system though they proposed that each symbol may have represented an individual name rather than working together and that the second and any other additional symbols may have been qualifiers – for example, the name of a relative, a rank or position, a group identity or an area of land (see Lee 2010, 162). However, their methodology and findings have been heavily critiqued (Sproat 2010).

The context of symbol deployment

Turning from historiography and how the symbols have been interpreted in the past, we can now examine the contexts in which the symbol tradition was deployed, examining two elements that archaeology is well placed to discuss – context and dating. Symbols are found in a wide variety of contexts. These include an association with burials, in caves, at settlements and forts, on personal objects and on standing stones, 'plaques', symbol-bearing cross-slabs and, more rarely, rock outcrops – the latter outwith Pictland. The relationship of Pictish symbol stones to burial has been widely discussed (for example, Wainwright 1955b, 87–96; Close-Brooks 1980; Driscoll 1988; Clarke 2007, 27–31; Mack 2007, 140, 232–37; Ritchie 2011, 133–34; Foster 2014, 64–65). There are, undoubtedly, examples of some sort of association between burials and monuments. Fragments of a Pictish symbol stone, for example, were found in 1974 at Garbeg, Inverness-shire, in association with one of the round cairns – Cairn 1 – (Wedderburn and Grime 1984, 151–52). And, similarly at Watenan, Caithness, part of a stone with a crescent and V-rod was located in 1977 in close proximity to a square cairn (Gourlay 1984). Two symbol stones have also been found at the cemetery at Ackergill, Caithness. Ackergill 1, decorated with a salmon, a rectangle and a short ogham inscription, is said to have been standing at the northern end of the mound upon which the cemetery was located until the 19th century and Ackergill 2, a very small fragment with a rectangle symbol and traces of a second symbol, was found lying on the surface of the mound next to the head end of a disturbed long cist (Ritchie 2011, 133–34). A further example of a burial cairn, at Dairy Park, Dunrobin, Sutherland (Figure 6.6), was found directly below where a symbol stone was found during ploughing in 1977 (Close-Brooks 1980, 328). At Tillytarmont, Aberdeenshire, symbol stones have also been found in the close vicinity of potential burial monuments (Woodham 1975, 6). Less certainly, long cist burials have been found near the Peterhead, Perthshire, Pictish symbol stone, though these were over 30m from the stone (Dingwall 2019, 51–53). It is also possible that the symbols at Covesea marked an area of burial in the later Roman Iron Age or memorialised a phase of burial (Armit and Büster 2020, 260). These examples suggest some relationship between the symbol tradition and burial but the numbers are generally quite small. Indeed, a geographic information system (GIS) study comparing the distribution of Pictish symbol stones and symbol-bearing cross-slab monuments to barrow, cairn and long cist cemeteries found that only 14 out of 337 carved stone monuments were found within 500m of a known cemetery location (Mitchell and Noble 2017, 31).

6.6 The Pictish symbol stone found over a cairn at Dairy Park, Dunrobin, Sutherland. (© Historic Environment Scotland)

Symbol-bearing objects and stones have also been found in association with a number of settlements. The carving of a bear was found at Scatness, Shetland. While not a conventional symbol stone, with only a single animal rather than a symbol pair, it is worth discussing its context and noting Samson's suggestion that animal symbols could also have represented names. The bear carving was found in Structure 11, the largest and most impressive building of the 7th- to 8th-century phases of the settlement (Colour Plate 23). It was found face down on an ash-rich floor deposit (Dockrill *et al.* 2010, 52, 304–05). It has been suggested that the stone could have been a pier end-slab from the wheelhouse but the deposit that it was found in association with was stratigraphically earlier than at least one of the piers in the building and the stone appears to have been reused for the top part of the stone was missing. It may, instead, have come from an earlier phase of occupation at Scatness. A stone with a very truncated carving of a salmon and part of a probable second symbol was also found in a reused context associated with Structure 11 from Scatness. This stone is likely to have been a more conventional symbol stone with paired symbols

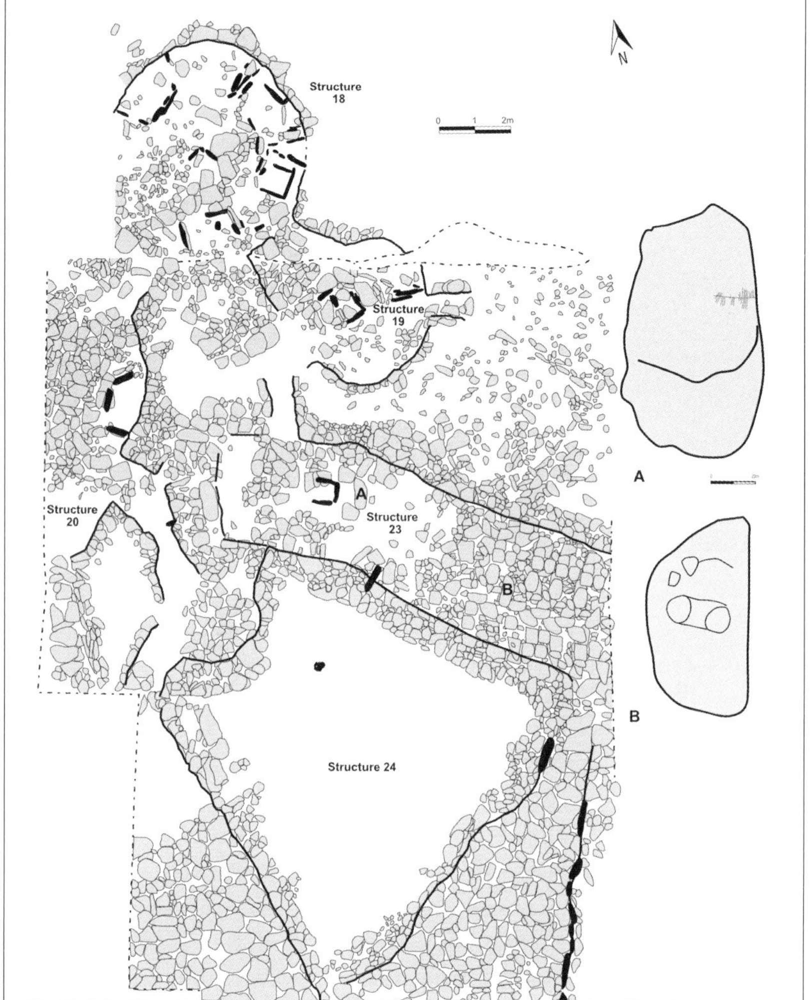

6.7 Pool, Orkney, Phases 6.1–6.6, showing rectangular Structure 23 with ogham (A) and symbol stone (B). Elaborate areas of paving and a range of buildings developed in the Pictish phases with Structure 23 the largest roofed structure. The ogham was found near the hearth of the western part of the building, while the symbol stone was found face down reused in paving of what may have been the byre of the dwelling. (After Hunter *et al.* 2007)

but only a small fragment was recovered and was again found out of context, face down within rubble just outside of one of the houses (Dockrill *et al.* 2010, 306). The carving of a boar on a small boulder was also reused in the hearth of Structure 5 at Scatness, a figure-of-eight building, and a pebble with a rudimentary crescent and V-rod was found in association with the same building. Little can be said about the context of these stones or their dating, other than they are likely to have all been earlier than the deposits they were found within.

Symbol-bearing objects have also been found at Pool, Sanday, Orkney (Hunter *et al.* 2007). These include a stone with what has been interpreted as rudimentary double disc and crescent designs – this was built into a flagstone floor of Structure 23 (for example, Hunter *et al.* 2007, 115; Alcock 1996; Foster 2014, 76) (Figure 6.7). The stone was used in the paving of

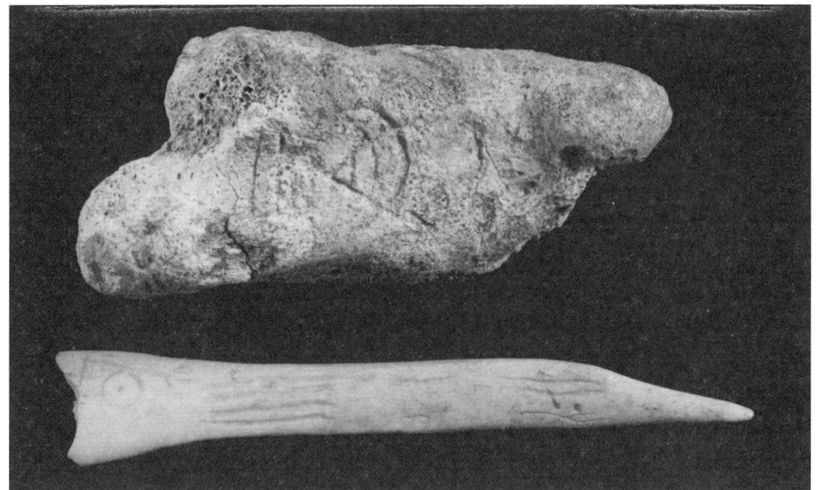

6.8 (Top) Ox phalange decorated with double disc, crescent and V-rod. (Bottom) A bone pin decorated with double disc and Z-rod from Pool, Sanday, Orkney. (© Roderick Richmond for Orkney Arts, Museums and Heritage)

the structure but again the symbols were found facing down in an apparently reused context – the dates for this phase of settlement have been modelled as AD 325–645 – 95% probability – or AD 425–575 – 68% probability (Noble *et al.* 2018a, 1339). In the same phase was a bone pin with a double disc and Z-rod of much more accomplished design (Chapter 2) (Figure 6.8). An ox phalange with a crescent and V-rod and a rectangular symbol appears to have been deposited in a broadly contemporary context dated to AD 410–570 with 95% probability – or AD 420–540 with 68% probability (Hunter *et al.* 2007, 509; Noble *et al.* 2018a, 1336) (Figure 6.8). Overall, at Pool, it is clear that symbols were being deployed on objects within a settlement context and objects bearing symbols were found discarded in the phases of settlement dating to the 5th to 6th centuries. Some of the objects with symbols could have been substantially earlier than the deposits they were found within. For example, the stone with the rudimentary symbols at Pool shows a much simpler carving style than the bone objects dated to this period and was lying face down in a 5th- to 6th-century building suggesting that the stone could have been reused from an earlier phase of the settlement.

In terms of the context of deployment, the set of symbols on the pin at Pool was added to an object that is likely to have been a personal accessory – a cloak or hair pin perhaps – while the ox phalange is likely to have been a gaming piece (Hunter *et al.* 2007, 509–10). A similar ox phalange, decorated with a crescent and V-rod and a mirror case, from late occupation at Broch of Burrian is also likely to have been a gaming piece for it shows heavy wear on the base (Hunter *et al.* 2007, 509–10). The use of the stone carved with the very basic symbols from Structure 23 is uncertain but conceivably could have come from an architectural setting in an earlier phase of settlement and was incidentally or deliberately reused in the floor

6.9 Plan of the earlier phases of the post-broch settlement at the Broch of Gurness, Orkney, showing the approximate findspot of the Pictish symbol stone. (After Hedges 1987)

of the largest building identified at Pool from the Pictish phases.

Two other likely settlement contexts for symbol-bearing stones occur in the Northern Isles. A magnificent slab with three warriors and two sets of symbols is known from the Brough of Birsay (RCAHMS 2008, 114). The stone was at first linked to a cemetery and to a particular grave at the ancient church site on the island but new phasing of the site has cast significant doubt on the links between the stone and graveyard (Morris 2021). We do know, however, that the Brough of Birsay is likely to have been an elite settlement of the Pictish era due to the finds found there (Chapters 3 and 4). Thus the stone may have been a monument of display within this Pictish site. What is likely to be a substantially earlier stone came from the nearby Broch of Gurness, a multi-period broch settlement on the north-west coast of Mainland, Orkney, not far from Birsay. The Gurness stone has relatively crude carvings of a mirror case and two rectangles (RCAHMS 2008, 114) (Figure 6.9). This stone was found on the wall between broch outbuildings 3 and 4. John Hedges (1987, 85) tentatively associated the stone with the shamrock building and annexe from the Pictish phases of the settlement. However, the position of the stone in relation to the wall of Buildings 3 and 4 is intriguing, with Buildings 3 and 4 appearing to belong to an earlier phase of occupation. The finding of the stone on the wall may again suggest an architectural context for this stone – on display in one of the post-broch rectilinear houses at Gurness. Its height, found *c.*0.7m off the ground level, would have been at eye level of anyone sitting in Buildings 3 or 4.

The Gurness stone is reminiscent of the carved stones from Dunnicaer, Aberdeenshire, both in carving style and context. Dunnicaer, the highly eroded promontory fort and settlement (see Chapter 3), has five symbol stones associated with the site. Like Gurness, the stones are modestly sized and would need to be incorporated in some sort of structural context for the symbols to be effectively displayed. At Dunnicaer, some of the stones have single symbols carved on them but they could have been paired in an architectural setting. The symbol stones were found in a low stone wall – most likely to have been the rampart of the fort (Noble *et al.* 2020a, 322).

At the Craw Stane complex at Rhynie, the Craw Stane, carved with a salmon and a Pictish beast, and possibly the Rhynie Man stood at the entranceway to the enclosure complex – a socket has been found near to the findspot of the stone (Noble *et al.* 2019b, 68). Both the Craw Stane and the stone socket were also located near to one of the buildings found at the complex – Structure 3. A smaller stone, Rhynie 8, more akin to the Dunnicaer and Gurness stones, was found in ploughing in the location of the complex but its exact context is unknown. Like the Dunnicaer examples, this latter stone is a very modestly sized stone and would have been most effectively displayed in an architectural context – perhaps it was part of the ramparts in the early ditched and banked phase of the elite complex. Similarly, the bulls from Burghead, Moray have been suggested to have been built into the rampart of the fort (Carver 1999, 30–31), though their forms, with many showing pointed ends, are unusual. The bull carvings were found in the north-east corner of the upper citadel around the entrance to the fort (MacDonald 1862, 356). They could conceivably have marked the routeway into the fort or could have been built into a gateway or entrance feature.

Symbol carvings are also found carved into the walls of caves. Several caves at East Wemyss, Fife, have symbols, including the caves known as the Court Cave, Doo Cave, Jonathan's Cave, Sliding Cave and the Glass Cave (RCAHMS 2008, 66). The symbols include double discs, rectangles,

6.10 Symbols at Covesea Cave. (© The Sculptor's Cave Publication Project, University of York)

arches, fish, serpents and a Pictish beast. Some appear to be paired but others are not obviously so. Covesea Cave, Moray, has a number of symbols carved around the twin entrances of the cave. On the rock above your head as you enter the cave is a well-carved triple disc and flower symbol (Figure 6.10) while, further into the cave, there are symbols including a salmon, crescents and V-rods, rectangular symbols and mirror cases (RCAHMS 2008, 106; Armit and Büster 2020, 57–74). Singular examples of symbols are also found in two caves at Caiplie and at Clashach Cove, Moray (RCAHMS 2008, 66, 106). At Wemyss and Covesea, the symbols appear to mark the threshold into the deeper spaces of the caves.

Finally, symbols also appear on material culture – as we have already seen, they are found on gaming pieces from Broch of Burrian and Pool, Sanday, and are also present on stone discs from Shetland at Jarlshof and Eswick (RCAHMS 2008, 139). There is also a small number of metalwork pieces with symbols on them. A plaque from the Norrie's Law hoard (see below) has a double disc and a beast head, while a silver chain terminal from Parkhill, Aberdeenshire, has an 'S' symbol and two pairs of three dots on one side and two triangles and another set of three dots on the other (Allen and Anderson 1903, 198–99; RCAHMS 2008, 138) (Colour Plate 24). Another silver chain terminal from Whitecleuch, Lanarkshire, found outwith Pictland, has a double disc and Z-rod and a notched rectangle (Allen and Anderson 1903, 472–73; RCAHMS 2008, 140). A very intriguing object, now unfortunately lost, was found in a barrow at Laws, Monifieth, during drain digging (Figure 6.11). A drawing survives of a small bronze or silver plaque around 12cm across that had a double disc and a beast head on one side and an elaborately decorated crescent and V-rod on the other side (Cruickshank 1880, 270; Allen and Anderson 1903, 280–81; Henderson and Henderson 2004, 225; RCAHMS 2008, 138).

Dating symbols

The dating of the symbol system has been as intense a debate as the meaning and context of the symbols. The seminal Allen and Anderson volume *The Early Christian Monuments of Scotland* set out the relative dates for their classes of monuments. They thought that the symbol system must have post-dated the emergence of the kingdom of Dál Riata, with the stones perhaps originating in the 7th and 8th centuries AD, with the Christian cross-slab monuments dating to the 9th and 10th centuries AD (Allen and Anderson 1903, cix). In the early 20th century, writers such as James Carnegie, 9th Earl of Southesk, suggested a 5th-century start date, with earlier non-monumental traditions such as tattooing argued to be the inspiration, a model followed by Diack who thought the first field monuments with symbols were carved in the 5th or 6th centuries AD (Carnegie

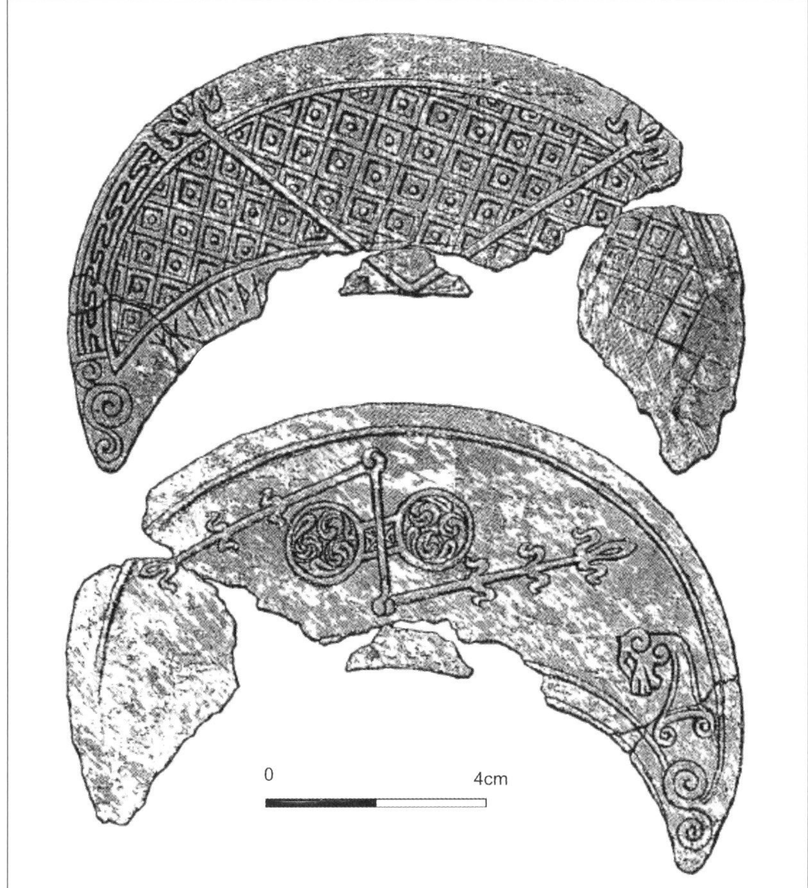

6.11 19th-century woodcut image of the now lost Laws of Monifieth, Angus, plaque. (Reproduced by kind permission of the Society of Antiquaries of Scotland)

1893; Diack 1944). Curle saw most of the Pictish monuments being the result of a short burst of creativity focussed on the 7th century AD. Others, such as Stevenson (1955, 1971, 1993) thought that the 7th century or later was more likely with the symbol designs influenced by Anglo-Saxon metal-work and manuscript art of the 7th and 8th centuries and that all the art was developed in a Christian context. The animal symbols in particular, Stevenson saw as derivative of Northumbrian and Irish Gospel book art (see discussion in Henderson and Henderson 2004, 31–35). Henderson (1958, 57) linked the development of the system to the powerful 6th century King Bridei, though following Stevenson, a 7th-century date for the origin of the symbol system came to the fore in Henderson's work in the 1960s and 1970s (1967, 1971).

Charles Thomas related certain symbols to late Iron Age art styles and consequently suggested a 5th century start date for the simpler Pictish symbol stones and, like Diack, sought an earlier origin in tattooing (Thomas 1961, 1963), a sentiment broadly followed by Laing and Laing who also identified the 4th or 5th centuries AD as a possible start date (1984, 1993; see also Noble *et al.* 2018a, Table 1). In 2004, the Hendersons briefly considered the origins of the symbol tradition, suggesting that the symbols were first established in a pre-Christian context with the practice of incising them on to stone first taking place in enclosed contexts such as caves, structures and 'remote locations' such as Dunnicaer (Henderson and Henderson 2004, 171), with the field monuments developed thereafter but specific dating was not commented upon. David Clarke saw the carving of symbols on monuments as part of a reaction to the Christianisation process in Pictland, presumably in a 6th- to 7th-century context (Clarke 2007). Overall, a range of dates has been proposed for the symbol tradition but dating has remained uncertain and there had been little in the way of application of absolute dating methods until recent years – dating had been based entirely on art-historical analysis, comparative study and speculation.

Nonetheless, in the 2000s, new methods of dating were piloted. In 2008, David Clarke and Andy Heald of the National Museum of Scotland dated the ox phalange from the Broch of Burrian to AD 570–655, the first absolute date on a symbol-bearing object (Clarke and Heald 2008). One further object was dated for a 2019 article on symbol dating – the ox phalange from Pool decorated with the crescent and V-rod and rectangular symbol (Noble *et al.* 2018a, 1336). The date for this object proved to be AD 410–570 pushing the absolute chronology for symbol-bearing objects further back in time. The dating for the bone pin from Pool, incised with the double disc and Z-rod, from the same settlement phase was able to be constrained by Bayesian modelling showing that the pin was in use somewhere between AD 325–645 and probably AD 425–575 (68% probability), broadly contemporary with the directly dated ox phalange. Of course, the symbols on both objects could have been carved on older bones (Clarke and Heald 2008, 293) but the dating for Phase 6.4 shows both symbol-bearing objects from Pool must have been in use and discarded within a phase of activity centring on the 5th and 6th centuries AD. The burial at Dairy Park, Dunrobin, found in the cairn located directly below the symbol stone discovered during ploughing there, has also been dated using high-precision methods – this showed the burial within the cairn belonged to AD 565–640 or AD 575–625 (95/68% probability) (Noble *et al.* 2018a, 1339). Through the extensive excavations at Dunnicaer, multiple radiocarbon dates were obtained on the settlement remains and defences of the fort. This allowed accurate models of the date of occupation of the fort to be sought. Radiocarbon modelling has produced an estimated start date of the 2nd or 3rd century AD for the settlement and an end date of the second half of the 4th century to earliest 5th century (Noble *et al.* 2020a). The rampart from which the stones appear to have been obtained was dated to the late 3rd century to the first half of the 4th century AD.

At Gurness, recent radiocarbon dating of archive materials from the earlier 20th century excavations at the broch settlement have allowed an absolute chronology and outline sequence for the settlement to be obtained (Noble and Allison forthcoming). Late occupation in the broch occurred in the 1st and 2nd centuries AD, when an extensive radial settlement of cellular and sub-rectangular buildings developed around the broch. Occupation in the surrounding settlement continued into the 5th century AD and perhaps the early 6th century AD, in association with the cellular shamrock building, but the whole settlement appears to have been abandoned by the mid 6th century at the latest. The dates of the cellular and sub-rectangular buildings are particularly interesting for, as noted above, the Pictish symbol stone seems to have been associated with a wall between Buildings 3 and 4, with radiocarbon dating suggesting the latest occupation of these buildings was in the 4th century AD. The evidence is not as secure as for Dunnicaer but, as well as the similarities in dating, there are the stylistic parallels between the Dunnicaer and Gurness slabs and also similarities in context. The Gurness stone, a small angular block, shares the small plaque-like or architectural form of the Dunnicaer examples and the symbols at both sites are simple and imprecisely carved. Like the Dunnicaer stones, the Gurness stone may have also been used in an architectural setting with the plaque visible from inside one of the houses.

The stones from Dunnicaer and Gurness share stylistic characteristics with the symbols found carved on cave walls – a context that Henderson and Henderson suggested was likely to be early in the sequence (Henderson and Henderson 2004, 171). The symbols in caves are currently impossible to date directly but it is important to note that there is no evidence for the use of the cave at Covesea after the 4th century AD, with a major phase of cave use in the 3rd and 4th centuries AD, to which the symbols could conceivably relate (Armit and Büster 2020, 260). Activity at Wemyss is more wide ranging but there was use of the caves throughout the Roman Iron Age. Overall, the evidence from Dunnicaer and more tentatively Gurness is suggestive of Late Roman Iron Age use for stones carved with symbols in a relatively rudimentary fashion.

The dates from Pool make it clear that symbols were definitely in circulation in the 5th and 6th centuries AD and this includes objects and stones with symbols which are either themselves radiocarbon dated or the settlement phases in which they were directly discarded. The evidence from Rhynie (see Chapter 3) also strongly supports a similar chronological horizon for the deployment of symbols, with extensive excavations having produced a very robust chronology for the settlement. Around 60 radiocarbon dates from the excavations suggest that activity at Rhynie began in the 4th century and had largely ceased by around AD 550. Dating evidence includes material from a stone socket that is likely to have held one of the

Pictish symbol stones from Rhynie. Objects and moulds from the settlement phases also include items that present close parallels for the animal designs and objects depicted on Pictish symbol stones and these are from closely dated contexts that fall within the 4th- to mid 6th-century dating range provided by the settlement evidence (Noble *et al.* 2018a, 1339; Noble *et al.* 2019b, 81). The moulds for producing animal figurines or decorations of some kind from the Craw Stane complex are particularly interesting for they show the circulation of sophisticated animal designs in metalwork, with the objects produced from the moulds an obvious parallel for the animals shown on Pictish symbol stones. Stevenson, in his influential dating scheme, did not consider that the Picts could have independently achieved the detailed representation of animals other than through the copying of manuscript art of the 7th and 8th centuries AD (Stevenson 1955, 1971, 1993). The Rhynie evidence shows this to have been a false assumption and that clearly animal depictions in metalwork was circulating in Pictland generations before the manuscript art achieved wide distribution. The Picts were indeed important innovators and contributors to the development of Insular art styles (Henderson and Henderson 2004, 31–35).

Unfortunately, at present, none of the other settlement sites where symbol-bearing objects are found provides much help in pinning down the chronologies of the tradition. As noted earlier, the bear from Scatness was found face down and broken in a layer that dates to the 7th to 8th centuries AD so only provides a date for when the stone was no longer in use. The other stones from Scatness were also in what are likely to be secondary contexts (Dockrill *et al.* 2010, 114–16, 307–11).

Turning to the metalwork, typological dating for metalwork objects provides broad ranges but few specifics. The date of silver chains, two of which have symbols on the terminal rings, has been extensively debated but, recently, an earlier date range has been favoured – *c.*AD 300–500 (Blackwell *et al.* 2017, 95). The triangular symbol on the Parkhill chain terminal is unusual but there are parallels on two stones from Dunnicaer – No. 2 and No. 3. The plaque at Norrie's Law comes from a hoard, the date for which has been debated, but the hoard has recently been suggested to belong to the 5th or 6th centuries AD (Noble *et al.* 2016, 734– 35), with the elaborate nature of the decoration of the symbols perhaps favouring a 6th-century date. The double disc on the Monifieth plaque has very similar internal design to that of the Norrie's Law plaque and, intriguingly, has the same symbol combination – double disc and beast head – though Monifieth also had a crescent and V-rod on the other side of the plaque. However, the Monifieth object clearly remained in circulation for a long time, having had runes added to it.

Overall, at present, the evidence on dating suggests a probable Late Roman Iron Age start date for the symbol tradition (Noble *et al.* 2018a), though more absolute dates would, of course, be very welcome. At present, the dates from Dunnicaer are perhaps the most secure but there are also strong possibilities that the Gurness stone may be from a similar context and dating horizon – built into the wall of a settlement of this date – and the cave carvings could also date from this era, sharing stylistic parallels with the Dunnicaer and Gurness carvings. Symbols were certainly in extensive use in the 5th and 6th centuries AD from Aberdeenshire to Orkney, with the evidence from Pool providing direct dates on symbol-bearing objects and settlement layers from which they came. The dates from Rhynie provide contextual dates for the stones but direct dates for objects that closely resemble motifs found on Pictish symbol stones provide supporting evidence. Regarding metalwork, the symbols on the two silver chain terminals from Parkhill and Whitecleuch may be relatively early in the sequence, given the recent re-evaluation of the dating of this artefact type. This is also supported by the composition of these objects – some of the chains show a high purity of Roman silver use, suggesting these were made directly from Roman bullion (Blackwell *et al.* 2017, 102). The symbols on the chains themselves are also relatively simple – particularly so on the Parkhill chain terminal whose unusual motifs find parallels at Dunnicaer.

With regards to stylistic development, there does seem to have been a growing complexity and boldness in the styles of the symbols over time. The plaques from Dunnicaer, the stones from Rhynie and the symbols from Pool all show a simplicity of line and form, whereas those symbols found in contexts with later dates show more elaboration. In miniature form, more elaborate symbols are found incised on to the gaming piece at Broch of Burrian dated to the 6th or 7th centuries AD, while the stone from Dairy Park, found in association with the burial monument dated to the same era, is also elaborately decorated compared to the Rhynie monuments. This elaboration of form is something that continued to develop. The symbols that were deployed on early Christian-era monuments began to be carved in relief with patterns of interlace and other elaborations boldly carved on increasingly impressive monuments of likely 7th century through to perhaps the later 9th century AD in origin (Henderson and Henderson 2004, 172), though the end date of this tradition is uncertain (see Chapter 7) (Figure 6.12).

6.12 Elaborate symbols on a cross-slab at Rosemarkie, Easter Ross. Later Christian monuments display the symbols but they were carved in relief and decorated with key pattern knotwork and other decoration of the kind found in Insular manuscripts. Image created through digital processing methods. (© Andy Hickie)

Overall, in the sequence sketched above, we can see changes to how symbols were carved from relatively plain, often relatively small-scale symbols on earlier monuments and objects to more complex incised designs on stones of the 6th to 7th centuries AD, with symbols carved in relief and decorated with key pattern and knotwork of the kind found in Insular manuscripts during the 7th to 9th centuries AD (Henderson and Henderson 2004, 172) (see Chapter 4). There also appears to be a general trend towards larger monuments through time, with the early monuments from

Dunnicaer and Gurness being on relatively modestly sized stones and also stones that are likely to have been incorporated into architectural settings such as ramparts and house walls. The standing stone monument with symbols may have become popular in the 5th to 6th centuries AD, developing into the dominant form of deployment – at least in surviving contexts – of the symbols for centuries to come.

Towards an interpretation and context

Bringing all the evidence together, what can we deduce about the Pictish symbol system, its status, distribution, function, origin and context of deployment? The distribution of the symbols, as noted as early as the 19th century, is heavily concentrated in eastern Scotland north of the Forth, particularly in Aberdeenshire, Moray and the Highlands, with fewer numbers in Fife, Perthshire, Angus and the Northern and Western Isles (see Chapter 1). There are many more symbol-bearing stones in northern Pictland than in the south – it could be that this was a tradition that originated in northern Pictland, with Stuart and Allen and Anderson preferring an Aberdeenshire origin, while Henderson suggested a Moray Firth origin. If the latter, it could have been a system developed in the context of the nascent kingdom of Fortriu and a tradition that spread to other areas of Pictland as the over-kingship of Pictland took shape, though associating numbers of stones with political geography may be a blunt instrument in terms of interpreting the pre-eminence of particular regions through time.

Symbols were certainly deployed in contexts associated with elites – the resources and wealth to commission a symbol stone, for example, would have been considerable (for example, Driscoll 1998, 228; Gondek 2006). Similarly, the metalwork objects upon which these symbols are found were certainly associated with elite forms of expression and dress and it is notable that all the surviving examples of symbols on metalwork are on silver rather than bronze or other less precious metals. The bone objects and stone discs from Shetland are less obviously elite objects, though gaming is likely to have been an important elite pursuit (see Chapter 3), and sites, such as Jarlshof, Pool and Broch of Burrian, are likely to have been, at least locally, important settlements. While at first glance the cave sites seem difficult to reconcile with high-status activity, it is worth noting that the Roman material from Covesea is the largest collection of Late Roman objects in northern Scotland of 3rd- to 4th-century date (Hunter 2007a, 34). Unfortunately, the East Wemyss caves appear to have been largely emptied in the medieval and post-medieval periods – when the caves stood below a castle of the Earls of Fife – meaning that little can be said about Roman Iron Age or early medieval activity here. Of course, it is entirely possible that the symbols had wider currency in mediums that do not survive but this is a point that is difficult to address with the evidence base as it stands.

With regard to function, it has been repeatedly noted that, due to the lack of any obvious geographical patterns or obvious clustering of individual or paired symbols, they could not have specifically denoted group affiliation or regional identities that endured for any length of time – such as Pictish regional divisions or sub-kingdoms (for example, Allen and Anderson 1903, xxxix, cxi–cxii, 108; Henderson 1971, 61; Samson 1992, 29, 60, Fig. 10). The function of the symbols must have been more general. Explanations have included a commemorative tradition or marking boundaries but this does not explain the specific function of the symbols. Curle connected them to pagan belief or 'hunting magic' (1940, 65) but this seems unlikely – the symbols were boldly deployed on cross-slab monuments of a probable 7th- to 9th-century date in an era when all of Pictland was fully Christianised (see Chapter 4).

As outlined earlier, the current most-favoured strand of interpretation is that this system conveyed information about individuals and their identity – or identities. For Thomas, these were 'pictograms' that conveyed simple messages about a person's rank and kin-group affiliation, whereas Samson suggested the meaning was more specific – it was the person's name and it could be qualified in some cases by their title or other supplementary information such as gender. The vertical format of many symbol inscriptions is certainly a strong characteristic of the tradition, with the vertical nature of the symbol layout similar to the way ogham and Latin inscriptions are carved on contemporary stones across Britain and Ireland (Forsyth 1997b; Edwards 2001).

That the symbols related directly to identity is suggested by symbol-bearing cross-slabs, some of which show individuals 'labelled' by symbols. One example of this is the Dunfallandy monument in Perthshire which shows two individuals seated on thrones and one mounted figure. The figures are 'labelled' with symbols – a Pictish beast, a double disc and crescent and V-rod, and a crescent and V-rod and Pictish beast (for example, Allen and Anderson 1903, xxxviii, 38; Stevenson 1955, 123; Noble *et al.* 2018a, 1333) (Figure 6.13). Other examples include the warrior from Collessie, Fife, who is labelled with the arch and rectangle symbols (Hall *et al.* 2020, 138), and mounted warriors from Kirriemuir and Woodwrae, both in Angus, and Meigle No. 6, Perthshire, who are directly next to symbols that include a double disc, a double disc and step, and a double disc and crescent respectively (RCAHMS 2008, 56, 130). Other possible examples include: the pair of symbols next to a rider at Balluderon, Angus; a large Pictish beast next to a rider on the stone from Scoonie, Fife; a large double disc and Z-rod and crescent and V-rod above the mounted figure on the Elgin, Moray, symbol-bearing cross-slab; the eagle, serpent and bull head above a mounted warrior at Mortlach; a Pictish beast and crescent

6.13 Examples of symbols labelling people on Pictish stones:
(a) Collessie, Fife;
(b)–(d) Dunfallandy, Perthshire;
(e) Meigle, Perthshire;
(f) Woodwrae, Angus.

and V-rod below the rider at Meigle No. 1; and the mirror case and Pictish beast on the side of Meigle No. 7 with a mounted warrior on the back of a small cross-slab (RCHAMS 2008, 70, 108, 112, 128, 130). In addition, there are three figures carved immediately next to mirrors and combs – one seated on a probable throne at Kirriemuir, Angus, one depicted standing at Western Denoon, Angus, and one mounted riding side saddle on the Hilton of Cadboll stone, Easter Ross (RCAHMS 2008, 56, 62, 88).

A naming tradition certainly makes the most sense in terms of what other contemporary forms of inscription and carving set out to achieve. Expressing the name and occasionally title, parentage, ethnic group or lineage of an individual was the format of almost all contemporary inscriptions across Britain and Ireland at this time (Samson 1992, 35; Forsyth 1997, 92; Edwards 2001, 17–18). In the majority of transcribable inscriptions of the period, the form of names identified was along the lines of 'X son of/descendant of Y', with two main elements plus linking words, perhaps similar to the symbol tradition where pairing of symbols is the most common format of deployment with auxiliary, or more rarely additional, symbols included. Short statements were also almost universal in other inscription traditions. Despite the fact that ogham – having an alphabet developed from Latin – could have been used for very long inscriptions for example, it was almost exclusively used for short inscriptions revolving around names. Likewise the Latin inscriptions in Wales and southern Scotland also focussed on the recording of names, usually as memorials (Swift 1997, 42–43; Edwards 2001). Looking further afield, the early runic tradition in Scandinavia, although again based on alphabetic system, also tends to have short inscriptions at least on earlier objects and stones and, in the majority of early cases, appears to have been carved to represent names – where they can be interpreted (Barnes 2012, 11). However, other possibilities are present such as the use of the symbols to identify other elements of identity – kindred groups, parentage, military units or rank but still identities of some kind, and names more specifically do seem the most likely form though the specificities of how what may have been a logographic system of representation worked with so few 'characters' does remain a puzzle (Forsyth 1997b; Gilbert Markus personal comment). A purely symbolic means of representing identity remains possible. It is likely that abstract symbols added to objects, in this case denoting Christ and a broader concept, were also known through Christianity – for instance, Adomnán stated that Columba opened the gates of Bridei's fortress after 'marking the sign of the Lord's cross' on them (II.35; Anderson and Anderson 1991, 146) and the white healing stone which miraculously healed Broichan and others was also marked with a sign by Columba's companions (II.33; Anderson and Anderson 1991, 142).

If the communication of identities using set symbols was the function of the symbols, then a system of use must have been in place from the beginning of the tradition and would share at least some consistency of use through time, which would explain why the symbol system shares many regularities across perhaps five or six centuries of use. That is not to say that things could not change. For example, as new names formed and came into fashion, the symbol repertoire might change too (Samson 1992, 57). This might explain some of the differences between early manifestations of the symbol system – for example, Dunnicaer and cave-carvings, which show single symbols more commonly – compared to the later Pictish symbol stones and symbol-bearing cross-slab examples, which show more regularity in symbols but also new symbols and combinations. Perhaps names or the identities being expressed also became more complex through time.

That the symbol system represented names or identities of some kind certainly explains why the symbols could exist in such a range of contexts – on items of personal adornment, on gaming pieces, on elite silver objects such as chains and plaques, in burial contexts and at settlements and in both probable pagan contexts – for example, 3rd- to 4th-century phases at Dunnicaer – and on Christian cross-slabs. Personal identifiers would have been appropriate for all of these contexts – as ownership marks on objects, as names or titles of the dead or group identity at cemetery locales or as names of powerful leaders, kindred groups or founding ancestors at elite settlements. In the caves, the names or identities referenced could perhaps have been of deities worshipped in pagan spaces or names of the deceased deposited there, as could have conceivably been the case at Covesea (Armit and Büster 2020, 260). The stones could have also marked boundaries as ogham stones did, with names or group symbols in prominent position to proclaim landownership and territory (Edwards 2001, 18, 36–38; Bhreathnach 2014, 42–44; for Pictland see RCHAMS 2007, 122–24).

It is also possible that stones and symbols could have been used in highly charged events such as inaugurations. There is, for example, an intriguing juxtaposition between stones and power centres in a number of cases, with stones positioned at important thresholds in architectural settings at sites of elite power. The excavations at Rhynie suggest the Craw Stane, a symbol stone decorated with a fish and a Pictish beast, and at least one other stone were located at the entranceway to a 4th- to 6th-century high-status enclosure complex and settlement and, at Burghead, the bull carvings appear to have been situated at the entrance to the upper citadel, which is likely to have been the most important space within the fort (MacDonald 1862, 356; see also Chapter 3). At Dunnicaer, the stones appear to have also been located near to the entrance to the fort (Noble *et al.* 2020a, 325).

The location of the stones at Dunnicaer, Rhynie and Burghead resembles the two contexts in which Pictish-style symbol carvings have been found outwith the core of Pictland – at Trusty's Hill, Dumfries and Galloway, and Dunadd, Argyll. At Trusty's Hill, a pair of Pictish-style symbols, a double disc and Z-rod and a serpent and sword, are carved on an exposed face of outcropping rock at the entrance to the summit enclosure of a probable early medieval royal fort (Toolis and Bowles 2017, 1) (The symbol stone found below Edinburgh Castle is also worth mentioning in this context – RCAHMS 2008, 64.) At Dunadd, a centre of Dál Riatan kingship, a carving of a boar, an ogham inscription, a footprint and a rock-cut basin are found close to the entrance of the summit citadel (Lane and Campbell 2000, 18). It has been argued that the symbols at both Dunadd and Trusty's Hill were used in royal inauguration ceremonies (Lane and Campbell 2000, 247–49; Toolis and Bowles 2017, 137; cf. Henderson and Henderson 2004, 172). The symbols at these forts could represent the founding ancestor of the royal lineage, an important ruler or over-king or could even relate to a tale or myth associated with an important place – for example, the Burghead bulls. Ceremonies conducted next to these carvings could indeed have been part of the inauguration of rulers whose leadership was confirmed next to the prominently displayed name or identity marker of an important ancestor or an important group symbol, deity or founding myth.

With regards to dating, the suggestion that the tradition began in the Roman Iron Age puts the symbol system in line with wider Western European patterns. Ogham in Ireland may have had a Late Roman origin (Ahlqvist 1982, 8–10; Harvey 1987, 9; Swift 1997, 49) and, in Scandinavia, the use of runes has been traced back to at least the 2nd century AD. Both were directly influenced by Latin, having been created by people with experience of Mediterranean language, reading and writing traditions through direct contacts including serving in the Roman military (Odenstedt 1990, 169; Barnes 2012, 10–11; Findell 2014, 15). Like runes and ogham, the Pictish symbols may have been created beyond the frontier in response to Roman influence but, in this case, they invented a system for representing identities that was radically different to the Latin alphabet and, although it had many commonalities with other inscription systems and traditions, the symbol tradition had a character all of its own that is found almost exclusively within areas of Pictish control. The unusual Newton Stone from Aberdeenshire (see Chapter 1 (Figure 1.20); Kilpatrick 2021) suggests the Picts also experimented with more direct uses of Late Roman script traditions, developing a monumental alphabet derived from Latin cursive. However, this form of inscription is only attested on the Newton Stone – perhaps this system never caught on or was mostly communicated in a medium that has largely not survived.

The symbol system may have been a particular expression of a Pictish identity – and, in its early guises, perhaps a strongly non-Roman identity. The system was very distinctive – instantly recognisable and prominently displayed in the landscape – and differed from all other carving traditions on stone monuments found in Britain and Ireland. It was a system found from Fife to the Northern and Western Isles, indicating cultural connections between these areas, in regions that spanned the likely core of Pictland at its height. Its absence in some areas, like Stirlingshire, Clackmannanshire, western Perthshire, Argyll and much of western Pictland, is interesting, since these were all, at various times, incorporated into the Pictish kingdom but may have been areas where the Pictish identity was less marked or where identities were expressed in different ways. It may be that areas, such as Stirlingshire and Clackmannanshire, for example, were more British and, when they were incorporated into the Pictish kingdom in whole or part after 685, the symbol tradition was not imported, possibly because of continuing British and perhaps Gaelic and Anglo-Saxon influences. Similarly, when Argyll was conquered in the 730s, it did not lead to the adoption of symbols in that region other than at the major hillfort at Dunadd.

Perhaps Pictish elites were not able or willing to impose, over a wide scale, a symbol tradition on areas without strong local Pictish leadership or many Pictish speakers. Through the conquests of Stirlingshire, Clackmannanshire and Argyll, the importance of a specifically Pictish identity may have also been reduced which perhaps brought about the end of the use of such symbols and hastened the transformation from Pictland to Alba (Chapter 7).

Conclusions

The symbols provide a fascinating and lasting testament to the Picts and their traditions of expressing identity on a variety of media. The symbol tradition was clearly a vibrant system that was found across most areas of Pictland and was deployed over the course of centuries. As we have seen in previous chapters, evidence would suggest major changes in the archaeological record for the Late Roman Iron Age that coincides with the first references to a Pictish identity. Major centres, such as Rhynie and Tap o' Noth, were emerging in the same chronological horizon (see Chapter 3). The fact that the Pictish symbol system may also originate in the Late Roman Iron Age would suggest a degree of complexity and shared practices across a widespread area centuries prior to the over-kingship that emerged in the 7th century. The use of monumental inscriptions in Roman Britain to the far south and on military installations closer to home is one possible inspiration for a distinctly Pictish system of identity marking that was radically different to the Latin alphabet in an era when a collective Pictish identity took shape. By the 9th century AD, some of the major royal and ecclesiastical centres rarely deployed the symbol system – its use as a distinctly Pictish means of communicating was coming to a close. As the Pictish kingdoms expanded in the 7th and 8th centuries and began to incorporate peoples and territories with perhaps a lesser allegiance to a Pictish identity, the importance of the system for identity marking at settlements and at monuments to the dead may have waned. This issue is one that is returned to in the next chapter. Overall, at present we can say little more about what the Pictish symbol system meant in terms of specifics but what we can do is continue to increase our archaeological knowledge of the symbol tradition, its dating and the context of its use and, through these endeavours, we may begin to understand the origin and demise of this enigmatic but hugely engaging tradition more fully.

CHAPTER SEVEN

Destroyed by 'the Strength of Spears and of Swords'?

The End of the Picts

Introduction

When the Gaelic poem 'The Prophecy of Berchan' allusively described the reign of Cináed mac Alpín (842/3–858) in the late 11th-century or later, it stated, 'He is the first king who will conquer in the east, from the men of Ireland in *Alba*. It was achieved through the strength of spears and of swords, after sudden death, after sudden slaughter' (Anderson 1990, 273; Skene 1867, 83–84). It then explains that Cináed tricked and massacred the Picts – 'the stupid savages of the east' – in pits in Scone. As was the case for the author of *Historia Norwegie* (see Chapter 1), for this later writer, the Picts no longer existed because they had been destroyed by the ancestors of the current ruling elite.

How the Pictish kingdom ended and was replaced with the Gaelic kingdom of Alba, the forerunner of the medieval kingdom of Scotland, has sparked debate for generations. A number of factors appear to have been at play. One is that the Pictish language – or languages – was replaced by Gaelic and Norse. For the elites, this linguistic transition had taken place by AD 1000 at the latest but, at a local level, pockets of Pictish speakers could potentially have survived longer. Another was the presence of Scandinavian raiders and settlers who made their greatest impact in the north and west but whose military ambitions and success created far-reaching effects across Pictland and the Insular world. A third factor must have been internal change and the strategies of rulership and identity making pursued by those seeking to shape the ideologies and frameworks of rule in Pictland. Through these factors, Pictland, by the 10th century, was no longer referred to – the new kingdom of Alba dominated northern Britain (Figure 7.1) and, by the start of the 11th century, its rulers clearly regarded themselves not as Picts but as Gaels, *Scotti* in Latin, men and women of Alba. The kings and the leading noble families of Alba now traced their ancestry back to the Gaelic kindreds of Dál Riata and thence back to Ireland. This chapter outlines the evidence we have for this transformative period and how we might interpret the changes that led to the demise of Pictish as an identity

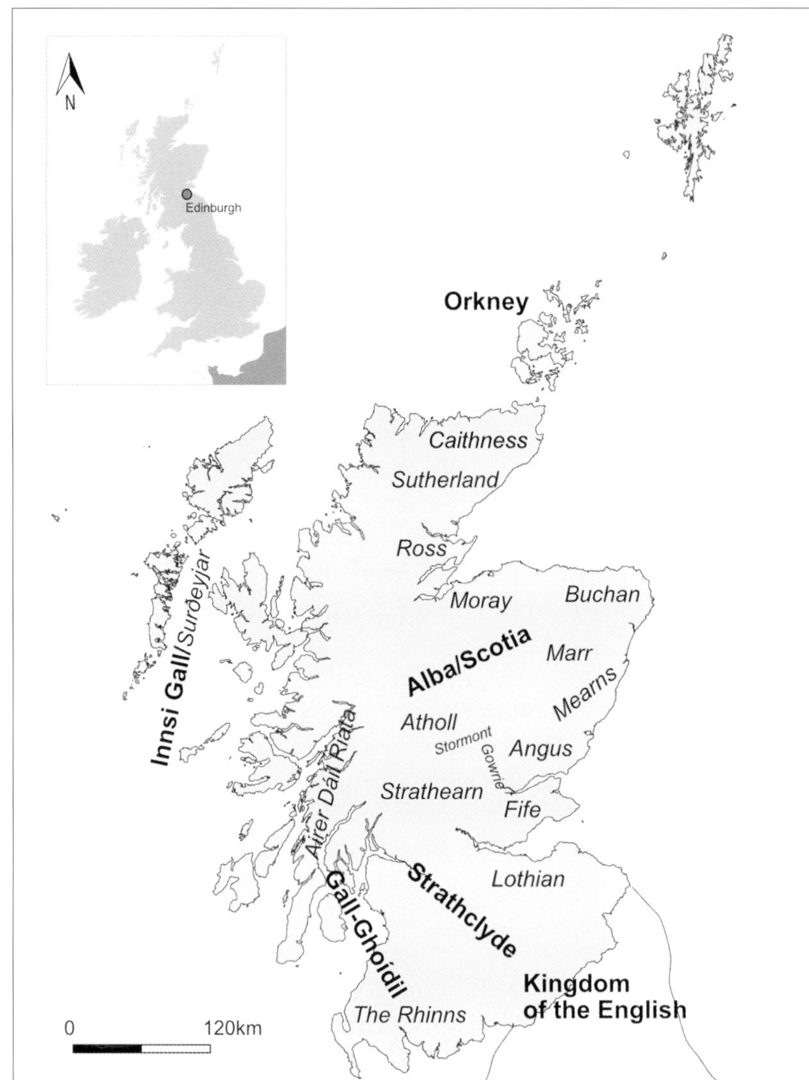

7.1 Scotland around AD 1000.

and a language, as well as the wider processes of change in what was a fascinating period for social, political and cultural transformation across Europe during the Viking Age.

Everything changes?

In the written sources, our last certain contemporary chronicle reference to the Picts occurs in AD 878 when Áed, son of Cináed mac Alpín, is described as 'king of the Picts' (*AU* 878.2). When the same text next records the death of a king in *AU* 900.6, Domnall son of Constantín is called 'king of Alba', *rí Alban*. A similar change occurs in the *Chronicle of the Kings of Alba* where the territory is called *Pictavia* in Domnall son of Constantín's reign (889–900) but had become *Albania* when events in 903 were recorded (Anderson 2011, 251). In the 10th century, Gaelic *Goídil* – 'Gaels' – and *Albanaig* or *fir Alban* – 'men of Alba' – as well as the Latin term *Scotti* came to be used for the inhabitants of Alba, replacing *Picti* and *fir Fortrenn* – 'men of Fortriu'. For the territory, Latin *Albania* and *Scotia* (which had originally denoted Ireland), Gaelic *Alba* and English *Scottaland* began to appear instead of *Pictavia* and Gaelic *Cruithentúath* (Broun 2007, 71–97; Charles-Edwards 2008). Clearly, in the late 9th and early 10th centuries, a Gaelic rather than Pictish identity came to the fore.

Indeed, by the early 11th century, the kings and leading noble families of Alba sought their ancestry amongst the kindreds of Dál Riata, rather than from the Picts. A genealogical tract from the reign of Máel Coluim II son of Cináed (1005–1034), for example, claimed Gaelic royal ancestry for the lords of the main territories of Alba (Woolf 2007a, 226; Broun 2019). Clearly, by the 11th century, change was perceived to have happened, with the main territorial families related to the royal line now all thought to have descended from figures supposed to have once lived in 6th-century Dál Riata.

As well as the eventual disappearance of the Pictish identity, the surviving historical evidence also underlines a shift in political importance from the former territories of northern Pictland to that of the south. As with all royal dynasties, the closer the relationship to the current king, the greater the prestige, so the fact that the nearest kindreds to the kings of Alba in Máel Coluim II's genealogical tract were the noble families of Gowrie, Fife and Strathearn is significant. In contrast, Moray, Angus and Ross were not even mentioned, perhaps only included as the descendants of the more distantly related *Conaing*, 'of the northern half' (Broun 2019, 238–40) (Figure 7.1). Ross may have been under Scandinavian control (Crawford and Taylor 2003) and Moray was semi-independent (Woolf 2000). Indeed, Moray had leaders like MacBethad who would later challenge for the kingship of Alba. After the defeat of MacBethad and Lulach of Moray in 1058, Moray's still separate but reduced status meant that the crucible of political control resided in the south in the kingdom of Alba, representing a marked shift from the period when Fortriu was the dominant polity among the Picts.

By the 12th century, the idea that the Picts had been destroyed by Cináed mac Alpín was established. The idea of ethnic destruction is exemplified by the tale, reflected in the 'Prophecy of Berchan', of the 'Treachery of Scone' in which Pictish nobles were invited to a feast by Cináed and then massacred by his followers (Anderson 1990, 1:271–74). In the later medieval period, it was clearly difficult to understand how the complete loss of the Pictish language and the Pictish identity took place without discrimination and ethnic replacement, which of course can happen as has been seen in more recent centuries. CKA (Anderson 2011, 249–50) presents the replacement of the Picts by the Gaels as a heavenly punishment, a Christian reading of history like that used in earlier centuries to justify the British to Anglo-Saxon transition elsewhere in Britain. In CKA, it has been plausibly suggested that the heavenly punishment angle was derived from a contemporary 9th-century interpretation proposed by the growing Gaelic *Céli Dé* reform movement that the defeats of the Picts at the hands of the Vikings in the 9th century were due to sinful ways (Wormald 1996). However, unfortunately, the CKA text has been subject to later alteration, making it an unreliable source and we know that Pictish identity continued for a generation later than the reign of Cináed mac Alpín.

Indeed, it is possible that the transition from Pictland to Alba was much less dramatic than it was later depicted. The name Alba, previously meaning 'Britain' (Dumville 1996), may have united both Picts and Gaels by including them all using a territorial rather than ethnic name for the polity (Broun 2007, 71–97). This term may have been relevant for a broader hegemony even if political reality meant that Alba later became restricted mainly to part of former Pictland. There is also some evidence for the use of Pictish territorial terms into the early 10th century, which suggests some continuity. The *Annals of Ulster*, for example, in AD 904 (*AU* 904.4), records that the men of Fortriu killed the Scandinavian leader Ímar. It is not certain whether the men of Fortriu referred to were inhabitants of the wider Pictish realm or only the province in northern Pictland but the appearance of Fortriu in an Irish text, which had four years earlier started to use the title *rí Alban*, demonstrates that Fortriu was still a relevant concept to the Irish chroniclers. Later, in 934, according to the northern English *Historia Regum Anglorum*, the English King Æthelstan wasted *Scotia* 'as far as Dunottar and *Wertermorum*' ('muir of Fortriu'), with the use of *Werter-* indicating that the Pictish form of Fortriu was still known and was the basis for more local – albeit substantial – features of the landscape (Woolf 2006, 197). After this, Fortriu no longer appears in contemporary chronicles but we do have Gaelic sources employing the term for events in the past. There is, therefore, some indication that the transition to Albanian and Gaelic terminology was not accompanied by an entire rejection of names based on the Pictish territory and former over-kingship of Fortriu.

The Gaelicisation of Pictland

In terms of the transition to Alba, a long-term process involving the Gaelicisation of Pictland was clearly one of the major factors at play. A political relationship between Pictland and the Gaelic west had a long track record. In the mid 8th century Onuist son of Uurguist conquered Dál Riata and, after perhaps a period of separation, *c.*768–792 at most, Dál Riata was again brought under Pictish control during the reign of King Constantín son of Uurguist *c.*788–820. It has been argued that Constantín was actually a Gael, the son of Fergus son of Eochaid, King of Dál Riata (778–781), rather than a Pict, so the period of his family's dominance from the 780s to 842/3 was regarded as a precursor to Cináed mac Alpín's reign (for example, Anderson 2011, 192). However, in the Irish chronicles, Constantín and his brother Onuist are given the title 'king of Fortriu' on their deaths in 820 and 834, and Constantín's battle in 789 or 790 with his rival, Conall son of Tadg, is described as being a conflict 'between the Picts' (*AU* 789.11). In addition, in the account of Blathmac's martyrdom on Iona in 825 by Walahfrid Strabo, Iona is described as an 'island of the Picts' (Clancy 2004). It is clear, therefore, that Pictish kings took over Dál Riata and likely that they were of the same dynasty as King Onuist son of Uurguist (732–761), ruling Dál Riata through subordinate leaders for significant periods (Broun 1998). This was a conquest not a union and the repeated warfare involved, from 731 to 736, 741, 768, during Constantín's conquest – probably in the period from 792 to 800 – and 807 would, alongside Scandinavian attacks, have disrupted pre-existing power structures in Dál Riata. In particular, it is likely that, after 781, other local leaders were preferred by the Picts to the line of Cenél nGabráin from which the two independent kings, Áed mac Echdach and Fergus mac Echdach, were derived, precipitating a decline in their fortunes. However, in 839, the dynasty of Onuist seems to have suffered a terminal setback; in that year King Unen – Eóganán in Gaelic – along with an Áed son of Boanta, who was presumably a sub-king of Dál Riata under Pictish overlordship, died in a battle against the Vikings (*AU* 839.9).

In 842 or 843, Cináed mac Alpín in his contemporary Gaelic form, Cinioid in Pictish, now often known as Kenneth mac Alpine, became king of the Picts. His origins, ethnic identity and whether he was already king of Dál Riata have all been intensely debated (for example, Woolf 2007a, 95–97; Charles-Edwards 2008). Cináed was certainly in retrospect a crucial figure – he was an ancestor of the royal dynasty which dominated the kingship of the Scots until the late 13th century, when Alexander III died. In contemporary sources, Cináed was named 'king of the Picts'. Both his and his father's personal names were originally Pictish but, by the 9th century, they were also used by Gaels, so we can only say that Cináed is likely to have come from somewhere in the Pictish kingdom but, in his lifetime, that included Dál Riata (Woolf 2007a, 96–97). However, two stanzas of near contemporary Gaelic verse added to the *Annals of Ulster* (*AU* 878.3) which lament the deaths of secular figures recorded in the annals for 877 and 878, indicate that Cináed had a connection to Argyll (Woolf 2007a, 116–17; Charles-Edwards 2008, 171–72). The first stanza links these rulers to places supposedly held by their ancestors, though one of the other connections is fictitious. Among the kings mentioned, the poem includes 'Áed from the lands of Kintyre', referring to a son of Cináed mac Alpín, the Áed who died as *rex Pictorum* in *AU* 878.2. While not necessarily accurate, it does indicate that Áed's forefathers were, by the late 9th or early 10th century, thought to have ruled Kintyre, which had earlier been controlled by the Cenél nGabráin dynasty who sometimes also provided kings of Dál Riata. By the late 10th century, Cináed mac Alpín was regarded as a great-grandson of direct descendants of Áed mac Echdach called king of Dál Riata when he died in 778 (Bannerman 1974, 65) but this connection has to be regarded with suspicion (Fraser 2009a, 293) since the offspring of this Áed would have been considered threats to Pictish control in the west.

A shift can probably be seen in the naming practice of Cináed's family. The earlier names, such as Alpin, Cináed and Constantín – king of the Picts (862–876), Cináed's son – are more Pictish and not found in our chronicle or genealogical sources for Cenél nGabráin. Cináed's brother Domnall (king 858–862), did, however, have a Gaelic name, though that name was used for a Pictish ruler of Dál Riata from 811 to 835 (Broun 1998, 79–82), so the choice of this name does not necessarily reflect a desire to make a connection with Cenél nGabráin. Those active and probably born later, after Cináed became king of the Picts in 842/3, do have Gaelic names, with Áed (king 876–878) and Eochaid (king 878–889), grandson of Cináed, attested among 8th-century Cenél nGabráin royalty.

Cináed's daughter, Máel Muire, adds to this picture. She had a Gaelic name, meaning 'servant/devotee of Mary', unattested among Cenél nGabráin but female names are very rare in our sources so that is not unexpected. However, Máel Muire married Áed Findliath mac Néill while he was the high-king of Ireland (862–879) and, following his death, she married his successor, Flann Sinna mac Maíle Sechnaill who died in 916 (Dobbs 1931, 186–88, 225–26). Máel Muire's name reflects an acceptance of Gaelic naming practices and her marriages indicate that kings of the Picts in the 860s or 870s sought connections with a leading Irish king. Máel Muire herself may have been a potential conduit for increased cultural and political contacts between Pictland and the Gaelic west (see Anderson 2011, 250–51; Broun 1999, 103–04). The naming practices of kings active after Cináed and the life of Máel Muire, his daughter, reflect a more general shift to Gaelic culture and outlook in the kingdom that may have promoted the desire to associate the Pictish royal dynasty with an established Gaelic past, linking the rulers of the east with Dál Riata and thus to Ireland. A similar positive attitude to Dál Riata's past may also be found in CKA, which stated that, during the reign of Domnall (858–862), the 'Gaels with their king made' the laws and rights of the kingdom of Áed mac Echdach at Forteviot (Anderson 2011, 250), perhaps a confirmation of the Gaelic laws and rights of Dál Riata (Woolf 2007, 105–06), given that substantial differences in social and legal structures between Argyll and Alba remained. While the original meaning is uncertain, this suggests continued connections to the Gaelic world, perhaps including continued overlordship over Dál Riata.

A similar shift to Gaelic identity, probably in the same period, has been thought to be indicated by two territorial names, Gowrie and Angus (Anderson 2011, 199) (Figure 7.1). These have been interpreted as containing the personal names found in the names of two of the leading kindreds of Dál Riata, Cenél nGabráin and Cenél nÓengusso. The use of these as territorial names in Alba has been considered to be the result of Gaelic migration to Pictland in response to Viking attacks on Dál Riata in the 9th century (Woolf 2007a, 341–42). However, these two territorial names only appear in sources later than the 9th century. In the case of Angus, CKA (Anderson 2011, 251) refers to the death of a Dubucán son of Indrechtach, *mormáer* of Óengus, in 938, indicating that the territory existed by that date and clearly contained the personal name. The situation with Gowrie is even less certain since this name appears after 1100 as *Gouerin* (Anderson 2011, 242), making it plausible that this does not derive from the personal name *Gabrán* at all. Indeed, it has to be suspected that, once Gaelic ancestry became attractive, connections with Dál Riata kindreds, some of which were virtually obsolete at the time, were invented or emphasised. Gowrie's similarity to Gabrán potentially enabled its *mormáer* lords to link themselves close to the royal kindred, and for the wider region allowed linkages to an ancestor called Onuist/Óengus – perhaps the famous King Onuist son of Uurguist, 732–761 (Jackson 1963, 319). This was later reinterpreted to provide their *mormáers* with a lineage stretching directly back to Dál Riata. However, while connections with Dál Riata as part of the Pictish realm might at times have been real, major migration of large population groups or Gaelic lords from the west into Pictland in the 9th or 10th century is not necessarily the explanation for the use of territorial names reflecting Gaelic influence, since Gaelic speakers had already been prominent in Pictland for centuries.

By the end of the 10th century, the Gaelic kingdom of Alba was certainly firmly established (Figure 7.1). Its territorial extent is uncertain and it is interesting to note that it was probably less extensive than Pictland at its height – reflecting perhaps some disintegration of the wider Pictish polity. The core territory of Alba was north of the Forth, south and east of the River Spey and east of *Druim Alban*, 'the ridge of Britain', the mountain watershed which divided it from Argyll. Its control further north was less certain – certainly, by the 11th century, the kings of Alba did not control the by then Scandinavian-held lands of Caithness and Sutherland and perhaps also areas of Ross (Crawford and Taylor 2003).

The dominant part of Pictland, Fortriu, no longer appears in our sources after the early 10th century, after seemingly being divided into the regions of Moray and Ross. As noted already, the relationship of Alba with Moray, a large region from Lochaber and the western seaboard at about Wester Ross to the Spey, perhaps into Strathbogie, was also strained at times and it is uncertain when Moray was regarded as part of Alba. The kings of Alba attempted to be overlords of the rulers of Moray, but their control was only sporadically effective (Woolf 2007a, 220–71; Ross 2011, 82–95). Given that Moray was at times an unwilling part of Alba and the core of the latter was in Fife, Angus and Perthshire, the balance of power in Pictland/Alba had clearly shifted southwards, away from the territory that formerly encompassed Fortriu to that of the core of what had been southern Pictland. In the far west and north, we also perhaps see the dissolution of control of the islands, for by the late 10th century at least the Hebrides and probably Orkney was under Scandinavian control (see below).

In older scholarship the nature of these transitions was obvious – conquests from outside were followed by rapid colonisation and cultural transformation, with a Gaelic takeover of southern and probably northern Pictland and a Scandinavian-led conquest of former Atlantic Pictland and territories around. But was cultural change really that wholesale and how quickly did these changes happen? With respect to Gaelicisation and a Gaelic takeover, from the 5th and 6th century at least, Gaelic influence in the form of at least some population movement bringing Gaelic speakers eastwards was an important factor that would have brought the Gaelic language and culture to the heart of Pictland – the Gaelicisation of Pictland had a long gestation.

The significance of Gaelic ecclesiastics in the conversion and establishment of the Church in Pictland has long been regarded as one factor which would have facilitated change. This can perhaps be seen in the dedications of the churches that were the major ecclesiastical centres in Pictland. Abernethy in Gowrie, for example, is dedicated to St Brigit of Kildare (Taylor 2005), while St Vigeans in Angus has a probable dedication to another Irish saint, St Féchín (Geddes *et al.* 2017, 38–56). In the Pictish territory of Atholl, meaning 'New or Second Ireland', the dedications are strongly Columban in nature – Dull is dedicated to St Adomnán, while Fortingall and Logierait are dedicated to Coeti of Iona (Taylor 1997). How far back some of these dedications go is uncertain but nearby Dunkeld in Stormont, one of the main church centres of Pictland, housed relics of St Columba himself by the 9th century (Woolf 2007a, 98–101).

The Gaelic Church may have become even more important in the early 10th century, the period in which Alba replaced Pictavia as the territorial term for the kingdom. According to CKA, in AD 906 at Scone, Constantín, king of Alba, and Bishop Cellach 'pledged to keep the laws and disciplines of the faith and the rights of the Church and the Gospels in the same manner as the Gaels' (Woolf 2007a, 134–35). Was this a confirmation of direct alignment of the Scottish Church with that of Dál Riata and Ireland in the era when Alba came into being (Clancy 1996, 122)? That is possible but the surviving text may have embroidered a contemporary description of this event in order to explain the Gaelic nature of the Church in a later period. However, the appearance of a Bishop Cellach, with a Gaelic name, as the key cleric – probably of St Andrews – tallies with other contemporary evidence that the Church of Pictland and latterly Alba was dominated by Gaelic-speakers which did, over time, enable Gaelic influence on Christian beliefs and practices, as well as perhaps over wider cultural norms, traditions and language.

Archaeological and linguistic evidence can perhaps contribute further to our understanding of the longer-term gestation of Gaelic influence on Pictland – perhaps, at first, largely administered through the Church. Ogham inscriptions, found across Pictland, indicate widespread Gaelic influence and language use in Pictland since ogham was a Gaelic cipher system and occasionally used for inscriptions in Gaelic itself (for example, Forsyth 1995b). There are around 25 ogham stones in likely areas of Pictish territory or influence (Figure 7.2). Ogham is also found on objects and an ogham inscribed knife handle from the Broch of Gurness, Orkney, has been directly dated to AD 340–540, showing that ogham had spread to the far north of Scotland by the early 6th century AD at the latest (Noble *et al.* 2018a, 1344). A spindle whorl from Buckquoy, Orkney, bears one of the ogham inscriptions in Gaelic to be found in Pictland. It reads '*bendact anim L*', 'a blessing on the soul of L' (Forsyth 1995b, 688). This suggests the probable presence of Irish speakers in Orkney in the 7th to 8th centuries AD – the date of the settlement phase the spindle whorl was found within (Forsyth 1995b, 693). The object could, of course, have been traded, but Gaelic Christian interest in travelling to Orkney and perhaps further north is suggested by sources such as the *Life of Columba* (*VSC* i.6, ii.42, iii.17) and Dicuil's description (Tierney with Bieler 1967, 72–77) of Gaels sailing to the Faroes and beyond in the century before he wrote in 825 (see Chapter 4).

In the majority of cases, there are serious problems in deciphering the ogham inscriptions of Pictland (Forsyth 1997a, 33). As well as the Irish inscription from Buckquoy, a few other inscriptions were in Gaelic but it would appear that the epigraphic tradition was mainly adapted to communicate in Pictish. Some inscriptions appear to represent personal names and others appear to be in the format of 'X son of Y', perhaps in the form of a memorial (Forsyth 1997a, 36). Personal identifiers include names such as Necton and Etharnon. Given that the Pictish symbols are likely to have been communicating names in the Pictish language (see Chapter 6), the juxtaposition of ogham and symbols could be suggestive of an audience who

7.2 Distribution of ogham inscriptions on stone in Scotland.

appreciated different cultural messages – valuing the indigenous symbol system but also the Gaelic connotations of the ogham tradition. It is difficult to date any of the stones with ogham on them in Pictland but the lack of a stem line from which the ogham letter forms were inscribed on the Auquhollie stone in Aberdeenshire suggests this was one of the earlier ogham stones in Scotland – perhaps dating to between the 5th and 7th centuries AD (Forsyth 1996, 41–54), the same era as the ogham inscribed knife handle from Gurness. Though the Auquhollie inscription's reading either VUUNON or VUONON probably includes the Pictish name Unen (Evans 2013, 18–19), this again shows widespread and early dissemination of what was originally a Gaelic means of communicating in Pictland.

Ogham on stone monuments is found on both Pictish symbol stones and symbol-bearing cross-slabs suggesting that in Pictland it was a long-lived tradition. The juxtaposition of ogham and the symbol system, along with the appearance of ogham on objects such as the knife handle from Gurness, is strong evidence for contact between Pictland and Gaelic-speaking areas, continuing contact from the Late Roman period when the *Scotti* and *Picti* colluded in attacking the Roman Empire. Ogham inscriptions are found both in southern and northern Pictland as well as Orkney and Shetland in Atlantic Pictland – this was clearly a widely used cipher system in Pictland. In contrast, in the Brittonic and Anglo-Saxon areas of early medieval Scotland, there is only one certain ogham inscription – it would appear the ogham tradition was much more widely used in Pictland than elsewhere in early medieval Scotland. Indeed, the 25 inscriptions found in Pictland are more than are known from Argyll, the locus of Dál Riata. The presence of ogham in Pictland indicates sustained and perhaps direct cultural contacts between Pictland and western Scotland and the wider Gaelic-speaking zone in the post-Roman period.

Archaeological science can also provide indicators of Gaelic influence in Pictland. In 1985, a long cist was discovered at Bridge of Tilt, Perthshire, in the area of Atholl. Inside the cist was the burial of a male around 45 years of age, who had been interred in the 5th or 6th century AD (Czére *et al.* 2021). Carbon and nitrogen isotope analyses show his dietary protein was dominated by terrestrial resources – as opposed to marine fish or migratory fish such as salmon. Most interestingly, strontium and oxygen isotopes indicate that he was an immigrant to the area at some stage with a west-coast origin likely. This individual may have been brought up as a Gaelic speaker but he moved to an area of Pictland that may have been a conduit for a large degree of Gaelic migration eastwards given the meaning of the name Atholl – *Áth Fhótla*, 'New Ireland' or 'Second Ireland' (Bölcskei 2014; Taylor with Márkus 2012, 92, 94, 287; Watson 1926, 228–29). Atholl is not mentioned in our sources till AD 739 but the Bridge of Tilt burial suggests some folk movement into Pictland from the west centuries before this reference and before Gaelic language and culture became dominant in Pictland in the 9th and 10th centuries AD.

Stable isotope studies show further diversity to Pictland's population. Analysis of the pre-monastic Phase 1 at Portmahomack demonstrated that three out of the four individuals sampled were probably not locals, with a female buried in a long cist consistent with a more westerly origin. Analysis of monastic Phase 2 individuals (*c.*AD 700–830) revealed other likely incomers, although only one probably originated in the west (Carver *et al.* 2016, Table 5.2.23) – though the sample size was small. While the 11th century genealogies stating that Cenél Loairn in Dál Riata migrated up the Great Glen and that the Cenél nGabráin kindred migrated further south should be taken with a large pinch of salt (Broun 2019, 231–34), archaeological science does show that the movement of people from the west to the east did occur and that this had a long pedigree. While 11th-century genealogies attempted to provide later rulers with connections to Dál Riata, the explanations in these texts may have reflected traditional routes of Gaelic expansion and migration into the east. It was not only clerics like Columba who travelled eastwards connecting the Gaelic west with the Pictish east. Folk movements and cultural exchanges involving multiple levels and elements of society would have provided long-term conduits for culture and language change.

Symbols of decline?

Does the archaeological record give us any other hints about the waning of Pictish as a language and identity? If the Pictish symbol system really did communicate names in the Pictish language, then the demise of this system may tell us more about the decline of Pictish. Unfortunately, while today we have a much better understanding of the dating for the origins of the Pictish symbol tradition (see Chapter 6), we have a much poorer understanding of its end. Symbols are found on cross-slabs at sites such as Nigg and Shandwick in Easter Ross and Meigle in Perthshire and these monuments are generally identified as being of 8th- or 9th-century date, but dating at this end of the symbol chronology relies on art historical analysis alone rather than absolute or even contextual dating. What is notable is the lack of symbols on sculpture from sites such as the documented mid 9th-century royal *palacium* at Forteviot, a site where Pictish burial and ritual activity stretched back to the first half of the first millennium AD (Campbell and Driscoll 2020; see also Chapter 3). The Dupplin or Constantine's Cross, for example, has no symbols carved on it but does have an alphabetic inscription (Forsyth 1995a) and, while the style of the monument retains some Pictish characteristics, the free-standing cross form looks west to Iona (Henderson 1997, 166, 175).

There are also further clues of Gaelic influence evident in other parts of the monument. As noted in Chapter 3, the Dupplin Cross has a dedication on it to Constantín son of Uurguist, who was king of Pictland from about AD 788 to 820 and overlord of Dál Riata (Forsyth 1995a). The inscription – *Custantin filius Fircus* – interestingly uses the Gaelic form of his name with Latin *filius*, 'son'. Clearly the creator of this inscription and at least some of the monument's audience were Gaelic speakers. Pictish symbols were not used on the monument, with the Roman alphabet chosen instead. The cross form and inscription fused art styles from Gaeldom and Pictland – for example, the mounted depiction of Constantín (Henderson and Henderson 2004, 125) – and this was perhaps thought appropriate on a monument to an individual and dynasty which managed to rule over both Picts and Gaels. Were the Pictish symbols already out of use in at least some areas of Pictland such as lower Strathearn by the 9th century? Or were such regional symbols simply not appropriate on a monument for a king whose name and monument spoke of his dynasty's pretensions to be seen as heirs to the Roman Empire (Campbell and Driscoll 2020, 209–10)?

Constantín son of Uurguist, the individual recorded on the Dupplin Cross, according to later medieval additions to the Pictish king-lists, founded the major church of Dunkeld (Anderson 2011, 100–01; Woolf 2007a, 65) and it was to this church in Stormont that a portion of the relics of Columba were brought from Iona in *c.*AD 849 (Woolf 2007a, 98–99). Clearly this transferral emphasised links between the Columban community and Pictland and for such an important church to be located in southern Pictland on a major routeway from the west already marked by Iona dedications at Fortingall, Dull and Logierait perhaps says a lot about the shifting cultural balance in Pictland in the 9th century. The foundation of Dunkeld as a major locus for Christianity in eastern Pictland reflected an extension of Gaelic influence, bringing a key saint into the protection of the kingdom.

There are no symbol stones known from Dunkeld or, indeed, other key royal centres or sites of patronage in southern Pictland such as St Andrews or the likely location of *Rathinveramon* around the confluence of the Almond and Tay. The lack of early medieval carved stones of any kind is also notable at Scone, the site that became the key one for royal inauguration for the later kings of Alba and Scotland (O'Grady 2018). Likewise, in northern Pictland, there are no symbols – other than a mirror and comb – on any of the cross-slabs from Kinneddar, an early Christian site that has clear evidence for royal patronage in the 8th century (Henderson 2018, 154–56; Fraser 2009a, 360; Noble *et al.* 2018c, 139). Only one monument with symbols is known from Rosemarkie, the probable bishopric centre of the northern Picts (see Chapter 4), albeit the symbols on the Rosemarkie cross-slab are prominently displayed in a richly decorated scheme on one of the largest monuments from the site. There is also a lack of obviously late stones with symbols from any of the nuclear or complex forts of Pictland such as Dundurn or Burghead (see Chapter 2). All of this begs the question of just how current and widely used was the Pictish symbols system by the 9th century?

It has been suggested that Pictish naming traditions had already begun to die out or become less commonly used by the 9th century or perhaps even earlier (Samson 1992, 62). The lack of Pictish names in current naming traditions could have led to the system's abandonment. However, Pictish names like Drust, Talorgen and Bred (Bridei?) continued to be used for kings into the 9th century, up to the reign of Cináed mac Alpín, 842/3–858 (Anderson 2011, 249, 273), when there was probably a shift to more

Gaelic names in the royal dynasty, and people with Gaelic names, like Flaithbertach son of Muirchertach, *princeps* of Dunkeld (*AU* 873.8), sometimes appear as ecclesiastical leaders. Pictish names that did endure after 900 (Forsyth *et al.* 2008, 137, 139, 141) were employed in a Gaelicised form – for example, Nechtan (Pictish *Naiton*), Fergus (*Uurguist*), Cináed (*Ciniod*), Feradach (*Uuredach*), Caustantín (*Constantinus*) and Ailpín (*Elpin*) (Evans 2019a; Ó Maolalaigh 2019). While recognising the small scale of the surviving corpus, the evidence indicates that the partial shift away from the most common Pictish names and Pictish orthography among the elite – presumably the most influential section of society affecting naming practices elsewhere – took place in the mid 9th century, broadly around the time the Dupplin Cross was commissioned. Perhaps the symbol system was on the wane in the generations before the commissioning of monuments such as Constantine's Cross. With Gaels, Britons, Scandinavians and probably Anglo-Saxons as subjects, kings such as Constantín and his successors may have seen the symbols as too regionally or culturally restrictive and unreflective of an increasingly multi-ethnic realm. The 9th-century rulers of Pictland perhaps had increasingly wide horizons and bigger aspirations.

The conspicuous absence of Pictish symbol stones from certain areas of Pictland may also hint at patterns of linguistic diversity and perhaps cultural identity in Pictland that had long historical trajectories. The modern parishes that make up the historical division of Atholl, for example, have only two Pictish symbol-bearing stones. These comprise a single Pictish symbol stone at Struan, Blair Atholl parish, and a symbol-bearing cross-slab at Dunfallandy, Logierait (Figure 7.3). Other notable gaps are present. There is a small number of Pictish symbol stones from Fife, none from Lewis and Harris (the two largest islands of the Western Isles), and a very sparse distribution on the west coast of Ross and Sutherland. Perhaps Gaelic had long been the main language group in the west in areas closer to Dál Riata, which may explain the only sporadic use of the symbol system in Atlantic Pictland. Likewise, in Fife, it may have been the proximity to Brittonic and Anglo-Saxon groups, as well as the presence of Gaelic speakers, at least from the 8th century (Taylor 1996), that led to the lesser deployment of the symbol tradition. Anglo-Saxon hegemony over southern Pictland in the 7th century may have been another limiting factor. Like the west, the southernmost areas of Pictland may have also been more linguistically and culturally diverse than areas to the north and east, with more Gaelic-, British- and perhaps English-speaking inhabitants.

New threats and new identities

As outlined in the introduction, another important factor in the demise of Pictish as a social and political identity was the presence of Scandinavian

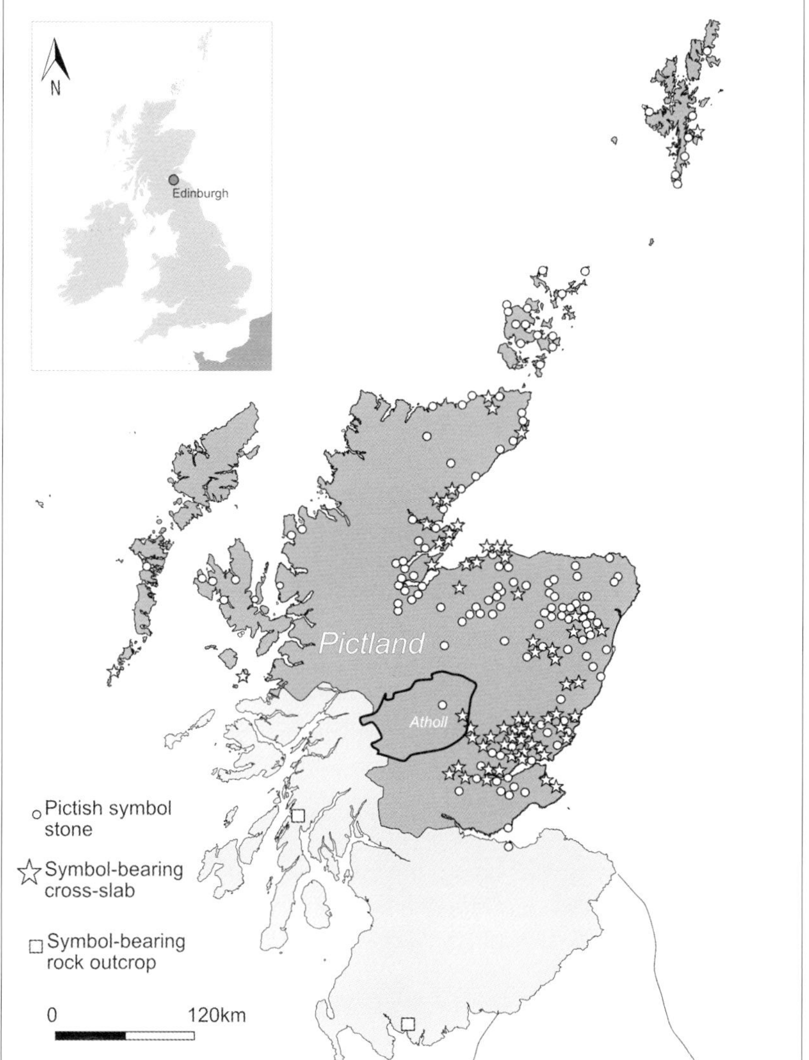

7.3 Distribution of Pictish symbol stones and symbol-bearing cross-slabs in relation to the later administrative area of Atholl.

raiders and settlers. The Viking diaspora from the late 8th century onwards was hugely significant, effecting large-scale change in many parts of Britain, Ireland and elsewhere in Europe. Early in the Viking Age, Scandinavian raiders made a major impression on Christian Europe in AD 793 with a raid on the monastery of Lindisfarne in Northumbria. In Scotland, the most infamous early raids were on the monastic community at Iona over a 30-year period beginning in AD 795, which led to a major downturn in the island's population and economy, albeit for a short period (Jones *et al.* 2020). In the period *c.*800–1100, the western seaboard area, the northern mainland south to at least Ross and the islands of Scotland were settled by Scandinavians, a process reflected in the archaeological record and place-names throughout the region (Jennings and Kruse 2009a, 2009b) though, as we shall see, the timings and tempos of this settlement and place-name adoption are difficult to judge. While the Pictish language did not survive in these areas, Gaelic language and culture did and was established or re-established as the dominant tongue in this zone, apart from in the Northern Isles (where the Norse language, Norn, was spoken until the 18th century) and part of Caithness (Clancy 2011).

We should not forget that the first documented Viking attack in Scotland may have actually targeted the Pictish kingdom, given the realm, at this time, is likely to have included Dál Riata. In the west, only Iona is recorded as being raided in the Irish chronicles though presumably many more episodes of conflict took place in other locations. From the mid 9th century, Scandinavian military campaigns in southern Pictland are attested in the annals. A major battle between the Scandinavians and Picts in 839 caused the deaths of the Pictish king Unen son of Unuist, his brother Bran and Áed son of Boanta, according to the *Annals of Ulster* (839.9). Áed was probably the sub-king of Dál Riata and the death of Unen probably broke the power of the Pictish dynasty established by Onuist son of Uurguist over a century earlier. In Cináed mac Alpín's reign (842/3–858), Vikings raided as far as Dunkeld and Clunie in Perthshire but the campaigns stepped up a gear while Constantín son of Cináed was king (862–876). These attacks occurred in the era when Scandinavian armies destroyed most of the Anglo-Saxon kingdoms to the south. Indeed, part of the Viking Great Army active among the Anglo-Saxons ventured north in 875, though Dublin seems to have been the main base for the attacks before this in 866 and 870–871. It is even possible that Constantín himself was killed in 876 by Scandinavians (Woolf 2007a, 111–12) though, after this, our sources largely fail us again, apart from a vague statement that relics of Columba were taken in flight from Vikings in 878 (*AU* 878.9).

There is then a gap in references to Scandinavian attacks until the reign of Domnall son of Constantín (889–900). During Domnall's reign, there was a battle in which the Scandinavians were defeated at *Inuisibsolian* – probably *innsib Solian*, on or at the isles including Seil off Argyll – and then King Domnall was killed by Scandinavians in 900, according to CKA (Anderson 2011, 251; Woolf 2007a, 122–25). In turn his successor, Constantín son of Áed, defeated Scandinavians in 904 (*AU* 904.4; Anderson 2011, 251). The Scandinavians in question were probably Ímar's grandchildren who had been rulers of Dublin until they were expelled in 902 (*AU* 902.2). However, by this time, there were known Scandinavian kingdoms and bases in England, Ireland and Wales, and Scandinavian conflict with what was now Alba would continue to be recorded intermittently for more than a century after this date.

Place-names can help us understand the potential impact of Scandina-

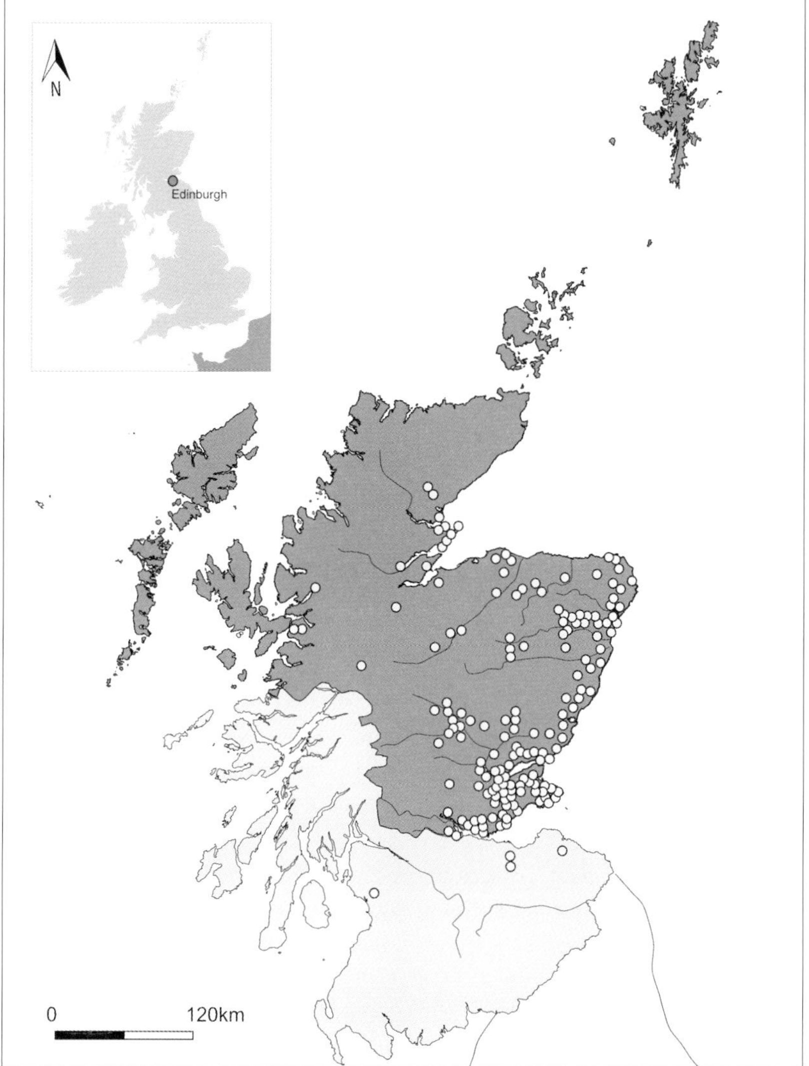

7.4 Distribution of place-names including the element *pett*.

vian settlement. In general, the place-name evidence for Scotland north of the Forth can be divided into two zones. The first was where Gaelic clearly succeeded Pictish south and east of Beauly Firth and Strathglass in the Highlands and encompassed eastern Scotland. A second zone, lying to the north of the first and also including the Hebrides, the north-west and Argyll, contains Scandinavian and Gaelic place-names. In the first zone, Pictish place-names are quite common, as are *pett* names – often now *pit* – used for a piece of land (Taylor 2011, 77–80, 103, 105). *Pett* appears in Scotland north of the Forth, with a few examples to the south of it, and generally in the eastern Lowlands (Taylor 2011, 79–80) (Figure 7.4). While *pett* names have been used for mapping out the potential territorial extent of Pictland, they are mainly now thought to date from after the Pictish period, after the element had been adopted by Gaelic speakers, since they are generally accompanied by Gaelic names and other Gaelic words (Taylor 2011).

In the second zone, Scandinavian and Gaelic names are found concentrated in Atlantic Pictland and further to the south on the western seaboard, continuing into the land that was Dál Riata and Brittonic and Anglo-Saxon areas (Figure 7.5). Pictish survivals are less frequent, with very few Pictish place-names north of the southern part of Sutherland, on the far north-west coast or in the Hebridean and Northern Isles. Scandinavian place-names are common in the islands and the coast in particular, reflecting sea-borne expansion of Scandinavian speakers, but there are also Scandinavian place-names inland, indicating that some wider settlement took place on the mainland (Fraser 1995; Jennings and Kruse 2009a). Regions such as Ross and Sutherland appear to have become frontier zones, with Scandinavian place-names intermixed with Gaelic and Pictish names (Waugh 1993; Gammeltoft 2001; Crawford and Taylor 2003). The general lack of Pictish place-names and the high density of Scandinavian names in coastal areas of Caithness indicate that it is likely to have seen relatively high levels of Scandinavian settlement, though a few names such as Duncansby and Canisbay attest to the continuing presence of Celtic speakers in the area (Waugh 2009). The more restricted distribution of secondary settlement names – including *bólstaðr* and *boll*, both meaning '(secondary) farm' – (Figure 7.5) indicates where Norse continued to be spoken later and where pre-Norse names generally are not found.

Clearly the long-term processes of Scandinavian settlement and political consolidation particularly affected the former Pictish territories of northern and Atlantic Pictland. However, while place-names suggest that the Norse language came to dominate or became particularly common in the north and west, the timings of these changes are uncertain. Some scholars have put place-names at the forefront of the debate regarding the Pictish to Norse transition in the isles, suggesting that the dominance of Norse place-names suggests wholesale replacement of the Pictish population (see Smith 2001 for the extremes of this view), since the surviving pre-Norse place-names are largely confined to island names (Gammeltoft 2004, 2007; Jennings and Kruse 2009a) (Figure 7.6).

However, there has been a tendency to attribute Scandinavian place-names primarily to an initial early Viking Age settlement phase, neglecting the possibility that later settlement, population movement, violence and changes in landownership and organisation in the 10th century and later could explain the high levels of place-name loss and replacement. Since there are few records including place-names in the north and west prior to the 13th century, the shifts in language and naming traditions could have been from longer-term processes of transformation (for example, Waugh

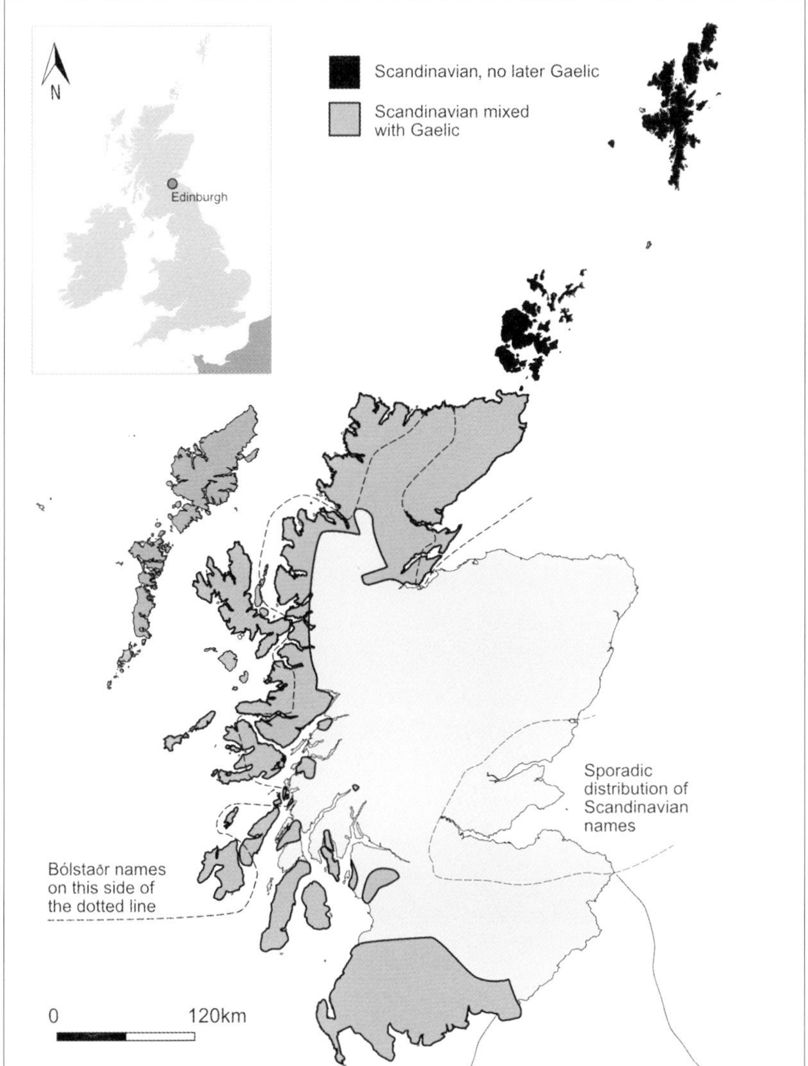

7.5 Distribution of Scandinavian place-names across Scotland.

1993, 121) continuing into the modern era, when our place-name evidence becomes abundant.

Interpretations that emphasise the lack of surviving Pictish names do not, in addition, allow for the possibility that Gaelic as well as Pictish was an important language in some areas of Atlantic Pictland by the time of Norse settlement. This is indicated for Skye and Orkney by the textual and inscription evidence, which is unfortunately non-existent for much of the region, including the Western Isles. Pointing in the same direction is the place-name Camas Thairbearnais on Canna in the Small Isles, including *Tairbearnais*, a word coined by Norse speakers who added *–nes*, 'headland', to the pre-existing Gaelic place-name *tairbert*, meaning a portage place or

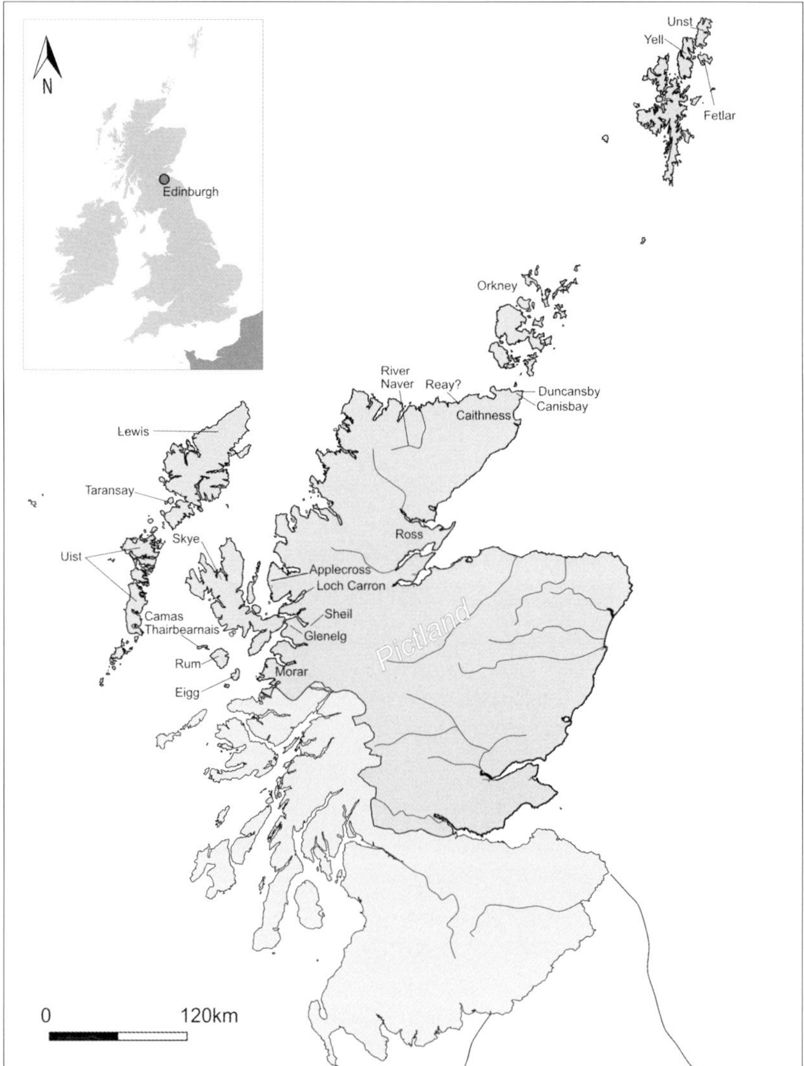

7.6 Non-Norse place-name survivals in the zone of Scandinavian settlement in Pictland.

isthmus (Cox 2007, 142). No similar evidence appears in the Western Isles, which are barely mentioned in early texts, though the island off Harris called Taransay, *Tarasaigh* in Gaelic means 'Taran's Isle', combining this Celtic, perhaps Pictish, personal name with a Norse specific element (Watson 1926, 300). This indicates the continued presence of Celtic speakers in a Norse context.

The combination of Pictish and Gaelic languages in Atlantic Pictland may have meant that Norse became dominant relatively early, though evidence for Gaelic in the Hebrides (Cox 2007) indicates that it may have survived or been reintroduced in the Viking Age through the arrival of newcomers, possibly including slaves (Jennings and Kruse 2005) or free settlers from the wider Scandinavian ruled region. It is also possible that later place-names in the Atlantic zone, especially *cill*, 'church', names accompanied by a saint in the Hebrides, may occasionally represent cultural survivals, as is plausible with Kildonan on Eigg, commemorating the St Donnán who was killed in *c.*617. However, caution with individual cases is necessary here, as primarily such names were created centuries later, themselves part of the process by which pre-existing names were replaced in the later medieval and modern eras. The key point is that, even if many of their pre-Norse inhabitants continued to live in these regions, we should not expect any pre-Norse place-names to survive from the Northern and Western Isles, given the history of these regions from AD 800 to 1500. Therefore, place-names alone do not provide strong evidence for the destruction by Vikings of the pre-existing Atlantic-zone society in the Pictish era.

Looking further south and east, the Scandinavian diaspora certainly had little long-term effect, with Scandinavian place-names few and far between on the southern side of the Moray Firth. It is fairly safe to say that there was little Scandinavian settlement in the easterly areas of northern Pictland or in southern Pictland south of Ross and the Black Isle, and within what became Moray and the core of the kingdom of Alba, apart from some limited settlement in Lowland regions from Fife to Angus, probably dating to the 10th century or later (Taylor 1995, 2004; Graham-Campbell and Batey 1998, 39).

Archaeology is another important source for assessing the Scandinavian impact. Based on the place-name evidence, the north and west are the most obvious places to look for early Scandinavian settlement of the 9th and 10th century AD – the key period when the Pictish to Albanian identity shift took place. Given that attacks on sites such as Iona and in the Irish Sea region began in the late 8th century, it is often assumed that the islands, particularly the Northern Isles, were being used as important stepping stones for Scandinavian settlement and attacks in this early horizon of Scandinavian impact on Britain and Ireland and that settlement was rapid and perhaps brutally enacted (for example, Wainwright 1962, 129–30; Smith 2001). This assumption has highly influenced researchers but there is, in fact, little secure evidence of rapid and dramatic change in the archaeological record or of such sweeping changes in the textual record and, as noted above, the place-name evidence is difficult to tie down chronologically.

As far as historical sources go, our contemporary Insular texts are largely silent on the Pictish to Norse transition. Later sources have often been used to date the settlement of the islands of the north and west but these are not reliable. *Orkneyinga Saga*, based on an earlier *Jarls' Saga* that was written *c.*1200 (Crawford 2013, 39–42), suggests that Norwegian control of the Northern Isles was consolidated in the reign of Harald Finehair – reputedly, but improbably, king of Norway *c.*872–932 – who conquered Orkney and Shetland because they had previously been used by Vikings as their winter bases, including for attacks on Norway itself (Pálsson and Edwards 1978, 26–27; Krag 2003, 185–91). Taken at face value – and ignoring the uncertainties over Harald's reign and even existence! – the saga would put permanent settlement and annexation of Orkney and Shetland sometime in the late 9th or early 10th century but the reliability of this source and other Icelandic texts for early settlement is hugely questionable (Woolf 2007a, 277–85).

The few contemporary sources that we do have are frustrating because they refer to raids on Iona but not to the political situation more widely in western or northern Scotland (Evans 2017), leaving us to make inferences from other evidence. We are also left with interpreting vague notices, such as the statement in *AU* 794.7 that all the islands of Britain were wasted by the pagans and the Frankish *Annals of St Bertin* entry for 847 that the Northmen, after raiding for many years, conquered and lingered on the islands around the *Scotti*. The latter could relate to the Hebridean islands of Dál Riata (Woolf 2007a, 99–100; see also Graham-Campbell and Batey 1998, 45, 71) but it is, perhaps, more likely that this referred to islands closer to Ireland. Any occupation may also have been short lived for, in the following year, the same annals record that ambassadors of the 'king of the *Scotti*' came to Frankia with news that their ruler had scored a major victory in Ireland over the Northmen. It is likely that the entry for 847 was based on the background context for the victory of 848 relayed by that king's ambassadors, who may have exaggerated the previous successes of their Scandinavian enemies. Since the 848 item probably relates to one or more of the four defeats inflicted by Irish kings on Viking forces recorded in 848 in the Irish chronicles, there is no need to regard this as evidence for occupation of islands apart from those immediately around the Irish coast.

What does seem clear from the situation in Ireland in the 840s is that substantial Scandinavian armies, including some from 848 onwards – and probably earlier – connected to at least one probably Norwegian polity, called Laithlinn in the Irish chronicles, were active in Ireland and there was a Scandinavian settlement on the coast north of Dublin by 827 (Etchingham 2010, 2014; Kruse 2017). The rulers of Dublin from 853 onwards were from Laithlinn's royal dynasty, so they may have travelled to Norway via the coast of Scotland. However, that was not the only route (Griffiths 2019) and, even if it was used, Scandinavians did not necessarily control part or its entirety at this point.

Apart from this, there is some evidence for continuity. In the west, for example, Iona, despite repeated attacks, continued to be a significant centre,

7.7 One of three King Alfred coins discovered at Burghead. Found with two holes, perhaps made to render them ornamental, they indicate connections between the Picts of Fortriu and Scandinavians, either friendly or antagonistic.

with the deaths of their abbots recorded in the Irish chronicles. Recently obtained environmental evidence at the monastery also shows that, after about 30 years of low activity starting in the late 8th century, there was increased activity again (Jones *et al.* 2020, 18, 20). The movement of relics in 849 to Ireland and Dunkeld probably reflects continued threats, perhaps relating to both raiding and inter-Viking conflict. Similarly, in 878 the taking of Columba's relics to Ireland in flight from Vikings (*AU* 878.9) probably resulted from unrest in the western seaboard or in eastern Pictland. At roughly this time, there was another temporary downturn in activity on Iona, which may or may not be connected (Jones *et al.* 2020, 18–20). Activity by the Vikings in Pictland is indicated by three Alfredian coins found at the fort at Burghead (Figure 7.7), because these are predominantly found in the Danelaw in England, not in West Saxon territory. Since an alliance with the Danelaw Vikings could make Fortriu the enemy of the rulers of Dublin, either possibility could explain why the Pictish realm was threatened by powerful Scandinavian groups around this time. Even if the relics were not moved from Iona, it is likely that the Pictish kingdom still had a role in Dál Riata, including Iona, up to the 10th century because, in the reign of Domnall mac Constantín (889–900), CKA records a victory by *Scotti* – most likely involving Domnall – at *Inuisibsolian*, probably at the islands just off Mid Argyll (Anderson 2011, 251).

It is only from the 930s that contemporary chronicle evidence for the Hebrides and the north starts to appear in sources. In the account of the campaign of Æthelstan in *Scotia* in 934, in the *Historia Regum*, a

12th-century chronicle including authentic northern English sources, the text states that his navy sailed north, travelling as far as Caithness. This is the first reference to that word (Woolf 2007a, 161) which combined the Pictish territorial name *Cait* with Old Norse *nes*, 'headland', indicating that some Scandinavian settlement had taken place there by that date. This is considerably earlier than our next reliable reference for this region which is to '*Siuchraidh m. Loduir iarla Innsi Orcc*' – 'Sigurðr son of Hlöðvir, jarl of the Orkney islands' – who died in the Battle of Clontarf in Ireland (*AU* 1014.2). How much earlier the jarls of these islands and Shetland can be traced is unclear but there is no reason to follow *Orkneyinga Saga* and other late Scandinavian texts in opting for the late 9th century or pegging the isles to Norway simply to mirror later Norwegian hegemony in the region (Griffiths 2019).

In the 10th century, Scandinavian involvement in the Hebrides also begins to be directly attested. The chronicle of Florence of Worcester described Óláfr Guðrøðsson (d. 941/2), a leader of the Dublin Vikings, as '*Hibernensium multarumque insularum rex*', 'king of the Irish and of the many islands', which was an exaggeration but a real connection with the Hebrides is likely given that his sons were based there in the 960s and 970s (Etchingham 2001, 167–72). Moreover, the *Annals of the Four Masters* (*AFM*) (O'Donovan 1848–1851), a 17th-century compilation of Irish annals which does contain late alterations but also some unique, contemporary early medieval material, refers to *Ladgmainn/Lagmainn* of the isles, probably a version of Norse *lǫgmenn*, 'law-men' (Etchingham 2001, 169, 172). These *lǫgmenn*, fighting in Ireland in *AFM* 960.14 (AD 961/2) and *AFM* 972.13 (AD 974) alongside the sons of Óláfr Guðrøðsson, were probably local leaders in the Hebrides (Etchingham 169, 172).

An earlier reference to a leader in the Hebrides is found in the *Annals of Clonmacnoise* (*AClon*) entry for the Battle of Brunanburh in 937 (*AClon* 931: Murphy 1896, 151) and, in this case, the leader appears to be of more local origin. *AClon* has a certain 'Gebeachan king of the Islands' fighting on Óláfr Guðrøðsson's side. Gebeachan is plausibly Gaelic in form (Etchingham 2001, 167) but is not found elsewhere. Given the large number of Gaelic names only attested once, that does not preclude it being Gaelic, though potentially it was a Dál Riata Gaelic name or a Pictish name in a Gaelicised form (Evans 2019, 30–34). The chronicles overall indicate that political control in the Hebrides was complex, with a non-Norse element still present, but, from the 940s, people with Scandinavian names, connected to Dublin and engaged in Viking activities in the countries surrounding the Irish Sea, emerged as the rulers of some, if not all, of the Hebrides.

The appearance of Scandinavian 'lawmen' in the 960s in the Hebrides indicates that the local leadership of some islands by this time was Norse, but it is unclear when the majority of the population was Scandinavian in language and culture. A hint might be provided in the Irish chronicles, where the Gaelic *Innsi Alban*, 'Isles of Alba', appears in the mid 10th century (*CS* 940. 5 (AD 941); Hennessy 1866; *ARC* AD 963; Jaski and Mc Carthy 2011, 62), then *na hInnsi*, 'the Isles' – seemingly for the Hebrides (*AFM* 972.13 [974]; *AU* 980.1; *Annals of Inisfallen* 986.4; Mac Airt 1951) – before *Innsi Gall*, the 'Isles of the Foreigners', makes its first contemporary appearance for its king, Gofraid (Guðrøðr) son of Harald, in 989 (Clancy 2008b, 26–27). It is likely, therefore, that it was only in the 10th century that the Hebrides were perceived in Ireland to have become Scandinavian. Before then, they were still regarded as primarily connected to Gaelic Alba and presumably, before that, to the kingdom of the Picts.

Airer Goídel, Argyll – but including much of the western seaboard further north – meaning 'shore or mainland of the Gaels', is also usually regarded as coined to contrast with *Innsi Gall*. However, place-names indicate that parts of Argyll experienced some Scandinavian settlement but not to the same extent as the isles and, soon afterwards, people coined Gaelic place-names again in such areas like Kintyre (Jennings and Kruse 2009a). Therefore, the contrast between Scandinavian Hebridean isles and Gaelic mainland may only have been apparent after Gaelic reasserted itself in Argyll and Norse became dominant in the isles. Moreover, *Airer Goídel* is not the term found in contemporary sources of the 10th century. Instead, Dál Riata reappears, once as the location where Gofraid was killed in 989 (*AU* 989.4) and it also appears in 986, when Gofraid's allies, called *Danair* (probably Danes), were defeated and hanged when they came *i n-airer Dail Riatai*, 'into the territory of Dál Riata' (*AU* 986.2). Soon after, the abbot of Iona was killed by *Danair* on Christmas Day (*AU* 986.3). The killing of the Ionan abbot indicates that it was the Scottish and not the Irish, County Antrim, part of Dál Riata that was the location for these events. We can again identify some level of continuity into the 10th century, with *airer Dáil Riatai* perhaps representing the stage before the region became *Airer Goídel*. It is likely, therefore, that both the Isles and the western seaboard, at least the part nearer to Ireland, remained primarily Gaelic in culture, with pockets of Norse speech, and was regarded as part of Alba, though perhaps sometimes relatively autonomous in practice into the 10th century. It may only have been in the mid 10th century that the kingdom of Alba lost all the Hebrides to the Norse and that a sufficient cultural contrast began to create the division between *Innsi Gall* and *Airer Goídel*.

A few other texts offer some useful evidence for the situation in the isles of western and northern Scotland. One is Dicuil's *Liber de Mensura Orbis Terrae*, written in 825 in Frankia on the Continent. Dicuil was a Gael, who had probably lived in the Hebrides (Tierney with Bieler, 1967; Charles-Edwards 2000, 586) and still had contacts in the islands. He mentions the isles around Britain, before discussing islands to the north visited by Gaels, including the Faroes (Tierney with Bieler 1967, 72–77). Dicuil states that the Faroes had once been inhabited by people but that they had all recently fled because of Scandinavian pirates and that this had resulted in the sheep running riot. What is significant is what he does not report. While stating that Gaelic travellers had previously set off to live on the Faroes for nearly a hundred years, he does not describe any other islands being inhabited or depopulated by Scandinavians. Orkney and Shetland were not worthy of specific comment at all, presumably because they were, to him, still unremarkable archipelagos inhabited by Picts and Gaels, not Scandinavians. The fact that Dicuil states that he knew that the Faroes had just innumerable sheep and many types of birds shows that someone had returned more recently to those islands. Dicuil also referred to a journey related to him by another cleric who sailed in a two-benched boat from 'northern islands of Britain' for two days and nights with continuously favourable winds and then disembarked on one of the islands to the north of Britain. Judging by the sailing time, this seems most likely to have been another journey to the Faroes, this time from Orkney (Lamb 1995, 13), presumably after the Vikings had driven people away. This again hints that clerics were still using Orkney as a base for sailing to the north, including as far north as the Faroes, the resulting information getting back to Dicuil. This supports the view that, if there was Scandinavian settlement in Orkney and Shetland by 825, it had, by this stage, left these societies predominantly intact, unlike Viking activity in the Faroes.

Supporting evidence for continuity of settlement in the 9th century can also be found in the 'Life of Findan of Rheinau', written in the late 9th century (Christiansen and Ó Nolan 1962, 148–64). Findan, raised in Leinster, was captured by Vikings in the 840s or 850s (Woolf 2007a, 287–88), then sold and re-sold as a slave while the raiders travelled north. At Orkney, they stopped off at an island enabling Findan to escape and hide for some days, before he miraculously managed to swim to another land where he climbed up a high hill or mountain. There, he found inhabitants and stayed with a bishop who spoke Gaelic as a second language, since he had trained in Ireland. The most plausible location for the bishop is Orkney. It is described as beyond the land of the Picts but that can probably be discounted as a natural way of thinking about an island (Woolf 2007a, 289), though it does raise the possibility that it was rather easy for such islands to have an identity detached from their neighbouring mainland, which could conceivably have eased the transition to a new social and political makeup in the Viking Age. Nevertheless, as with Dicuil's account but about a generation later, it can be inferred that Orkney was still part of a wider Pictish and Gaelic world (Woolf 2007a, 288–89) and that there was no Scandinavian authority to force Findan, a runaway slave, back into

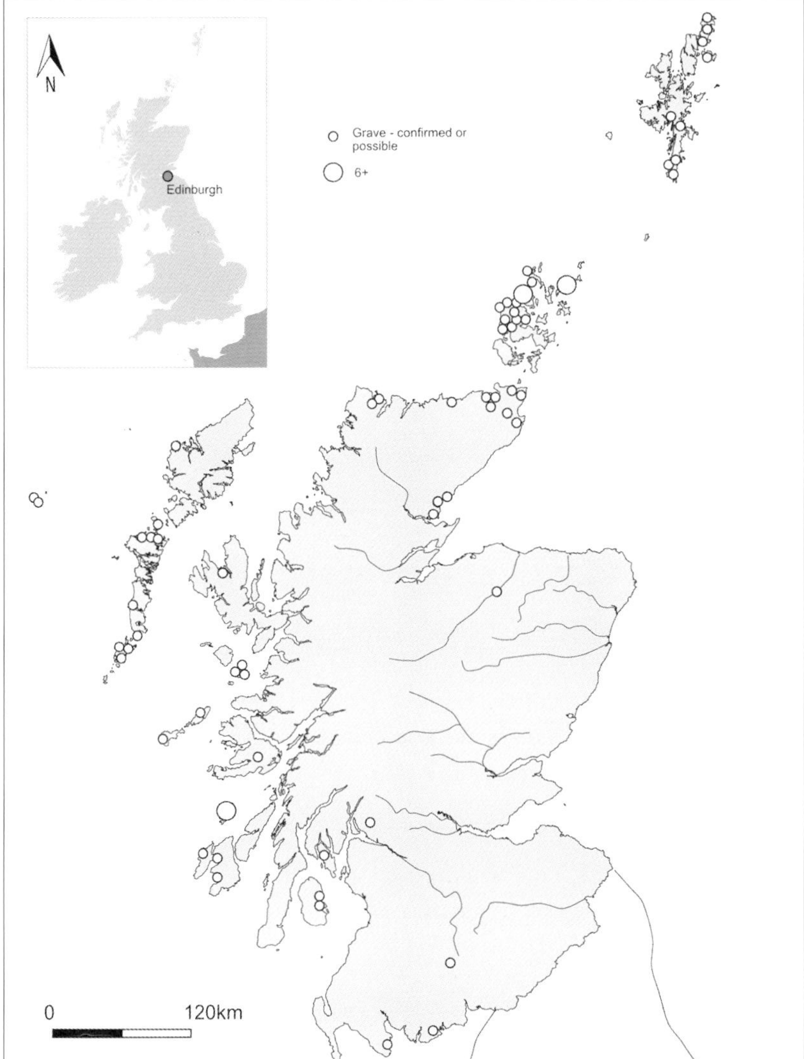

7.8 Scandinavian-style furnished burials from Scotland – distribution of confirmed and possible examples.

captivity. Though the presence of Viking raiders looms in both sources, it is unclear whether Scandinavian settlement as opposed to raiding had already taken place.

In terms of Viking Age archaeology, Viking-style furnished burials are known from Shetland to the Inner Hebrides (Graham-Campbell and Batey 1998, 47) (Figure 7.8). Orkney represents a particular concentration of these furnished graves, with one important cemetery being Westness, Rousay, Orkney, where furnished burials and boat graves have been dated to the 9th to 11th century AD (Barrett and Richards 2004, Table 1). In general, the furnished 'Viking' burials of northern and western Scotland have been dated to *c.*AD 850–950 through typological dating of the artefacts

(Graham-Campbell and Batey 1998, 152–54) – though note that the dating is partly influenced by the assumed chronology of Viking settlement in the west and north (Maldonado 2021, 76). The furnished nature of the burials in the Northern Isles is certainly in sharp contrast to the unfurnished burials known from Pictland and early medieval Scotland more generally (see Chapter 5). These graves are strongly suggestive of incoming Scandinavian populations, if not substantial influence from Scandinavian traditions. Having said that, the furnished burials from Westness, Orkney, the largest 'Viking' cemetery known, were within a cemetery that was founded in the Pictish period, suggesting some sort of continuity in place of burial at least (Graham-Campbell and Batey 1998, 56, 136; Barrett and Richards 2004, Table 1; Kaland 1993, 312; Sellevold 2010). It is also the case that long cist burial without any accompanying grave goods continued alongside and after the phase of furnished burial, suggesting further elements of continuity or at least cultural hybridity and interchange (Sellevold 2010). In Shetland, Viking-style burials are rare and generally poorly furnished. This may be partly due to a lack of survival of evidence but, if the pattern is real, it could also contradict the expectation that Shetland might have been settled prior to Orkney and areas further south (Graham-Campbell and Batey 1998, 64).

Turning to the habitation evidence for Orkney and Shetland, it has long been assumed that settlement in these islands must have begun around AD 800 or within a few generations of this date. The logic for this is that the Northern Isles were used as a base for attacks further south – such as on the Hebrides and Ireland (for example, Graham-Campbell and Batey 1998, 24, 44–45) – but this is an assumption rather than a fact and it is possible that these areas only saw minimal settlement in the early decades of the Viking Age as Scandinavians focussed on more populous and perhaps richer areas in the Irish Sea zone (Woolf 2007a, 55–56; see also Griffiths 2019) and, as noted above, the limited historical evidence does not actually support Scandinavian takeover in the north and west till the 10th century. Indeed, when we examine the current evidence from Orkney and Shetland, the settlement sequences likewise suggest little in the way of abrupt change till the 10th century (see also Maldonado 2021, 78–79). For example, at the substantial settlement at Scatness, Shetland, the wheelhouse (Structure 11), where the Pictish-style carving of a bear was found (Chapters 3 and 6), continued in use till at least the late 9th century and probably the 10th century AD. In a late floor level of Structure 11, there were some probable Norwegian-style objects, including imported steatite vessels, but, as well as the continuing use of the wheelhouse, the pottery traditions, metalworking styles and the economic base of the settlement largely continued as in previous phases (Dockrill *et al.* 2010, 299–301, 361–69). These traditions are unlikely to have continued without a substantial level of continuity in population. More definitive traces of Norse occupation could, of course, have occurred outwith the excavation area but the currently available evidence suggests broad continuity in architectural traditions, material culture, and economic and crafting traditions into the 10th century AD.

Jarlshof in Shetland, just a stone's throw away from Scatness, has been identified as a classic case of Norse takeover of a Pictish site, with Norse settlement assumed to have occurred from around AD 800 at another multi-period settlement mound (Hamilton 1956), but it is important to note that the Jarlshof sequence is not actually supported by absolute dating and there are problems with the stratigraphy and conflation of deposits (Graham-Campbell and Batey 1998, 155–60). That aside, the artefactual evidence might suggest a much later Norse arrival than the excavator put forward, with the early phases of 'Norse settlement', the 'parent farmstead' having artefact styles that suggest a 10th-century or later date for this phase (Maldonado 2021, 77). Likewise, at Pool, Sanday, Orkney, it was only really in the 10th century AD that major changes in settlement architecture and material culture occurred, with a well-preserved building – Structure 29 – resembling a more classic 'Late Norse' longhouse dating to the late 10th century or later – Pool, Phase 8 (Hunter *et al.* 2007, 147–48). Prior to Phase 8 at Pool, economic changes and the use of steatite as a crafting medium *might* reflect Scandinavian influence but this was within a settlement context that displayed continuities with the Pictish phases – Phase 7 (Hunter *et al.* 2007, 121). Material culture traditions such as pottery and pin forms continued throughout Phase 7 and, indeed, into Phase 8 (Hunter *et al.* 2007, 131, 138). Phase 7 was thought to be a Scandinavian 'interface' horizon, prior to full-blown Scandinavian settlement in Phase 8 but one difficulty is that the excavators assumed a 9th-century date for Scandinavian takeover rather than critically assessing this possibility. While the continuities of architecture and material culture were acknowledged, the significance of this was perhaps not fully explored in terms of allowing for longer-term changes in cultural norms and identities and divergence from traditional narratives.

One possible early Viking longhouse settlement pre-dating the 10th century has been found at Norwick Bay on Unst, in Shetland, but the dating at this site is uncertain given that there was Pictish settlement prior to the longhouse phase (Ballin Smith 2013, 217–33; Turner and Owen 2013, 234). Indeed, the Viking Unst project found little in the way of clear traces of Norse-style buildings or material culture prior to the 10th century or later (Turner and Owen 2013, 234–35). Likewise, recent excavations at Snusgar and East Mound, at the Bay of Skaill on Orkney's West Mainland, identified two groups of longhouses, with their main phases of occupation dating from the later 10th to early 11th centuries AD (Griffiths *et al.* 2019). Similarly, another longhouse settlement at Quoygrew, excavated in recent years and benefitting from robust dating, developed from the 10th century AD onwards (Barrett 2012). At Snusgar, Bay of Skaill and Quoygrew, the settlements were founded anew in the 10th century on land that had been little used previously.

Buckquoy, Birsay, on Orkney, has also often been cited as the type-site for a Pictish–Norse transition, with rectangular dwellings identified here assumed to be Norse – demonstrating what shaky ground our ideas of cultural change can be based on – and for that change to have taken place relatively early. However, recent dating at Buckquoy has shown that the rectangular buildings belong to the 8th century with no definitively Norse-style material culture within the dwellings of this phase which confirms earlier doubts about the Viking Age date of these dwellings (see discussion in Morris 2021, 568). The rectangular buildings of Buckquoy now comfortably fit within the broader settlement traditions of Pictland (see Chapter 2) and there is no need to seek external influence for the evolution of rectilinear forms of architecture at this site. At Buckquoy, the only probable evidence for Scandinavian influence is the artefacts found within a burial of 10th-century date dug into the abandoned settlement mound and this grave itself may be an interesting case of cultural hybridity (see below and Chapter 3). Other sites may need to be similarly reassessed – at Skaill, Orkney, for example, some of the 'Norse' period rectangular structures have only local styles of artefact and, throughout the assemblages, there was a lack of demonstrable 9th-century Scandinavian finds (Buteux 1997; Graham-Campbell and Batey 1998, 168–71).

Rather than being widespread, it has been suggested that the earliest Norse presence in the Northern Isles may have focussed upon pre-existing high-status Pictish sites such as the Brough of Birsay in Orkney. According to *Orkneyinga Saga*, the 11th-century Earl of Orkney, Thorfinn, had his permanent residence at Birsay and built a minster there for the first Bishop of Orkney (Morris 1993, 286). On the Brough of Birsay, there are the remains of a 12th-century church along with 'hall houses' and a blacksmith's workshop from Scandinavian settlement along with much more limited traces of pre-Norse settlement including a Pictish symbol stone (Henderson and Henderson 2004, 65–66; RCAHMS 2007, 114), three ogham stones, some of which at least may have been from buildings on the brough (Forsyth 2021, 374–87; Morris 2021, 567), metalworking and a well (see Chapter 3 and Curle 1982; Morris 2021, 566). The metalworking at least would suggest some sort of high-status activity on the Brough of Birsay in the Pictish period (see Chapter 3) but the relationship with the Scandinavian remains is uncertain, as is the chronological development of the site through time. Certainly, recent re-analysis of the site sequence does not provide clear chronological resolution for the Pictish to Norse transition or evidence of abrupt change (Morris 2021, 560). Modelling available radiocarbon dates for the Birsay area suggests overlap between 'Pictish' and 'Viking' phases (Morris 2021, 568), a situation also suggested by the artefactual evidence with mixed assemblages of 'Pictish' and 'Norse' character in the later phases of the settlement on the Brough of Birsay itself (Curle 1982). On the Brough of Birsay, the Norse phase has been dated to the period AD 890–1190 (Outram 2021, 140–41, Table 9.4, Illus. 9.26; Morris 2021, 568), suggesting that it was the 10th century, as the evidence stands, before major transitions were consolidated in the character of the settlement.

One other important strand of evidence is the continuity at church sites, though the evidence from only a very few early examples can contribute. In Orkney and Shetland, incoming Scandinavians would have been pagans early in the Viking Age but, at St Ninian's Isle, Shetland, there is evidence of continuity of use and burial at this church site at least till the 10th century AD. At St Ninian's Isle, E–W burial continued into the 10th century AD, with a furnished burial with weaponry of an 11th- to 12th-century date suggesting some change in this relatively late period (Barrowman 2011, 198–200).

The Western Isles provide similar evidence to that of the Northern Isles. There are a number of probable Viking-style burials of a 9th- to 10th-century date. These include individual examples as well as a cemetery at Cnip, Lewis (Graham-Campbell and Batey 1998, 74–75; Dunwell *et al.* 1995a, b). The Cnip cemetery included a 10th-century burial of a female with a range of grave goods including two oval brooches, a glass-bead necklace, a ringed pin, a knife, a whetstone, a needle case and a sickle. Thus, there is certainly evidence for some sort of Scandinavian impact in the Western Isles but the settlement record is less clear cut – though admittedly not as well explored or dated as that of the Northern Isles. At present, the published documentation provides little in the way of concrete evidence of Scandinavian settlement prior to the 10th century. At Bornais, South Uist, the use of longhouses associated with Scandinavian settlement appears to have started around the mid 10th century AD (Sharples 2019, Fig. 399) and settlement at Cille Pheadair, South Uist, began in the 11th century AD (Parker Pearson *et al.* 2018). A longhouse, built into the figure-of-eight building complex (see Chapter 3), at Tràigh Bhòstadh, Lewis, may date to the 9th century (Neighbour and Burgess 1996) but the site is not fully published to allow assessment of the sequence in more detail or the cultural background of its occupants to be pinpointed definitively without further evidence. The transition to Norse material culture and architecture has been claimed to occur in the 9th century at the Udal but none of the current dating aids precision and nor, like Tràigh Bhòstadh, does the lack of final publication for the site. It is notable, however, that there was little evidence for any sort of substantial longhouses in the early 'Norse' phases (Crawford and Switsur 1977, 131). The 'Norse' house at Drimore, South Uist, a small sub-oval structure, has been dated by artefact typology that draws on parallels with Jarlshof, the difficulties of dating of which have already been outlined (MacLaren 1974). Thus, the settlement evidence in the Western Isles has, at present, little conclusive to say about Pictish–Norse transitions towards the end of the first millennium AD.

Nonetheless, archaeological science can again contribute important direct evidence for population movement and change in the Northern and Western Isles in the Viking Age, though the results don't always perhaps match expectations. Isotopic study of individuals from the 'Viking' Cnip cemetery, Isle of Lewis, has certainly suggested population movement, though of two female burials, one may have come from England (Burial E: 9th–10th century AD) and the other from mainland Scotland or north-east England (Burial A: later 10th century) rather than Scandinavia (Dunwell *et al.* 1995a, 242–43; Montgomery *et al.* 2014, 64). Isotopic analysis from burials at Westness, Orkney, of probable 9th- to 10th-century date, identified one female who probably grew up on mainland Scotland or Ireland, while two males may have had a Scandinavian upbringing (Montgomery *et al.* 2014, 64; Barrett and Richards 2004, Table 1).

The isotopic evidence suggests that identities could perhaps be adopted – or, indeed, imposed – and were not always the result of direct migration from Scandinavia. Ancient DNA evidence may paint a similar – if, at present, sketchy – image. Ancient DNA studies are in their infancy – especially for early medieval Scotland where there is only one study to date for the period. This has shown that two individuals from Newark Bay, Orkney – a medieval-period chapel and cemetery from which a Pictish cross-slab is known – had what appeared to be mixed Scottish or Irish and probable Scandinavian parentage – it is difficult to be more exact given the limited range of current datasets. However, only one of these burials is directly dated and is probably 11th century AD in date – that is after the 9th and 10th centuries AD that are of prime interest in discussing the end of the Pictish period (Margaryan *et al.* 2020, supplementary data 55–56). A 10th-century man from a Viking-style grave at Buckquoy, Orkney, was buried with a coin of Edmund I (939–946), a ring-headed pin, an iron knife, a whetstone and an iron javelin head. Despite the exotic Viking style of his burial, he was likely of local descent though, again, only identifiable at present as being related primarily to the modern population of Scotland and Ireland, (Margaryan *et al.* 2020, supplementary data 55, 139–40). A flexed inhumation of the 10th to early 12th century AD, from Brough Road, Birsay, unaccompanied by grave goods, was similarly of probable local or at least Insular origin (Margaryan *et al.* 2020, supplementary data 56, 139–40).

The preliminary data suggests the continuation of what seems most likely to have been local genetic lineages into the second millennium AD in Orkney though much more work needs to be done to test and refine these results and other possibilities regarding the origins of these individuals remain – for example, it is not impossible that there was the transplantation of genetic lines through slave raiding and Viking forces themselves were of mixed ancestry. However, the data tentatively argues against any sort of rapid genocide characterising the late 8th- and 9th-century period in the Northern Isles (contra Smith 2001). The evidence might again suggest that a Norse identity could be assumed by individuals with no direct connection – on a genetic level at least – to Scandinavia, though the genetic data tell us little about the cultural identity, language or upbringing of these individuals.

The modern DNA of the Northern and Western Isles may be another evidence strand, though we have little ancient DNA to compare it to and the patterns sketched out at present are largely ahistorical. There are certainly significant levels of Scandinavian DNA in the modern genetic makeup of the islands today (Gilbert *et al.* 2019) but we cannot as yet identify how and when the genetics of these places began to shift and how rapid and extensive that shift was. It may have been substantially later than the period in which the Pictish identity ceased to exist. All in all, ancient DNA approaches will undoubtedly play an important role in disentangling the changes in this period but it is early days with these techniques and there is the danger of making false assumptions in interpretations. Nonetheless, even the limited evidence at present illuminates the potential complexity of the cultural situation in the Viking Age.

There is certainly no doubt that Scandinavian influence over the north and west of Scotland became extensive over the long term. While there could still be shifts in cultural elements such as language and ethnic identity long after the Picts, the Hebrides came under Scandinavian control and remained subject to Norway till 1266 when they became part of the kingdom of the Scots. However, by the mid 12th century, the rulers of the region were predominantly Gaelic speakers and, gradually, Gaelic became dominant more widely, though connections with Norway remained since the Lordship of the Isles stayed in the ecclesiastical diocese of Nidaros near Trondheim. Caithness, part of the Orkney earldom, was also settled by Norse speakers but, from the 12th century, was increasingly regarded as part of the Scottish realm and the Gaelic language expanded in this area (Clancy 2011; Crawford 2013). However, Orkney and Shetland remained under Scandinavian rule until 1468–9 so that, although Scots was increasingly spoken from the 14th century onwards, there were still many centuries for settlement, cultural and language shift to have taken place and these were recorded in sources that are largely 14th century or later (Crawford 2013).

Overall, our current understanding of the transition to Norse-speaking societies in Scotland is still either based on later evidence, such as late medieval or modern documents with place-names, or patchy and difficult archaeological and textual material. Given the differences within Atlantic Pictland, in which islands and coastal regions can be very diverse, we should also not expect there to be a single picture for Scandinavian raiding, control and settlement. Certainly the image based on the archaeology of the region – and, indeed, looking at our limited historical sources in a new light – is that there was greater and longer continuity of local settlement and culture into the 10th century than, until recently, was considered plausible. The Picts and other occupants of the islands interacted with Scandinavian culture and lived alongside Scandinavians. Newcomers came from diverse geographical backgrounds; some of them embraced Scandinavian forms of material culture and identity marking, despite not being of direct Scandinavian descent themselves. The evidence is limited but it does seem possible that the Pictish kingdom and its successor, Alba, maintained control of part or all of the north and west into the 10th century or at least to the mid 10th century when other rulers appear in our sources.

Nevertheless, it would be wrong to portray the development of Atlantic Pictland and the west and north more generally as uneventful. There is plenty of evidence for massacres, such as the repeated raids on Iona, and, in the case of the Faroes, of people fleeing from Vikings. Conquest and the creation of bases before 900 is also likely in some cases, most plausibly at strategic locations like Islay and perhaps on some of the islands of Orkney though, as elsewhere, these pioneer settlements could often be transient or of short duration, being abandoned, attacked and destroyed. In fact, the traditional narrative of a single, total and permanent Scandinavian settlement neglects the possibility that raiding, conquest and settlement processes could repeatedly affect the same islands over generations. In Ireland, as well as Scandinavian campaigns, local rulers attacked Vikings and Scandinavians, and perhaps even more fought each other for supremacy, their followers and subjects the protagonists, beneficiaries and victims of these conflicts. This is the situation we see in the 10th century when the Hebrides reappear in the chronicles (Etchingham 2001) and to some extent for the Northern Isles in the 11th century and later (Crawford 2013). Especially on the islands, the repeated killing and movement out and in of people would have made long-term continuity difficult, so it is not surprising that the surviving pre-Norse place-names are largely confined to the islands themselves, as they are the biggest landscape features. Nor is it strange, especially if some Gaelic as well as Pictish was spoken on Orkney and perhaps elsewhere, that another language, Norse, could replace them so completely. In places, these processes were already taking place in the 9th century, as indicated by the traditions about *Peti* in Orkney as well as by the existence of the Pentland Firth, 'Pictland Firth', but the key transitions were perhaps mainly in the 10th century and, in some locations, perhaps even later. An implication of this is that the full process of Scandinavianisation of the Atlantic region may have taken place largely after Pictish identity had ceased to exist.

Continuity vs change?

Shifting focus from the Atlantic to southern and northern Pictland, what can we say about continuity and change in this period in these more easterly and southerly regions of Pictland? The 9th and 10th centuries in eastern Scotland are perhaps an even more difficult period to identify in the archaeological record than the earlier centuries of the first millennium AD. There are only limited numbers of settlement sites or cemeteries belonging to this period that illuminate in any detail what changes – or lack of changes – were occurring. In the uplands of Perthshire, there were certainly settlement continuities with the sequences at Pitcarmick-style buildings at Lair and Pitcarmick itself extending into at least the 10th century AD. However, in the Lowlands, the lack of a consistent settlement pattern makes it unfortunately difficult to say anything valuable about settlement continuity or otherwise (see Chapter 2).

In terms of elite centres, it has been suggested that there was a broad shift towards Lowland royal centres in the late first millennium AD (Driscoll 1998b, 169–70) but there are some hillfort sites, such as Craig Phadrig, Inverness-shire, and Doune of Relugas, Moray, that have radiocarbon dates stretching to the 11th and 12th centuries AD and there are historical references to sites such as Dunsinane and Dundurn, Perthshire, and to Dunnottar, Aberdeenshire, in the 9th and 10th centuries (Anderson 2011, 251, 267, 274–75, 283–4). Nonetheless, some fortified centres do appear to have fallen out of use in the Viking Age. The massive promontory fort at Burghead, Moray, the largest early medieval fort of its kind known, appears to have been abandoned sometime between the late 9th and the mid 10th century, the period in which the references to the Picts and Pictish territories cease. Lowland power centres, such as Forteviot and Cinnbelathoir, perhaps just north of Perth, continued in use into the high medieval period but any impact on sites like these in the late 9th or 10th centuries AD is difficult to assess given the limited archaeological and historical information we have at our disposal.

With regards to ecclesiastical centres, we know that these were major targets for Viking raiding elsewhere, as occurred at Iona. In the late 8th or early 9th century, just across the Moray Firth, the Pictish monastery at Portmahomack is argued to have been destroyed by Viking attack in the period, though other perpetrators or causes could have also been responsible for the changes evident at the site (Griffiths 2019, 470; Maldonado 2021, 40). Certainly there was no major hiatus of occupation at the site, though the character of production did alter towards a more mercantile orientation, with the casting of dress items, weights and other tradable commodities. Other ecclesiastical centres show some level of continuity, perhaps even expansion in the late first millennium AD. Dates from the vallum at Kinneddar, Moray, suggest the ecclesiastical enclosure there went on in use till the 11th century (Noble *et al.* 2018c). In southern Pictland, recent reassessments of sculpture from St Vigeans, Abernethy and Dunkeld suggest that significant investments in sculpture may have been happening at these ecclesiastical centres through the 10th century and perhaps later (Geddes 2017; Maldonado 2021, 178–85).

Transformations

Bringing all these complex strands together, what can we really say about the later first millennium AD when Pictish identity disappeared? We can certainly see changes in the limited historical and archaeological sources we have for the 9th and early 10th centuries AD. Looking at the elite level in Pictland or Alba, we can see that there was a shift in royal titles – rulers became kings of Alba rather than kings of Fortriu or Pictland. The territory formerly known as Pictland also came to be known as *Albania* and *Scotia* in Latin or *Alba* in Gaelic. By the 11th century, lineages were sought for the kings and aristocrats of Alba in the Gaelic west in Dál Riata and, by the 12th century, the idea that the Picts had been destroyed by the Gaels had arisen. Thus it is clear that change did occur and that it led to the demise of the Pictish over-kingdom, Pictish identity and the Pictish language. Later tradition ascribed these changes to rapid cataclysmic events. Nonetheless, these changes may not have been as wholesale as scholars once thought. There are no contemporary references to major episodes of ethnic cleansing or wholesale population movements, which surely would have attracted the attention of even distant annals writers and commentators. These changes must have been at least partly enacted by the Picts themselves and by people within the existing social and political frameworks shaping a new polity and identity to suit lords and rulers and perhaps an increasingly diverse subject population. Some of these changes may have been rapid but others may have been largely imperceptible to the people of the time.

The main factors at play in these changes appear to have been a combination of pressures – some long-term internal processes of change, others external factors in a changing social and political environment. One important long-term factor was undoubtedly language shift with Gaelic rising in prominence in eastern Scotland and clearly dominating in the east by the end of the first millennium AD. The rise in Gaelic may have been prompted by its use in the Church, through folk movement of Gaelic speakers eastwards, as may have been the case with the Bridge of Tilt individual, and perhaps through its increasing use in courtly circles through kings and elites with Gaelic connections or ancestry. The Pictish overlordship of Dál Riata in the 8th century may have actually set the foundations for this elite shift, enabling more leaders who spoke Gaelic or with Gaelic connections to assume positions of authority and rule within Pictland. Other language groups are likely to have been present in Pictland through time, with increasing Norse influence in the west and north perhaps particularly keenly felt, but also some Scandinavian and other influences elsewhere in Pictland and Alba. Indeed, in the king-lists and chronicles of 10th-century Alba, we can see kings, nobles and leading clerics with names of likely Pictish, Gaelic and even perhaps Norse or Continental descent – the polity and its rulers were becoming increasingly multilingual and multi-ethnic (Woolf 2007a, 192–93, 206; Evans 2019).

In terms of the wider context, we should also not underestimate just how uncertain and fluctuating the social and political situations were in early medieval Britain and Ireland towards the end of the first millennium AD. It was a time of transformation for the majority of the polities that existed in Britain and Ireland in this period. One major factor in this disruption was, of course, the Viking presence with Scandinavians launching full-scale campaigns in regions such as eastern Ireland from the 9th century onwards, with permanent bases established around the coast from the 830s and 840s. The 'Great Heathen Army' that landed in England in AD 865 similarly wreaked havoc in the later 9th century across England leading to the demise of the kingdoms of Northumbria and East Anglia and this army came close to defeating Wessex and Mercia. Closer to home, in AD 870 Dumbarton Rock, the main centre of the British kingdom of Alt Clut, was sacked by Ímar and Amlaíb, king of Dublin. This event led to the demise of the kingdom of Alt Clut with 200 ships of plunder and slaves (including Picts) taken to Ireland, destined to be sold in the markets of Dublin. However, the Britons did reorganise themselves within a new kingdom known as Strathclyde. As noted earlier, the Scandinavians also targeted Pictland, whose kings were killed in 839, perhaps 876, and 900, and Pictland was occupied for considerable periods in 866 and 875–876 (*AU* 839.9; Anderson 2011, 250, 251; Woolf 2007a, 66–67, 106, 122–23), these events may have kick-started a similar process of transformation through external and internal processes of influence and change.

In Pictland, the impact of Viking attacks is hard to document in the archaeological record. As shown above, the archaeological record for the Northern and Western Isles suggests some change, principally in the appearance of furnished burials, but we can also identify broad continuities in settlement into the late first millennium AD. However, it must be said that the chronological and contextual resolution of Viking Age settlement in the Northern and Western Isles is very poor and certainly requires new programmes of dating and analysis. That aside, the evidence that is present would favour continuities of Pictish-style architectural and material culture traditions into the 10th century AD and this perhaps contradicts the oft-presumed role of the islands as early forward bases involved in a rapidly changing social and political geography driven by Scandinavian incomers.

Nonetheless, the burial evidence in particular and the possible presence of Scandinavian material culture in late phases of native settlements in Orkney and Shetland at sites such as Scatness and Pool do suggest some level of cultural contact and transformation. Given the presence of furnished burials with Scandinavian-style objects and cemeteries that include furnished burials of a probable *c.*AD 850–950 date, there is likely to have been a degree of settlement by non-locals in the 9th and early 10th centuries, although how widespread and permanent that was is difficult to ascertain with the present levels of evidence and chronological certainty. Associated with early Norse settlement may have been processes that sapped local resources such as the use of local food supplies and the extracting of tribute from local groups.

However, change may not have simply pitted newcomers against Picts but may have also brought wider changes in social and political circumstances. From a Pictish perspective, for example, there could have been some local collusion with Norse incomers in Atlantic Pictland, in order to promote the standing of the Northern and Western Isles vis-à-vis the Pictish over-kingship centred on mainland areas to the south, with individuals perhaps tapping into the wider changing social and political climate in a world with increasingly international horizons and connections. Certainly the albeit limited isotopic and ancient DNA (aDNA) evidence provides food for thought, with Scandinavian identities being heterogeneous and perhaps assumed as well as being inherited – some locals may have gone 'Viking', using a new Scandinavian identity to assert power and influence outwith the over-kingships of the Picts and Gaels. We also shouldn't underestimate the level of conflict that may have happened internally within the society of Scandinavian settlers or the possibility that Scandinavian groups could be used by local leaders in settling scores and assuming power or new positions of authority within indigenous society – new cultural connections had great potential to shake up the status quo.

The Vikings were certainly a threat and an important new force to contend with. While the 9th century was an important horizon of change, it was perhaps in the 10th century that some of the wider trajectories of change came to the fore. The mid 10th century is when a new hoarding tradition of silver coin and mixed objects including hacksilver, ring money and other finds of Viking character really takes off, the deposition of hoards perhaps an important indicator of the forging of new social, political and economic relations in the far north (Graham-Campbell 1993, Fig. 7.3; Graham-Campbell and Batey 1998, 226–47). This latter tradition endured for almost a century and, by the time it had ceased, former Atlantic Pictland was very much a Scandinavian dominion.

What the Scandinavian impacts may have done is catalyse dramatic and perhaps irreversible transformations to power structures in the north and west which then had wider repercussions in Pictland. In the earlier Viking Age, the activities of Vikings in the Northern and Western Isles may have, over time, restricted or entirely stopped the flow of tribute and resources south to Fortriu, for example. In the 9th and early 10th centuries, the occupations of parts of Pictland on the mainland and killing of kings and other leaders in eastern Scotland will have similarly drained and diverted resources and power since these attacks struck at the very heart of what became the core regions of Alba. Certainly, the balance of power in Pictland shifted in the 9th century, with sources of this period emphasising the importance of royal centres in southern Pictland such as Forteviot.

Moreover, in 9th- and 10th-century northern Britain, the Viking presence was not the only threat to stability – there were always other forces to contend with. For example, the *Chronicle of the Kings of Alba* states that, in the reign of Cináed mac Alpín (842/3–858), the Britons of Dumbarton Rock burned *Dulblaan* (Dunblane) (Anderson 2011, 250). Internal unrest is also evident in the 10th century, according to the *Chronicle of the Kings of Alba*, Máel Choluim mac Domnaill, king of Alba (943–954), led his army to Moray and killed a certain Cellach. All of these events suggest significant periods of unrest in addition to those caused by Vikings.

During periods of instability, one way to respond to threats is through transformation (Woolf 2007a, 116–34, 312–42). With regard to Viking threats, the Anglo-Saxon realm that did succeed in defeating the Vikings was that of the West Saxons. After experiencing occupation, bloody loss in battle and paying enormous levels of tribute, the West Saxons under King Alfred and his successors reorganised their defence through the creation of *burhs*, appropriated Church lands to provide themselves with more patronage and revenues and reorganised the political landscape of Anglo-Saxon England to combat Viking dominance. In Pictland, the Viking campaigns of the 860s and 870s were conducted by the Dublin Vikings and the same leaders who broke the power of the Anglo-Saxon kings of East Anglia, Northumbria and Mercia. It is perhaps no surprise that it is in this same era that references to the Picts and Fortriu wane – being replaced by Alba – and it is tempting to link structural changes to this era. It is possible that the small local unit called the davoch, from Gaelic *dabach*, 'vat', became a render imposed throughout much of the Pictish kingdom as a result of the Scandinavian threat, in the decades around AD 900, either to pay tribute to the Vikings (Broun forthcoming b) or to raise and maintain armies to fight them off. The lack of the davoch in former Dál Riata, Menteith and Strathearn may have been because such areas already had alternatively named systems for levying resources and men (as seen in Dál Riata's case in *Míniugud Senchasa Fher nAlban* (*Senchus*), the smaller unit is the *tech*, 'house'). However it was achieved, the increasing usage of the *dabach* unit is indicative of a more systematic approach to extracting resources throughout the kingdom in the face of external challenges.

In addition, the position of *mormáer* may have been created or extended in the same period to coordinate military responses to Scandinavian attacks throughout the kingdom. The first reference to *mormáer* is in a battle of the men of Alba against Irish Vikings in *AU* 918.3. When the position of *mormáer* was created is unclear though, at some point after the last reference to a king of Atholl in 739 the region's leader became a *mormáer* and similarly the name Morvern, probably meaning '*mormáer*dom', indicates that part of Cenél Loairn territory in Argyll had a *mormáer* after the Pictish conquest was completed in 741 (Broun forthcoming a). Given the lack of references in our admittedly scanty contemporary records to a *mormáer* or any of the *mormáer* territories except Fife before the reign of Constantín mac Áeda (900–943), the late 9th century may have been the period in which the office of *mormáer* was established.

In eastern Pictland, the creation of *mormáer* positions in a Gaelicising context would have provided an opportunity to re-imagine the landscape of Pictland to create connections to Dál Riata in provinces such as Angus and Gowrie. Moreover, in the south the new prominence of significant territories like Strathearn, Stormont, Gowrie and Angus, and the Mearns made the pre-existing Pictish territorial name Circin redundant, explaining its demise. Similar processes might explain the rise of Buchan – and Mar? – instead of Ce, and perhaps Moray and Ross instead of Fortriu. The depiction in the *Series longior* Pictish king-list during the reign of Constantín son of Cináeda (862–876) of the sons of Cruithne, including the older territories of Fortriu, Fib, Fidach, Fotla, Cat, Circin and Ce, would have increasingly seemed antiquated and irrelevant. With the *mormáer* leading his men into battle for the king, these newly elevated territories became the foci of regional sentiment, the conflicts engaged in by these armies not only killing a proportion of the pre-existing Pictish nobility, but also bringing new ideas and identities. Thus, the threats to the realm in this period may have allowed new lineages to come to the fore and for transformations to a society similar to those that occurred in England to have taken place in the far north.

By around AD 900, external commentators at least saw the occupants of much of the Pictish realm as now belonging to the kingdom of Alba.

The adoption of the name Alba for the kingdom is intriguing – as noted earlier, it is a geographical term rather than an ethnic one (Broun 2007, 71–97). It is perhaps a term that recognised that the kings no longer simply ruled over Picts but over a kingdom that had a growing contingent – perhaps a majority – of Gaelic speakers. The kingdom may have also comprised Norse and perhaps even Brittonic and English speakers given the likely refugee movements that may have occurred with the mainly but not exclusively Viking-led occupation and destruction that occurred across Britain in the 9th and 10th centuries AD. By the late 9th century, Picts and Pictland were terms that may no longer have captured the diversity of the kingdom or perhaps the real or perceived ancestry of its leaders who came to the fore in the later 9th century in such uncertain times. The fluid political situation allowed major transformations in leadership, identity and allegiances to occur. The uncertainties of the period and the opportunities that it could bring may also have inspired the kings of the Picts and those of Alba to think in broader terms about a wider overlordship, perhaps foreshadowed by their attempt to dominate British Strathclyde. *AU* 872 records that Artgal, king of Strathclyde, was killed 'at the instigation of Constantine son of Cináed', king of the Picts, and, in 878, the son of the Strathclyde king, Eochaid son of Rhun, became king of the Picts, as the grandson of Cináed mac Alpín. This indicates a period in the late 9th century when the Pictish and British polities were closely connected. The situation is shadowy but it is possible that a desire to claim overlordship over the Britons and others and to rule over an area comprising multiple ethnicities and language groups influenced the adoption of the name Alba, meaning 'Britain'. Whatever the case – and the changes of this period will certainly be debated for generations to come – times had most definitely changed and the Pictish identity was relegated to history.

CHAPTER EIGHT

Coda

The Pictish Legacy

This book has attempted to sketch out how the Picts played key roles in the history of Britain for more than half a millennium. The emergence of the Picts occurred during a period in which small-scale native groups coexisted with an Empire to the south – the very formation of the Picts was perhaps an ultimate symbol of the Romans' failure to conquer and assimilate all of Britain. In turn, the dramatic assaults on Roman Britain that the Picts helped lead were a violent part of the transition of that province from imperial rule to local control. The victory of Fortriu in 685 at Nechtanesmere marked another major turning point, when the expansion northwards of Anglo-Saxon Northumbria was decisively halted. The kingdom of the Picts then reached new heights, the power and extent of this polity acting as a precursor to the emergence of Alba and Scotland itself. The extensive area over which the Picts ruled was unusual for the period, with major figures such as Onuist son of Uurguist (*c.*729–761) establishing a regional hegemony and defeating enemies across an area close to the entirety of modern Scotland.

Just how the Picts achieved this has at times perplexed historians (for example, Wickham 2009, 155). As has been shown in this book, the regions of Scotland where people identified themselves as Picts were diverse and it was perhaps the acceptance of this diversity that allowed for such an extensive polity to coalesce and eventually to transform into Alba and latterly Scotland. We can identify diversity throughout the Pictish period in the building and settlement types found even within a single area and there were various lowland and upland elite centres too, all reflecting different landscapes, resources, traditions, priorities and ideologies that had shared characteristics but also important individualities. Unifying elements included shared enemies, language, for some, and symbols of identity such as the Pictish symbol tradition. However, even the unique features of the Picts such as their language and symbols did not occur in all reaches of the polity – Pictish symbols did not represent or identify all Picts and there were alternative means of conveying identity which coexisted with the symbols, in particular the ogham and Roman alphabet traditions. These different methods of conveying identity were reflections of both internal divergences and markers of local and regional individuality as well as the influence and legacies of external connections, such as the trade and diplomatic contacts epitomised by the Roman, Frankish and Byzantine glass and ceramics found at sites like Dunnicaer and Rhynie and, from the 7th century at the latest, the increasingly internationalising networks of the Church. Even the Pictish symbols, their unintelligibility to outsiders perhaps emblematic of their local origins, were perhaps invented as a creative response to the images and monumental traditions of the wider Late Roman world.

The linguistic situation epitomises the cultural hybridism at the heart of the Picts and, indeed, found in most historical groups. There was a Celtic Pictish language, most closely related to British, reflected in place, personal, territorial and population names in Pictland but the Pictish kingdom also contained many who spoke other languages – in particular, British and Gaelic. When Bede wrote (*HE* I.12: Colgrave and Mynors 1969, 42–43) that the name *Peanfahel*, modern Kinneil, on the Antonine Wall was Pictish, even though the name is a mixture of British or Pictish *pean* and Gaelic *fahel*, we should not dismiss this as a mistake. Language and ethnic identity did not have to align because the kingdom of the Picts, through which personal ties of allegiance bound society from top to bottom to the monarch, could act as a unifying force. However, it was also this diversity that perhaps led to the abandonment of the name Picts – its singularity, origins and implications perhaps not capturing the zeitgeist or realities of identity in what became the territory of Alba in the Viking Age.

A consequence of the material, cultural and linguistic differences found in Pictland was that it produced not a singular but a variety of legacies for Scotland in more recent centuries. Later political, cultural and linguistic contexts, such as whether an area became Norse or Gaelicised, complicate the picture, with more continuity displayed outside the zone of Scandinavian settlement. Nevertheless, it is possible to identify direct and indirect inheritances from the Picts. The most striking of the direct legacies of the Picts was the Christian Church, with many key ecclesiastical centres of the region, such as St Andrews, Dunkeld, Dunblane, Rosemarkie and Kinneddar, continuing to be significant into the 12th century and beyond. In addition, at a local level, Pictish sculpture can be found at many lesser churches, most famously at Meigle and St Vigeans but also at sites like Dyce, in Aberdeenshire, and Fowlis Wester, in Perth and Kinross, showing that many later parish churches had visible markers of their earlier Pictish past.

In the secular sphere, the transition from Pictland and Alba, combined with the disruption caused by the Scandinavians and later change, means that continuity is perhaps harder to identify today. The *mormáer* and their provincial territories were Pictish innovations which remained a key feature of the Gaelic political landscape, before being transformed into the earls and earldoms of later medieval Scotland. The position of *mormáer* was also adopted in the west, underlying the name Morvern and explaining why three *mormaír* of Alba, one with a Norse patronymic, died fighting in a battle in Ireland in 976 (*AT* 975, vol. 2, 231). After 900, perhaps as a result of the structural and cultural changes in the kingdom many territories, such as Strathearn, Angus, Moray and Ross, come to prominence in our sources and some Pictish regional terms, like Fortriu, Circin and Ce, ceased to be used. However, other names, like Atholl, Fife and the Mearns, all Pictish in origin, remain in use in the 21st century. In addition, secular centres like Forteviot, Clunie, Cinnbelathoir, Dunnottar and Dundurn saw use that straddled the change to Alba, even if most of these did not retain their significance later, as the burghs and new castles of the 12th century increasingly attracted royal and noble attention. To a considerable extent, the later people of Scotland built on foundations, transformed to meet the challenges of the Viking Age, established by the Picts.

At a local level, the landscape of eastern Scotland north of the Forth contains many Pictish place-names, the most prominent now being Aberdeen, Dundee and Perth, but there are others across the land containing Pictish elements such as *cupar* and *aber*. In addition, the Picts had an indirect legacy in words like *pett*, *carden* and *cair* borrowed into Gaelic or in Gaelic words which have meanings that seem to derive from their Pictish equivalent, like *foithir* – found in Dunnottar, Kinneddar and Fetteresso – used for an administrative unit in Pictland (Taylor 2011). Many of these words are found in important local place-names for parishes or davochs, which themselves probably have Pictish origins. Therefore, it is likely that much of the social landscape of Scotland was influenced by the Picts, notwithstanding that the physical landscape of Scotland was shaped by generations of Pictish families farming the land, building forts and monuments, the legacies and ruins of which can still be seen today.

How much of broader Pictish culture and society was continued in later Scotland is an open question, requiring further, careful investigation. It has been argued here that Pictish society continued, often in a modified form and alongside Scandinavian culture, in the Northern Isles and Hebrides for much longer than previously thought into the 10th century. This raises the question of how much this affected the nature of later communities in these islands, even after Norse had come to completely dominate and Pictish-era names were replaced. In Alba, after 900, society was Gaelic in language and culture but, in addition to the continuities already mentioned, it has been suggested that Pictish affected Scottish Gaelic at a structural level as well as through loanwords (Rhys 2020b; Greene 1994). Moreover, the adoption of the 'Law of the Innocents' among the Picts indicates that their legal and therefore social practices may have been broadly compatible with Dál Riata and Ireland. Therefore, while change was always taking place, as can be seen by the rise and fall of sites such as Rhynie and Tap o' Noth in the Pictish period, and the period from 900–1100 was also important in shaping the country, it is plausible that some significant aspects of Albanian and later Scottish society, legal forms, land division and customs had important legacies at least partly derived from Pictish ways of life.

The Picts, however, have a more enduring additional significance – the material legacy that has survived and speaks to us today and forms one of the most tangible means of getting in touch with the Pictish past. The Pictish symbols carved on stone and cast in metal, the forts and potentially vast settlements only just identified through new campaigns of archaeological investigation and, increasingly, the houses, halls, churches, possessions and burials provide immediate and palpable expressions of Pictish lifeways. The Picts did not, as the author of *Historia Norwegie* claimed, live a semi-subterranean existence but, by digging underground, as well as in the archives and the library, we continue to discover more about the fascinating Picts.

Bibliography

Abbreviations

AClon Murphy, D. (ed.) 1896 *The Annals of Clonmacnoise, being annals of Ireland from the earliest period to A.D. 1408, translated into English, A.D. 1627 by Conell Mageoghagan* (Dublin: University Press).

AFM O'Donovan, J. (ed. and trans.) 1848–1851 *Annála Ríoghachta Éireann, Annals of the Kingdom of Ireland by the Four Masters from the earliest period to the year 1616*, 7 vols (Dublin: Hodges and Smith).

ARC Jaski, B. and Mc Carthy, D. (eds) 2011 *A facsimile edition of the Annals of Roscrea*, https://www.scss.tcd.ie/misc/kronos/editions/ AR_portal.htm, (accessed 13 December 2021).

AT Stokes, W. (ed. and trans.) 1993 *The Annals of Tigernach*, 2 vols (Felinfach: Llanerch).

AU Mac Airt, S. and Mac Niocaill, G. (eds and trans.) 1983 *The Annals of Ulster (To A.D. 1131) Part I Text and Translation* (Dublin: Dublin Institute for Advanced Studies).

CKA Anderson, M. O. (ed.) 2011 'The Chronicle of the Kings of Alba', in *Kings and Kingship in Early Scotland* (Edinburgh: John Donald), pp. 249–53.

CS Hennessy, W. M. (ed. and trans.) 1866 *Chronicum Scotorum. A Chronicle of Irish Affairs, from the Earliest Times to A.D. 1135; with a Supplement, containing the Events from 1141 to 1150* (London: HMSO).

eDIL *Electronic Dictionary of the Irish Language*, http://www.dil.ie (accessed 9 February 2022).

HE Colgrave, B. and Mynors, R. A. B. (eds and trans.) 1969 *Bede's Ecclesiastical History of the English People* (Oxford: Clarendon Press).

PSAS *Proceedings of the Society of Antiquaries of Scotland*.

VSC Sharpe, R. (trans.) 1995 *Adomnán of Iona: Life of St Columba* (Harmondsworth: Penguin Books); Anderson, A. O. and Anderson, M. O. (ed. and trans.) 1991 *Adomnán's Life of Columba* (rev. edn) (Oxford: Clarendon Press).

Primary Sources

Ahlqvist, A. 1982 *The Early Irish Linguist: An Edition of the Canonical Part of the Auraicept na nÉces* (Helsinki: Societas Scientiarum Fennica).

Anderson, A. O. 1990 [1922], *Early Sources of Scottish History A.D. 500 to 1286*, 2 vols (Stamford: Paul Watkins).

Anderson, A. O. and Anderson, M. O. (ed. and trans.) 1991 *Adomnán's Life of Columba* (rev. edn) (Oxford: Clarendon Press).

Barney, S. A. *et al.* (trans.) 2006 *The Etymologies of Isidore of Seville* (Cambridge: Cambridge University Press).

Binchy, D. A. (ed.) 1979 *Crith Gablach* (Dublin: Dublin Institute for Advanced Studies).

Bisagni, J. 2019 *Amrae Coluimb Chille: a critical edition* (Dublin: Dublin Institute for Advanced Studies).

Burgess, R. W. 2001 'The Gallic Chronicle of 452: A New Critical Edition with a Brief Introduction', in R. W. Mathisen and D. Schanzer (eds), *Society and Culture in Late Antique Gaul: Revisiting the Sources* (London: Ashgate), pp. 52–84.

Cary, E. 1927, *Dio's Roman History*, 9 vols (London: William Heinemann).

Christiansen, R. with Nolan, K. Ó. 1962 'The People of the North', *Lochlann: A Review of Celtic Studies* 2, pp. 137–64.

Clancy, T. O. (ed.) 1998 *The Triumph Tree: Scotland's Earliest Poetry, 550–1350* (Edinburgh: Canongate).

Colgrave, B. and Mynors, R. A. B. (eds and trans.) 1969 *Bede's Ecclesiastical History of the English People* (Oxford: The Clarendon Press).

Dobbs, M. C. 1931 'The Ban-shenchus', *Revue Celtique* 48, pp. 163–233.

Dowden, J. (ed.) 1903 *Chartulary of the Abbey of Lindores 1195–1479*, Scottish History Society 42 (Edinburgh: Scottish History Society).

Ekrem, I. and Mortensen, L. B. (eds) and Fisher, P. (trans.) 2003 *Historia Norwegie* (Copenhagen: Museum Tusculanum Press).

Hood, A. B. E. (ed. and trans.) 1978 Patrick, 'Letter to the Soldiers of Coroticus', in *St Patrick: His Writings and Muirchu's Life* (London: Phillimore), pp. 35–38, 55–59.

Kinsella, T. (trans.) 1969 *The Táin* (Oxford: Oxford University Press).

Koch, J. T. 1997 *The Gododdin of Aneurin: Text and Context from Dark Age North Britain* (Cardiff: University of Wales Press).

Levison, W. (ed.) 1920 '*Vita Germani Episcopi Autissiodorensis auctore Constantio*', in B. Krusch and W. Levison (eds), *Passiones Vitaeque Sanctorum Aevi Merovingici*, Monumenta Germaniae Historica, Scriptores Rerum Merovingici 7 (Hannover: Hahn), 225–83.

Mac Airt, S. (ed. and trans.) 1951 *The Annals of Inisfallen (MS Rawlinson B. 503)* (Dublin: Dublin Institute for Advanced Studies).

Mac Airt, S. and Mac Niocaill, G. (eds and trans.) 1983 *The Annals of Ulster (To A.D. 1131) Part I Text and Translation* (Dublin: Dublin Institute for Advanced Studies).

Márkus, G. 2008, *Adomnán's 'Law of the Innocents' – Cáin Adomnáin* (Kilmartin: Kilmartin House Trust).

Morris, J. (ed. and trans.) 1980 *Nennius: British History and The Welsh Annals* (London: Phillimore).

Murphy, D. (ed.) 1896 *The Annals of Clonmacnoise being Annals of Ireland from the earliest period to A.D. 1408* (Dublin: University Press, repr. Felinfach: Llanerch Publishers, 1993).

O'Donovan, J. (ed. and trans.) 1848–1851 *Annála Ríoghachta Éireann: Annals of the Kingdom of Ireland, by the Four Masters, from the Earliest Period to the Year 1616*, 7 vols (Dublin: Hodges and Smith).

Pálsson, H. and Edwards, P. (trans.) 1978 *Orkneyinga Saga: The History of the Earls of Orkney* (London: Penguin).

Seyfarth, W., Jacob-Karau, L. and Ulmann, I. (eds) 1978 *Ammiani Marcellini Rerum gestarum libri qui supersunt*. 2 vols (Stuttgart and Leipzig: B. G. Teubner).

Sharpe, R. (trans.) 1995 *Adomnán of Iona. Life of St Columba* (Harmondsworth: Penguin).

Skene, W. F. (ed.) 1867 *Chronicles of the Picts, Chronicles of the Scots, and other Early Memorials of Scottish History* (Edinburgh: H. M. General Register House).

Stokes, W. 1905 *Félire Óengusso Céli Dé: The Martyrology of Oengus the Culdee* (London: Henry Bradshaw Society; reprinted 1984, Dublin: Dublin Institute for Advanced Studies).

Swanton, M. (ed. and trans.) 1978 *Beowulf* (Manchester: Manchester University Press).

Tierney, J. J. with Bieler, L. (eds and trans.) 1967 *Dicuili Liber de Mensura Orbis Terrae* (Dublin: Dublin Institute for Advanced Studies).

Webb, J. F. (trans.) 2004 'Life of Wilfrid', in D. H. Farmer (ed.), *The Age of Bede* (rev. edn) (London: Penguin), pp. 105–84.

Whittaker, C. R. (ed. and trans.) 1969 *Herodian*, 2 vols (London: William Heinemann).
Williams, I. (ed.) and Bromwich, R. (trans.) 1982 *Armes Prydein: The Prophecy of Britain From the Book of Taliesin* (Dublin: Dublin Institute for Advanced Studies).
Winterbottom, M. (ed. and trans.) 1978 *Gildas: The Ruin of Britain and Other Works* (London: Phillimore).

Secondary Sources

Addyman, P. V., Pearson, N. and Tweddle, D. 1982 'The Coppergate helmet', *Antiquity* 56, pp. 189–94.
Aitchison, N. 2006 *Forteviot: A Pictish and Scottish Royal Centre* (Stroud: Tempus).
Alcock, L. 1976 'A multi-disciplinary chronology for Alt Clut, Castle Rock, Dumbarton', *PSAS* 107, pp. 103–13.
Alcock, L. 1988a 'The activities of potentates in Celtic Britain, AD 500–800: a positivist approach', in S. T. Driscoll and M. R. Nieke (eds), *Power and Politics in Early Medieval Britain and Ireland* (Edinburgh: Edinburgh University Press), pp. 22–46.
Alcock, L. 1988b The Rhind Lectures 1988–89: a synopsis. 'An Heroic Age: war and society in northern Britain, AD 450–850', *PSAS* 118, pp. 327–34.
Alcock, L. 1996 'Ur-symbols in the pictograph-system of the Picts', *Pictish Arts Society Journal* 9, pp. 2–5.
Alcock, L. 2003 *Kings and Warriors, Craftsmen and Priests in Northern Britain AD 550–850* (Edinburgh: Society of Antiquaries of Scotland).
Alcock, L. and Alcock, E. A. 1990 'Reconnaissance excavations on Early Historic fortifications and other royal sites in Scotland, 1974–84: excavations at Alt Clut, Clyde Rock, Strathclyde, 1974–75', *PSAS* 120, pp. 95–149.
Alcock, L. and Alcock, E. A. 1992 'Reconnaissance excavations on Early Historic fortifications and other royal sites in Scotland, 1974–84; 5: A, Excavations and other fieldwork at Forteviot, Perthshire, 1981; B, Excavations at Urquhart Castle, Inverness-shire, 1983; C, Excavations at Dunnottar, Kincardineshire, 1984', *PSAS* 122, pp. 215–827.
Alcock, L., Alcock, E. A. and Driscoll, S. T. 1989 'Reconnaissance Excavations on Early Historic Fortifications and Other Royal Sites in Scotland, 1974–84; 3: Excavations at Dundurn, Strathearn, Perthshire, 1976–77', *PSAS* 119, pp. 189–226.
Aldhouse-Green, M. 2004 *An Archaeology of Images: Iconology and Cosmology in Iron Age and Roman Europe* (London: Routledge).
Alexander, D. 2005 'Redcastle, Lunan Bay, Angus: the excavation of an Iron Age timber lined souterrain and a Pictish barrow cemetery', *PSAS* 135, pp. 41–118.
Allen, R. J. and Anderson, J. 1903 *The Early Christian Monuments of Scotland*, vols 1 and 2 (reprinted 1993 Balgavies, Angus: Pinkfoot Press).
Anderson, B. 1991 *Imagined Communities: reflections on the Origins and Spread of Nationalism* (London: Verso).
Anderson, J. 1891 'Notice of the Excavation of the brochs of Yarhouse, Brounaben, Bowermadden, Old Stirkoke, and Dunbeath, in Caithness, with remarks on the period of the brochs; and an appendix, containing a collected list of the brochs of Scotland, and early notices of many of them', *Archaeologia Scotica* 5, pp. 131–98.
Anderson, M. O. 2011 *Kings and Kingship in Early Scotland* (Edinburgh: John Donald).
Arbuthnot, S. and Hollo, K. (eds) 2007, *Fil súil nglais: A Grey Eye Looks Back: A Festschrift in Honour of Colm Ó Baoill* (Drochaid: Clann Tuirc).
Armit, I. 1992 *The Later Prehistory of the Western Isles of Scotland* (Oxford: BAR British Series 221).
Armit, I. 2006 *Anatomy of an Iron Age Roundhouse: The Cnip Wheelhouse Excavations, Lewis* (Edinburgh: Society of Antiquaries of Scotland).
Armit, I. 2008 'Excavation of an Iron Age, Early Historic and medieval settlement and metalworking site at Eilean Olabhat, North Uist', *PSAS* 138, pp. 27–104.
Armit, I. 2016 *Celtic Scotland* (Edinburgh: Birlinn).
Armit, I. and Büster, L. 2020 *Darkness Visible: The Sculptor's Cave, Covesea, from the Bronze Age to the Picts* (Edinburgh: Society of Antiquaries of Scotland).
Armit, I. and Ginn, V. 2007 'Beyond the Grave: Human Remains from Domestic Contexts in Iron Age Atlantic Scotland', *Proceedings of the Prehistoric Society* 73, pp. 113–34.
Ashmore, P. J. 1980 'Low cairns, long cists and symbol stones', *PSAS* 110, pp. 346–55.
Ashmore, P. J. 2003 'Orkney burials in the first millennium AD', in Downes and Ritchie 2003, pp. 33–50.
Atkinson, D. 2007 'Mither Tap, Bennachie, Aberdeenshire (Oyne parish), watching brief, radiocarbon dating', *Discovery and Excavation in Scotland* 8, p. 28.
Badcock, A. and Downes, J. 2000 'Excavation of Iron Age Burials at An Corran, Boreray, Outer Hebrides', *PSAS*, 130, pp. 197–222.
Bailey, G. 2006 'An Early Timber Hall at Callendar Park', *Calatria* 23, pp. 37–57.
Ballin Smith, B. 1994 *Howe: Four Millennia of Orkney Prehistory* (Edinburgh: Society of Antiquaries of Scotland).
Ballin Smith, B. 2013 'Norwick – Shetland's Earliest Viking Settlement?', in V. E. Turner, J. M. Bond and A. Larsen (eds), *Viking Unst: Excavation and Survey in Northern Shetland 2006–2010* (Lerwick: Shetland Heritage Publications), pp. 217–33.

Bannerman, J. 1974 *Studies in the History of Dalriada* (Edinburgh: Scottish Academic Press).

Bannerman, J. 2016 'The Clàrsach and the Clàrsair', in J. W. M. Bannerman, *Kinship, Church and Culture: Collected Essays and Studies* (Edinburgh: John Donald, 2016), pp. 398–417.

Barclay, G. J. 2001 'The excavation of an early medieval enclosure at Upper Gothens, Meikleour, Perthshire', *Tayside and Fife Archaeological Journal* 7, pp. 34–44.

Barclay, G. J. and Maxwell, G. S. 1998 *The Cleaven Dyke and Littleour: Monuments in the Neolithic of Tayside*, Society of Antiquaries of Scotland Monograph Series 13 (Edinburgh: Society of Antiquaries of Scotland).

Barclay, G. J., Brophy, K. and MacGregor, G. 2002 'Claish, Stirling: an Early Neolithic structure in its contexts', *PSAS* 132, pp. 65–137.

Barnes, M. P. 2012 *Runes: A Handbook* (Woodbridge: Boydell Press).

Barrett, J. C. 1994 *Fragments From Antiquity: An Archaeology of Social Life in Britain, 2900–1200 BC* (Oxford: Blackwell).

Barrett, J. H. (ed.) 2012 *Being an Islander: Production and identity at Quoygrew, Orkney, AD 900–1600* (Cambridge: McDonald Institute for Archaeological Research).

Barrett, J. H. and Richards, M. P. 2004 'Identity, gender, religion and economy', *European Journal of Archaeology* 7(3), pp. 249–71.

Barrett, J. H. and Slater, A. 2009 'The Brough of Deerness Excavations 2008: Research Context and Data Structure Report' (unpublished report, Cambridge: McDonald Institute for Archaeological Research).

Barrow, G. W. S. 1983 'The Childhood of Scottish Christianity: a Note on Some Place-Name Evidence', *Scottish Studies* 27, pp. 1–15.

Barrow, G. W. S. 2003 *The Kingdom of the Scots*, 2nd edn (Edinburgh: Edinburgh University Press).

Barrowman, R. 2011 *The Chapel and Burial Ground on St Ninian's Isle, Shetland: Excavations Past and Present* (Abingdon: Routledge/Society for Medieval Archaeology Monographs).

Batey, C. E. 1993 'The Viking and Late Norse Graves of Caithness and Sutherland', in Batey, Jesch and Morris 1993, pp. 148–64

Batey, C. E., Jesch J. and Morris, C. D. (eds) 1993 *The Viking Age in Caithness, Orkney and the North Atlantic* (Edinburgh: Edinburgh University Press).

Bazelmans, J. 1999 *By Weapons Made Worthy: Lords, Retainers and their Relationship in 'Beowulf'* (Amsterdam: Amsterdam University Press).

Bell, C. 1992 *Ritual Theory, Ritual Practice* (Oxford: Oxford University Press).

Bhreathnach, E. 2014 *Ireland in the Medieval World, AD 400–1000: Landscape, Kingship and Religion* (Dublin: Four Courts Press).

Birch, S. 2018 'Rosemarkie Caves Excavations: Interpreting the results of three years of excavations – 2016 to 2018': http://www.spanglefish.com/ rosemarkiecavesproject/excavations2016–2018.asp.

Birch, S. and Noble, G. 2019 'Tarradale Through Time: Archaeological Excavations at the Tarradale Barrow Cemetery' (unpublished Data Structure Report).

Blackwell, A., Goldberg, M. and Hunter, F. 2017 *Scotland's Early Silver* (Edinburgh: National Museums Scotland).

Blair, J. 1995 'Anglo-Saxon shrines and their prototypes', *Anglo-Saxon Studies in Archaeology and History* 38, pp. 1–28.

Blair, J. 2018 *Building Anglo-Saxon England* (Princeton, NJ: Princeton University Press).

Bland, R., Moorhead, S. and Walton P. 2013, 'Finds of late Roman silver coins from Britain: the contribution of the Portable Antiquities Scheme', in Hunter and Painter 2013, pp. 117–66.

Boardman, S., Davies, J. R. and Williamson, E. (eds) 2009 *Saints' Cults in the Celtic World* (Woodbridge: Boydell).

Bölcskei A. 2014 'Traces of Ancient Celtic Religiosity in the Place Names of the British Isles', in V. Ruttkay, and B. Gárdos (eds), *Proceedings of the 11th Conference of the Hungarian Society for the Study of English* (Budapest: L'Harmattan Publishing House), pp. 103–12.

Bourke, C. 1983 'The hand-bells of the early Scottish church', *PSAS* 113, pp. 464–68.

Bourke, C. 2020 *The Early Medieval Handbells of Ireland and Britain* (Dublin: National Museum of Ireland).

Boyle, A. 2020 'Cowboys and Indians? A Biocultural Study of Violence and Conflict in South-East Scotland, c. AD 400 to c. AD 800' (unpublished PhD thesis, University of Edinburgh).

Bradley, J. 2011 'An early medieval crannog at Moynagh Lough, Co. Meath', in C. Corlett and M. Potterton (eds), *Settlement in Early Medieval Ireland in the Light of Recent Archaeological Excavations*, Research Papers in Irish Archaeology 3 (Dublin: Wordwell), pp. 11–34.

Bradley, R. 2000 *The Good Stones: A New Investigation of the Clava Cairns* (Edinburgh: Society of Antiquaries of Scotland).

Bradley, R. 2007 *The Prehistory of Britain and Ireland* (Cambridge: Cambridge University Press).

Brady, K., Lelong, O. and Batey, C. E. 2007 'A Pictish Burial and Late Norse/Medieval Settlement at Sangobeg, Durness, Sutherland', *Scottish Archaeological Journal* 29(1): pp. 51–82.

Bramwell, D. 1994 'Bird remains', in Ballin Smith 1994, pp. 153–57.

Britton, K. 2017 'A stable relationship: isotopes and bioarchaeology are in it for the long haul', *Antiquity* 91 (358), pp. 853–63.

Broun, D. 1998 'Pictish kings 761–839: integration with Dál Riata or separate development?', in S. M. Foster (ed.), *The St Andrews Sarcophagus and its International Connections* (Dublin: Four Courts Press, 1998), pp. 71–83.

Broun, D. 1999 'Dunkeld and the origin of Scottish Identity', in D. Broun and T. O. Clancy, *Spes Scotorum: Hope of Scots. Saint Columba, Iona and Scotland* (Edinburgh: T&T Clark), pp. 95–111.

Broun, D. 2000a 'The seven kingdoms in *De situ Albanie*: a record of Pictish political geography or an imaginary map of Alba?', in E. J. Cowan and R. Andrew McDonald (eds), *Alba: Celtic Scotland in the Middle Ages* (East Linton: Tuckwell Press), pp. 24–42.

Broun, D. 2000b 'The church of St Andrews and its foundation legend in the early twelfth century: recovering the full text of version A of the foundation legend', in Taylor 2000b, pp. 108–14.

Broun, D. 2007 *Scottish Independence and the Idea of Britain* (Edinburgh: Edinburgh University Press).

Broun, D. 2008 'The property records in the Book of Deer as a source for early Scottish society', in Forsyth 2008a, pp. 313–60.

Broun, D. 2015 'Statehood and lordship in "Scotland" before the mid-twelfth century', *The Innes Review* 66(1), pp. 1–71.

Broun, D. 2019 'The genealogy of the king of Scots as charter and panegyric', in J. R. Davies and S. Bhattacharya (eds), *Copper, Parchment and Stone: Studies in the Sources for Landholding and Lordship in Early Medieval Bengal and Medieval Scotland* (Glasgow: University of Glasgow), pp. 209–60.

Broun, D. (forthcoming a) 'The origins of the *mormaer*', in M. Brown (ed.), *Earls and Earldoms in Medieval Scotland* (Woodbridge: Boydell).

Broun, D. (forthcoming b) '*Doldauha* and the origins of the *dabach* in Pictland', in T. O. Clancy, C. Hough and E. Williamson (eds), *Onomastications: A Festschrift for Simon Taylor* (Glasgow: Clò Gàidhlig Oilthigh Ghlaschu).

Brown, L. D. and Reay, D. 2015 'Painted quartz pebbles' in Dockrill *et al.* 2015, pp. 377–84.

Buckley, A. 2005 'Music in Ireland to c. 1500', in D. Ó Cróinín (ed.), *A New History of Ireland I. Prehistoric and Early Ireland* (Oxford: Oxford University Press), pp. 744–814.

Busset, A. and Evemalm-Graham, S. 2020 'Places of Belief in Medieval Glen Lyon and Beyond: Onomastic and Archaeological Perspectives', *Journal of Scottish Name Studies* 14, pp. 59–120.

Buteux, S. 1997 *Settlements at Skaill, Deerness, Orkney: Excavations by Peter Gelling of the Prehistoric, Pictish, Viking and Later Periods, 1963–1981* (Oxford: BAR British Series 260).

Campbell, E. 1999 *Saints and Sea-kings. The First Kingdom of the Scots* (Edinburgh: Canongate).

Campbell, E. 2001 'Were the Scots Irish?', *Antiquity* 75, pp. 285–92.

Campbell, E. 2007 *Continental and Mediterranean Imports to Atlantic Britain and Ireland, AD 400–800* (York: Council of British Archaeology Research Report 157).

Campbell, E., Driscoll, S., Gondek, M. and Maldonado, A. 2019 'An early medieval and prehistoric nexus: the "Strathearn Environs and Royal Forteviot" project' in A. E. Blackwell (ed.), *Scotland in Early Medieval Europe* (Leiden: Sidestone), pp. 85–102.

Campbell, E. and Driscoll, S. T. (eds) 2020 *Royal Forteviot: Excavations at a Pictish Power Centre in Eastern Scotland* (London: Council for British Archaeology): https://archaeologydataservice.ac.uk/library/browse/ issue.xhtml?recordId=1181734.

Campbell, E. and Maldonado, A. 2020 'A New Jerusalem "at the ends of the earth": interpreting Charles Thomas's excavations at Iona Abbey 1956–63', *Antiquaries Journal* 100, pp. 33–85.

Carey, J. 2019 *Magic, Metallurgy and Imagination in Medieval Ireland: Three Studies* (Aberystwyth: Celtic Studies Publications).

Carnegie, J., 9th Earl of Southesk, 1893 *Origins of Pictish Symbolism with Notes on the Sun Boar and a New Reading of the Newton Inscriptions* (Edinburgh: David Douglas).

Carter, S. and Fraser, D. 1996 'The Sands of Breckon, Yell, Shetland', *PSAS* 126, pp. 271–301.

Carver, M. 1999 *Surviving in Symbols: A Visit to the Pictish Nation* (Edinburgh: Birlinn).

Carver, M. 2002 'Reflections on the meaning of Anglo-Saxon barrows', in Lucy and Reynolds 2002, pp. 132–43.

Carver, M. 2005 *Sutton Hoo: A Seventh-Century Princely Burial Ground and its Context* (London: British Museum Press).

Carver, M. 2009 *Archaeological Investigation* (London: Routledge)

Carver, M. 2019 *Formative Britain: An Archaeology Britain, Fifth to Eleventh Century AD* (London: Routledge).

Carver, M., Barrett, J., Downes, J. and Hooper, J. 2012 'Pictish Byre-houses at Pitcarmick and their landscape: investigations 1993–5', *PSAS* 142, pp. 145–99.

Carver, M., Garner-Lahire, J. and Spall, C. 2016 *Portmahomack on Tarbat Ness: Changing Ideologies in North-East Scotland, Sixth to Sixteenth Century AD* (Edinburgh: Society of Antiquaries of Scotland).

Charles-Edwards, T. M. 2000 *Early Christian Ireland* (Cambridge: Cambridge University Press).

Charles-Edwards, T. M. (ed.), 2003 *After Rome* (Oxford: Oxford University Press).

Charles-Edwards, T. M. 2008 'Picts and Scots: A review of Alex Woolf, *From Pictland to Alba 789–1070*', *Innes Review* 59, pp. 168–88.

Charles-Edwards, T. M. 2013 *Wales and the Britons 350–1064* (Oxford: Oxford University Press).

Clancy, T. O. 1996 'Iona, Scotland and the Celi De', in Crawford 1996, pp. 111–30.

Clancy, T. O. 2001 'The real St. Ninian', *Innes Review* 52, pp. 1–28.

Clancy, T. O. 2004 'Iona in the kingdom of the Picts: a note', *Innes Review* 55, pp. 73–76.

Clancy, T. O. 2008a 'Deer and the early church in North-Eastern Scotland', in Forsyth 2008a, pp. 363–97.

Clancy, T. O. 2008b 'The Gall-Ghàidheil and Galloway', *Journal of Scottish Name Studies* 2, pp. 19–50.

Clancy, T. O. 2009 'The cults of Saints Patrick and Palladius in early medieval Scotland', in Boardman, Davies and Williamson 2009, pp. 18–40.

Clancy, T. O. 2011 'Gaelic in Medieval Scotland: advent and expansion' (The Sir John Rhys Memorial Lecture 2009), *Proceedings of the British Academy* 167, pp. 349–92.

Clancy, T. O. 2017 'VIG001 (The Drosten Stone): The Inscription', in Geddes 2017, pp. 107–18.

Clancy, T. O., Butter, R., Márkus, G. and Barr, M. *Saints in Scottish Place-Names* https://saintsplaces.gla.ac.uk/ (accessed 14 Feb. 2022).

Clarke, D. V. 2007 'Reading the multiple lives of Pictish symbol stones', *Medieval Archaeology* 51, pp. 19–39.

Clarke, D. V. 2012 'Communities', in Clarke, Blackwell and Goldberg 2012, pp. 69–140.

Clarke, D. V. and Heald, A. 2008 'A new date for "Pictish" symbols', *Medieval Archaeology* 52(1), pp. 291–310.

Clarke, D. V., Blackwell, A. and Goldberg, M. 2012 *Early Medieval Scotland: Individuals, Communities and Ideas* (Edinburgh: National Museum of Scotland).

Close-Brooks, J. 1980 'Excavations in the Dairy Park, Dunrobin, Sutherland, 1977', *PSAS* 110, pp. 328–45.

Close-Brooks, J. 1984 'Pictish and other burials', in Friell and Watson 1984, pp. 87–114.

Close-Brooks, J. 1986 'Excavations at Clatchard Craig, Fife', *PSAS* 116, pp. 117–84.

Coleman, R. and Hunter, F. 2002 'The Excavation of a Souterrain at Shanzie Farm, Alyth, Perthshire', *Tayside and Fife Archaeological Journal* 8, pp. 77–101.

Collins, R. 2013 'Soldiers to warriors: renegotiating the Roman frontier in the fifth century', in Hunter and Painter 2013, pp. 29–44.

Cooijmans, C. (ed.) 2017 *Traversing the Inner Seas: Contacts and Continuity in and around Scotland, the Hebrides, and the North of Ireland* (Edinburgh: The Scottish Society for Northern Studies).

Cook, M. 2011a 'Maiden Castle, Insch, Aberdeenshire: choice and architecture in Pictland', *Tayside and Fife Archaeological Journal* 17, pp. 25–35.

Cook, M. 2011b 'New evidence for the activities of Pictish potentates in Aberdeenshire: the hillforts of Strathdon', *PSAS* 141, pp. 207–31.

Cook, M. 2016 'Prehistoric Settlement Patterns in the North-east of Scotland: Excavations at Grantown Road, Forres 2002–2013', *Scottish Archaeological Internet Reports* 61.

Cook, M. and Dunbar, L. 2008 *Rituals, Roundhouses and Romans: Excavations at Kintore, Aberdeenshire, 2000–2006* (Edinburgh: Scottish Trust for Archaeological Research).

Cowie, T. G. 1978 'Excavations at the Catstane, Midlothian 1977' *PSAS* 109, pp. 166–201.

Cowley, D. C. 1996 'Square Barrows in Dumfries and Galloway', *Transactions of the Dumfriesshire and Galloway Natural History and Antiquarian Society* 71, pp. 107–13.

Cowley, D. 2011 'Remote sensing for archaeology and heritage management – site discovery, interpretation and registration', in D. Cowley (ed.), *Remote Sensing for Archaeological Heritage Management* (Brussels: Europae Archaeologia Consilium), pp. 43–58.

Cowley, D. 2016 'Creating the cropmark archaeological record in East Lothian, South-East Scotland', in Crellin, Fowler and Tipping 2016, pp. 59–70.

Cox, R. A. V. 2007 'Notes on the Norse Impact on Hebridean Place-Names', *Journal of Scottish Name Studies* 1, pp. 139–44.

Craddock, P. 1989 'Metalworking techniques', in Youngs 1989b, pp. 170–213.

Cramond, W. 1887 'The stone circles at Ley: excursion to Deskford', *Transactions of the Banffshire Field Club*, pp. 92–93.

Crawford, B. E. 2011 'F. T. Wainwright and *The Problem of the Picts*', in Driscoll *et al.* 2011, pp. 3–14.

Crawford, B. E. 2013 *The Northern Earldoms. Orkney and Caithness from* AD *870 to 1470* (Edinburgh: John Donald).

Crawford, B. E. (ed.) 1995 *Scandinavian Settlement in Northern Britain* (London: Leicester University Press).

Crawford, B. E. (ed.) 1996 *Scotland in Dark Age Britain* (Aberdeen: Scottish Cultural Press).

Crawford, B. E. and Taylor, S. 2003 'The Southern Frontier of Norse Settlement in North Scotland', *Northern Scotland* 23, pp. 1–76.

Crawford, I. A. and Switsur, R. 1977 'Sandscaping and C14: the Udal, N. Uist', *Antiquity* 51, pp. 124–36.

Crellin, R., Fowler, C. and Tipping, R. (eds) 2016 *Prehistory Without Borders: The Prehistoric Archaeology of the Tyne–Forth Region* (Oxford: Oxbow Books),

Crellin, R. and Harris, O. 2020 'Beyond binaries. Interrogating ancient DNA', *Archaeological Dialogues* 27(1), pp. 37–56.

Cruickshank, R. G. 1880 'Notice of a Drawing of a Bronze Crescent-shaped Plate, which was dug up at Laws, Parish of Monifieth, in 1796', *PSAS* 14, pp. 268–74.

Cummins, W. A. 1999 *The Picts and Their Symbols* (Stroud: Sutton).

Curle, A. O. 1912 'Excavation of a Galleried Structure at Langwell, Caithness', *PSAS* 46, pp. 77–89.

Curle, A. O. 1941 'An account of the partial excavation of a "wag" or galleried building at Forse, in the parish of Latheron, Caithness', *PSAS* 75, pp. 23–39.

Curle, A. O. 1948 'The excavation of the "wag" or prehistoric cattle-fold at Forse, Caithness', *PSAS* 82–83, pp. 11–12.

Curle, C. L. 1940 'The Chronology of the Early Christian Monuments of Scotland', *PSAS* 74, pp. 60–116.

Curle, C. L. 1982 *Pictish and Norse Finds from the Brough of Birsay*, vol. 1 (Edinburgh: Society of Antiquaries of Scotland).

Curtis-Summers, S., Pearson, J. A. and Lamb, A. L. 2020 'From Picts to Parish: Stable isotope evidence of dietary change at medieval Portmahomack, Scotland', *Journal of Archaeological Science Reports* 31, pp. 1–21.

Czére, O., Fawcett, J., Evans, J., Sayle, K., Müldner, G., Hall, M., Will, B., Mitchell, J., Noble, G. and Britton, K. 2021 'Multi-isotope analysis of the human skeletal remains from Blair Atholl, Perth and Kinross, Scotland', *Tayside and Fife Archaeological Journal* 27, pp. 31–44.

Dark, K. R. 1994 *From Civitas to Kingdom: British Political Continuity, 300–800* (London: Leicester University Press).

Dark, K. R. 2000 *Britain and the End of the Roman Empire* (Stroud: Tempus).

Diack, F. C. 1944 *The Inscriptions of Pictland* (Aberdeen: Spalding Club).

Dickinson, T. M. 2011 'Overview: Mortuary ritual', in Hamerow *et al.* 2011, pp. 221–37.

Dickinson, T. M. and Griffiths D. (eds) 1999 *The Making of Kingdoms: Anglo-Saxon Studies in Archaeology and History 10* (Oxford: Oxford University Press).

Dingwall, K. 2019 'Redating and rethinking: the discovery of a cropmark enclosure, burials and kilns at Peterhead, Perth and Kinross', *Tayside and Fife Archaeological Journal* 25, pp. 47–59.

Ditchburn, D. and MacDonald A., 2001 'Medieval Scotland, 1100–1560', in R. A. Houston and W. W. J. Knox (eds), *The New Penguin History of Scotland* (London: Allen Lane, 2001), pp. 96–181.

Dobat, A. S. 2006 'The king and his cult: the axe-hammer from Sutton Hoo and its implications for the concept of sacral leadership in early medieval Europe', *Antiquity* 80, pp. 880–93.

Dobbs, M. E. 1949 'Cé: the Pictish name of a district in eastern Scotland', *Scottish Gaelic Studies* 6, pp. 137–38.

Dockrill, S. J., Bond, J. M. and Turner, V. E. 2010 *Excavations at Old Scatness, Shetland. Volume 1: The Pictish Village and Viking Settlement* (Lerwick: Shetland Heritage Publications).

Dockrill, S. J., Bond, J. M., Turner, V. E., Brown, L. D., Bashford, D. J., Cussans, J. E. M. and Nicholson, R. A. 2015 *The Broch and Iron Age Village: Excavations at Old Scatness, Shetland*, vol. 2 (Lerwick: Shetland Heritage Publications).

Doherty, C. 1985 'The monastic towns in early medieval Ireland', in P. Ní Chatháin and M. Richter (eds), *Ireland and Europe: The Early Church* (Stuttgart: Klett-Cotta), pp. 89–101.

Downes, A. and Ritchie, A. (eds) 2003 *Sea Change. Orkney and Northern Europe in the Later Iron Age AD 300–800* (Balgavies, Angus: Pinkfoot Press).

Dransart, P. 2001 'Two Shrine Fragments from Kinneddar, Moray', in M. Redknap, N. Edwards, S. Youngs, A. Lane and J. Knight (eds), *Pattern and Purpose in Insular Art* (Oxford: Oxbow Books), pp. 233–40.

Dransart, P. 2016 'Bishop's Palaces in the Medieval Dioceses of Aberdeen and Moray', *Transactions of the British Archaeology Association* 49, pp. 58–81.

Driscoll, S. T. 1988 'Power and authority in early historic Scotland: Pictish symbol stones and other documents', in J. Gledhill, B. Bender and M. Larsen (eds), *State and Society: The Emergence and Development of Social Hierarchy and Political Centralization* (London: Taylor & Francis), pp. 215–36.

Driscoll, S. T. 1997 'A Pictish settlement in north-east Fife: the Scottish Field School of Archaeology excavations at Easter Kinnear', *Tayside and Fife Archaeological Journal* 3, pp. 74–118.

Driscoll, S. T. 1998a 'Picts and prehistory: cultural resource management in early medieval Scotland, *World Archaeology* 30(1), pp. 142–58.

Driscoll, S. T. 1998b 'Political discourse and the growth of Christian ceremonialism in Pictland, the place of the St Andrews Sarcophagus', in Foster 1998a, pp. 168–78.

Driscoll, S. T. 2011 'Pictish archaeology: persistent problems and structural solutions', in Driscoll *et al.* 2011, pp. 245–80.

Driscoll, S. T., Hall, M. and Geddes, J. (eds) 2011 *Pictish Progress: New Studies on Northern Britain in the Early Middle Ages* (Leiden: Brill).

Dumville, D. N. 1976 'A note on the Picts in Orkney', *Scottish Gaelic Studies* 12 (1971–76), p. 266.

Dumville, D. N. *et al.* 1993 *Saint Patrick, A.D. 493–1993* (Woodbridge: Boydell).

Dumville, D. N. 1996 'Britain and Ireland in *Táin Bó Fráich*', *Études Celtiques* 32, pp. 175–87.

Dumville, D. N. 2002 'Ireland and north Britain in the earlier Middle Ages: contexts for *Míniugud Senchasa Fher nAlban*', in C. Ó Baoill and N. R. McGuire (eds), *Rannsachadh na Gàidhlig 2000* (Aberdeen: An Clò Gaidhealach), pp. 185–211.

Dunbar, L. 2012 'Greshop Farm cropmark (Site 13), Forres (River Findhorn and Pilmuir) FAS, topsoil strip, evaluation and excavation: data structure report' (unpublished report, AOC Archaeology).

Dunbar, L. and Maldonado, A. 2012 'A long cist cemetery near Auchterforfar Farm, Forfar, Angus – Christian or pre-Christian?', *Tayside and Fife Archaeological Journal* 18, pp. 63–80.

Duncan, A. M., 1975 *Scotland, The Making of the Kingdom* (Edinburgh: Oliver and Boyd).

Dunshea, P. M. 2013 'Druim Alban, Dorsum Britanniae – 'the Spine of Britain'', *Scottish Historical Review* 92(2), pp. 275–89.

Dunwell, A. J., Cowie, T. G., Bruce, M. F., Neighbour, T. and Rees, A. R. 1995 'A Viking Age cemetery at Cnip, Uig, Isle of Lewis', *PSAS* 125, pp. 719–52.

Dunwell, A. J., Neighbour, T. and Cowie, T. G. 1995 'A cist burial adjacent to the Bronze Age cairn at Cnip, Uig, Isle of Lewis'. *PSAS* 125, pp. 279–88.

Dunwell, A. and Ralston, I. B. M. 2008 *Archaeology and Early History of Angus* (Stroud: Tempus).

Edel, D. 2015 *Inside the Táin: exploring Cú Chulainn, Fergus, Ailill, and Medb* (Berlin: Curach Bhán).

Edwards, A. J. H. 1926 'Excavation of a number of graves in a mound at Ackergill, Caithness', *PSAS* 50, pp. 160–82.

Edwards, N. 2001 'Early-Medieval Inscribed Stones and Stone Sculpture in Wales: Context and Function', *Medieval Archaeology* 45(1), pp. 15–39.

Edwards, N. (ed) 2009 *The Archaeology of the Early Medieval Celtic Churches*, Society for Medieval Archaeology Monograph 29 (Leeds: Maney).

Ellis, C., Cruickshanks, G., Hall, D., Ballin, T. B., Ramsay, S. and Anderson, S. 2021 'The Logierait terraces, a place of significance', *Tayside and Fife Archaeological Journal* 27: https://www.tafac.org.uk/category/ journals/.

Enright, M. J. 1982 'The Sutton Hoo whetstone sceptre: a study in iconography and cultural milieu', *Anglo-Saxon England* 11, pp. 119–34.

Enright, M. J. 1996 *Lady with a Mead Cup: Ritual, Prophecy, and Lordship in the Warband from La Tène to the Viking Age* (Dublin: Four Courts Press).

Esmonde Cleary, A. S. 1989 *The Ending of Roman Britain* (London: B. T. Batsford).

Etchingham, C. 1999 *Church Organisation in Ireland A.D. 650 to 1000* (Maynooth: Laigin Publications).

Etchingham, C. 2001 'North Wales, Ireland and the Isles: the Insular Viking Zone', *Peritia* 15, pp. 145–87.

Etchingham, C. 2010 '*Laithlinn*, "Fair Foreigners" and "Dark Foreigners": the identity and provenance of Vikings in ninth-century Ireland', in Sheehan and Ó Corráin 2010, pp. 80–88.

Etchingham, C. 2014 'Names for the Vikings in Irish annals', in Jón Viðar Sigurðsson and T. Bolton (eds), *Celtic-Norse Relationships in the Irish Sea in the Middle Ages 800–1200*, Northern World 65 (Leiden: Brill), pp. 23–38.

Etchingham, C. and Swift, C. N. 2004 'English and Pictish Terms for Brooch in an 8th-century Irish Law-Text', *Medieval Archaeology* 48:1, pp. 31–49.

Evans, N. 2008 'Royal succession and kingship among the Picts', *Innes Review* 59(1), pp. 1–48.

Evans, N. 2011 'Ideology, Literacy and Matriliny: Approaches to Medieval Texts on the Pictish Past', in Driscoll *et al.* 2011, pp. 45–65.

Evans, N. 2013 'Circin and Mag Gerginn: Pictish Territories in Irish and Scottish Sources', *Cambrian Medieval Celtic Studies* 66, pp. 1–36.

Evans, N. 2014 *A Historical Introduction to the Northern Picts* (Aberdeen: Tarbat Discovery Centre/University of Aberdeen).

Evans, N. 2017 'News Recording and Cultural Connections between Early Medieval Ireland and Northern Britain', in Cooijmans 2017, pp. 140–70.

Evans, N. 2018 'Irish chronicles as sources for the history of northern Britain, A.D. 660–800', *Innes Review* 69(1), pp. 1–48.

Evans, N. 2019a 'Personal Names in Early Medieval Gaelic Chronicles', in Hammond 2019, pp. 18–40.

Evans, N. 2019b 'Ideas of origins and ethnicity in Early Medieval Scotland', in A. E. Blackwell (ed.), *Scotland in Early Medieval Europe* (Leiden: Sidestone Press), pp. 149–60.

Evans, N. 2022 '*Picti*: from Roman Name to Internal Identity', *Journal of Medieval History*, 48(3), pp. 291–322.

Evans, N. (forthcoming), 'A Delfina, the Desert and the Saint among the Picts in the Lives of Cuthbert', in T. O. Clancy, C. Hough and E. Williamson (eds), *Onomastications: A Festschrift for Simon Taylor* (Glasgow: Clò Gàidhlig Oilthigh Ghlaschu).

Fairweather, A. D. and Ralston, I. B. M. 1993 'The Neolithic timber hall at Balbridie, Grampian Region, Scotland: the building, the date, the plant macrofossils', *Antiquity* 67, pp. 313–23.

Feachem, R. W. 1955 'Fortifications', in Wainwright 1955a, pp. 66–86.

Findell, M. 2014 *Runes* (London: British Museum).

Fisher, I. 2001 *Early Medieval Sculpture in the West Highlands and Islands* (Edinburgh: Society of Antiquaries of Scotland).

Fitzpatrick, A. 2007 'Druids: towards an archaeology', in C. Gosden, H. Hamerow, P. de Jersey and G. Lock (eds), *Communities and Connections: Essays in Honour of Barry Cunliffe* (Oxford: Oxford University Press), pp. 287–315.

Fleming, R. 2010 *Britain after Rome: The Fall and Rise 400 to 1070* (London: Allen Lane).

Forsyth, K. 1995a 'The inscriptions on the Dupplin Cross', in C. Bourke (ed.), *From the Isles of the North: Medieval Art in Ireland and Britain* (Belfast: HMSO), pp. 237–44.

Forsyth, K. 1995b 'The ogham-inscribed spindle whorl from Buckquoy: evidence for the Irish language in pre-Viking Orkney?', *PSAS* 125, pp. 677–96.

Forsyth, K. 1996 *The Ogham Inscriptions of Scotland: An Edited Corpus* (Ann Arbor, MI: Harvard University).

Forsyth, K. 1997a *Language in Pictland: The Case Against 'non-Indo-European Pictish'* (Utrecht: Nodus).

Forsyth, K. 1997b 'Some thoughts on Pictish symbols as a formal writing system', in Henry 1997, pp. 85–98.

Forsyth, K. 1998 'Literacy in Pictland', in H. Pryce (ed), *Literacy in Medieval Celtic Societies* (Cambridge: Cambridge University Press), pp. 39–61.

Forsyth, K. with an appendix by Koch, J. T. 2000 'Evidence of a lost Pictish source in the Historia Regum Anglorum of Symeon of Durham', in Taylor 2000b, pp. 19–34.

Forsyth, K. 2005 'HIC MEMORIA PERPETUA: the inscribed stones of sub-Roman southern Scotland', in S. M. Foster and M. Cross. (eds), *Able Minds and Practised Hands: Scotland's Early Medieval Sculpture in the Twenty-First Century* (Edinburgh: Society for Medieval Archaeology Monograph Series (23)/Historic Scotland), pp. 113–34.

Forsyth, K. (ed.) 2008a *Studies on the Book of Deer* (Dublin: Four Courts Press).

Forsyth, K. 2008b 'The Stones of Deer', in Forsyth 2008a, pp. 398–438.

Forsyth, K. 2021 'Ogham inscriptions from the Brough of Birsay', in Morris 2021, pp. 374–87.

Forsyth, K., Broun, D. and Clancy, T. 2008 'The property records: text and translation', in Forsyth 2008a, pp. 131–44.

Foster, S. (ed.) 1998a *The St Andrews Sarcophagus: A Pictish Masterpiece and its International Connections* (Edinburgh: Historic Scotland).

Foster, S. 1998b 'Discovery, Recovery, Context and Display', in Foster 1998a, pp. 36–62.

Foster, S. M. 2014 *Picts, Gaels and Scots* (Edinburgh: Birlinn).

Foster, S. M. 2015 'Physical evidence for the early church in Scotland', in P. S. Barnwell (ed.), *Places of Worship in Britain and Ireland*, 300–950 (Donington: Paul Watkins), pp. 68–91.

Fowler, E. 1963 'Celtic metalwork of the fifth and sixth centuries AD. A reappraisal', *Archaeological Journal* 120, pp. 98–160.

Fraser, I. A. 1995 'Norse settlement on the north-west seaboard', in Crawford 1995, pp. 92–107.

Fraser, J. E. 2004 'The Iona Chronicle, the Descendants of Áedán mac Gabráin, and the "Principal Kindreds of Dál Riata"', *Northern Studies* 38, pp. 77–96.

Fraser, J. E. 2005a *The Roman Conquest of Scotland: The Battle of Mons Graupius AD 84* (Stroud: The History Press).

Fraser, J. E. 2005b 'Illustrations relating to Fraser's article, "The Iona Chronicle"', *Northern Studies* 39, pp. 125–30.

Fraser, J. E. 2009a *From Caledonia to Pictland: Scotland to 795* (Edinburgh: Edinburgh University Press).

Fraser, J. E. 2009b 'Rochester, Hexham and Cennrígmonaid: the movements of St Andrew in Britain, 604–747', in Boardman, Davies and Williamson 2009, pp. 1–17.

Fraser, J. E. 2011 'From Ancient Scythia to *The Problem of the Picts*: Thoughts on the Quest for Pictish Origins', in Driscoll *et al.* 2011, pp. 15–43.

Friell, J. G. P. and Watson, W. G. (eds) 1984 *Pictish Studies: Settlement, Burial and Art in Dark Age Northern Britain* (Oxford: British Archaeological Reports British Series 125).

Fyles, C. 2008 'Excavations at School Wynd, Abernethy', *Tayside and Fife Archaeological Journal* 14, pp. 16–25.

Gammeltoft, P. 2001 *The Place-Name Element* bólstaðr *in the North Atlantic Area* (Copenhagen: C. A. Reitzel).

Gammeltoft, P. 2004 'Contact or Conflict? What Can We Learn from the Island-Names of the Northern Isles?', in J. Adams and K. Holman (eds), *Scandinavia and Europe 800–1350* (Turnhout: Brepols), pp. 87–95.

Gammeltoft, P. 2007 'Scandinavian Naming-Systems in the Hebrides: A Way of Understanding how the Scandinavians were in Contact with Gaels and Picts?', in B. Ballin Smith, S. Taylor, G. Williams (eds), *West over Sea: Studies in Scandinavian Sea-borne Expansion and Settlement before 1300. A Festschrift in Honour of Dr. Barbara E. Crawford* (Turnhout: Brill), pp. 479–95.

Gavin, F. 2013 'Insular military-style silver pins in late Iron Age Ireland', in Hunter and Painter 2013, pp. 427–41.

Geake, H. 1992 'Burial practice in seventh- and eighth-century England', in M. Carver (ed), *The Age of Sutton Hoo: The Seventh Century in North-Western England* (Suffolk: Boydell), pp. 83–94.

Geddes, J. 2017 *Hunting Picts: Medieval Sculpture at St Vigeans, Angus* (Edinburgh: Historic Environment Scotland).

Geddes, J. (forthcoming) *Historic Environment Scotland Statement of Significance: Early Medieval Carved Stones at St Andrews Cathedral, Fife* (Edinburgh: Historic Environment Scotland).

Geddes, J., Murray, H. K. and Murray, J. C. 2015 'Tullich, Aberdeenshire: a reappraisal of an early ecclesiastical site and its carved stones in the light of recent excavations', *PSAS* 145, pp. 229–81.

Gilbert, E. *et al.* 2019 'The genetic landscape of Scotland and the Isles', *Proceedings of the National Academy of Sciences* 116(38), pp. 19064–19070; DOI: 10.1073/pnas.1904761116

Gilmour, S. M. D. 2000 'Late Prehistoric and Early Historic Settlement Archaeology of the Western Seaways' (unpublished PhD thesis, University of Edinburgh).

Gleeson, P. 2017 'Converting kingship in early Ireland: re-defining practices, ideologies and identities', in M. Ní Mhaonáigh, R. Flechner and N. Edwards. (eds), *Transforming Landscapes of Belief in the Early Medieval Insular World and Beyond: Converting the Isles* (Turnhout: Brepols), pp. 287–318.

Goldberg, E. J. 2020 *In the Manner of the Franks: Hunting, Kingship, and Masculinity in Early Medieval Europe* (Philadelphia, PA: University of Pennsylvania).

Goldberg, M. 2015 'At the western edge of the Christian world, c. AD600–90', in J. Farley and F. Hunter (eds), *Celts: Art and Identity* (London: British Museum/National Museums Scotland), pp. 172–205.

Goldberg, M. and Blackwell, A. 2013 'The different histories of the Norrie's Law hoard', in J. Hawkes (ed), *Making histories. Proceedings of the Sixth International Insular Arts Conference, York 2011* (Donington: Shaun Tyas), pp. 326–38.

Gondek, M. 2006 'Investing in Sculpture: Power in early historic Scotland', *Medieval Archaeology* 50, pp. 105–42.

Gondek, M. M. and Jeffrey, S. 2003 'The re-use of a figurative panel from Eigg', *Medieval Archaeology* 47, pp. 178–85.

Gooney, D. 2015 'Life and death in Iron Age Orkney: an osteoarchaeological examination of the human skeletal remains from the burial ground at Knowe of Skea, Westray' (unpublished PhD thesis, University of Edinburgh).

Gourlay, R. 1984 'A symbol stone and cairn at Watenan, Caithness', in Friell and Watson 1984, pp. 131–34.

Graham, B. J. 1987 'Urban genesis in early medieval Ireland', *Journal of Historical Geography* 13(1), pp. 3–16.

Graham-Campbell, J. 1985 'A lost Pictish treasure (and two Viking-age gold arm-rings) from the Broch of Burgar, Orkney', *PSAS* 115, pp. 241–61.

Graham-Campbell, J. 1991 'Norrie's Law, Fife: on the nature and dating of the silver hoard', *PSAS* 121, pp. 241–59.

Graham-Campbell, J. 1993 'The Northern Hoards of Viking-Age Scotland', in Batey, Jesch and Morris 1993, pp. 173–86.

Graham-Campbell, J. and Batey, C. E. 1998 *Vikings in Scotland: An Archaeological Survey* (Edinburgh: Edinburgh University Press).

Greene, D, 1994 'Gaelic: syntax, similarities with British syntax', in D. Thomson (ed.), *The Companion to Gaelic Scotland* (Glasgow: Gairm), pp. 107–08.

Gregory, R. A. and Jones, G. D. B. 2001 'Survey and excavation at Tarradale, Highland', *PSAS* 131, pp. 241–66.

Greig, J. C. 1970 'Excavations at Castle Point, Troup, Banffshire', *Aberdeen University Review* 43, pp. 274–83.

Greig, J. C. 1971 'Excavations at Cullykhan, Castle Point, Troup, Banffshire', *Scottish Archaeological Forum* 3, pp. 15–21.

Greig, J. C, Greig, M. and Ashmore, P. 2000 'Excavation of a cairn cemetery at Lundin Links, Fife, in 1965–6', *PSAS* 130, pp. 586–636.

Griffiths, D. 2019 'Rethinking the Viking Age in the West', *Antiquity* 93(368), pp. 468–77.

Griffiths, D., Harrison, J. and Athanson, M. 2019 *Beside the Ocean: Coastal Landscapes at the Bay of Skaill, Marwick and Birsay Bay, Orkney* (Oxford: Oxbow).

Griffiths, D. and Ovenden, S. 2021 'Birsay Bay Landscape Geophysical Surveys 2003–6', in Morris 2021, pp. 533–42.

Grigg, J. 2015 *The Philosopher King and the Pictish Nation* (Dublin: Four Courts Press).

Haldane, A. R. B. 1973 *The Drove Roads of Scotland* (Newton Abbot: David and Charles)

Hall, D. 1995 'Pre-Burghal St Andrews. Towards an Archaeological Research Design', *Tayside and Fife Archaeological Journal* 1, pp. 23–27.

Hall, M. 2007 *Playtime in Pictland: The Material Culture of Gaming in Early Medieval Scotland* (Rosemarkie: Groam House Museum).

Hall, M., Evans, N., Hamilton, D., Mitchell, J., O'Driscoll, J. and Noble, G. 2020 'Warrior ideologies in first millennium AD Europe: new light on monumental warrior stelae from Scotland', *Antiquity* 94(373), pp. 127–44.

Hall, M. A. and Forsyth, K. 2011 'Roman rules? The introduction of board games to Britain and Ireland', *Antiquity* 85 (330), pp. 1325–38.

Halliday, S. 2019 'Re-visiting the morphology of Pitcarmick buildings', in Strachan, Sneddon and Tipping 2019, pp. 123–29.

Halsall, G. 2012 'Northern Britain and the fall of the Roman Empire', *Medieval Journal* 2(2), pp. 1–25.

Halsall, G. 2013 *Worlds of Arthur. Facts and Fictions of the Dark Ages* (Oxford: Oxford University Press).

Hamerow, H. 1993 *Excavations at Mucking, Vol. 2: The Anglo-Saxon Settlement*, English Heritage Archaeological Report 21 (London: English Heritage).

Hamerow, H. 2012 *Rural Settlements and Society in Anglo-Saxon England* (Oxford: Oxford University Press).

Hamerow, H., Bogaard, A., Charles, M., Forster, E., Holmes, M., McKerracher, M. and Thomas, R. 2020 'An Integrated Bioarchaeological Approach to the Medieval "Agricultural Revolution": A Case Study from Stafford, England, c. AD 800–1200', *European Journal of Archaeology* 23(4), pp. 585–609.

Hamerow, H., Hinton, D. A. and Crawford, S. (eds) 2011 *The Oxford Handbook of Anglo-Saxon Archaeology* (Oxford: Oxford University Press).

Hamilton, D. W., Haselgrove, C. and Gosden, C. 2015 'The impact of Bayesian chronologies on the British Iron Age', *World Archaeology* 47(4), pp. 642–60.

Hamilton, J. R. C. 1956 *Excavations at Jarlshof, Shetland* (Edinburgh: HMSO).

Hammond M. (ed.) 2019 *Personal Names and Naming Practices in Medieval Scotland* (Woodbridge: Boydell Press).

Harding, D. W. 2009 *The Iron Age Round-House: Later Prehistoric Building in Britain and Beyond* (Oxford: Oxford University Press).

Harding, D. W. 2012 *Iron Age Hillforts in Britain and Beyond* (Oxford: Oxford University Press).

Harding, D. W. and Gilmour, S. 2000 *The Iron Age settlement at Beirgh, Riof, Isle of Lewis: Excavations 1985–95 Volume 1: The Structures and Stratigraphy*, Calanais Research Monograph 1 (Edinburgh: University of Edinburgh).

Härke, H. 1990 '"Warrior graves"? The background of the Anglo-Saxon weapon burial rite', *Past & Present* 126, pp. 22–43.

Härke, H. 2001 'Cemeteries as places of power', in M. de Jong, F. Theuws and C. van Rhijn (eds), *Topographies of Power in the Early Middle Ages. Volume 6: The Transformation of the Roman World* (Leiden: Brill), pp. 9–30.

Härke, H. 2014 'Grave goods in early medieval burials: messages and meanings', *Mortality* 19: pp. 41–60.

Harvey, A. 1987 'Early literacy in Ireland: the evidence from Ogam', *Cambridge Medieval Celtic Studies* 14, pp. 1–15.

Heald, A. 2001 'Knobbed spearbutts of the British and Irish Iron Age: new examples and new thoughts', *Antiquity* 290, pp. 689–96.

Heald, A. 2011 'The interpretation of non-ferrous metalworking in Early Historic Scotland', in Driscoll *et al.* 2011, pp. 221–44.

Heather, P. 2009 *Empires and Barbarians: Migration, Development and the Birth of Empire* (London: Macmillan).

Hedeager, L. 1999 'Myth and art: a passport to political authority in Scandinavia during the Migration Period' in Dickinson and Griffiths 1999, pp. 151–56.

Hedges, J. W. 1987 *Bu, Gurness and the Brochs of Orkney*, Part 2: Gurness. BAR British Series 165 (Oxford: BAR).

Hencken, H. O'N. 1950 'Lagore Crannog: an Irish royal residence of the seventh to tenth centuries AD', *Proceedings of the Royal Irish Academy* 53, pp. 1–248.

Henderson, G. 1972 *Early Medieval (Style and Civilisation)* (London: Pelican).

Henderson, G. and Henderson, I. 2004 *The Art of the Picts: Sculpture and Metalwork in Early Medieval Scotland* (London: Thames and Hudson).

Henderson, I. 1958 'The origin centre of the Pictish symbol stones', *PSAS* 91, pp. 44–60.

Henderson, I. 1967 *The Picts* (London: Thames and Hudson).

Henderson, I. 1971 'North Pictland', *The Dark Ages in the Highlands: ancient peoples, local history, archaeology* (Inverness: Inverness Field Club), pp. 37–52.

Henderson, I. 1987 'Early Christian monuments of Scotland displaying crosses but no other ornament', in Small 1987, pp. 45–58.

Henderson, I. 1993 'The Making of The Early Christian Monuments of Scotland', in Allen and Anderson 1903, pp. 13–38.

Henderson, I. 1994, 'The Picts: Written Records and Pictorial Images', in J. R. F. Burt (ed.), *Stones, Symbols and Stories: Aspects of Pictish Studies*, Proceedings of the Conferences of the Pictish Arts Society, 1992 (Edinburgh: Pictish Arts Society), pp. 44–66.

Henderson, I. 1996 *Pictish Monsters: Symbol, Text and Image*, H. M. Chadwick Memorial Lecture 7 (Cambridge: Department of Anglo-Saxon, Norse and Celtic, University of Cambridge).

Henderson, J. A. 1907 *Aberdeenshire Epitaphs and Inscriptions: with Historical, Biographical, Genealogical, and Antiquarian Notes* (Aberdeen: Aberdeen Daily Journal Press).

Henning, J. 2009 'Revolution or relapse? Technology, agriculture and early medieval archaeology in Germanic Central Europe', in G. Ausenda, P. Delogu and C. Wickham (eds), *The Langobards Before the Frankish Conquest: An Ethnographic Perspective* (Woodbridge: Boydell Press), pp. 149–73.

Henry, D. (ed.) 1997 *The Worm, the Germ and the Thorn: Pictish and Related Studies Presented to Isabel Henderson* (Balgavies, Angus: Pinkfoot Press).

Henshall, A. S. 1956 'A long cist cemetery at Parkburn Sand Pit, Lasswade, Midlothian', *PSAS* 89, pp. 252–83.

Higgitt, J. 1982 'The Pictish Latin inscription at Tarbat in Ross-shire', *PSAS* 112, pp. 300–21.

Hill, P. 2003 'The Stone of Destiny examined: an overview and discussion', in Welander, Clancy and Breeze 2003, pp. 11–31.

Hind, J. G. F. 1983 'Caledonia and its occupation under the Flavians', *PSAS* 113, pp. 373–78.

Hines, J. A. and Bayliss, A. L. (eds), 2013 *Anglo-Saxon Graves and Grave Goods of the 6th and 7th Centuries AD: a Chronological Framework*, Society for Medieval Archaeology Monograph 33 (Leeds: Society for Medieval Archaeology).

Hingley, R. 1996 'Ancestors and identity in the later prehistory of Atlantic Scotland: the reuse and reinvention of Neolithic monuments and material culture', *World Archaeology* 28, pp. 231–43.

Hingley, R., Moore, H., Triscott, J. and Wilson, G. 1997 'The excavation of two later Iron Age homesteads at Aldclune, Blair Atholl, Perth & Kinross', *PSAS* 127, pp. 407–66.

Hope-Taylor, B. 1977 *Yeavering: An Anglo-British Centre of Early Northumbria* (London: HMSO).

Hughes, K. 1970 *Early Christianity in Pictland*, Jarrow Lecture 1970 (Jarrow: St Paul's Church). Reprinted in Hughes 1980, pp. 1–21.

Hughes, K. (ed. D. Dumville) 1980 *Celtic Britain in the Early Middle Ages: Studies in Scottish and Welsh Sources*, Studies in Celtic History II (Woodbridge: Boydell).

Hunter, F. 2007a *Beyond the Edge of the Empire: Caledonians, Picts and Romans* (Rosemarkie: Groam House Museum).

Hunter, F. 2007b 'Silver for the barbarians: interpreting denarii hoards in north Britain and beyond', in R. Hingley and S. Wills (eds), *Roman Finds: Context and Theory* (Oxford: Oxbow), pp. 214–24.

Hunter, F. and Painter, K. (eds) 2013 *Late Roman Silver: The Traprain Treasure in Context* (Edinburgh: Society of Antiquaries of Scotland).

Hunter, F. and Ralston, I. B. M. (eds) 2015 *Scotland in Later Prehistoric Europe* (Edinburgh: Society of Antiquaries of Scotland).

Hunter, J., Bond, J. M. and Smith, A. N. 2007 *Investigations in Sanday, Orkney: Excavations at Pool, Sanday* (Kirkwall: Orcadian).

Hunter Blair, A. 2004 'Ackergill, Wick (Wick parish), cemetery', *Discovery and Excavation in Scotland* 5, p. 82.

Isaac, G. R. 2005 'Scotland', in J. de Hoz, E. R. Luján and P. Sims-Williams (eds), *New Approaches to Celtic Place-Names in Ptolemy's Geography* (Madrid: Ediciones Clásicas), pp. 189–214.

Iversen, F. 2013 'Concilium and Pagus – Revisiting the Early Germanic Thing System of Northern Europe', *Journal of the North Atlantic Special Volume 5: Debating the Thing in the North I: Selected Papers from Workshops Organized by The Assembly Project*, pp. 5–17.

Jackson, A. 1984 *The Symbol Stones of Scotland: A Social Anthropological Resolution of the Problem of the Picts* (Stromness: Orkney Press).

Jackson, K. 1954 'Two Early Scottish Names', *Scottish Historical Review* 33, pp. 14–18.

Jackson, K. 1955 'The Pictish Language', in Wainwright 1955a, pp. 129–76.

Jackson, K. (ed. with trans. and notes by A. O. Anderson and M. O. Anderson) 1963 'Review of *Adomnán's Life of Columba* (Edinburgh: Nelson, 1961)', *English Historical Review* 78(307), pp. 317–20.

James, A. G. 2013 'P-Celtic in Southern Scotland and Cumbria: a review of the place-name evidence for possible Pictish phonology', *Journal of Scottish Name Studies* 7, pp. 29–78.

James, H. and Yeoman, P. 2008 *Excavations at St. Ethernan's Monastery, Isle of May, Fife 1992–7* (Brechin: Tayside and Fife Archaeological Committee, Monograph No. 6).

Jaski, B. 2000 *Early Irish Kingship and Succession* (Dublin: Four Courts Press).

Jennings, A. and Kruse, A. 2005 'An Ethnic Enigma: Norse, Pict and Gael in the Western Isles', in A. Mortensen and S. V. Arge (eds), *Viking and Norse in the North Atlantic: Selected Papers from the Proceedings of the Fourteenth Viking Congress, Torshavn 19–30 July 2001* (Torshavn: Føroya Fróðskaparfelag), pp. 251–63.

Jennings, A. and Kruse, A. 2009a 'One Coast – Three Peoples: Names and Ethnicity in the Scottish West During the Early Viking Period', in Woolf 2009, pp. 75–102.

Jennings, A., and Kruse, A. 2009b 'From Dál Riata to the Gall-Ghàidheil', *Viking and Medieval Scandinavia* 5, pp. 123–49.

Jones, S. E. *et al.* 2020, 'Identifying Social Transformations and Crisis during the Pre-Monastic to Post-Viking era on Iona: New Insights from a Palynological and Palaeoentomological Perspective', *Environmental Archaeology* (prepublication DOI: 10.1080/14614103.2020.1713581).

Jones, S. E. *et al.* 2021 'Settlement, landscape and land-use change at a Pictish Elite Centre: Assessing the palaeoecological record for economic continuity and social change at Rhynie in NE Scotland', *The Holocene* 31(6), pp. 897–914.

Kaland, S. H. 1993 'The Settlement of Westness, Rousay', in Batey, Jesch and Morris 1993, pp. 308–17.

Kelly, F. 1988 *A Guide to Early Irish Law* (Dublin: Dublin Institute for Advanced Studies).

Kelly, F. 1997 *Early Irish Farming* (Dublin: Dublin Institute for Advanced Studies).

Kennet, D. A., Timpson, A., Balding, D. J. and Thomas, M. G. 2018 'The Rise and Fall of Britain's DNA: A Tale of Misleading Claims, Media Manipulation and Threats to Academic Freedom', *Genealogy* 2, p. 47: https://doi.org/10.3390/ genealogy2040047.

Kilbride-Jones, H. 1980 *Zoomorphic Penannular Brooches* (London: Thames and Hudson).

Kilpatrick, K. 2011 'The iconography of the Papil Stone: sculptural and literary comparisons with a Pictish motif', *PSAS* 141, pp. 159–205.

Kilpatrick, K. 2021 'The Newton Stones and writing in Pictland, part 2: the Newton Stone ogham, Pictish Latin-letter alphabetic inscription and the Pictish symbol system', *PSAS* 150, pp. 407–34.

King, J. 2005 '"Lochy" names and Adomnán's *Nigra Dea*', *Nomina* 28, pp. 69–91.

Kirby, M. 2012 'Lockerbie Academy: Neolithic and Early Historic timber halls, a Bronze Age cemetery, an undated enclosure and a post-medieval corn-drying kiln in south-west Scotland', *Scottish Archaeological Internet Reports* 46 (2011): https://archaeologydataservice.ac.uk/archives/view/sair/contents. cfm?vol=46.

Krag, C. 2003 'The early unification of Norway', in K. Helle (ed.), *The Cambridge History of Scandinavia. Volume I Prehistory to 1520* (Cambridge: Cambridge University Press), pp. 184–201.

Kruse, A. 2017 'The Norway to Be: *Laithlind* and Avaldsnes', in Cooijmans 2017, pp. 198–231.

Laing, L. and Laing, J. 1984 'The date and origin of the Pictish symbols', *PSAS* 114, pp. 261–76.

Laing, L. and Laing, J. 1993 *The Picts and the Scots* (Stroud: Alan Sutton).

Lamb, R. G. 1973 'Coastal settlements of the north', *Scottish Archaeological Forum* 5, pp. 76–98.

Lamb, R. G. 1995 'Papil, Picts and Papar', in B. E. Crawford (ed.), *Northern Isles Connections: Essays from Orkney and Shetland presented to Per Sveaas Andersen* (Kirkwall: Orkney Press), pp. 9–27.

Lamb, R. G. 1998 'Pictland, Northumbria and the Carolingian Empire', in B. Crawford (ed.), *Conversion and Christianity in the North Sea World* (St Andrews: Committee for Dark Age Studies, University of St Andrews), pp. 41–56.

Lane, A. and Campbell, E. 2000 *Dunadd: An Early Dalriadic Capital* (Oxford: Oxbow).

Lee, R. 2010 'The use of information theory to determine the language character type of Pictish symbols', *Scottish Archaeological Journal* 32(2), pp. 137–76.

Lee, R., Jonathan, P. and Ziman, P. 2010 'Pictish symbols revealed as a written language through application of Shannon entropy', *Proceedings of the Royal Society* 10, pp. 1–16.

Logan, J. 1929 'Observations on several monumental stones in the north of Scotland', *Archaeologia* 22, pp. 55–58.

Loggie, R. 2020 'A Revisit to Sueno's Stone' (unpublished MSc dissertation, University of Aberdeen).

Longley, D. 2009 'Early medieval burial in Wales', in Edwards 2009, pp. 105–34.

Lorimer, D. 2000 'Familial Traits', in Greig *et al.* 2000, pp. 602–03.

Lucas, A. T. 1963 'The Sacred Trees of Ireland', *Journal of the Cork Historical and Archaeological Society* 68, pp. 16–54.

Lucy, S. and Reynolds, A. (eds) 2002 *Burial in Early Medieval England and Wales*, Society for Medieval Archaeology Monograph 17 (Leeds: Maney).

Lynn, C. J. 1994 'Houses in Rural Ireland, A.D. 500–1000', *Journal of Irish Archaeology* 57, pp. 81–94.

McCormick, M. 2001 *The Origins of the European Economy: Communications and Commerce AD 300–900* (Cambridge: Cambridge University Press).

MacCotter, P. 2008 *Medieval Ireland: Territorial, Political and Economic Divisions* (Dublin: Four Courts Press).

MacDonald, A. 1994 *Curadán, Boniface and the Early Church of Rosemarkie*, Groam House Lecture (Rosemarkie: Groam House Museum).

MacDonald, A. 2002 'The *papar* and some Problems: a brief Review', in B. E. Crawford (ed.), *The* Papar *in the North Atlantic: Environment and History* (St Andrews: Committee for Dark Age Studies, University of St Andrews), pp. 13–30.

MacDonald, A. D. S. and Laing, L. R. 1970 'Early ecclesiastical sites in Scotland: a field survey, Part II', *PSAS* 102, pp. 129–45.

MacDonald, J. 1862 'Historical notices of "the Broch" or Burghead, in Moray, with an account of its antiquities', *PSAS* 4, pp. 321–69.

MacGregor, A. 1974 'The Broch of Burrian, North Ronaldsay, Orkney', *PSAS* 105, pp. 63–118.

MacGregor, G. 2004 'Excavation of an Iron Age burial mound, Loch Borralie, Durness, Sutherland', *SAIR* 9, https://doi.org/10.5284/1017938.

MacGregor, G. 2010 'Legends, Traditions or Coincidences: Remembrance of Historic Settlement in the Central Highlands of Scotland', *International Journal of Historical Archaeology* 14(3), pp. 398–413.

MacIver, C., Cook, M., Heald, A., Robertson, A., McLaren, D., Strachan, D. and Henderson, C. 2019 'King's Seat, Dunkeld, Perth and Kinross: Archaeological Evaluation Phase 3 Data Structure Report' (unpublished report, AOC Archaeology): https://www.pkht.org.uk/wp-content/uploads/2021/08/Kings_Seat_Hillfort_Archaeology_Project_DSR_2019.pdf.

McKerracher, M. 2018 *Farming Transformed in Anglo-Saxon England* (Oxford: Windgather Press).

MacKie, E. 2000 'Excavations at Dun Ardtreck, Skye, in 1964 and 1965', *PSAS* 130, pp. 301–411.

MacLaren, A. 1974 'A Norse house on Drimore Machair, South Uist', *Glasgow Archaeological Journal* 3, pp. 9–18.

McNeill, P. G. B. and MacQueen, H. L. (eds) 1996 *The Atlas of Scottish History to 1707* (Edinburgh: Scottish Medievalists and Department of Geography, University of Edinburgh).

McNiven, P. E. 2011 'Gaelic Place-names and the Social History of Gaelic Speakers in Medieval Menteith' (unpublished PhD thesis, University of Glasgow).

MacQuarrie, A. (ed.), with Butter, R. and contributions by Taylor S. and Márkus, G. 2012 *Legends of the Scottish Saints: Readings, Hymns and Prayers for the Commemorations of Scottish Saints in the Aberdeen Breviary* (Dublin: Four Courts Press).

Mack, A. 1997 *Field Guide to the Pictish Symbol Stones* (Balgavies, Angus: Pinkfoot Press).

Mack, A. 2007 *Symbols and Pictures: The Pictish Legacy in Stone* (Balgavies, Angus: Pinkfoot Press).

Maldonado, A. 2013 'Burial in early Medieval Scotland: New questions', *Medieval Archaeology* 57, pp. 1–34.

Maldonado, A. 2016 'Death and the formation of Early Christian Scotland', in T. Ó Carragáin, and S. Turner (eds), *Making Christian Landscapes in Atlantic Europe: Conversion and Consolidation in the Early Middle Ages* (Cork: Cork University Press), pp. 225–45.

Maldonado, A. 2021 *Crucible of Nations: Scotland from Viking Age to Medieval Kingdom* (Edinburgh: National Museums Scotland).

Mann, J. C. and Penman, R. G. 1996 *Literary Sources for Roman Britain (Lactor 11)* (London: London Association of Classical Teachers).

Margaryan, A., Lawson, D. J., Sikora, M. *et al.* 2020 'Population genomics of the Viking world', *Nature* 585, pp. 390–96: https://doi.org/10.1038/s41586-020-2688-8.

Márkus, G. 2017 *Conceiving a Nation: Scotland to* AD *900* (Edinburgh: Birlinn).

Mauss, M. 1925 *The Gift: Forms and Functions of Exchange in Archaic Societies* (reprinted 2002, London: Routledge).

Maxwell, G. S. 1978 'Air photography and the work of the Royal Commission for the Ancient and Historical Monuments of Scotland', *Aerial Archaeology* 2, pp. 37–45.

Maxwell, G. S. 1987 'Settlement in Southern Pictland: A New Overview', in Small 1987, pp. 31–44.

Maxwell, G. S. 1989 *The Romans in Scotland* (Edinburgh: James Thin, Mercat Press).

Mitchell, J. 2020 'Monumental landscapes: the early medieval barrow and cairn cemeteries of northern and eastern Scotland' (unpublished PhD thesis, University of Aberdeen).

Mitchell, J. and Noble, G. 2017 'The monumental cemeteries of northern Pictland', *Medieval Archaeology* 61, pp. 1–40.

Mitchell, J., Cook, M., Dunbar, L., Ives, R. and Noble, G. 2020 'Monumental Cemeteries of Pictland: Excavation and Dating Evidence from Greshop, Moray, and Bankhead of Kinloch, Perthshire', *Tayside and Fife Archaeological Journal* 26, pp. 21–34.

Montgomery, J., Grimes, V., Buckberry, J., Evans, J. A., Richards, M. P. and Barrett, J. H. 2014 'Finding Vikings with isotope analysis: the view from wet and windy islands', *Journal of the North Atlantic* 7, pp. 54–70.

Morris, C. D. 1993 'The Birsay Bay Project: A Resume', in Batey, Jesch and Morris (eds) 1993, pp. 285–307.

Morris, C. D. 2021 *The Birsay Bay Project Vol. 3: The Brough of Birsay Investigations 1954–2014* (Oxford: Oxbow).

Morris, C. D. and Emery, N. 1986 'The chapel and enclosure on the Brough of Deerness, Orkney: Survey and excavations, 1975–1977', *PSAS* 116, pp. 301–74.

Murray, H. K., Murray, J. C. and Fraser, S. M. 2009 *A Tale of the Unknown Unknowns: a Mesolithic Pit Alignment and a Neolithic Timber Hall at Warren Field, Crathes, Aberdeenshire* (Oxford: Oxbow).

Neighbour, T. and Burgess, C. 1996 'Traigh Bostadh (Uig Parish)', *Discovery and Excavation in Scotland*, pp. 113–14.

Neighbour, T., Knott, C., Bruce, M. F. and Kerr, N. W. 2000 'Excavation of Two Burials at Galson, Isle of Lewis, 1993 and 1996', *PSAS* 130, pp. 559–84.

Newman, C. 2009 'The Sword in the Stone: previously unrecognised archaeological evidence of ceremonies of the later Iron Age and early medieval period' in G. Cooney *et al.* (eds), *Relics of Old Decency: Archaeological Studies in Later Prehistory. Festschrift for Barry Raftery* (Wordwell: Dublin), pp. 425–36.

Nicolaisen, W. F. H. 1995 'Scandinavians and Celts in Caithness: the Place-Name Evidence', in J. Baldwin (ed.), *Caithness: A Cultural Crossroads* (Edinburgh: Edinburgh University Press), pp. 75–85.

Nicolay, J. A. W. 2014 *The Splendour of Power: Early medieval kingship and the use of gold and silver in the southern North Sea area* (Groningen: Barkhuis and University of Groningen).

Nieke, M. R. 1993 'Penannular and related brooches: secular ornament or symbol in action?', in Spearman and Higgitt 1993, pp. 128–34.

Noble, G. and Evans, N. 2019 *The King In the North: The Pictish Realms of Fortriu and Ce* (Edinburgh: Birlinn).

Noble, G., Gondek, M., Campbell, E. and Cook, M. 2013 'Between prehistory and history: the archaeological detection of social change among the Picts', *Antiquity* 87, pp. 1136–50.

Noble, G., Goldberg, M., McPherson, A. and Sveinbjarnarson, O. 2016 '(Re)discovering the Gaulcross hoard', *Antiquity* 90, pp. 726–41.

Noble, G., Goldberg, M. and Hamilton, D. 2018a 'The development of the Pictish symbol system: inscribing identity beyond the edges of Empire', *Antiquity* 92, pp. 1329–48.

Noble, G., Turner, J., Hamilton, D., Hastie, L., Knecht, R., Stirling, L., Sveinbjarnarson, O., Upex, B. and Milek, K. 2018b 'Early Medieval Shellfish Exploitation in Northwest Europe: Investigations at the Sands of Forvie Shell Middens, Eastern Scotland, and the Role of Coastal Resources in the First Millennium AD', *Journal of Island and Coastal Archaeology* 13(4), pp. 582–605.

Noble, G., Cruickshanks, G., Dunbar, L., Evans, N., Hall, D., Hamilton, D., MacIver, C., Masson-MacLean, E., O'Driscoll, J., Paskulin, L. and Sveinbjarnarson, O. 2018c 'Kinneddar: a major ecclesiastical centre of the Picts', *PSAS* 148, pp. 113–45.

Noble, G., Lamont, P. and Masson-Maclean, E. 2019a 'Assessing the ploughzone: the impact of cultivation on artefact survival and the cost/benefits of topsoil stripping prior to excavation', *Journal of Archaeological Science Reports* 23, pp. 549–58.

Noble, G., Gondek, M., Campbell, E., Evans, N., Hamilton, D. and Taylor, S. 2019b 'A Powerful Place of Pictland: Interdisciplinary Perspectives on a Power Centre of the 4th to 6th Centuries AD', *Medieval Archaeology* 63(1), pp. 56–94.

Noble, G., Evans, N., Hamilton, D., MacIver, C., Masson-MacLean, E., O'Driscoll, J., Cruickshanks, G., Hunter, F., Ingemark, D., Mainland, I., Taylor, S. and Wallace, C. 2020a 'Dunnicaer, Aberdeenshire, Scotland: a Roman Iron Age promontory fort beyond the frontier', *Archaeological Journal* 177, pp. 256–338.

Noble, G., O'Driscoll, J., MacIver, C., Masson-MacLean, E. and Sveinbjarnarson, O. 2020b 'New Dates for enclosed sites in north-east Scotland', *PSAS* 149, pp. 165–96.

Noble, G., Evans, N., Goldberg, M. and Hamilton, D. W. (forthcoming) 'Burning Matters: the Rise and Fall of an Early Medieval Fortified Centre: a New Chronology for Clatchard Craig', *Medieval Archaeology*.

Noble, G. and Allison, J. (forthcoming) 'A new chronology for the Broch of Gurness' (manuscript in preparation).

O'Brien, E. 1999 *Post-Roman Britain to Anglo-Saxon England: Burial Practices Reviewed*, British Archaeological Report British Series 289 (Oxford: BAR).

O'Brien, E. 2009 'Pagan or Christian? Burial in Ireland during the 5th to 8th centuries AD', in Edwards 2009, pp. 135–54.

O'Brien, E. 2020 *Mapping Death: Burial in Late Iron Age and Early Medieval Ireland* (Dublin: Four Courts Press).

O'Brien, E. and Bhreathnach, E. 2011 'Irish Boundary *Ferta*, their Physical Manifestation and Historical Context', in F. Edmonds and P. Russell (eds), *Tome: Studies in Medieval Celtic History and Law in Honour of Thomas Charles-Edwards*, Studies in Celtic History 31 (Woodbridge: Boydell Press), pp. 53–64.

Ó Carragáin, T. 2010 *Churches in Early Medieval Ireland: Architecture, Ritual and Memory* (Yale, CT: Yale University Press).

Ó Corráin, D. 1998 'Creating the past: the early Irish genealogical tradition', *Peritia* 12, pp. 177–208.

Ó Cróinín, D. 1995 *Early Medieval Ireland 400–1200* (London: Routledge).

Odenstedt, B. 1990 *On the Origin and Early History of the Runic Script: Typology and Graphic Variation in the Older Futhark* (Stockholm: Almqvist and Wiksell).

O'Driscoll, J. and Noble, G. 2019 'Geophysical Survey at Dunkeld, Perth and Kinross' (unpublished Data Structure Report, University of Aberdeen).

Ó Floinn, R. 1989 'Secular metalwork in the eighth and ninth centuries', in Youngs 1989b, pp. 170–213.

Oggins, R. S. 2004 *The Kings and Their Hawks: Falconry in Medieval England* (Yale, CT: Yale University Press).

O'Grady, O. J. T. 2008 'The setting and practice of open-air judicial assemblies in medieval Scotland: a multidisciplinary study' (unpublished PhD thesis, University of Glasgow).

O'Grady, O. J. T. 2011 'Culdee Archaeology Project (Pilot Phase 2): Fortingall, Glen Lyon, Perth and Kinross: Geophysical Survey and Trial Excavation' (unpublished Data Structure Report).

O'Grady, O. J. T. 2014 'Judicial assembly sites in Scotland: archaeological and place-name evidence of the Scottish court hill', *Medieval Archaeology* 58, pp. 104–35.

O'Grady, O. J. T. 2018 'Accumulating Kingship: the archaeology of elite assembly in medieval Scotland', *World Archaeology* 50(1), pp. 137–49.

Okasha, E. 1985 'The non-Ogam Inscriptions of Pictland', *Cambridge Medieval Celtic Studies* 9, pp. 43–69.

Ó Maolalaigh, R. 2019 'Gaelic Personal Names and Name Elements in Scottish Charters, 1093–1286', in Hammond 2019, pp. 41–99.

Oosthuizen, Susan, 2011 'Archaeology, common rights and the origins of Anglo-Saxon identity, *Early Medieval Europe* 19(2), pp. 153–81.

Oram, R. 2007 'Capital tales or Burghead bull?' in S. Arbuthnot and K. Hollo (eds) 2007, pp. 241–62.

Ó Riain, P. 2011 *A Dictionary of Irish Saints* (Dublin: Four Courts Press).

O'Sullivan, A. 2008 'Early medieval houses in Ireland: social identity and dwelling spaces', *Peritia* 20, pp. 225–56.

O'Sullivan, A., McCormick, F., Kerr, T. R. and Harney, L. 2014 *Early Medieval Ireland AD 400–1100: The Evidence from Archaeological Excavation* (Dublin: Royal Irish Academy Monograph).

Outram, Z. 2021 'The radiocarbon dating reconsidered', in Morris 2021, pp. 140–41.

Outram, Z. and Batt, C. 2010 'Dating at Old Scatness' in Dockrill *et al.* 2010, pp. 161–204

Owen, O. and Lowe, C. 1999 *Kebister: The Four-thousand-year-old Story of One Shetland Township* (Edinburgh: Society of Antiquaries of Scotland).

Painter, K. 2013 'Hacksilber: a means of exchange', in Hunter and Painter 2013, pp. 215–42.

Pantos, A. and Semple, S. J. (eds) 2004 *Assembly Places and Practices in Medieval Europe* (Dublin: Four Courts Press).

Parker Pearson, M. 2018 'The Pictish Burial Cairn, cal AD 640–780', in Parker Pearson, Brennand, Mulville and Smith 2018, pp. 21–41.

Parker Pearson, M. and Sharples, N. 1999 *Between Land and Sea: Excavations at Dun Vulan* (Sheffield: Sheffield Academic Press).

Parker Pearson, M., Brennand, M., Mulville, J. and Smith, H. 2018 *Cille Pheadair: a Norse farmstead and Pictish cairn in South Uist*, SEARCH vol. 7 (Oxford: Oxbow).

Peteranna, M. and Birch, S. 2018 'Storm Damage at Craig Phadrig Hillfort, Inverness: Results of the Emergency Archaeological Evaluation', *PSAS* 148, pp. 61–81.

Peters, C. N. 2016 'Translating Food Shortages in the Irish Chronicles, A.D. 500–1170', *Cambrian Medieval Celtic Studies* 71, pp. 29–58.

Phillips, E., McMillan, M. and Forty, N. 2003 'The geology of the Stone of Destiny', in Welander, Clancy and Breeze 2003, pp. 33–40.

Plumb, O. 2020 *Picts and Britons in the Early Medieval Irish Church* (Turnhout: Brepols).

Price, N. 2002 *The Viking Way: Religion and War in Late Iron Age Scandinavia* (Uppsala: Department of Archaeology and Ancient History, University of Uppsala).

Proudfoot, E. 1996 'Excavations at the long cist cemetery on the Hallow Hill, St Andrews, Fife', *PSAS* 126, pp. 387–454.

Proudfoot, E. 1997 'Abernethy and Mugdrum: towards reassessment', in Henry 1997, pp. 47–63.

Radford, C. A. R. 1959 *The Early Christian and Norse Settlements at Birsay, Orkney* (Edinburgh: RCAHMS).

Rae, A. and Rae, V. 1953 'A bowl barrow at Pityoulish, in Strathspey', *PSAS* 87, pp. 153–60.

Rahtz, P. A. 1978 'Grave Orientation', *Archaeological Journal* 135, pp. 1–14.

Rains, M. and Hall, D. W. (eds) 1997 *Excavations in St Andrews 1980–89: A Decade of Archaeology in a Historic Scottish Burgh* (Glenrothes: Tayside and Fife Archaeological Committee Monograph).

Ralston, I. B. M. 1980 'The Green Castle and the promontory forts of North-East Scotland', *Scottish Archaeological Forum* 10, pp. 27–40.

Ralston, I. B. M. 1987 'Portknockie: promontory forts and Pictish settlement in the North-East', in Small 1987, pp. 15–26.

Ralston, I. B. M. 1997 'Pictish homes', in Henry 1997, pp. 18–34.

Ralston I. B. M. 2004 *The Hill-forts of Pictland since 'The Problem of the Picts'* (Rosemarkie: Groam House Museum).

Ralston, I. B. M. 2015 'The hillforts and enclosed settlements of Scotland: an overview', in Hunter and Ralston 2015, pp. 201–10.

Ralston, I. B. M. 2019 'Going back in time: re-assessment of the timber halls at Doon Hill, Dunbar', *Transactions of the East Lothian Antiquarian and Natural History Society* 32, pp. 4–27.

Rankin, D. 1996 *Celts and the Classical World* (London: Routledge).

Rau, A. 2013 'Where did the late empire end? Hacksilber and coins in continental and northern Barbaricum', in Hunter and Painter 2013, pp. 339–58.

RCAHMS 1990 *North-East Perth: An Archaeological Landscape* (Edinburgh: HMSO).

RCAHMS 1994 *South-East Perth: An Archaeological Landscape* (Edinburgh: HMSO).

RCAHMS 2007 *In the Shadow of Bennachie: A Field Archaeology of Donside, Aberdeenshire* (Edinburgh: RCAHMS).

RCAHMS 2008 *The Pictish Symbol Stones of Scotland* (Edinburgh: RCAHMS).

Rees, A. 2009 'The excavation of an unenclosed settlement and an Early Historic multiple burial and metalworking area at Hawkhill, Lunan Bay, Angus', *Tayside and Fife Archaeological Journal* 15, pp. 22–72.

Reynolds, N. 1980 'Dark Age Timber Halls and the Background to Excavation at Balbridie', *Scottish Archaeological Forum* 10, pp. 55–59.

Rhys, G. 2015 'Approaching the Pictish language: historiography, early evidence and the question of Pritenic' (unpublished PhD thesis, University of Glasgow).

Rhys, G. 2020a 'The Pictish Language', *History Scotland*, pp. 16–22.

Rhys, G. 2020b 'The Non-Operation of the "New Quantity System" in Pictish', *Cambrian Medieval Celtic Studies* 79, pp. 37–45.

Rideout, J. S. 1995 'Carn Dubh, Moulin, Perthshire: survey and excavation of an archaeological landscape 1987–90', *PSAS* 125, pp. 139–95.

Ringtved, J. 1999 'The geography of power: South Scandinavia before the Danish kingdom', in Dickinson and Griffiths 1999, pp. 49–64.

Ritchie, A. 1972 'Painted Pebbles In Early Scotland', *PSAS* 104, pp. 297–301.

Ritchie, A. 1977 'Excavation of Pictish and Viking-age farmsteads at Buckquoy, Orkney', *PSAS* 108, pp. 174–227.

Ritchie, A. 1989 *Picts* (Edinburgh: HMSO).

Ritchie, A. 2003 'Paganism among the Picts and the conversion of Orkney', in Downes and Ritchie 2003, pp. 3–10.

Ritchie, A. 2011 'Cemeteries of platform cairns and long cists around Sinclair's Bay, Caithness', *PSAS* 141, pp. 125–43.

Ritchie, J. N. G. 1976 'The Stones of Stenness, Orkney', *PSAS* 107, pp. 1–60.

Rivet, A. L. F. and Smith, C. 1979 *The Place-Names of Roman Britain* (London: Batsford).

Robertson, N. M. 1997 'The Early Medieval Carved Stones of Fortingall', in Henry 1997, pp. 133–48,

Rogers, J. M. 1992 'The Formation of the Parish Unit and Community in Perthshire' (unpublished PhD thesis, University of Edinburgh)

Ross, A. 1999 'Pictish matriliny?', *Northern Studies* 34, pp. 11–22.

Ross, A. 2011 *The Kings of Alba* c. *1000*–c. *1130* (Edinburgh: John Donald).

Ross, A. 2015, *Land Assessment and Lordship in Medieval Northern Scotland* (Turnhout: Brepols).

Roy, W. 1793 *Military Antiquities of the Romans in North Britain*: https://maps.nls.uk/roy/antiquities/.

Russell, N. 2012 *Social Zooarchaeology: Humans and Animals in Prehistory* (Cambridge: Cambridge University Press).

Samson, R. 1992 'The reinterpretation of the Pictish symbols', *Journal of the British Archaeological Association* 145, pp. 29–65.

Scott, I. G. and Ritchie, A. 2009 *Pictish and Viking-Age carvings from Shetland* (Edinburgh: RCAHMS).

Scott, I. G. and Ritchie, A. 2014 'Pictish symbol stones and early cross-slabs from Orkney', *PSAS* 144, pp. 169–204.

Scragg, D. (ed.) 1991 *The Battle of Maldon* AD *991* (Oxford: Basil Blackwell).

Scull, C. 2009 *Early Medieval (Late 5th–Early 8th Centuries* AD*) Cemeteries at Boss Hall and Buttermarket, Ipswich, Suffolk*, Society for Medieval Archaeology Monograph 27 (London: Society for Medieval Archaeology).

Seaman, A. P. 2006 'Conversion, Christianity and the Late Roman Transition in South-East Wales', *Archaeologia Cambrensis* 155, pp. 137–42.

Seaman, A. P. 2014 '*Tempora Christiana*? Conversion and Christianization in Western Britain AD 300–700', *Church Archaeology* 16, pp. 1–22.

Sellevold, B. J. 2010 'Life and death among the Picts and Vikings at Westness', in Sheehan and Ó Corráin 2010, pp. 369–79.

Semple, S. J. 2013 *Perceptions of the Prehistoric in Anglo-Saxon England: Religion, Ritual and Rulership in the Landscape* (Oxford: Oxford University Press).

Semple, S. J. and Sanmark, A. 2013 'Assembly in North West Europe: collective concerns for early societies?', *Journal of European Archaeology* 16(3), pp. 518–42.

Semple, S. J., Sanmark, A., Iversen, F. and Mehler, N. 2021 *Negotiating the North: Meeting-places in the Middle Ages in the North Sea Zone* (London: Society for Medieval Archaeology Monograph 41).

Sharples, N. 1998 *Scalloway: A Broch, Late Iron Age Settlement and Medieval Cemetery in Shetland* (Oxford: Oxbow).

Sharples, N. (ed.) 2019 *The Economy of a Norse Settlement in the Outer Hebrides: Excavations at mounds 2 and 2A Bornais, South Uist* (Oxford: Oxbow Books).

Sheehan, J. and Ó Corráin, D. (eds), *The Viking Age in Ireland and the West* (Dublin: Four Courts Press).

Shepherd, A. 1994 'Howe: A Review of the Sequence', in Ballin Smith 1994, pp. 267–89.

Shepherd, I. A. G. 1993 'The Picts in Moray', in W. D. H. Sellar (ed.), *Moray: Province and People* (Edinburgh: Scottish Society for Northern Studies), pp. 75–90.

Sheridan, A. 2004 'The National Museums Of Scotland Radiocarbon Dating Programmes: Results Obtained During 2003/4', *Discovery and Excavation Scotland*, pp. 174–76

Sheridan, J. A. S. *et al.* 2019 'Scottish Archaeological Radiocarbon Dates Associated with National Museums Scotland, 2018/9', *Discovery and Excavation Scotland*, pp. 226–27.

Sinfield, L. 2005 'Human Remains', in Alexander 2005, pp. 201–04.

Small, A. 1969 'Burghead', *Scottish Archaeological Forum* 1, pp. 61–69.

Small A. (ed.) 1987 *The Picts: A New Look at Old Problems* (Dundee: University of Dundee).

Small, A. and Cottam, M. B. 1972 'Craig Phadrig', Department of Geography Occasional Paper 1 (Dundee: University of Dundee).

Small, A., Thomas, C. and Wilson, D. M. 1973 *St Ninian's Isle and its treasure*, 2 vols, Aberdeen University Studies 152 (Oxford: Oxford University Press).

Smart, I. H. M. and Campbell-Wilson, M. 2000 'Analysis of Human Remains Immediately Following Excavations in 1965–6', in Greig *et al.* 2000, pp. 601–02.

Smith, B. 2001, 'The Picts and the Martyrs or Did Vikings Kill the Native Population of Orkney and Shetland?', *Northern Studies* 36, pp. 7–32.

Sneddon, D. 2018 'Adomnán of Iona's Vita Sancti Columbae: a literary analysis' (unpublished PhD thesis, University of Edinburgh).

Southern, P. 1996 'Men and mountains, or geographical determinism and the conquest of Scotland', *PSAS* 126, pp. 371–86.

Spearman, R. M. and Higgitt, J. (eds) 1993 *The Age of Migrating Ideas: Early Medieval Art in Northern Britain and Ireland* (Edinburgh: National Museums Scotland).

Sproat, R. 2010 'Ancient symbols, computational linguistics, and the reviewing practices of the general science journals', *Computational Linguistics* 36(3), pp. 585–94.

Stanton, L. 2018 'The Northernmost Picts: A Synthesis of the Archaeological Evidence for Pictish Orkney and Shetland' (unpublished MSc dissertation, University of Aberdeen).

Stevenson, J. B. 1984, 'Garbeg and Whitebridge: two square-barrow cemeteries in Inverness-shire', in Friell and Watson 1984, pp. 145–50.

Stevenson, R. B. K. 1952 'Long cist burials, particularly those at Galson (Lewis) and Gairloch (Wester Ross) with a symbol stone at Gairloch', *PSAS* 86, pp. 106–15.

Stevenson, R. B. K. 1955 'Pictish art', in Wainwright 1955, pp. 97–128.

Stevenson, R. B. K. 1971 'Sculpture in Scotland in the 6th–9th centuries AD', in V. Milojcic (ed.) 1971, *Kolloquium über spätantike und frühmittelalterliche Skulptur* 2 (Mainz: Heidelberg), pp. 65–74.

Stevenson, R. B. K. 1993 'Further thoughts on some well-known problems' in Spearman and Higgitt 1993, pp. 16–26.

Stewart, M. E. C. 1969 'The Ring Forts of Central Perthshire', *Proceedings and Transactions of the Perthshire Society for Natural Science* 12, pp. 21–32.

Strachan, D. 2013 *Excavations at the Black Spout, Pitlochry and the Iron Age Monumental Roundhouses of North West Perthshire* (Perth: Perth and Kinross Heritage Trust).

Strachan, D., Sneddon, D. and Tipping, R. (eds) 2019 *Early Medieval Settlement in Upland Perthshire: Excavations at Lair, Glen Shee 2012–17* (Oxford: Archaeopress).

Stuart, J. 1867 *Sculptured Stones of Scotland*, vol. 2 (Aberdeen: Spalding Club).

Swift, C. 1997 *Ogam Stones and the Earliest Irish Christians* (Maynooth: Maynooth Monograph Series Minor 2).

Swift, C. 1998 'Forts and fields: a study of "monastic towns" in seventh and eighth century Ireland', *Journal of Irish Archaeology* 9, pp. 105–25.

Swift, C. 2013 *Pictish Brooches and Pictish Hens: Status and Currency in Early Scotland* (Rosemarkie: Groam House Museum).

Taylor, A. 2009 '*Leges Scocie* and the Lawcodes of David I, William the Lion and Alexander II', *Scottish Historical Review* 88, pp. 207–88.

Taylor, A. 2016 *The Shape of the State in Medieval Scotland 1124–1290* (Oxford: Oxford University Press).

Taylor, D. B. 1990 *Circular Homesteads in North West Perthshire*, Abertay Historical Society publication no. 29 (Dundee: Abertay Historical Society).

Taylor, S. 1995 'The Scandinavians in Fife and Kinross: the onomastic evidence', in Crawford 1995, pp. 141–68.

Taylor, S. 1996 'Place-Names and the Early Church in Eastern Scotland', in Crawford 1996, pp. 93–110.

Taylor, S. 1997 'Seventh-century Iona abbots in Scottish place-names', *Innes Review* 48(1), pp. 45–72.

Taylor, S. 2000a 'Columba east of Drumalban: some aspects of the cult of Columba in eastern Scotland', *Innes Review* 51(2), pp. 109–30.

Taylor, S. (ed.) 2000b *Kings, Clerics and Chronicles in Scotland 500–1297: Essays in Honour of Marjorie Ogilvie Anderson on the Occasion of her Ninetieth Birthday* (Dublin: Four Courts Press)

Taylor, S. 2000c 'The coming of the Augustinians to St Andrews and version B of the St Andrews foundation legend', in Taylor 2000b, pp. 115–23.

Taylor, S. 2004 'Scandinavians in Central Scotland – bý-place-names and their context', in G. Williams and P. Bibire (eds), *Sagas, Saints and Settlements* (Leiden: Brill), pp. 125–45.

Taylor, S. 2005 'The Abernethy Foundation Account and its Place-Names', *History Scotland* July/Aug 2005, pp. 14–16.

Taylor, S. 2011 'Pictish Place-names Revisited', in Driscoll *et al.* 2011, pp. 67–118.

Taylor, S. 2017 'St Vigeans: Place, Place-names and Saints' in Geddes 2017, pp. 38–51.

Taylor, S. (forthcoming) *Fortrose, Fortriu and the Place-names of Northern Pictland* (Rosemarkie: Groam House Museum).

Taylor, S. with Clancy, T. O., McNiven, P. and Williamson, E. 2020 *The Place-Names of Clackmannanshire* (Donington: Shaun Tyas).

Taylor, S. with Márkus, G. 2008 *The Place-Names of Fife. Volume Two: Central Fife between the Rivers Leven and Eden* (Donington: Shaun Tyas).

Taylor, S. with Márkus, G. 2009 *The Place-Names of Fife. Volume Three: St Andrews and the East Neuk* (Donington: Shaun Tyas).

Taylor, S. with Márkus, G. 2010 *The Place-Names of Fife. Volume Four: North Fife between Eden and Tay* (Donington: Shaun Tyas).

Taylor, S. with Márkus, G. 2012 *The Place-Names of Fife. Volume Five: Discussion, Glossaries and Edited Texts, with Addenda and Corrigenda of Volumes 1–4* (Donington: Shaun Tyas).

Thickpenny, C. R. 2019 'Abstract pattern on stone fragments from Applecross: the master carver of northern Pictland?', *PSAS* 148, pp. 147–76.

Thomas, A. C. 1971 *The Early Christian Archaeology of North Britain: the Hunter Marshall Lectures delivered at the University of Glasgow in January and February 1968* (Oxford: Oxford University Press for University of Glasgow).

Thomas, C. 1961 'The animal art of the Scottish Iron Age and its origins', *Archaeological Journal* 117, pp. 14–64.

Thomas, C. 1963 'The interpretation of the Pictish symbols', *Archaeological Journal* 120, pp. 31–64.

Thomas, G. 2018 'Mead-halls of the Oiscingas: a new Kentish perspective on the Anglo-Saxon great hall complex phenomenon', *Medieval Archaeology* 62(2), pp. 262–303.

Thomson, A. 1859 'Notice of Sculptured Stones found at "Dinnacair", near Stonehaven', *PSAS* 3, pp. 69–75.

Tipping, R. 1994 'The form and the fate of Scotland's woodlands', *PSAS* 124, pp. 1–54.

Toolis, R. and Bowles, C. 2016 *The Lost Dark Age Kingdom of Rheged: the Discovery of a Royal Stronghold at Trusty's Hill, Galloway* (Oxford: Oxbow Books).

Traill, W. 1890 'Results of Excavations at the Broch of Burrian, North Ronaldsay, Orkney, during the summers of 1870 and 1871', *Archaeologia Scotica* 5, pp. 341–64.

Tucker, F. and Armit, I. 2009 'Human Remains from Iron Age Atlantic Scotland Dating Project: results obtained during 2009', *Discovery and Excavation in Scotland* 10, pp. 214–16.

Turner, V. 1994 'The Mail stone: an incised Pictish figure from Mail, Cunningsburgh, Shetland', *PSAS* 124, pp. 315–25.

Turner, V. E. and Owen, O. 2013 'The Legacy of the Viking Unst Project', in Turner, Bond and Larsen 2013, pp. 234–52.

Turner, V. E., Bond, J. M. and Larsen, A.-C. (eds) 2013 *Viking Unst: Excavation and Survey in Northern Shetland 2006–2010* (Lerwick: Shetland Heritage Publications).

University of Edinburgh 2007 Database of Dedications to Saints in Medieval Scotland: https://saints.shca.ed.ac.uk/ (accessed 14 Feb 2022).

Valante, M. A. 1998 'Reassessing the Irish monastic town', *Irish Historical Studies* 31, pp. 1–18.

Veitch, K. 1997 'The Columban Church in northern Britain, 664–717: a reassessment', *PSAS* 17, pp. 627–47.

Wainwright, F. T. (ed.) 1955a *The Problem of the Picts* (Edinburgh: Nelson; reprinted 1980, Perth: Melven Press).

Wainwright, F. T. 1955b 'Houses and graves', in Wainwright 1955a, pp. 87–96.

Wainwright, F. T. (ed.) 1962 *The Northern Isles* (Edinburgh: Nelson).

Walther, L., Montgomery, J. and Evans, J. 2016 'Combined strontium and oxygen isotope data at Portmahomack', in Carver *et al.* 2016, Digest 4.4.

Watson, R. R. B. 1929 'Note on a Celtic Bell found at Mare's Craig, near Newburgh', *Transactions of the Perthshire Society Natural Science* 7(6), pp. 149–52.

Watson, W. J. 1926 *The Celtic Place-Names of Scotland* (Edinburgh: William Blackwood; reprinted with an introduction by Simon Taylor, Edinburgh: Birlinn, 2004).
Waugh, D. 1993 'Caithness: An Onomastic Frontier Zone', in Batey, Jesch and Morris 1993, pp. 120–28.
Waugh, D. 2009 'Caithness: Another Dip in the Sweerag Well', in Woolf 2009, pp. 31–48.
Wedderburn, L. M. and Grime, D. 1984 'The cairn cemetery at Garbeg, Drumnadrochit', in Friell and Watson 1984, pp. 151–68.
Welander, R., Clancy, T. O. and Breeze, D. J. (eds), *The Stone of Destiny: Artefact and Icon* (Edinburgh: Society of Antiquaries of Scotland).
Welch, M. 2011 'The Mid Saxon "Final Phase"', in Hamerow *et al.* 2011, pp. 266–87.
Whitfield, N. 2004 'More thoughts on the wearing of brooches in early medieval Ireland', in C. Hourihane (ed.), *Irish art historical studies in honour of Peter Harbison* (Dublin: Four Courts Press), pp. 70–108.
Wickham, C. 2009 *The Inheritance of Rome: A History of Europe from 400 to 1000* (London: Allen Lane).
Will, R. S., Forsyth, K., Clancy, T. O. and Charles-Edwards, G. 2003 'An eighth-century inscribed cross-slab in Dull, Perthshire', *Scottish Archaeological Journal* 25(1), pp. 57–71.
Williams, H. 2007 'Depicting the dead: commemoration through cists, cairns and symbols in early medieval Britain', *Cambridge Archaeological Journal* 17(2), pp. 145–64.
Williams, M. 2003 'Growing Metaphors: The Agricultural Cycle as Metaphor in the Later Prehistoric Period of Britain and North-Western Europe', *Journal of Social Archaeology* 3(2), pp. 223–55.
Wilson, D. M. 1973 'The treasure', in Small, Thomas and Wilson 1973, pp. 45–148.
Winlow, S. 2011 'A review of Pictish burial practices in Tayside and Fife', in Driscoll *et al.* 2011, pp. 335–50.
Winlow, S. and Cook, G. 2010 'Two new dates from two old investigations: a reconsideration of The Women's Knowe, Inchtuthil and Kingoodie long cist cemetery, Invergowrie', *Tayside and Fife Archaeological Journal* 16, pp. 4–56.
Woodham, A. A. 1975 'Tillytarmont cairn', *Discovery and Excavation in Scotland*, p. 6.
Woolf, A. 1998 'Pictish matriliny reconsidered', *Innes Review* 49, pp. 147–67.
Woolf, A. 2000, 'The "Moray Question" and the kingship of Alba in the tenth and eleventh centuries', *Scottish Historical Review* 79, pp. 145–64.
Woolf, A. 2006 'Dún Nechtain, Fortriu and the Geography of the Picts', *Scottish Historical Review* 85, pp. 182–201.
Woolf, A. 2007a *From Pictland to Alba, 789–1070*, New Edinburgh History of Scotland 2 (Edinburgh: Edinburgh University Press).
Woolf, A. 2007b 'The cult of Moluag, the see of Mortlach and Church organisation in northern Scotland in the eleventh and twelfth centuries', in Arbuthnot and Hollo 2007, pp. 311–22.
Woolf A. (ed.) 2009 *Scandinavian Scotland – Twenty Years After* (St Andrews: Committee for Dark Age Studies, University of St Andrews).
Woolf, A. 2013 *The Churches of Pictavia*, Kathleen Hughes Memorial Lecture 11 (Cambridge: Department of Anglo-Saxon, Norse and Celtic, University of Cambridge).
Woolf, A. 2017a 'Review of Alasdair Ross, *Land Assessment and Lordship in Medieval Northern Scotland*', *Scottish Historical Review* 96(1), pp. 110–12.
Woolf, A. 2017b 'On the Nature of the Picts', *Scottish Historical Review* 96(2), pp. 214–17.
Wormald, P. 1996 'The emergence of the *Regnum Scottorum*: a Carolingian hegemony?', in Crawford 1996, pp. 131–60.
Young, A. 1996 'The Skeletal Material', in Proudfoot 1996, pp. 429–31.
Young, H. W. 1890 'The ancient bath at Burghead, with remarks on its origin, as shown by existing baths of the same shape and design', *PSAS* 24, pp. 147–56.
Young, H. W. 1891 'Notes on the ramparts of Burghead, as revealed by recent excavations', *PSAS* 25, pp. 435–47.
Young, H. W. 1893 'Notes on further excavations at Burghead', *PSAS* 27, pp. 86–91.
Youngs, S. 1989a 'Fine metalwork to c. AD 650', in Youngs 1989b, pp. 20–71.
Youngs, S. (ed.) 1989b *The Work of Angels: Masterpieces of Celtic Metalwork, 6th–9th Centuries* AD (London: British Museum Press).
Youngs, S. 2007 'Britain, Wales and Ireland: holding things together', in K. Jankulak and J. Wooding (eds), *Ireland and Wales in the Middle Ages* (Dublin: Four Courts Press), pp. 80–101.
Youngs, S. 2013 'From chains to brooches: the uses and hoarding of silver in north Britain in the Early Historic period' in Hunter and Painter 2013, pp. 403–26.

Sites to Visit

Below is a list of sites from Fife to Shetland to visit. Canmore is the searchable online catalogue of the National Record of the Historic Environment and each site featured or the nearest landmark to it – for example, a parish church – has its own Canmore number. More information on a specific site can be obtained by entering its number at https://canmore.org.uk. The Canmore number is followed by an OS map grid reference.

Aberdeenshire

Canmore 18978, NJ 70378 24714
Chapel of Garioch To the north-west of Inverurie is the Maiden Stone, perhaps Aberdeenshire's most impressive Pictish stone. The tall, pink granite slab has an elaborate but faded ring-headed cross with a human figure and two fish monsters above on one face and a series of figures and symbols on the reverse. These include the mirror and comb on the bottom, a Pictish beast, a notched rectangle and Z-rod, and a group of centaurs and other four-legged beasts. The stone stands in the shadow of the Pictish fort, Mither Tap o' Bennachie.

Canmore 19464, NJ 8752 1541
Dyce There are a number of Pictish symbol stones and carved crosses at St Fergus' Church indicating that this was an important site in the early medieval period and the focus of an early church. The stones include one with symbols only – a Pictish beast and double disc and Z-rod. Another has an elaborate interlaced cross with a crescent and V-rod and triple disc on the left and a double disc and Z-rod and mirror case on the right. There is also an ogham inscription on the side of this stone. The others are simple cross-inscribed stones. The stones are within a recess in the ruined chapel.

Canmore 18294, NJ 60994 30259
Insch Just over a mile to the north-west of Insch stands the Picardy Stone, an imposing pillar of whinstone with prominent veins of quartz. On one face are a mirror, snake and Z-rod and a double disc and Z-rod. Fine views of Dunnideer hillfort can be obtained from here.

Canmore 18894, NJ 75992 22403
Inverurie Now in the middle of a housing estate, the Brandsbutt stone was broken up for a field dyke in the 19th century but is now re-assembled and redisplayed. It has a crescent and V-rod, a serpent and Z-rod and an ogham inscription on the front. The stone may have been associated with and reused from a Late Neolithic or Bronze Age stone circle that stood nearby.

Canmore 18872, NJ 78043 20611
Inverurie Kirkyard Four symbol stones are displayed near the motte here. All but one – a charismatic horse carved on a small standing stone – are damaged. The other three have the more abstract symbols including double discs and a crescent and V-rod, although a serpent does make an appearance on the largest stone of the three.

Canmore 17199, NJ 49749 26345 and 17219, NJ 4992 2649
Rhynie The Craw Stane is a block of granite that sits on top of a prominent rise just to the west of Rhynie churchyard. A salmon and a Pictish beast are carved on one side. Further stones can be found in a shelter built near the churchyard on the outskirts of the village down by the Water of Bogie. These are part of a group of eight stones known from Rhynie that include the fearsome axe-wielding Rhynie Man, who now stands in the foyer of Aberdeenshire Council's building, Woodhill House in Aberdeen. The village of Rhynie is overlooked by Tap o' Noth, a stern walk up the steep hill rewards the hardy hillwalker with magnificent views from the Iron Age summit fort.

Canmore 229637, NO 39050 97548
Tullich A Pictish symbol stone and cross-incised slabs can be found in the churchyard of St Nathalan's Kirk. These relate to an important early church site of the early medieval period.

Angus

Canmore 34806, NO 52239 55554
Aberlemno Within the grounds of Aberlemno Church stands a huge cross-slab with the elaborate battle scene featured in Chapter 3. Nearby, along the roadside that leads though the village centre, are three other Pictish monuments including two symbol stones and another magnificent cross-slab.

Canmore 33868, NO 40083 50019
Cossans Standing in situ towards the edge of a former area of wetland, St Orland's Stone is a cross-slab that includes the depiction of a Pictish rowing boat – a rare representation of a boat in early medieval sculpture in Scotland.

Canmore 32092, NO 3526 4745
Eassie A wonderful cross-slab now housed in a purpose-built shelter within the ruins of Eassie Old Parish Church. The stone features an interlace and a key-pattern decorated cross on one side along with a hunter carrying a spear, the hunter's prey and a dog, and two other figures, one an angel. The back has two Pictish symbols, figures processing left to right, a tree and cattle.

Canmore 35559, NO 63842 42912
St Vigeans St Vigeans Church sits dramatically atop a steep glacial knoll. Over 30 monuments and fragments including numerous cross-slabs, a house shrine, recumbent grave-markers and a free-standing cross, all likely to be of 8th- to 9th-century date, are known from St Vigeans. The majority of monuments are held within St Vigeans museum, generally only open by appointment, but some monuments are built into the walls of the church itself and the setting of the church mound is worth seeing in its own right.

Fife

Canmore 29881, NO 24422 06192
East Lomond Fort East Lomond was a complex Roman Iron Age and Pictish era fort and settlement. The summit fort comprises a sub-oval enclosure with two lower ramparts encircling the hill and a massive rampart and ditch on the south-west. Recent excavations on terraces below the fort have identified extensive buildings and finds from the Roman Iron Age to 7th century AD in date.

Canmore 53979, NT 3456 9723
East Wemyss The caves on the south Fife coast at East Wemyss hold a remarkable series of Pictish-style carvings. These are now most easily seen in two caves today – Jonathan's Cave and Court Cave – but other caves have symbols and more have been lost to cave collapse and erosion. The caves are looked after by the Save Wemyss Ancient Caves Society (SWACS) which arranges regular tours to the caves – https://wemysscaves.org.

Canmore 34299, NO 51415 16687
St Andrews Cathedral Over 80 pieces of early medieval sculpture are known from St Andrews and a number can be seen in the visitor centre in the cathedral including the magnificent St Andrew's shrine.

Highlands

Canmore 11740, NG 71355 45838
Applecross, Wester Ross A monastery was founded here by Máel Ruba of Bangor, Co. Down, Ireland, in 672. At the site today, the ruins of the 19th-century parish church stand in a modern burial ground. Within the grounds of the church is a tall, plain cross-slab. A much more impressively decorated cross-slab is represented by a series of richly decorated fragments that can be seen in the Applecross Heritage Centre.

NH 54954 58772
Dingwall Only discovered in 2019, the Conan Stone is now on display in the Dingwall Museum. The stone is richly decorated with a Christian cross protected by two massive beast heads and on the reverse are Pictish symbols including a crescent and V-rod, a hippocamp and an animal-headed warrior wielding a sword and shield.

Canmore 7328, NC 9673 6482
Reay, Caithness Near Reay Parish Church stands an older church with the remains of a burial aisle of a local family, the MacKays of Bighouse. Within the aisle is a much earlier monument, a rectangular cross-slab of grey sandstone, almost 2m high. The cross is decorated with knotwork and key pattern and is probably of a 9th-century date.

Canmore 12458, NH 4845 5852
Strathpeffer, Ross and Cromarty The Clach an Tiompain or the Eagle Stone is a striking Pictish symbol stone incised with an arch and an eagle. The stone stands on a small mound near the main road through the village of Strathpeffer with wonderful views down the strath towards Dingwall.

Inverness-shire and Easter Ross

Canmore 14653, NH 70833 85074
Edderton Here, an impressively tall standing stone called the Clach Chairidh – the 'pointed stone' – can be found. The stone may have originally been erected in the Bronze Age but bears on one face a salmon and double disc and Z-rod symbols. The stone was recorded in the 18th century as standing on a circular mound of earth which has now largely disappeared. At nearby Old Edderton Parish Church is an impressive cross-slab with a ring-headed cross on one side and three riders on the other side.

Canmore 13486, NH 6400 4527
Inverness Originally built in the Iron Age, Craig Phadrig is an impressive fort overlooking Inverness. The site was reoccupied in the Pictish period. Excavations in 1971 uncovered fragments of moulds and imported pottery dating to the 7th century AD. The site is one of the likely candidates for being the fort of king Bridei, whom Columba visited in the late 6th century at Bridei's fort at the head of the River Ness.

Canmore 13507, NH 6567 4134
Knocknagael Until the 1990s, this huge slab of slate, known as the Boar Stone, stood in a field on the farm of Knocknagael to the south of Inverness. With its impressive carving of a boar and a mirror case, the stone now stands in the foyer of the Highland Council Headquarters, Glenurquhart Road, Inverness.

Canmore 15280, NH 8045 7171
Nigg One of a series of elaborately decorated cross-slabs from the Tarbat peninsula, the Nigg Stone is located in the present-day church. It displays on one side an impressively carved cross with representations of St Paul and St Anthony above the cross. On the back are scenes from the story of David and a series of Pictish symbols.

Canmore 15278, NH 85544 74718
Shandwick The imposing monument Clach a' Charridh stands in a glass box overlooking a beautiful sandy bay. The front has a cross that is decorated with carved spiral bosses and on the back is an elaborate hunting scene with incredible panels of spirals, interlace and key pattern.

Islands

Canmore 1796, HY 23977 28513
Brough of Birsay, Orkney The main centre for the Norse earldom of Orkney in later centuries, its role may have been due to its elite status in the Pictish period. Pictish finds from this tidal islet include a magnificent carved stone monument showing three warriors armed with spears and shields and four Pictish symbols above, cross-incised stones and a portable cross-slab. The standing stone on site is a replica as the original is in the National Museum of Scotland. Settlement remains from the adjacent Mainland at Saever Howe and Buckquoy suggest further important Pictish foci in the Birsay area.

Canmore 2201, HY 38179 26850
Gurness, Orkney One of the most spectacular visitor sites in Scotland is the Broch of Gurness, a multi-period prehistoric to Viking Age settlement on Mainland Orkney. The later phases of Gurness included the development of rectilinear dwellings outside the broch entrance in the early centuries AD which, in turn, were replaced by a series of cellular buildings, including a shamrock-style building with an oval central room with a series of small cells opening from it. A large rectangular building attached to the north-east side of the shamrock building may also belong to this phase too. A small Pictish symbol stone can be seen in the little visitor centre.

Canmore 513, HU 39819 09551
Jarlshof, Shetland At Jarlshof, the late first millennium AD settlement was dominated by impressive wheelhouse-style buildings that were built within an earlier courtyard attached to an Iron Age broch tower. At least three wheelhouses were constructed and a wheelhouse-style building may have been inserted into the broch too. Late additions to the settlement at Jarlshof were the so-called passage-houses and other cellular types of building. Wheelhouse 2 at Jarlshof is one of the best-preserved buildings of the Pictish period with the corbelled roof of the building and cells still partly in place.

Canmore 556, HU 3898 1065
Old Scatness, Shetland One of the most important sites for elucidating first millennium AD settlement transitions in Shetland is Old Scatness, near the southern tip of Mainland Shetland, now a visitor centre managed by the Shetland Amenity Trust. The site includes Pictish-era wheelhouses, roundhouses and cellular structures.

Canmore 11475, NG 5467 3677
Raasay In the grounds of Raasay House, on the Isle of Raasay, stands a striking cross-slab with incised cross-of-arcs depicted atop of a slender cusped shaft. Below are the tuning fork and crescent and V-rod symbols. There is a similar cross carved on a rock outcrop nearby.

Canmore 587, HU 3685 2090
St Ninian's Isle, Shetland St Ninian's Isle is linked to Mainland Shetland by a spectacular sand bar. Excavations in the 1950s found traces of an early chapel, of probable 7th- to 9th-century AD date, below the ruins of later church buildings. The St Ninian's Isle hoard of silver vessels, brooches and pieces of weaponry came from an early phase of the church. A cemetery of long cists and dug graves was associated with the early church, along with fragments of at least two composite shrines, ten cross-marked slabs, an ogham stone, a cruciform-shaped stone and a recumbent grave-marker.

Canmore 11276, NG 4210 4908
Tote, Skye Not far from Dunvegan Castle in the village of Tote on Skye is Clach Ard, a symbol stone with a crescent and V-rod, a double disc and Z-rod and a mirror and comb.

Moray

Canmore 15529, NH 98425 57665
Brodie Positioned by the driveway at the entrance to Brodie Castle is Rodney's Stone. This symbol stone was originally found during excavations of the foundations for Dyke Church in 1781. It bears, on one face, an elaborately carved interlaced cross and, on the back, two fish monsters, a Pictish beast and a double disc and Z-rod. On the sides and back is the longest ogham inscription in Pictland, which includes the name EDDARRNON. The inscription may be a dedication.

Canmore 16146, NJ 1090 6914
Burghead At Burghead lie the remains of a very substantial promontory fort. The complex defences included a triple rampart cutting the promontory off from the headland and an upper and lower enclosure within. Excavations and radiocarbon dating suggest the fort was in use from the 6th century AD to the 10th. Six carved stones of bulls from a much larger group found in the 19th century survive. Additional sculpture found near the churchyard and around, including fragments of a cross-slab and shrine, indicate an important Christian establishment here in the later first millennium AD. Within the fort is an impressive rock-cut well. Some of the stones can be seen in the visitor centre at the end of the promontory.

Canmore 16278, NJ 1750 7072
Covesea The most well-known of the Covesea caves is Sculptor's Cave. Here, carved into the rock, are Pictish symbols that include a fish, a crescent and V-rod, stars and a keyhole shape. The symbols are found near the mouths of the two entrance passages seemingly marking the transition between outside and in. Within the cave, a substantial number of human bones have been found including remains indicative of decapitation. Late Bronze Age metalwork and Roman coins and jewellery have also been found. Take great care accessing the site as the cave is cut off at high tide.

Canmore 15785, NJ 04655 59533
Forres Sueno's Stone is a remarkable example of early medieval carving dating to the late first millennium AD. Featured in Chapter 3, it is around 6m high, carved from sandstone and displays a great battle scene on one side and an enormous ring-headed cross on the other.

Canmore 16010, NJ 18287 37599
Inveravon Four well-displayed Pictish symbol stones can be found in the foyer of Inveravon Parish Church located on a bluff above the River Spey close to its confluence with the River Avon. The symbols include an impressive eagle, a Pictish beast, a triple disc and the mirror and comb.

Perthshire

Canmore 27924, NO 18990 16392
Abernethy A Pictish symbol stone, depicting a hammer, anvils, tuning fork and a crescent and V-rod, is now displayed on the wall of one of only two Irish-style round towers known in Scotland, located at the heart of the town at the edge of the churchyard. The round tower is likely to be of 11th-century date, while the symbol stone may be of the 7th century. A small number of other Pictish stones from Abernethy can be seen in the Museum of Abernethy, located in a former 18th-century barn and stable.

Canmore 24873, NN 70819 23257
Dundurn This site is mentioned twice in Irish annals of the 7th and 9th centuries AD. Excavations in the 1970s revealed a prominent summit citadel enclosure with a series of lower enclosures on top of a craggy outcrop overlooking the upper Earn river valley. Little is evident of the fort today, other than a well and some earthworks denoting what would have been complex defences, but the site has impressive views up and down the Earn valley.

Canmore 26295, NN 94629 56530

Dunfallandy This spectacular cross-slab is unsatisfactorily displayed where it was found at an old chapel site. On one side is an imposing equal-armed cross on a shaft decorated with high relief spiral bosses, interlace and key pattern. Angels along with animals, one playing with a human head, flank the cross, the latter perhaps representing the torments of hell. On the back, lower relief carving shows two seated and one mounted figures, all three labelled with symbols – see Chapter 6. Images of power and wealth are towards the base of the stone – the hammer, anvil or crucible and tongs of the metalworker.

Canmore 27156, NO 02393 42595

Dunkeld The current cathedral was not begun until around the 13th century but it clearly sits atop a site of earlier significance. A range of early medieval sculpture is now held within the cathedral museum. Geophysical survey has indicated that the site was enclosed by a ditched vallum in the 9th century AD that enclosed an area of around 8–10 hectares.

Canmore 26683, NO 01905 14490

Dunning Originally located overlooking Forteviot around 5km to the east, the Dupplin or Constantine's Cross was moved to St Serf's Church, Dunning, in 2002 for safekeeping and conservation. The cross can be visited during the summer months. The Romanesque church tower at Dunning itself is one of the earliest surviving in Scotland and excavations at the church and in the village suggest the site was established as a major early Christian site during the 7th and 8th centuries AD.

Canmore 79662, NO 05144 17480

Forteviot This is the site of the *palatium* of Cináed mac Alpín (Kenneth mac Alpine), who died here in AD 858. At the heart of the small village today is a modern Pictish-inspired cross-slab put up in 2017 to commemorate Kenneth mac Alpine, carved by the sculptor David McGovern. Inside the church, a 9th-century handbell and fragments of early medieval sculpture can be seen when the church is open – by appointment. In the fields to the south and east lay the Pictish cemetery and an earlier prehistoric monument complex but there are no visible traces of these on the ground today.

Canmore 26195, NN 92805 24080
Fowlis Wester Within the parish church at Fowlis Wester is a magnificent cross-slab carved in relief on both sides. On one is an equal-armed cross with spiral bosses, interlace and key pattern, while on the reverse is a busy scene with multiple human figures and animals, a large double disc and Z-rod and a crescent and V-rod. A replica of the cross stands in its place in the village square. In the church is a further cross-slab and a fragment of a cross-slab, with the former displaying a ringed cross and decoration includes two enthroned figures or seated figures, their feet on footstools.

Canmore 30837, NO 28722 44558
Meigle Meigle was a 9th century royal centre. The extensive sculptural assemblage from the site includes a range of cross-slabs, grave-markers and architectural fragments which suggest the site had an important church here too. The assemblage is similar in size and range to that at St Vigeans and the museum at Meigle offers an excellent introduction to the Picts and their stone-carving.

Canmore 28191, NO 11448 26643
Scone At Moot Hill, there a large artificial mound that is thought to have been a royal assembly and ceremonial site for the kings of Alba and latterly Scotland. Kings were inaugurated on the Stone of Destiny, a block of Roman masonry atop the mound. The site is located next to Scone Palace and a former royal abbey.

Museums

Dunrobin Castle Museum, Sutherland This small museum is worth the entry fee to the castle alone. More than 20 Pictish carved stones can be seen, including examples from the castle environs itself, set within a museum that has the old-school charms and curiosity of a museum retaining its Victorian early 20th-century arrangement. The most impressive monument on show is the magnificent cross-slab from nearby Golspie which has an impressively decorated cross on one side along with Pictish symbols and an ogham inscription. The depictions on the back of the monument include a Rhynie Man style figure wielding an axe and a dagger.

Elgin Museum, Moray Situated in Elgin town centre, this is Scotland's oldest independent museum. It holds an impressive collection of Pictish sculpture including bulls from Burghead and a collection of sculpture from Kinneddar. It also has a small display on Covesea Cave. A Pictish cross-slab can also be seen at nearby Elgin Cathedral.

Groam House Museum, Black Isle, Easter Ross Located in the centre of the lovely village of Rosemarkie, on the Black Isle, north of Inverness, it holds extensive collections of Pictish sculpture including a magnificent cross-slab that was found in the floor of the old parish church.

Inverness Museum and Art Gallery This museum has a number of Pictish carved stones on display including a beautiful slab with a wolf from Ardross and one with a bull from Kingsmills.

The McManus Art Gallery and Museum, Dundee Here a range of Pictish sculpture from sites such as Dunnichen, Benvie, Aberlemno and Strathmartine is on display, along with a reconstructed long cist from Lundin Links, Fife.

Meffan Museum and Art Gallery, Forfar An excellent range of Pictish stones is on display with collections from Forfar and the Angus area.

National Museum of Scotland, Edinburgh There are wonderful Pictish collections here including the Hilton of Cadboll cross-slab, a range of Pictish symbol stones and major finds such as the Norrie's Law, Gaulcross and St Ninian's Isle hoards. Other star finds include the Monymusk reliquary and the Forteviot arch.

North Coast Visitor Centre, Thurso, Caithness The displays include three Pictish carved stone monuments including a symbol stone from Watenan and two cross-slabs from Ulbster and Skinnet.

Orkney Museum, Kirkwall, Orkney Excellent Pictish and Viking Age displays are held at Tankerness House, Kirkwall, including finds from settlement sites such as Pool, Howe and Buckquoy. A range of Pictish stones as well as Viking grave assemblages are also on display along with general archaeology and history displays outlining the settlement of Orkney from the Stone Age to the present day.

Perth Museum and Art Gallery A range of Pictish sculpture is on display from sites such as Inchyra, Gellyburn and St Madoes, as well as an excellent overview of local archaeology and history.

Shetland Museum A real gem of a cultural centre in the north, Shetland Museum holds fascinating and brilliantly displayed material on the archaeology and early history of Shetland. The early medieval collections include painted pebbles, finds from Pictish-era settlements, sculpture from Mail, Cunningsburgh, and an impressive shrine panel from Papil, Shetland.

Tarbat Discovery Centre, Portmahomack A wonderful museum located in the former church of St Colman's, Portmahomack, it displays material found during the University of York excavations. The excavations, from 1996 to 2007, uncovered the remains of a major monastery of the Picts on land immediately to the south of the church. The displays include artefacts from the dig, information on the Picts and an impressive collection of early medieval sculpture.

Online resources

The hundreds of Pictish monuments known can be found by searching through the national and regional databases of sites and monuments records. A good place to start is with the National Record of the Historic Environment accessed through Canmore – https://canmore.org.uk/

Teachers! Find out more. Forestry and Land Scotland has produced a wonderful learning resource for the Picts. It contains excellent material to inspire young audiences – https://forestryandland.gov.scot/what-we-do/biodiversity-and-conservation/ historic-environment-conservation/learning/the-picts

When visiting sites, use the maps on Canmore and regional Sites and Monuments records. There are also regional guides such as the Highland Pictish Trail – https:// highlandpictishtrail.co.uk

On social media the University of Aberdeen Northern Picts project has popular Facebook – www.facebook.com/northernpicts – and Twitter streams – @northernpicts

Index